Allen Lane · King Penguin

BY THE SAME AUTHOR

American Excursion
Charles Lamb and Elia
The Penguin History of the United States
(with R. B. Nye)
The Road to Athens
Barnes Wallis: A Biography
Treason at West Point
Their Majesties' Royall Colledge

J. E. MORPURGO

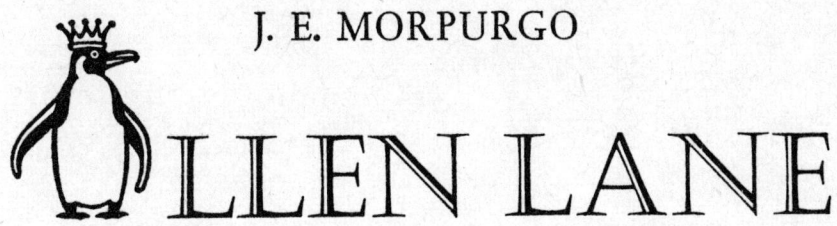LLEN LANE

KING PENGUIN

A Biography

Hutchinson of London

Hutchinson & Co. (Publishers) Ltd
3 Fitzroy Square, London WIP 6JD

London Melbourne Sydney Auckland
Wellington Johannesburg and agencies
throughout the world

First published 1979
Reprinted 1980
© J. E. Morpurgo 1979

Set in Monotype Spectrum

Printed and bound in Great Britain
by Redwood Burn Ltd
Trowbridge and Esher

British Library Cataloguing in Publication Data

Morpurgo, J. E.
  Allen Lane, King Penguin
  1. Lane, *Sir* Allen
  2. Penguin Books Limited – Biography
  3. Publishers and publishing – Great Britain
  – Biography
  I. Title
338.7'61'0705730924   Z325.L/

ISBN 0 09 139690 5

FOR
SEBASTIAN, HORATIO AND ROSALIND,
ALLEN'S GRANDCHILDREN – AND MINE

CONTENTS

List of Illustrations	9
Chapter One	11
Chapter Two	46
Chapter Three	80
Chapter Four	116
Chapter Five	155
Chapter Six	195
Chapter Seven	235
Chapter Eight	264
Chapter Nine	305
Chapter Ten	354
A Personal Afterword	387
Index	397

The King Penguin masquerading as an 'A' on the title-page was designed by Percy Metcalfe, probably in the early 1940s, but never used.

The devices shown at chapter beginnings are:

CHAPTER ONE: John Lane The Bodley Head, about 1888

CHAPTER TWO: Long-bow by Eric Gill from the binding of the first Bodley Head edition of *Ulysses*, 1936

CHAPTER THREE: Original Penguin by Edward Young, 1935

CHAPTER FOUR: Original Pelican by Edward Young, 1937

CHAPTER FIVE: Original Puffin, designer unknown, 1941

CHAPTER SIX: Definitive Penguin as redesigned by Jan Tschichold, 1949

CHAPTER SEVEN: Silver jubilee Penguin by Elizabeth Friedlander, 1960

CHAPTER EIGHT: 'Pelican in her piety', for *The Pelican History of Art*, by Berthold Wolpe, 1953

CHAPTER NINE: Peregrine by Hans Schleger, 1962

CHAPTER TEN: Allen Lane The Penguin Press by Hans Schleger, 1966

ILLUSTRATIONS

Plates (between pages 192 and 193)

The Williams family c. 1912 *(Clare Morpurgo)*
Richard and Allen Williams as choirboys *(Clare Morpurgo)*
Allen Lane in 1919
Allen Lane aged about 30 *(Clare Morpurgo)*
Lead box from the original Harmondsworth building
  (Penguin Books)
The Lane brothers, 1940 *(Radio Times Hulton)*
Allen Lane at work, 1940 *(Radio Times Hulton)*
John Lane at work, 1940 *(Radio Times Hulton)*
Richard Lane at work, 1940 *(Radio Times Hulton)*
Allen and Lettice Lane after their wedding, 1941 *(Clare Morpurgo)*
'After the Conference' by Rodrigo Moynihan RA *(Penguin Books;
  photo – Rodney Todd-White)*
E. V. Rieu
Sir William Emrys Williams *(Lotte Meitner-Graf)*
Sir Allen Lane after the *Lady Chatterley* verdict *(Press Association)*

In the text (page 63)

Christmas card sent by the Lane brothers, 1934

CHAPTER ONE

ALLEN LANE was in his early thirties and already a veteran publisher when he began preparation for the venture which was to make him famous. He left school and home before he was seventeen and had started work, by his own account as an office-boy, earning only a few shillings a week. Yet within five years of that seemingly inauspicious novitiate he established himself as a leading personality in the British book world, known among the professionals for his adventurousness, admired by the younger generation and regarded with suspicion by some of their seniors. Already before the creation of Penguin he was the instigator and central figure in several publishing exploits which, if he had done nothing else in all his days, would still have won him a mention in at very least a footnote to the history of letters.

But it was Penguin which lifted him above his contemporaries in publishing, who remain to the public-at-large generally anonymous, their personalities obscure and uninteresting, their names unnoticed despite interminable repetition on title-pages and book-spines. It was Penguin which gave him international fame, which made his activities, as those of no other publisher, enthralling to a world-wide audience. It was Penguin that made him rich, the owner of four houses in three countries, two flats and an ever-thickening portfolio of investments. He was knighted and garlanded with honorary degrees. He became notable among his innumerable acquaintances as a *bon viveur* and notorious among his many enemies as a ruthless tycoon. For many years Penguin's prestige so dimmed the lustre of all rivals that the name Penguin had almost universal currency and, much to his displeasure, came to be a synonym for paperback books.

Many thought of Allen Lane in terms that were in truth somewhat exaggerated, as the creator of a great commercial empire, as a Mond or a Rockefeller of the publishing world. But that he had created something more than a publishing house is undeniable; for the last twenty or so years of his life the half-grasped realization that in its brief history Penguin had become an institution of national and international importance, like *The Times* or the BBC, fostered anxiety about the future of the firm far beyond the inner circle and made every rumour of plans for its perpetuation a matter for widespread and excited press comment. It is equally certain that he was a pioneer in communications and, in the broadest sense, educational techniques, a man to be considered alongside such very different characters as Hearst, Northcliffe, Reith and the Hollywood moguls. Allen Lane made the book, for the first time in its long history, one of the mass media.

This braggart introduction, this breathless summary of rapid transformation from rags to riches, from obscurity to universal and presumably lasting influence, has the hall-mark of nineteenth-century moralizing fiction. In his later years Allen himself loved to tell his story as if it had been written by Horatio Alger and Samuel Smiles in collaboration. There is, however, a flaw in the cliché, an elided parenthesis; when this is corrected, though the achievement still stands unique in its generation, some of the romantic gloss is removed from the tale.

Allen Williams was not born with a silver spoon in his mouth but there was, within easy reach of his infant grasp, a gilded colophon. His father changed the family name to Williams-Lane in the year when Allen left Bristol Grammar School and went to work for a distant cousin – known always as Uncle John – in the firm of John Lane The Bodley Head.

Uncle John was alone in the family: he was settled, successful and at times even notorious in the great world of London. All the other Lanes, Williamses and Williams-Lanes were solidly and even stolidly middle class and provincial. The stock was yeoman, part-Welsh and part-Devonian, and Allen often (as his brother Richard invariably) looked in his middle years as if he were a country farmer who had somehow got himself into the hands of the best barber and the most expensive tailor in London.

However, by the time that Allen was born, on 21 September 1902, the Williamses were comfortably established as city-dwellers in Bristol. Allen was the first child; the rest followed at decent three-year intervals: Richard in 1905, John in 1908 and Nora in 1911.

In those years between the South African War and the First World War, Bristol remained, as it had been for many centuries (and continued to be until the Second World War), in essence a provincial capital with a thriving commercial, social and artistic life of its own, generally unaffected by the powerful magnetism of London. The majority of Bristolians went from school in Bristol to work in Bristol. They lived, they died and they were buried in Bristol. For all its urban qualities and all its self-sufficiency, however, Bristol, perhaps more than any other major British city, was in a very real sense a country town. Unlike Manchester, Birmingham, Leeds or Newcastle it was comparatively free of heavy industry. The sensational Avon Gorge is in the city, the lovely Gloucestershire and Somerset countryside immediately and easily accessible. As they grew up the Williams brothers indulged in all the pastimes common to country-bred children. They climbed in the Gorge, they picked bluebells in Leigh Woods, they caught sticklebacks with home-made rods and bent pins at Coombe Dingle and brought them home in jam-jars, they collected birds'-eggs and butterflies. This bucolic apprenticeship was furthered in the school holidays. Mrs Williams had several relatives who owned farms in North Devon, and on these farms the boys learned at first hand something of agriculture. In those early days the closest that any of them came to commerce was helping in the grocery store owned by an uncle at Winkleigh.

When compared to the spaciousness of Devon farms and in contrast even to the liberating excursions into the country around Bristol, Broomcroft, the house in the Bristol suburbs to which the family moved when Allen was six years old, was gloomy and restricted. Built of heavy grey stone, it stood four storeys high but there was little light on the ground floor – and no running water on the top two. The family atmosphere was more cheerful than the house; unsophisticated but by the standards of the time remarkably relaxed. Comics were forbidden and the house had no vast library, but there was a complete run of *The Strand Magazine*; from 1912, when he brought out *Tarzan of the Apes*,

Edgar Rice Burroughs was added to the superb stable of authors in *The Strand* as the boys' favourite reading.

On Sunday mornings the family was mustered for church. On Sunday evenings they sang hymns around the family piano. Mr Williams had a fine bass voice; all his sons graduated eventually to church choirs and Allen to the madrigal society. Once he sang 'Oh for the Wings of a Dove' solo at a concert in St Mary Redcliffe.

For boys of the Bristol middle class a boarding-school education was at that time inconceivable. Parents with social aspirations and enough money sent their sons as day boys to Clifton College. For the rest there was, first of all, Bristol Grammar School; if, for financial or academic reasons, that could not be achieved, there were several other good but less prestigious independent secondary schools. Clifton was beyond the Williamses, and beyond Allen, but they had hopes that he might get into the Grammar School. In preparation they sent him to an appallingly bad private school, Telesford House.

The school was ruled over by a vigorous sadist but Allen, who even at that early age had developed some refinements in the art of avoiding crises, practised considerable ingenuity in keeping out of the Head's path. To this end he set himself even to the unpalatable task of mastering Latin and mathematics.

The peaceful days at Telesford House ended when Richard joined Allen at the school. Allen was not ready to be outdone by his younger brother even in mischief or the tribulations that followed upon mischief; it came to be said at Telesford House that the Williams boys were, like packets of Seidlitz powders, explosive only when mixed. Nevertheless Allen managed to pass the entrance examination to the Grammar School.

At Bristol Grammar School Allen was neither a success nor a failure. In fact he passed through the school almost unnoticed by the staff and his contemporaries; sixty years later, when the school was asked to provide for a survey a list of its distinguished twentieth-century *alumni*, it did not remember the founder of the modern paperback movement – though it did write into its record some men who, perhaps justly, have no other memorial. Allen had no love for team games and in all his life never showed any interest or aptitude for competitive sport of any kind. He was neither notably academic nor sensationally unscholarly. He was not at that time the kind of boy whom schoolmasters and schoolboys pick out as a potential leader of men, the kind of boy who would have attracted the attention of his first Grammar School headmaster, Cyril Norwood. Norwood, one of the great public-school headmasters of this century, dragged Bristol Grammar School out of its nineteenth-century decline, and later became Head of Marlborough and then of Harrow. But Allen was fortunate in Norwood's successor, J. E. Barton, a teacher with a broader view of education than was common among his schoolmaster contemporaries. Allen learnt from Barton an appreciation of the visual arts; it was Barton who first opened Allen's eyes to the significance of design and form, a revelation which was useful preparation for collaboration in the more limited and yet more explicit work of the great exponent of the importance of book-design, his Uncle John. In time, it would make Allen's dedication to typographical excellence and careful design one of the most endearing aspects of his professional character – and one of the most influential. Barton was among the very few men for whom Allen's respect and affection never faltered.

For Allen, as for all who were at school at that time, those were years of foreboding. He was only twelve years old when war broke out and too young to comprehend the sense of fulfilment, of destiny accepted with rapture, which swept over those who were five or ten years his senior in August 1914. But his schooldays were punctuated by the names of grim battles. The sad roll of honour read over at assemblies grew longer with each year; what was in 1914 no more personal to him than a recital of the names of the dead at Agincourt had become by 1918 immediate, personal, abrupt and threatening. The list now included the names of boys who only a few months before had been among his acquaintances, and he could not hide from himself the knowledge that a few more months would see him going the way of all boys from Britain's grammar and public schools.

Allen was sixteen in 1918. In 1939 he was thirty-seven. He was a member of that fortunate but in some sense emotionally deprived generation which lived through both world wars and yet missed both. The fact that he came to adolescence during the Great War rendered him incapable of sustained consideration of a future career. Even early in 1918 the one future open to a middle-class English boy was a commission in the Services, and the life-expectancy of an infantry subaltern in Flanders was reckoned to be just a little over three weeks.

The Armistice saved Allen from the necessity to go soldiering, but it was a minor mishap of war which opened the way to his life's work. During a Zeppelin raid on London John Lane's house in Lancaster Gate was hit by a bomb. The damage was slight and there were no casualties, but Lane decided to move to the safety of a furnished house in Bath. He took to visiting his Williams relatives and, having no children of his own, soon conceived the idea of taking Allen into The Bodley Head and making him heir-apparent.

Allen was not enamoured of the plan. He ploughed dutifully through the books that Uncle John provided for his intellectual improvement and professional indoctrination – a strange assortment which included both Oscar Wilde and Sir Edward Coke. But he was almost sixteen and had discovered interests more intriguing and more time-consuming than the printed word.

Most of the family believed that he had taken to breeding rabbits. It was, they thought, a surprisingly childish hobby for Allen but the evidence was clear: one of his schoolfellows was much involved with rabbit-breeding; Allen was not thought to be notably friendly with this boy yet he was forever visiting him, his home and his rabbit-hutches. Only Dick, watching with the suspicious eyes of a younger brother, came soon to understand what was going on. That same schoolfellow had two attractive and not disobliging sisters; Allen's one difficulty, apart from keeping his assignations secret from his parents, was that he could not make up his mind as to which of the two he favoured. This indecision forced him to arrange more frequent meetings at the rabbit-hutches; so urgent was his love-fever that once it persuaded him to interrupt Uncle John mid-way through a sermon on the advantages of life in a publishing house with the slim explanation that he had to leave immediately to take care of his rabbits. Lane was affronted. If Allen found rabbits more enthralling than books he must take not to publishing but to farming. Lane could not know that this trivial episode with its overt and furtive alternatives might serve as a parable for much of Allen's life.

Still unenthusiastic about the future designed for him by others, Allen left Bristol Grammar School at the end of the first term of 1919. He joined The Bodley Head on 23 April, Shakespeare's birthday and St George's Day – a coincidence in which later he took some engaging pride. His status as heir-apparent was confirmed by the change of family name; soon he dropped the hyphen and called himself just Allen Lane. But his wages did not match his high estate: he was paid only a guinea a week. He boarded with an uncle and aunt at Raynes Park in the South London suburbs and contributed ten shillings a week to the household budget. He was not yet benefiting from publishers' expense accounts and business lunches. For the best part of a year his only entertainments were Sunday church and an occasional visit to Paddington Station, where he would gaze wistfully down the line towards Bristol, sad in the knowledge that the return fare home was twelve shillings and sixpence.

The lives of great men, no less than the lives of the rest of us, are rich with paradox. It remains to be proved that Allen Lane was a great man; that there were in his character more shattering paradoxes than is common either among the great or the rest of us is undeniable. Of all these paradoxes not the least confusing to those who knew him well – and to his biographer – is his attitude to his family. He was in his youth devoted to his parents, more particularly to his mother, and the devotion held firm until the end of their days. Until early middle age he had no friends who could compete with his brothers as intimates, and perhaps in all his life he never found a travelling companion he preferred to his sister. Nor did his involvement stop at the boundaries of the immediate family group. If there was in his make-up one element which identified him with the yeoman society which he liked to claim as his true environment it was his concern with an extended family, his generosity towards cousins, second cousins, aunts and uncles. Yet, even in his relations with his father and mother, his patience could never match his aspirations. His good intentions were often thwarted by his ambition and by his overweening concern for what was going on in a greater world of which they had no knowledge. Later, when he had a family of his own, his expeditions into parental responsibility were spasmodic, almost hysterical, as if he knew what was expected of him and intended to do it wholeheartedly –

until interrupted by demands from the world that he had made his empire; demands at once more intriguing and more challenging than the duties of fatherhood. From the day he left home for London he lost all sense of awe for any member of his family except his mother; she, a woman with a will as strong as his own, maintained some kind of sway over him until she died. To his father he was always dutiful and frequently genuinely loving but from him he neither sought nor accepted advice. As she grew up Allen was drawn to his sister, but for him and for the most part she was outside his real, his professional existence. His brothers were good drinking companions but, as each came in turn into publishing, they were also both business partners and competitors. When he married he was already too old and too well-established in his career to permit his wife to affect his work. With no Prince of Wales in the blood-line he dreamed for a while of making one of his daughters an heir to his throne, but she was just one of many candidates for the role and the dream was short-lived.

Of all the family only Uncle John exercised an influence over Allen which stayed with him throughout his life.

In his mature years Allen liked to suggest that he had inherited from John Lane many characteristics, both personal and professional. He reinforced the notion with actions, some trivial or sentimental but all designed to prove, as much to himself as to the knowledgeable in his audience, that the line of descent was clear and explicit. Thus, for example, the return to Vigo Street late in his publishing career was at once a salute to his own novitiate and to John Lane's; the much-publicized impulsiveness of the decision to set up a new hardback firm exactly where John Lane – and after him Allen – had started was to all who knew publishing history an almost exact re-enactment of the impetuosity which had brought John Lane to that street in the summer of 1887. Even the name which Allen chose for his latter-day venture, Allen Lane The Penguin Press, echoed John Lane The Bodley Head.

Unravelling the skeins of heredity and influence is always a complicated exercise, no easier for the man who sees himself as a palpable successor than for the dispassionate historian. Investigating the relationship between John Lane and his *soi-disant* nephew is made no easier by Allen's excursions into imitation;

but there are remarkable and indisputable congruities between the careers, personalities, skills and foibles of the two men, even if it is almost impossible to decide whether these congruities were the consequence of heredity, of training or of Allen's deliberate attempts to make history repeat itself.

John Lane was a devout Devonian; for this reason he chose Sir Thomas Bodley – 'The most pious of founders . . . one of the most notable worthies of Devon, my native county' – as his patron saint. That must serve as sufficient explanation for Allen's undoubtedly genuine conviction (against most of the evidence of his upbringing and family-tree) that North Devon was his real home, the one place where he could be of the people, uninhibited by the need to be a tycoon on show which obsessed him almost everywhere else. John Lane was a collector of beautiful objects and cared more for acquisition than for profit. In time Allen, too, became a collector; of pictures, furniture and antique snuff-boxes; but not even his most fervent admirer could ever say of Allen, as many said of John Lane, that his love of the beautiful rather than his zest for success made him a great publisher. Both men came to the London publishing scene raw, hesitant and rustic, both were adaptable, both quick, and both became famous and almost notorious for their urbanity. Both pretended and perhaps aspired to a democratic manner which neither could ever achieve. Both were shrewd and even harsh in their business dealings, and yet each in his time (if in very different ways) made errors of judgement so hideous as to bring his creation to the edge of disaster.

Allen undoubtedly inherited, learnt or imitated John Lane's manner of running a publishing house as if it was a great sport in which he wanted all his colleagues to share. Unfortunately for those colleagues Allen, in this unlike John Lane, changed the rules – and the team – as often as possible. And, unfortunately for those who would wish to hold up John Lane's loyalty to his subordinates as a model, Allen's methods proved, in almost every worldly sense, far more successful.

When Allen joined John Lane at The Bodley Head his uncle was only sixty-one years old and the firm only half that age. Even so both publisher and publishing house were already showing signs of decline. But the decline was comparative. In the last decade of the nineteenth century and the first of the twentieth The Bodley Head had been Britain's most original publishing house – and sometimes the most notorious; the head of the firm had achieved what is seldom granted to publishers, a fame beyond the close fraternity of the book world.

John Lane had arrived in London from North Devon to take up an undistinguished post as a junior clerk in the Railway Clearing House. His manner at that time was clumsy; he spoke with a marked Devon accent; he had few friends in London, and among those few none were in any way associated with the literary set. But he watched and he imitated. Soon, even on the meagre wages of his clerkship, he contrived for himself virtually a new character. Refinement overlaid the burr; he was always well-groomed, even debonair, his hair and sandy beard neatly brushed. And he began to make friends: women friends by the dozen, some of them the wives or daughters of men who exercised influence; men friends who were not as yet themselves influential but, many of them, settled in places where influence was within their grasp. There was, for example, R. W. Wilson of the British Museum, in whose company Lane discovered the premises in Vigo Street suitable for the ambition which had been in his mind for some time, the setting-up of a bookshop.

It was, however, a friend from Devon, Elkin Mathews, who became Lane's first partner. Mathews ran the bookshop for four years before Lane abandoned the Railway Clearing House for a full-time career as a bookman.

Soon after its inception, and some time before Lane resigned from the railway service, The Bodley Head had ventured from bookselling into publishing. The inaugural title, Richard Le Gallienne's *My Ladies' Sonnets*, was also the author's first book. Lane's choice proved at one and the same time the rapidity with which he had acquired literary sophistication and his shrewdness as an editor. Le Gallienne lived on until after the Second World War; though a prolific writer, he never achieved popularity either in Britain or in the United States. His poetry is mannered, exquisite, even pretty rather than sensitive; but in the late 1880s Le Gallienne was as near as a new publisher could come to a foot-hold in the heart-land of the aesthetes where Swinburne and Wilde reigned supreme. Latter-day readers find Le Gallienne's verse pious; the delicacy of phrase which his contemporaries thought admirable we now regard as artificial, and his sentiment as saccharine. Yet his work was ideally suited to Lane, who had it in mind to produce titles in a manner that would make them collectors' items, worthy of consideration for their appearance as for their contents by that small group of connoisseurs worthy of collecting them. The significance of this first publication, both for The Bodley Head and for British publishing, is revealed most obviously in Lane's production technique. Few publishers before him had been as scrupulous as Lane in matching design and typography to subject matter. William Morris, his senior by twenty years, had been preaching for several decades on the text of the book as object, but Morris's Kelmscott Press was not established until three years after The Bodley Head had exhausted its first edition of *My Ladies' Sonnets*, exquisitely printed on hand-made paper by one of the best printers in the country. There were in that edition only 300 copies but that was all that Lane intended, and those 300 made the reputation of his firm.

At the end of The Bodley Head's second year as a publishing house the *St James Gazette* wrote: ' . . . they have managed, by means of limited editions and charming workmanship, to impress book-buyers with the belief that a volume may have an aesthetic and commercial value.' In his first fifteen years as a publisher John Lane seldom attempted large-scale publication. He saw himself as a specialist publisher to the *cognoscenti*, issuing carefully selected books in carefully produced and always limited editions. Very few titles in the Bodley Head list had an initial run of more than 1000 copies; most appeared in editions of 300 to 500.

John Lane's dedication to excellence in book production was one of the qualities he passed on to Allen – and also, if in a sense that must seem at first sight paradoxical, his determination to remain a specialist. Certainly Allen neither recognized himself nor accepted when it was brought to his notice by others any substantial contradiction between his uncle's preference for limited editions and his own attack upon the popular market. A man not much given to generalization – or to overt tutelage – nevertheless on one day he twice produced aphorisms for the benefit of an apprentice colleague. 'Penguins,' he said, 'are not intended for the mass market; they are limited editions; editions limited to the size of the audience who can read them.' And again: 'There are only two prices at which a book is commercial, six pence and six guineas.'

John Lane's reputation for shrewdness grew at a remarkable pace. He built upon it eagerly, seizing every opportunity to make himself, The Bodley Head and Bodley Head authors acceptable in those places where literary prestige is created. By 1890 his opinion was sought by leaders of taste; when it was not sought it was given gratuitously and usually to the advantage of his list. It was, for example, no ordinary achievement for a publisher who had been in business effectively for only five years that when Clement Shorter resigned as its literary critic the editor of the *Star* turned to Lane for advice about a successor. Lane nominated his very first author, Richard Le Gallienne, and Le Gallienne was appointed to serve alongside two colleagues whose skills, percipience, immediate impact and eventual fame were far greater: A. B. Walkley as theatre critic and Bernard Shaw as music critic. Lane made doubly-sure that Le Gallienne's new eminence would serve The Bodley Head: he gave him a retainer as reader for the firm.

Most remarkable of all, however, was the growth of the list and its extension to include not only new authors of promise but also authors who had already arrived. In less than ten years The Bodley Head was publishing Alice Meynell, Francis Thompson, J. A. Symonds, Katherine Tynan, Lionel Johnson and William Watson. The galaxy of artists commissioned to design or decorate Bodley Head books was in some senses even more impressive; among them were Aubrey Beardsley, C. S. Ricketts, William Rothenstein, Selwyn Image, C. W. Furse and R. Anning Bell.

Lane's most sensational acquisition was contrived very early in his career and stayed with him for only a few years; in that time he was almost consistently antipathetic to Lane and always ready to voice his antipathy in waspish and public comment and by irritable and irritating objections to his publisher's methods. Late in 1891 The Bodley Head agreed to take over sheets of Oscar Wilde's poems left over from the bankrupt stock of David Bogue, who had first published the book ten years earlier. Charles Ricketts was paid five guineas to design a title-page, half-title and cover for a new Bodley Head edition limited to 220 copies, signed by the author and selling at fifteen shillings. The book appeared in May 1892, and a few weeks later The Bodley Head issued a contract for Wilde's *The Sphinx*.

Wilde offered Lane a sharp lesson in the business of publishing. The word 'author', customarily used in publishing contracts for the creators of books of all kinds, he would not have applied to himself. 'The maker of a poem is a "poet", not an "author"; author is misleading.' And Wilde went on to demonstrate that he considered his publisher no more than an unpleasant and insignificant mechanic; his activities were unfortunately necessary but he must never be allowed to think of himself as equal to his 'poet', nor yet be granted the comfort of imagining that he knew as much as the 'poet', even about the business of publishing:

> A book of this kind – very rare and curious – must not be thrown into the gutter of English journalism. . . . I hope that the book will be subscribed for before publication and that as few as possible will be sent for review. . . .
> With regard to the copies given to other than reviewers. I will have six myself. You and Mr Mathews will of course have a copy each, besides a copy to be kept in your place of business, and Mr Ricketts will have a copy.
> I did not contemplate assigning to you the copyright of so important a poem for so small an honorarium as 10 per cent, but will do so, it being clearly understood that no new edition is to be brought out without my sanction. . . .

Wilde ended his lesson with a magnanimous peroration. The book would undoubtedly be a success and – whether for this reason or because justice must be done to be seen – Lane would come to accept that all Wilde's demands were reasonable.

Lane accepted no such thing, but he kept his doubts and his resentment from any but his closest colleagues. Wilde was at that time the centre and the master of the world which Lane aspired to conquer; as reward for his forbearance Lane was granted the book-rights for *Salomé* – and was treated to another, even more ferocious disquisition on the manifold responsibilities and limited privileges of a publisher.

The key letter in the correspondence between Wilde and John Lane about *Salomé* was written in February 1893. It merits extensive quotation even in a biography of Allen Lane, not so much because it must shift some of the reader's sympathy from the abused and ambitious publisher to the resentful if arrogant author as because it serves as an apposite preface to many incidents in Allen's career. The record it reveals – of procrastination, of promises made and not kept, of casual attention to the minutiae of business and scant concern for the interests of the other party to a deal – tends to prove that Allen inherited or imitated from Uncle John, as well as characteristics quintessential to publishing success, some unlovely traits that made him at best infuriating and at worst undeserving of the trust of his authors and employees. When, in 1962, Rupert Hart-Davis published his edition of Wilde's letters one commentator who had been both Penguin author and Penguin editor remarked, scathingly and with feeling, that this one letter proved that the relationship between John and Allen Lane was in reality as close as the two men had pretended; with only a change of date, it could be copied and marketed as a memento of their sorrows to all who had business dealings with Allen:

... You see now [wrote Wilde] how right I was in continually pressing you for a written agreement, and I cannot understand why you would not do so. I spoke to you on the subject at your own place; you promised to forward the agreement next day; this was in November last; I spoke to you about it at the Hogarth Club, you made the same promise. I wrote to you endless letters . . . ; I received promises, excuses, apologies, but no agreement. . . .

Lane had already angered Wilde by advertising *Salomé* in the end-papers of J. A. Symonds's *In the Key of Blue and Other Essays* as 'the play the Lord Chamberlain refused to license'. But, perhaps because he accepted that Lane was 'interested in literature and curious works of art' (the words are Wilde's own), he did not take away from Lane the book rights to his plays, and even sent him a ticket for the first night of *Salomé* – 'the front row of the dress-circle; I think the best seat in the house', and a privilege which he had 'been obliged to refuse to many dear and delightful people'.

Wilde continued to be exasperated by Lane's casual business methods. Nevertheless, when Lane and Elkin Matthews inevitably went their separate ways, Lane had Wilde's agreement to retain the more profitable part of Wilde's works. The severance of the partnership between Lane and Matthews in the autumn of 1894 was amicable, at least according to Lane, who kept not only Wilde but also most of the better-known authors on the list.

Lane moved the firm and its sign across Vigo Street to the back of Albany; freed from the few inhibitions forced upon him by the necessity to consult a less thrusting partner, he seemed set firmly on the pinnacle of literary publishing. Already he was being paid the compliment of mild lampoons in the press:

> How doth the busy little Lane
> Improve the Bodley Head.
> He gathers round him, day by day
> The authors who are read.

But that year and the next Lane would remember for the rest of his life in his nightmares; from that time on, although he never abdicated from his intention to be above all a literary publisher nor abandoned his scrupulous care for the appearance of his books, he was never again truly *avant garde*. The multiple crises of the mid-nineties brought home the realization that he had gone too far. By his own confession a puritan, he found that he had thrust so far forward that he had come to be recognized as the entrepreneur of decadence. The public teasing, which at first he had found flattering and exceptionally useful to his business, had now turned sour and menacing:

> Give us more of the godly heart
> And less of the Bodley Head

was harmless enough, but Owen Seaman's verses were different and dangerous:

> The erotic affairs that you fiddle around
> Are as vulgar as coin of the mint;
> And you merely distinguish yourself from the crowd
> By the fact that you put 'em in print.
>
> For your dull little vices we don't care a fig,
> It is this that we deeply deplore,
> You were cast for a common or usual pig
> But play the invincible bore.

Overtly the lines were addressed to a 'boy-poet of the decadence' but the salvo was aimed at Lane. He knew it, and removed himself from the target-area. Immediately he invited Seaman to dinner, courted him with Lane charm and the best wines in the Lane cellar, and so lured his assailant into the Bodley Head list. This trivial cunning was just one move in a serious policy of recantation and self-purification.

Lane's troubles – one might almost write, his conversion to respectability – had begun with that same English translation of *Salomé* which had exposed him to Wilde's fury. He must have known that he was courting danger by accepting *Salomé*: not only had it already aroused the censor but it had even created difficulties with the management which proposed to stage it in London and with Sarah Bernhardt who was cast for the title role. But he had not expected the animus which the book exploded all around him.

Aubrey Beardsley, whom Lane liked and admired both for his artistic genius and for the interest (which he shared with Lane) in adapting new printing techniques to the purposes of book-illustration, had made the first attempt to translate *Salomé* from Wilde's French. Wilde, too, was inclined to admire Beardsley as an artist, but the admiration was tinged with jealousy and did not extend to Beardsley's gifts as a translator. The Beardsley version of *Salomé* Wilde rejected out of hand. Lord Alfred Douglas, for whom neither Lane nor Beardsley felt either affection or respect, made the next version. Wilde's 'worship' of his 'dearest of all boys' did not blind him to the infelicities in Douglas's translation. Later Wilde wrote to Douglas in particularly venomous terms, insisting that the work was as unworthy of him 'as an ordinary Oxonian as it was of the work he sought to render'; for the moment he condescended to accept the translation, if only after he had himself amended several passages. He deigned to dedicate the book 'to my friend Lord Alfred Bruce Douglas, the translator of my play' but he conspired, even with the 'wicked Lane', to keep Douglas's name from the title-page. Beardsley confounded Lane and Wilde by withdrawing at the last moment three illustrations which had been accepted by all concerned. He substituted 'three new ones (simply beautiful but quite irrelevant)', and stung Lane by agreeing with Wilde, his arch-enemy, that the coarse Irish linen binding on the small-paper edition of *Salomé* was 'simply dreadful'.

All this was confusing enough for Lane. More sinister was the virtually unanimous view of the critics that *Salomé* was, in the words of *The Times*, 'an arrangement in blood and ferocity, morbid, bizarre, repulsive and very offensive in its adaptation of scriptural phraseology to situations the reverse of sacred', for this was close to accusing the publisher of dealing in blasphemy and pornography. Publicly Wilde protested that the opinion of English critics did not interest him, but for his publisher he had a different story. The verdict of the critics, he claimed, was by no means unanimous; through Lane's habitual inefficiency none of the critics who might have appreciated his art had received the copies that Wilde had instructed should be sent; not Shaw, Archer, Pater, Swinburne nor even Le Gallienne.

For Lane, however, the furore over *Salomé* was a comparatively mild foretaste of what was to follow almost immediately.

More than any other achievement in his career, Lane's connection with *The Yellow Book* has won for him a place where few publishers are admitted, in the annals of literature. More than any other literary journal, *The Yellow Book* is associated in the popular imagination with *fin-de-siècle* aestheticism and decadence. By extension, Lane is remembered as publisher by self-appointment to festering genius.

In conception and in fact *The Yellow Book* was not very different from the many other journals launched by book publishers to publicize their more substantial properties, to offering the authors on their list an opportunity to present to the public work that did not run to book length, to lure into the list new authors, and, perhaps above all, to gather for the enlargement of the publishers' prestige authors whose commitment to other firms made their books unavailable. In the early months of 1894 Lane's ambitions for his *Yellow Book* were similar to those of any other book publisher who plans a new journal: it would attract the best contemporary writers and artists, be they conservative or *avant garde*. To a remarkable extent he succeeded: Sir Frederick Leighton (President of the Royal Academy), Sargent, Henry James, George Saintsbury, Richard Garnett, William Watson, Kenneth Grahame, A. C. Benson, John Davidson; not one of them could be regarded, even by his contemporaries, as in any way shocking. Many were stalwart representatives of Victorian respectability.

Henry Harland, the literary editor of *The Yellow Book*, was an American who, under the pseudonym Sidney Luska, had made a reputation in the United States as the author of realistic novels about Jewish life in New York City. His later novels, written for The Bodley Head under his own name whilst he was living in England, are saccharine historical romances, and the themes of his several contributions to *The Yellow Book* are as innocuous as the style is noxious.

Max Beerbohm was in the first volume of *The Yellow Book* and in several of its successors. He could be called arrogant; though still in his early twenties he was preparing for Lane his first book, *The Works of Max Beerbohm*. He was marked down as 'incomparably silly' by one or two of the more pompous reviewers, but the irony of his essays was too mild to cause him to be reviled even by philistines. The closest that he ever came to giving real cause for offence to respectable opinion with any of his contributions to *The Yellow Book* was when the journal published his caricature of George the Fourth. (Beerbohm remained throughout his life ambivalent about royalty: 'he loved it, and loved to think of the possibility of its being ridiculous'.) Nor was Max then or at any time in tune with the more obviously decadent representatives of the nineties. Always he loathed 'the latest thing' and already he pretended that he had read little except *The Four Georges* and Lear's *Book of Nonsense*.

There is missing from the roll-call of *The Yellow Book* one name which by all conventional publishing precedents should have been there. It would seem that Oscar Wilde was never asked to contribute. Without him the journal could never be, as was intended, a significant gathering of both experimental and conservative writing. Without him it could never be what the myth-makers have come to consider it: the apotheosis of Bunthorne-ism. Without him, the most sensational and outrageous author on the Bodley Head list, it could not even claim to be truly representative of Lane's house.

It is not likely that the exclusion of Wilde was engineered by Lane. His loathing for Wilde was not yet so perfervid as to overcome his commercial sense. Almost certainly it was Beardsley who kept out Wilde. Later, when Leonard Smithers invited him to edit another journal Beardsley agreed providing that '*it is quite agreed that Oscar Wilde contributes nothing to the magazine, anonymously, pseudonymously, or otherwise*'.

The proscription which kept him from *The Yellow Book* Wilde accepted in disdainful silence. Only once did he allow himself to show that it rankled; indeed, only twice in all his voluminous correspondence did he mention the journal which dignity demanded that he despise. When the first number appeared Wilde released his habitual venom – but not his habitual wit – first in a letter to Douglas: '*The Yellow Book* has appeared. It is dull and loathsome, a great failure. I am so glad.' And, in the next week, also to Douglas: 'Max on Cosmetics . . . is wonderful . . . quite delightfully wrong and fascinating.'

But, if Beardsley kept out of *The Yellow Book* the Bodley Head author most inimical to the publisher, it was Beardsley, one of Lane's favourites, who almost alone made *The Yellow Book* if not exactly the failure which soothed Wilde's bruised pride then at best a *succès de scandale*, and it was Beardsley's cover designs and illustrations which brought the publisher of *The Yellow Book* to consider the risks of adventurousness.

Lane had gone far in his eager search for fame, and had made the journey rapidly and in style. Overnight Beardsley took him to the brink of notoriety. Lane had lacked the perspicacity to see the dangers for himself or he was blinded by his genuine enthusiasm for Beardsley's exquisite draughtmanship, but there were watch-dogs baying in Fleet Street. *The Times* pontificated: 'Its note appearing to be a combination of English rowdyism with French lubricity . . . ,' and the *Westminster Gazette* pointed to Beardsley as the arch-villain: 'His offence is that he had undoubted skill as a line draughtsman. . . . But as regards certain of his inventions in this number . . . we do not know that anything would meet the case except a short Act of Parliament to make this kind of thing illegal.' Even more persuasive to Lane, many of the protesters who came knocking at the doors of Vigo Street were prized contributors to *The Yellow Book* and some of them were also his patrons in London society. Leighton, for example, had already more public honours than any artist of his time but there were rumours that what had been granted to the last Poet Laureate might now be conferred upon him. He was not prepared to forego being the first President of the Royal Academy to enter the House of Lords just because he had foolishly accepted Lane's invitation to produce a frontispiece for his journal. Man enough to admit privately that he admired Beardsley's work, nonetheless he insisted that Lane must make some demonstration which would prove to the public that Leighton was free from guilt by association with a purveyor of obscenity.

William Watson's anger was even more intense and his threats more direct. Beardsley must go, or Lane would lose the poet whom all sensitive critics – Watson most sensitive of them all and most vociferous – regarded as the only true heir to Tennyson's still-vacant laureateship and to the rest of Tennyson's poetic laurels. And, if The Bodley Head lost Watson then with him it would lose also those few other poets who were high enough on the slopes of Parnassus to glimpse him at its summit.

Lane capitulated. After the publication of volume four the publisher himself took over as art editor of *The Yellow Book*. Beardsley went to the short-lived *Savoy*; though his friendship with Lane survived, for the few years that remained to him his talents were at the disposal of 'the most learned erotomaniac in Europe', Leonard Smithers.

Lane must have felt relief when he saw Beardsley's illustrations to *The Rape of the Lock* and *Under the Hill* but when he let Beardsley go he removed a collaborator of genius and one of the few men who could maintain him in his appointed role, against the tenor of all his puritan instincts, as publisher to a bold new movement in English letters. Once it became impeccably virtuous *The Yellow Book* lost its character. Nine more volumes appeared but what they contained was little more venturesome and far less thrilling than the contents of *Blackwood's*.

The Lane invasion of journal publishing ended with a strategic withdrawal. It was not renewed in John Lane's lifetime but when, in 1935, John Lehmann's restless, confused plans for a magazine '... began to crystallize ... ' he turned first to The Bodley Head. Of that and of all that followed more must come later but, apart altogether from the Lane connection, one fact links *The Yellow Book* to *New Writing*. Rare among journals, both appeared bound in hard covers.

In all the history of British publishing it is difficult to match the rise of John Lane. Starting without the advantages of money, influential friends or family connections, without even an apprenticeship in some established publishing house, in less than a decade he made The Bodley Head the equal of firms such as Longmans and Murray whose histories stretched back more than a century. His success he owed almost entirely to his own bustling energy and to innate shrewdness which held him from competing with the traditional and traditionalist firms. Instead, he first identified the possibility of commercial and prestigious success in collectors' editions, and then created the market from which he intended to prosper. Nor was his fabulous rise limited to the world of literature. In that same decade the Devon rustic transformed himself into a man-about-town, immaculately groomed, lively in conversation, a member of several of the best clubs, a frequent guest at the best dinner-tables, and comfortably established at what was, for his purposes, the best address in London. Not only was Albany a convenient annexe to his office but also it was close to being an annexe to the Hogarth Club, the Reform and the Café Royal; its tradition and contemporary reputation made it both the symbolic and geographical centre of that small part of London where high living and high thinking meet and merge.

It was, indeed, part of Lane's genius as a publisher that, at the beginning of his career as for most of his life and unlike more conservative competitors, he made no distinction between his professional and his social life. A new author or an idea for a book might come his way at the most unlikely and unliterary dinner-party. He recognized, too, that the social columns provided publicity for The Bodley Head no less valuable than the literary pages.

Lane's rise to prominence had been so fast, and he so busy in achieving it, that he had no time to consider the problems that came with fame. The hysteria over the English version of *Salomé* gave him his first lesson; it was not always pleasant to be talked at, even by such brilliant talkers as Wilde and Beardsley. The outcry against *The Yellow Book* was even more salutary; for the first time he realized that it is not always healthy to be talked about.

On February 1895 Lane's *amour-propre* suffered another if seemingly insignificant jolt. That night the St James's Theatre staged for the first time Wilde's 'exquisitely trivial ... delicate bubble of fancy, *The Importance of Being Earnest*'. As with all Wilde's plays, the book rights were promised to The Bodley Head; yet there on the stage at the St James's was a bit-part player acting a stock character, an English manservant with only three lines to speak. The playwright had called this insignificant menial just Lane. It was a private joke – and if typical of Wilde's spitefulness by no means typical of his wit – but many saw the point and laughed. John Lane saw the point, and did not laugh.

Retribution followed swiftly. When Wilde was arrested, Lane was making his first visit to New York, where he planned to open an American office. Later Lane himself said that the first he knew was a newspaper headline reading 'OSCAR WILDE ARRESTED. YELLOW BOOK UNDER HIS ARM' and 'it nearly killed me'. In fact the book Wilde was carrying was a copy, bound in yellow, of *Aphrodite*, by the young French author, Pierre Louys (who had sat next to Lane in the dress circle for the first night of *Salomé*) and the *furore* over *The Yellow Book* had reached its peak several months before Lane left for New York. Nevertheless, Lane was near to a metaphorical truth. The Wilde affair came close to killing the originality which had thrust him forward as a publisher. As a year earlier when the first volume of *The Yellow Book* appeared so now, as Wilde's futile libel action against the Marquess of Queensberry turned against him and led to Wilde's arrest and trial, pious and respectable Bodley Head authors turned upon their publisher and demanded that he clean out his stable. Cablegrams from Watson and the rest battered Lane in New York. The news reached him that his name had actually been mentioned in court in the most damaging manner, as a man who had introduced to Wilde and to Wilde's 'unnatural vices' one of his young employees. Goaded by his authors, and by this hideous culmination to the long sequence of slights that he had received from the pen of Wilde, Lane blurted out his instructions to Vigo Street. The manuscript of *Mr W.H.* to be returned to Wilde. All stocks of Wilde's books to be withdrawn from the booksellers. All contractual obligations to Wilde to be cancelled. His name to be removed from the Bodley Head catalogue.

Wilde was suffering tribulations more bruising to his spirit than the petulance of his publisher but even so it is impossible to withhold some admiration for his reticence. At the time when they had been useful to each other and Wilde was at the height of his fame, he had called him 'wicked Lane'. Now, in the moment of his public infamy when Lane's support would have been enormously valuable, when even silence and inaction from his publisher would have been some comfort, he called him just 'silly'. Wilde offered his books to the eager Smithers, the flagrant pornographer who affronted all respectable London by putting a notice in the window of his Bond Street office which read: 'Smut is cheap today.'

Lane's craven performance in the Wilde affair did not trouble his many apologists. Some defended him just because they hated Wilde, others because vociferous condemnation of Wilde was the best way to divert public attention from their own dubious activities. (Gleeson White, the art critic, said at the moment of Wilde's condemnation, '[Wilde] will never lift his head again, for he has against him all men of infamous life.') Lane's faithful authors and employers defended him then, and continued to defend him in their autobiographies: the interests of The Bodley Head transcended any responsibility to one Bodley Head author. They could do none other for they had harassed and blackmailed Lane to act as he did, and they benefited as much as Lane from the overt and almost ritualistic purification of The Bodley Head.

Later commentators, amongst them John Lane's heir, Allen, have used a different and weaker argument. Lane, they say, behaved no differently from most of his contemporaries. Even the manager of the St James's Theatre took Wilde's name off the playbills, and men far greater than a leading theatre-manager or a leading publisher turned their backs on Wilde. They point almost proudly to the fact that Bernard Shaw, George Meredith and Emile Zola ignored or refused requests to sign petitions seeking some slight amelioration of Wilde's circumstances in prison.

To the larger consideration of the case of Oscar Wilde the charge against Lane is irrelevant but its significance for the future of The Bodley Head is considerable. In this, the first great crisis of his career, Lane lost his nerve. He never again recovered it in its entirety. Up to that time the progress of The Bodley Head had been fantastic, the genius and originality which inspired that success unmistakable and unique. Thereafter, and although Lane continued to toy with the experimental in literature, he was always on his guard lest the experimental might prove to be the scandalous. Thereafter, though he claimed that his publishing methods were not as those of others, the Bodley Head list began to look more and more like that of any other middle-of-the road, commercial publishing house, its few *avant-garde* titles outnumbered by solid biographies, novels that were meritorious but never meretricious, and books of verse by poets who, though overtly modern, were also obvious candidates for respectable acclaim.

It is tempting to argue more than can be proved from Lane's cowardice at the time of Wilde's distress and from his disloyalty to his most prominent and successful author; it is not without interest that, for one reason or another, many of his best writers – Max Beerbohm, Theodore Dreiser, Rupert Brooke, G. K. Chesterton and H. G. Wells among them – stayed with him for only one or two books.

When Beardsley and Wilde were helping to make Lane famous and threatening to make him infamous, the works of one other Bodley Head writer created a stir almost equal to the sensation over *The Yellow Book* or *Salomé*. The manuscript of George Egerton's first book, *Keynotes*, had arrived unheralded in Vigo Street sometime early in 1893. Le Gallienne reported on it enthusiastically but no one had ever heard of Egerton and the author had forgotten to provide an address. Several months later George Egerton called at The Bodley Head, 'a very attractive young woman, slim, dark-haired and dressed all in white'. George Egerton was in fact Mrs Egerton Clairmonte. She had been Miss Mary Dunne and Mrs Melville (and she later married the theatrical agent Reginald Golding Bright). Today *Keynotes* reads as a tepid account of the intimate life of a young woman who is inseparable from a stupid and insensitive husband; when Lane published the book in 1895 it was thought shocking, perhaps more particularly because of Beardsley's impudent cover design and the author's flamboyant and smirk-provoking dedication, 'To Knut Hamsun, In Memory of a day when the wind and the rainbow met'.

Upon the basis of this one book Lane developed a Keynotes series. Many titles were by authors such as Henry Harland, Fiona Macleod and Arthur Machen who could be depended upon to maintain the aesthetic and stylistic poses of the period without incurring the risks inherent in an extravagantly eccentric genius like Oscar Wilde. They offered token allegiance to the cult of modernism, enough to allow Lane to convince himself and the public that his policies had not changed. They came often close to the boundary between the frank and the shocking, but they seldom strayed into disreputable territory.

There is not one book in the series which held the respect or affection of critics and readers for fifty years (and this is commonly the fate of publisher's prized series) but there is a whisper of things to come in Lane's initial plans for *Keynotes*, and in the frustration of those plans more than a hint of objections which would be raised against Allen's innovations in 1934 and 1935.

John Lane thought to produce *Keynotes* in paper covers and in a longer run than was then customary for Bodley Head books. His small staff tested the market. Booksellers were adamant: discriminating book-buyers would not consider paper-bound books. Both booksellers and librarians insisted that the shelf-life of books bound in this way would be so short as to make them uneconomical for bookshops, libraries and readers.

It is inconceivable that Allen was ignorant of this unfulfilled ambition of Uncle John: from the time when John Lane began to visit Bristol until his death, Allen was the principal beneficiary of his zest for publishing reminiscences. If Allen knew of *Keynotes* and even if it contributed to his inspiration, its presentation was in a sense antithetical to a production tenet to which Allen held firm almost to the end of his days. Beardsley's cover drawing for the first book in the series – a tall dark woman in a huge hat, a Pierrot and a tiny imp playing a guitar – was only remotely relevant to the text. For its own period and for all Beardsley's skill it was an example of the kind of cover design which sixty years later Allen described, pungently and despisingly, as 'bosoms and bottoms'.

From his beginnings as a publisher John Lane had been energetic and successful in selling the American rights of books on his list. His first visit to New York achieved all that he had hoped. Although he spent so much time reading and writing cables about Oscar Wilde he was able to complete preparations for his own American branch office. In the next two decades, although he never came to compete on equal terms with the major American houses and was not averse to placing Bodley Head titles with rival firms if the terms were right, he managed to exploit the American market, mostly with books originated in Vigo Street but with a leavening of transatlantic writers, among them Theodore Dreiser, Sherwood Anderson and Stephen Leacock.

Lane's capacity for delegation was minimal. His failure to accommodate to the ambiguities of partnership had been a major cause of the breach with Elkin Mathews; though he expected his subordinates to work as hard as he did himself, he neither doubted nor left for doubt in the minds of others that they were subordinates. For him there could be no plenipotentiary, not even on the other side of the Atlantic; it was inevitable that, once the New York branch was established, Lane was forever crossing and re-crossing the ocean. He enjoyed New York, he liked the United States and, because he had a very strong sense of family tradition, he liked it even more when he discovered that the country was full of distant cousins. Above all he relished the sense of bustling achievement which came with being busy about his business on two continents.

However, the greatest benefit that came to him by way of America was initiated only indirectly through his professional concerns. When he was forty he married a rich American widow. The marriage was a surprise to most of his acquaintances: Lane was known to be attractive to women and fond of their company -- he was not nicknamed Petticoat Lane because of his skill as a salesman -- but all had thought him so obsessed with publishing that he would never find time for courtship. Lane met Annie Eichberg King at a reception in London, chased her to Boston, returned to London without her, and finally overcame her doubts with fifty-page letters and more personal transatlantic visits. He acquired not only a wife but also an elegant hostess, a persuasive literary adviser, and, not least important, a financial backer.

Lane had launched his business by shrewd dealing in the old books which he and Mathews had bought in their youth and put in the joint pool. Since that time he had borrowed £2000 – from a lady friend – but had developed The Bodley Head and lived well enough entirely on the proceeds of publishing. Now with his wife's money he bought a large house in Lancaster Gate Terrace, entertained lavishly, and enlarged the Bodley Head list.

Lewis May, who was working for Lane at the time of his marriage (and who later wrote an effusive but satisfactory biography of the publisher), was not impressed by Mrs Lane, whom he found 'rather hard and pragmatical' but Lane was happy in his marriage. The gossip about his attention to ladies was not so common after his wedding – and what there was referred always to his behaviour when he was in Paris and out of Annie's suzerainty – and he was also content to allow her to add a new dimension to his social and professional life. Though his loathing of music was not eradicated he was proud of his wife's musical accomplishments and more particularly of her musical antecedents. (She was the daughter of Julius Eichberg, director of the Boston Conservatory.) Even through the anguish caused to him by the scraping of fiddles and the twanging of pianos, he could but recognize that chamber music and solo performances added class to the receptions and tea-parties at Lancaster Gate Terrace such as was not always or inevitably provided by the conversation of egocentric authors and amiable peers.

Annie Lane had many talents. In adolescence she had thought herself a poet; in this fallacy she had been encouraged by a pat on the head from Longfellow and by the applause of her countrymen for a more than ordinarily nauseating patriotic song she wrote to a mangled version of her father's music. Fortunately she grew out of verse-writing and developed a sensible reticence in considering the work of poets so that she seldom interfered between Lane and his better-informed poetic advisers. Consequently The Bodley Head continued to publish poets of quality; if in the final analysis only a few of them can be numbered amongst the truly great, still the roll-call of Bodley Head's poets is in all English publishing history surpassed only by the list built up from the mid twenties by Faber and Faber under the editorial and poetic genius of T. S. Eliot. Francis Thompson, Alice Meynell, William Watson, Ernest Dowson, John Davidson, Laurence Binyon, Stephen Phillips, Lascelles Abercrombie, Rupert Brooke, A. E. and the Belgian poet Emile Cammaerts all appeared at some time or another under Lane's publishing patronage. He himself thought that Watson was the greatest of them all, but the solecism can be forgiven him because he made poetry pay – even for his poets.

One of Lane's poets, John Davidson, wrote: 'To discover or create a buying public for minor and other poetry must always be a great feat; to have achieved it nowadays, and in the manner in which it has been done at The Bodley Head, is to have established a record.'

Annie Lane's influence on the major and prose section of The Bodley Head was more considerable. Before his marriage Lane had begun to move from the publication of limited editions for an esoteric audience into conventional and comparatively long runs of more obviously popular books. Annie furthered this development with her fortune, and by her tastes set its direction.

John Lane was no linguist. Even in French he was not merely illiterate but almost inarticulate. Wilde had known it. 'Any desire on the part of Mr Lane,' he had written at the time of the *Salomé* controversy, 'to have the manuscript of my French play submitted to him for his approval would I fear have excited considerable amusement in myself and in others.' (Thirty years later, Allen benefited hugely from Lane's linguistic impotence. Uncle John was so over-awed by Allen's schoolboy French that he thought him competent to serve as an interpreter and frequently used him in this capacity during visits to Paris – which must have amazed the French.) Annie Lane, on the other hand, was almost as fluent in German and French as she was in English, and was capable of reading manuscripts in both Spanish and Italian. With Frederick Chapman, she was largely responsible for persuading her husband to move boldly into the publication of translations. The works chosen were, for the most part, biographies poor in literary value but rich in immediate sales potential. It was, however, through his wife's intercession that Lane became the English publisher of Anatole France; it was she who brought into The Bodley Head André Maurois. It was Maurois who, by way of his *Ariel*, became as it were the symbol of and the link between the achievements of two generations of Lanes.

Annie Lane was with her husband when Anatole France was first visited in Paris to discuss the English rights of his works. She it must have been who did all the material negotiation, for his command of English made Lane's French seem almost respectable. It was she, too, who made that first meeting business-like: Lane was so overcome by covetousness at the sight of the author's superb collection of antique furniture that for once he forgot The Bodley Head. One of Anatole France's friends who was present when John Lane called on the author reported unkindly, '*Il regardait autour de lui comme un commissaire-priseur.*'

There is a suggestion supported by many of his contemporaries that Lane never read any of the books by France that he published, not even the one translated by Annie, and that the only aspect of his work which attracted Lane was its overt secularism. Lane liked to call himself a Quaker though he never attended Meeting, and he was rabidly anti-Catholic. For this prejudice Lane appears to have been damned by Fate; from Wilde, Beardsley and Dowson onwards the path from Vigo Street to Rome was well-trodden by Bodley Head authors.

France was almost sixty before ever one of his books was translated into English; thereafter, once The Bodley Head had taken him on, he owed his phenomenal success in the English language almost entirely to Lane's skill as publisher and publicist. First Lane produced immaculately designed editions, almost in the manner of the limited editions of the nineties. These he himself hawked around the bookshops, converting reluctant booksellers by his own evangelical zeal; he suborned, seduced and bullied critics to write fulsome articles on France; he flattered the booksellers by pointing out that the good sense and good taste they had shown by ordering France had preceded the verdict of the literary arbiters, and he strengthened their commercial resolve by ensuring that favourable press comment would continue. He created a cult and kept its altar-fires burning with new titles and new editions of previously published translations. There were de luxe versions, illustrated versions and, finally and most successfully, France's caviare offered to the general, a half-crown popular edition. For this cheap edition Lane used the plates of the more expensive Library Edition but the size was crown octavo, so that the margins were meagre – and the production costs much reduced. For the lavish red and gold bindings of the earlier editions he substituted bright orange covers.

> These little orange-covered books were soon to be seen everywhere [writes Lewis May]; everywhere Anatole France was the great topic of conversation. Clerks and typists, tea-shop waitresses, the intelligentsia of Bloomsbury, the *virtuosi* of Chelsea, all eagerly began to imbibe the easy scepticism, the graceful if somewhat libidinous philosophy of the Sage of the Villa Saïd.

As the orange edition of Anatole France was the zenith of Lane's career as a publisher for the many, so did his stage-management of France's visit to London in 1913 mark the high point of his powers as publicity man. Never before in English literary history, and certainly never since, has a foreign writer been fêted as was France in London. A banquet at the Savoy, a tea-party at Number Ten Downing Street, a reception by the Fabian Society, and crowds waiting in the streets for a glimpse of the author; no publisher could ask for more or arrange better.

When Anatole France died John Lane was himself a sick man, no longer capable of the cunning in puffery which had persuaded the public to accept France as the greatest literary figure of his time, which had helped to win him the Nobel Prize, and which had seduced critics into hyperbole such as that which came from W. J. Locke (admittedly himself a Bodley Head bestseller) who wrote: 'he hovers over the world like a disembodied spirit, wise with the learning of all times and with the knowledge of all hearts that have beaten...'. Even on his sick-bed, Lane must have known a twinge of regret in that he could not boast responsibility for arranging Anatole France's funeral. Full military honours, in attendance the President of the Republic, the entire French Cabinet, most of the Diplomatic Corps and, to deliver the funeral oration, M. Léon Blum: that was indeed a publicity party for an author to arouse envy in the heart of any publisher – even John Lane.

Not all Annie Lane's advice about European authors was as fruitful as her intervention on behalf of Anatole France. For no other writer, English, American or European, did Lane operate so lavishly or so triumphantly as he did for France, not even for Maurois. But the customary success of translations gave to The Bodley Head an extra dimension, an extra specialization of a kind enjoyed in a later generation by firms such as Secker and Warburg, and an opportunity for making reciprocal arrangements on behalf of English authors. Nevertheless, when as is inevitable, the career of John Lane is considered not so much for itself as for the sly nudges which the history of one generation offers to those who consider the next, then, of all Bodley Head excursions into translations the most significant are not Lane's manoeuvrings on behalf of Anatole France nor yet any of his bright successes, but the story of his near-failures.

The publishing history of the English-language versions of Herman Sudermann's *The Song of Songs* is simple enough. First translated into English by an American called Seltzer, the book was originally published in the United States where it sold well and without impediment from the authorities. Lane imported sheets; then, discovering that he was about to be prosecuted for publishing an obscene book, he withdrew the edition, employed another translator to produce a version which he described, quaintly and ambiguously, as 'while in no sense bowdlerised [nevertheless] a model of good taste'. This new translation appeared under The Bodley Head imprint complete with several prefatory comments by eminent and eminently respectable men and women who vouched for the genius and integrity of Sudermann and for the essentially moral quality of his book.

The parallels between this and the trial of Penguin Books for publishing *Lady Chatterley's Lover* are so striking that they merit a break in chronological narrative. When the police came to serve a writ on The Bodley Head, John Lane was conveniently away from the office (ostensibly with a cold) just as Allen was not present when the writ was served on Penguin. In both cases, it might be argued, the absence of the head of the firm could have been accidental and the sense of history repeating itself merely a coincidence. Yet John Lane made a habit of absenting himself when crisis was imminent; Allen transformed the habit into an art. And, if it cannot be proven that Allen was remembering the prefaces to *The Song of Songs* when he published a full-scale account of the 1960 case *Regina* v. *Penguin Books Ltd*, then the coincidence is so sensational as to be unbelievable. It is far easier to accept that Uncle John's tutelage and example persuaded Allen to adopt throughout his working life two seemingly conflicting principles; the first that a commander should never risk himself in preliminary skirmishes; the second that, to the success of a publicist, impertinence is often remarkably pertinent.

The translations which Annie Lane helped to bring into The Bodley Head were, for all that they came from across the Channel, not so very different in literary texture from the British and American titles which made up the bulk of the list once, through fear of the consequences and by commercial necessity, Lane was moved from his original intention to be at the same time adventurous and esoteric. His wife's influence also lured Lane into another field which was to him novel, which earlier he would have regarded as out of bounds to the publisher of *The Yellow Book*, but which he was to explore with considerable success for the next twenty years. Annie had abandoned her poetic ambitions and had taken to writing ostensibly satirical books about British society. Inevitably Lane became his wife's publisher and almost inevitably her taste for the kind of book which she herself wrote soon began to colour the list. Lane's own sense of humour was not acute, though he could accept a joke against himself with grace, providing always that it could be given wide currency and so serve as effective publicity. He was more comfortable with the humorists who came his way through Annie's introduction and later through his editor, Herbert Jenkins (himself a successful author of light-hearted novels), than ever he had been with Wilde or Beerbohm. True, he found Chesterton for himself but he promptly lost him as a novelist (though The Bodley Head did publish both *Heretics* and *Orthodoxy*), but generally his second-generation humorists were more rumbustious and slighter than those he had coralled in the nineties. They were also, with two exceptions, ephemeral.

The two exceptions were Stephen Leacock and Saki. Both would not have been acceptable to Lane in his earlier, more precious days. Both owed their popularity on the two sides of the Atlantic largely to Lane's adroitness and yet neither can be regarded in any real sense as Lane discoveries.

When his first humorous book, *Literary Lapses*, appeared under the Bodley Head imprint in 1910 Leacock was already forty. The sketches in it had all been written in the nineties when the author was engaged in the 'most dreary, most thankless and the worst-paid profession in the world', as a schoolmaster at Upper Canada College; most of them had been published at that time in American and Canadian journals. Later, when Leacock had made his reputation as a scholar with his *Elements of Political Economy*, he gathered together his sketches and sent them off to his academic publishers:

> They thought I had gone mad. I therefore printed the sketches on my own account and we sold them through a news company. We sold 3000 copies in two months. In this modest form the book fell into the hands of ... Mr John Lane. ... He cabled me an offer to publish the book in regular form.

Fortunately for the reputation of Canadian letters, fortunately for readers of English, and most fortunately for The Bodley Head, thereafter Lane kept the Head of the Department of Political Science and Economics at McGill University from wasting much time writing on economics and political science. It was no easy task, as Leacock explained:

Many of my friends are under the impression that I write humorous nothings in idle moments when the wearied brain is unable to perform the serious labours of the economist. My own experience is exactly the other way. The writing of solid, instructive stuff, fortified by facts and figures, is easy enough. But to write something out of one's own mind, worth reading for its own sake, is an arduous contrivance only to be achieved in fortunate moments, few and far between.

And, he added, in a phrase appropriate to a man who lived and worked close to the Heights of Abraham, 'I would rather have written *Alice in Wonderland* than *the whole Encyclopaedia Britannica*'.

As with Leacock so also with Saki: Lane fostered a reputation that had already been made in magazines and journals. Unlike Leacock, Saki never became an intimate of the Lanes and, though The Bodley Head did well with his finely wrought, whimsical and high-spirited short stories and novels, Lane did not come to appreciate fully the genius of the man until after his death as a corporal in the Royal Fusiliers at Beaumont-Hamel in 1916.

Neither John Lane nor any literary historian could classify W. J. Locke among the humorists, but Lane made a mistake which no literary historian has compounded in pairing Locke with Anatole France as the most significant novelists on his list. The publisher's confidence and persuasiveness fooled librarians, booksellers and through them the reading public for almost a quarter of a century; more than the works of any of his poets and humorists, the frothy, sentimental novels of this one writer – like Leacock a refugee from schoolmastering – typified, in the second phase of the firm's history, the Bodley Head list.

The history of publishing is made grim by examples of publishers who, having offered up nightly prayers to the Almighty that He send them bestselling authors, come at last to the awful realization that their pleas have been answered by another agency: in exchange for a catalogue-full of popular successes they have mortgaged their souls to the Devil and their premises, goodwill and independence to the bank. The decline of The Bodley Head had begun with Lane's move from the limited editions which he and Mathews had planned to make their own preserve into competition with well-established general houses with healthier finances. For several years Annie's fortune held Lane from reality. The triumphs which they engineered together had to be sustained, an expensive process – too expensive to be contrived with Annie's money alone, especially as she was called upon to support also their expensive domestic arrangements and their rich-blooded entertaining. The Bodley Head could manage only whilst it stayed small and specialized; once it grew to medium size and embraced the kind of publishing which only a large house could finance the fragility created by under-capitalization became obvious and progressively dangerous. Lane was supremely capable of publicizing France or W. J. Locke; perhaps no other publisher in London could have done it with as much *panache*; but *panache* would not pay the bills that had to be met when the publicity had its rewards. Public response made it imperative that *Penguin Island*, *The Morals of Marcus Ordeyne* and *Beloved Vagabond* be kept in print.

The financial problems that Lane was creating for himself by manufacturing bestsellers did not become insistent for many years. Nor did he suffer over-much for his casual attention and naïve attitude to the political portents which were lowering over Europe in the years immediately before the First World War. He earned justifiable opprobrium when he published a translation of a book by an author whose name, surprisingly for a German, was Houston Stewart Chamberlain, who contended that the Germans deserved to rule the earth and would undoubtedly gain their deserts. But Lane defended himself on the grounds that he had not read the book ('Oscar Wilde, thou shouldst be living at this hour'); as if that was not defence enough, he followed it up with a statement which later generations, gifted with knowledge of the activities of some of the Mitfords, find even more amazing. The book must be reputable: had it not been translated by Lord Redesdale?

Despite these aberrations, in the period between the Boer War and the Great War Lane remained in the eyes of the public, as he had been in the nineties, a major power in British and American publishing; he was (as he had most certainly not been when Wilde, Beardsley and *The Yellow Book* first helped establish his fame) a much-honoured figure in the world of books and in society.

So it was when, after the bombing of Lancaster Gate Terrace, he moved his home to Bath and became a frequent visitor at the house of his Williams relations; the full effects of his prodigality had still not punctured either his self-esteem or his confidence in the future of his *alter ego*, The Bodley Head. Nevertheless the effects of war on his private life were inescapable, and war-time restrictions and regulations added considerably to his burdens as the autocrat of Vigo Street. Still he believed, without reservation, that the spirit of a publishing house was created in the image of the founder and head. Haunted by the memory of his few years with Elkin Mathews, he had no difficulty in persuading himself that the miseries of partnership must be arithmetically compounded by the existence of a board of directors, each one obstinate that he alone could plot the correct course for the firm, each selecting a different route, and all insisting upon the democracy of the board-room. His arrogance was undiminished and his energy to all outward appearance undiminished, but the whisper of time was in his ears. He knew that he could not sustain for long the sole direction of two publishing houses, one in London and one in New York. He had no heir. One after the other his editors had deserted him; he worked them so hard that their health broke, or else (in his opinion) he taught them so well that they felt qualified to set up as publishers on their own account. The best of the latest had gone off to the war. He recognized that he must start the process again. This time he would select a young man who would do as he did, not a competitor for the hegemony of his empire, but one whose obligation to him would be entire, who would not be easily tempted to convert the benefits of apprenticeship to the service of some rival firm. Lane's strong family loyalty and the sense of deprivation that is inescapable for a childless man made the discovery of young Allen Williams seem a message from Heaven. It needed only the simple magic of a change of name to convince him that all had been done that needed to be done to secure for all time the glories of John Lane The Bodley Head.

Yet John Lane was too shrewd to concede all at once. Allen must learn his trade; if he did not prove himself worthy of the role for which he was cast, John Lane could still somehow be rid of him. He could find him a place with his friend William Heinemann, with his former employee, Herbert Jenkins, or he could somehow shuffle him back to Bristol.

CHAPTER TWO

THERE is no way to learn the trade of publisher except by observation and imitation, but Allen was a shrewd observer and a quick study. The Bodley Head had a great reputation but a small staff; although he was at first little more than an office-boy, his new name and the privilege that came from his relationship with the head of the firm gave him the right to eavesdrop and to peer over shoulders. It was not long before he had mastered the limited techniques of the editorial department and the uncomplicated accounting system. Out on the road, at first in the company of John Lane himself or of one of the three senior travellers, but very soon as a plenipotentiary, Allen's ready sociability was immediately acceptable to that species of bookseller who likes to fill his orders and his glass in the public bar at lunch-time. Even booksellers of the sterner sort, the dour men who look upon publishers' representatives as garrulous interrupters of the leisurely communion between bookseller, reader and unseen author, were not unwilling to receive John Lane's 'nephew'; nor were they disinclined to bolster his inexperience with advice and with their reminiscences of past achievements and distant failures. He had then, as for the rest of his life, a remarkable memory for book titles and some skill in discussing the contents of books which he had never read; these two gifts (perhaps the most useful of all advantages accessible to a bookman) and his civilized eagerness to talk in an informed manner about books published by rival firms made him popular with booksellers of both kinds.

By going out as a representative early in his career Allen built for himself a benefit which he shared with very few of his publishing contemporaries (and notably in his generation only with Jonathan Cape). His intimacy with booksellers was to stand him in good stead in later years; though he could never bridge the chasm which separates the two sides of the book trade, he was, more than most of his fellow-publishers, socially acceptable on the other side of the gap.

John Lane encouraged him to make early forays also into the world of printing. There the warmth of the reception was even more palpable than among booksellers. Book-printers – even those who printed on what was, for that time, a large scale – were just beginning to reap the rewards of the doctrines which John Lane had been trying to expound for thirty years; a print-buyer who bore the name of Lane and came from The Bodley Head was welcomed immediately by printers who were concerning themselves as never before with the importance of good book design.

In many of the major printing houses a new generation was active. Like Allen several were heirs-presumptive to management but, being just a little older than he, they had experienced that strange amalgam of independence from convention and dependence upon remote authority which makes up Service life in war-time. In the war years both leaders and subordinates, they were now at one and the same time chafing to be masters in the firms that they knew must soon be theirs, and ready to accept some even bolder spirit whom they could acknowledge as their leader.

This was a time when, as never before in British history, the young possessed knowledge which their seniors could not acquire, knowledge which had come their way in the mud of Flanders and the sands of Mesopotamia. It left them despising anything that was pre-war, impatient with antique formulae, and in their social *mores* utterly unlike their fathers. Young printers and young publishers alike no longer believed that because they were about to inherit solid respectable businesses they must behave like solid, respectable and essentially middle-class businessmen. As professionals they were impatient for innovation, and as men they were unconventional, spontaneous, ready to seize upon any excuse – or none – to start a party.

In the company of such as these, more even than from Uncle John, Allen quickly acquired the sophistication that Bristol and his family had never given him. He was as yet without money or tangible authority, but more than any other member of that loosely-knit group he had come to know his way around all the trades that made up the book world and so came to be regarded as the link between them all. More obviously than any other young aspirant to power, his manner seemed to epitomize their disdain for convention. At twenty he could manage drink or girls as well as any recently demobilized infantry subaltern, and could manage both drink and girls more frequently and more enthusiastically than most. His fund of trade gossip was inexhaustible and uninhibited. And yet his professional seriousness was obvious and undeniable.

He acquired cronies by the dozen who were not passed on to him by Uncle John, and not a few friends, themselves up-and-coming members of the book trade. There was, for example, Raymond Hazell, of the printing firm of Hazell, Watson and Viney, Allen's companion by choice for some of his less reputable excursions and the prime recipient of his confidences about his plans for his publishing future. There was also, actually in The Bodley Head, a new novelist, a man considerably older than Allen – with already behind him six years in the Royal Naval Air Service and the Royal Air Force. Ben Travers would soon make his own name famous and with it the names of Ralph Lynn, Tom Walls, Robertson Hare, Mary Brough and the Aldwych Theatre. For the moment Travers shared many of Allen's enthusiasms and supported his ebullience with his own cheerful maturity. He never persuaded Allen to take on his passion for cricket.

Indeed Allen was disinclined to take any exercise at all. He did envy the competence as horsemen common among his immediate seniors and so, like many young men of that time who could not afford a civilian riding-master, he joined the Territorial Army. His soldierly zeal was not intense and he resented sacrificing part of his precious holidays to the annual camp, but he liked to look smart; as in publishing, so also as a trooper in the Surrey and Sussex Yeomanry, his powers of imitation and his quick memory made him stand out. He was soon offered a commission. As a newly joined subaltern in the Essex Yeomanry he was summoned to a levée at Buckingham Palace and there his military career almost ended. When he was called to be presented to the King he marched forward six paces, halted, faced right smartly, and set off to advance another six paces before saluting. But, in the process of facing right his spurs had locked, and he slid towards his Sovereign like a one-legged ice skater.

The ceremonious indignity was forgiven. He remained in the Territorials for many years, was eventually promoted to captain, learnt to ride well, and in the Yeomanry gathered round him another band of racketing cronies utterly unlike his book world companions in all but their zest for girls and parties.

John Lane was too shrewd to condemn Allen's energetic adventures among his contemporaries, but he did temper them by inviting him more and ever more frequently to Lancaster Gate Terrace where he could meet the staider, older and more notable men and women of literature and the other arts. Even he engineered for Allen opportunities for coming face-to-face with men not ordinarily accessible to publishers' staffs nor even to the publishers themselves.

As a collector of highly considered trifles, Lane discovered a drinking-goblet that had once belonged to a Prince of Wales. He obtained permission to present it to the then holder of the title, who expressed a wish to add his signature to that inscribed on the glass by his predecessor. Recognizing that even the most tenuous acquaintance with the Prince, the symbolic leader of Allen's generation, could only be useful to the young man he had selected to be Prince of Wales at The Bodley Head, John Lane made Allen responsible for handling the affair. So that he might more effectively instruct royalty in the art of writing on glass Allen practised assiduously with a diamond-pencil, using the window-panes of the Vigo Street office as scribbling-blocks. On the appointed day Allen took to Clarence House the antique goblet and a modern glass. Patiently he explained the technique to the Prince, ending by engraving his own signature on the practice-glass. The Prince took over the diamond-pencil, essayed his skill by writing his name above Allen's, and then, satisfied that he had mastered the art, he repeated the signature on the goblet. Allen's career as a collector had begun, the first item in that collection a drinking-glass signed *Allen Lane* and *Edward P.*

As an opportunist he was making progress.

For John Lane, however, the task of creating an heir-apparent had scarcely begun. It pleased Lane that Allen was impressing his contemporaries. It pleased him, too, that when Allen attended the Sunday tea-parties and musical soirées at Lancaster Gate Terrace he was no longer blatantly obvious as a flat-footed plebeian only a few years out of a provincial grammar school. Lane had never succeeded in losing entirely his Devon burr but no such vulgarity could be permitted to Allen. All evidence of Bristol must go. A publisher needs contacts anywhere and everywhere but Lane, encouraged by his wife, preferred the *haute-monde* to all other worlds. Allen must learn to move easily in high society. Raynes Park was not even bohemian; Annie Lane doubted that it existed at all, and John knew that in Raynes Park no one made any contacts worth the making. He decided to move Allen to 8 Lancaster Gate Terrace.

The change of address was accompanied by an increase in salary and by a considerable increase in responsibility. There was no longer any hesitancy in John Lane's attitude; he had presented his Prince of Wales to the people. Though Allen was not yet a member of the Bodley Head board, he was from then on encouraged to act as a brevet-director. He was given almost dictatorial powers in the sales department, even above Crockett, the ostensible sales manager. He was let loose to seek out new authors; he was usually present in Lane's office when the head of the firm discussed contracts with his more distinguished writers and was summoned to join dinner-parties whenever John and Annie entertained the eminent. Thus Allen came to know among others Conan Doyle, Bernard Shaw, W. J. Locke, John Galsworthy, Max Beerbohm and Lane's favourite rival, William Heinemann.

Locke invited him to stay at his villa in the South of France; Allen went with Uncle John's blessing. From the villa he wrote to his brother Richard a letter which said very little about France, nothing at all about Locke's personality but a great deal about Locke's seven bathrooms.

He asked Bernard Shaw for his autograph and was told that he should not waste time seeking other men's signatures but should instead work at making his own worth collecting.

Allen's equivocal position in the firm's hierarchy might have been acceptable before the War, when Lane was undisputed emperor, Annie the power behind the throne, and the rest of the staff no more than respected hirelings; but things were changing faster than Lane could understand. Because of heightened competition from other and newer houses whose editorial policies were not so very different, because costs were rising, and because neither John nor Annie could bring themselves to temper their extravagance, The Bodley Head was now faced with disaster. Regretfully Lane closed his American company. So that he might solve his immediate cash-flow problem he turned The Bodley Head into a private company and offered a stake in the firm to some of his senior employees. Both Willett, the production manager, and Crockett, the sales manager, responded but their financial contribution was small. Lane cast about for new and more substantial transfusions of capital.

Most putative investors could see from the accounts that the business affairs of The Bodley Head were more affairs than business; it took no great shrewdness to realize that the stock was grossly over-valued. But the fame of John Lane was still immense and the editorial reputation of The Bodley Head still high, and so two young men, Ronald Boswell and Carr-Gomm, each put up £10,000 to purchase a directorship. Neither had much publishing experience – not even as much as Allen – but their arrival in Vigo Street created unease. There were now five working directors, too many for a house whose total staff was not more than thirty; four were not members of the family and the fifth, John Lane himself, was tiring, his mind turning more and ever more to reminiscence about the great days when he had burst upon the London publishing scene. There was also Allen, not as yet a director but very much his Uncle John's favourite, and endowed with privileges not granted to the others.

Late in 1924 John tried to ease the awkwardness by promoting Allen to the board. It was almost his last act as a publisher.

One night in January 1925 he attended a dinner in aid of the French Hospital, a charity to which he was much devoted because his connection with it emphasized his Huguenot ancestry. From the dinner he went to catch a train to Brighton, stood around on a dreary, fog-swept platform, and caught a chill. He was persuaded to take to his bed, but not even Annie could order him to rest. From his sick-room he issued a stream of telephoned orders. He read manuscripts. He summoned his colleagues to conferences. Two weeks later he was dead.

Allen's grief for John Lane was short-lived and muted. He had admired Uncle John for his past achievements and he was grateful to him, but his own knowledge of publishing had made him impatient with Lane's archaic methods and with his dedication to a tradition that, in Allen's opinion, would no longer hold The Bodley Head in the advance guard of publishing. John Lane had taught him to be bold, efficient and hard-headed, but only by exhortation reinforced with example from a distant past; the John Lane Allen had actually watched at work had been less businesslike and far less adventurous than many of Allen's close acquaintances in the younger generation. Conscience told him that he owed much to John Lane, but common sense urged him to repay his debt by leaving the easy road to bankruptcy which Uncle John had been following for several years. Instead he would revive and make appropriate to the twenties the courageous originality that had first made The Bodley Head notable. By his efforts The Bodley Head would become once more exciting.

The ambition fitted his ebullient personality well but it brought him immediately into conflict with his fellow-directors: with Willett (now Managing Director) and Crockett because they saw themselves as guardians of the sober Bodley Head style which they had known throughout their working days; with the newcomers, Carr-Gomm and Boswell, because they did not wish to see their investments dissipated by the mad-cap indiscretions of a brash youngster. But Allen had advantages in addition to his unflagging energy. As yet he owned no shares in the firm beyond the nominal holding which allowed him to sit on the board, but he lived at Lancaster Gate Terrace, he was a Lane, and he had the tacit support of Annie, the majority shareholder.

Despite these advantages his exuberance led him into an error which gave his colleagues the chance that they coveted to put this upstart in his place.

Hesketh Pearson was then in his early forties and a successful actor who was not known to have put a professional pen to paper. Allen knew him as a drinking companion and as a man with a wide range of acquaintances. When Pearson told him that he could bring to The Bodley Head the sensational, salacious and undiplomatic memoirs of a very distinguished diplomat, Allen not only believed him but accepted without hesitation the mysterious condition that the identity of the author must be known only to Pearson and himself. When Allen announced his *coup* to the board he made no attempt to disguise the sense of triumph he felt at having acquired a book in the modern vogue of unrestrained revelation which was certain to make a bestseller, nor did he hide his impish pleasure in possessing knowledge which they could not share. For their part, so eager were they for profits that they did not press him to name the diplomat, contenting themselves with Allen's assurance (which may or may not have been true) that the public career of the person whose name he knew had followed the pattern outlined in the book.

Hesketh Pearson was to edit *The Whispering Gallery*, and it was to him that The Bodley Head paid an advance of £100. The firm ordered a long run, sent out review copies and waited for the sensation and the sales.

The sensation came, but not the sales. The *Daily Mail* devoted its leading article to an attack on The Bodley Head. *The Whispering Gallery* was beyond belief; the one conceivable explanation was that The Bodley Head had conspired to deceive the public. Other newspapers followed suit. The only way that the horrified Bodley Head directors could justify themselves in the eyes of the public was by taking libel actions against most of Fleet Street, but their chances of winning the actions would be derisory unless they could prove that the book was genuine. To do this they must have the name of the author.

Forty years later Ronald Boswell recalled the events of the days after the publication of *The Whispering Gallery*; the phrases he used still revealed not only resentment of this particular treacherous act of Allen's but also something of the relationship between the junior director and his partners. 'We had Allen Lane up before us,' he said, as if he were describing a defaulter appearing before his company commander, 'and we told him, "You must tell us the name given to you by Hesketh Pearson." '

Allen was unabashed, but he conceded the name. *The Whispering Gallery* was by Sir Rennell Rodd, the British Ambassador in Rome. Had they been told that the author was Queen Mary, the board could hardly have been shocked more than on hearing that the scabrous book was the product of one of the most diplomatic and respectable members of His Majesty's much-respected Diplomatic Service. 'We all nearly had a fit,' reported Boswell. '. . , The Ambassador was protocol enshrined.' Had Allen been in touch with Sir Rennell? He had not. Had he any written assurance of authorship? He had not. They sent him off to see Pearson. He came back with devasting news. Pearson admitted that the memoirs were fabricated; when he had suggested that the anonymous author was Rodd, he had meant it as a joke. Frantically The Bodley Head withdrew from the bookshops all copies of *The Whispering Gallery* and instituted proceedings against Pearson for seeking financial gain by false pretences.

By this time Printing House Square had been roused by Rodd, and *The Times* weighed in with an editorial attacking The Bodley Head in unequivocal terms. Allen tried to explain his actions, to his partners, to *The Times* and, through an intermediary, to Rodd himself, but only made a bad situation worse. Faced with the opprobrium of most of Fleet Street, with portentous letters from Rodd's solicitors and with the august displeasure of Sir Rennell Rodd, The Bodley Head board cravenly decided to place all the blame where blame was in truth due. Abandoning all pretexts of communal responsibility, they sent out in all directions letters which Uriah Heep would have been proud to have drafted.

To Rodd's solicitors, Willett wrote that all this sorrow had been caused 'by the youngest partner of the Firm in the course of business' and 'did not come to the knowledge of the other Directors until it was too late'. Allen, he said, had prepared an explanation for publication in the press in which he intended to convey that 'alone he personally knew the name' of the author of *The Whispering Gallery*. Willett had not seen the letter, which, he insisted, none of his fellow-directors had been shown, because Allen had heard that legal proceedings were impending.

To Rodd, Willett wrote in even more obsequious terms. He would call on him, if possible on that very day, to apologize and to explain how it had come about that Sir Rennell's name had been dragged into this unfortunate business. And, he concluded, 'we are taking steps to bring to justice the miscreant who has made use of your name in this disgraceful way'.

In this last phrase is a nice ambiguity which must have pleased Willett as he wrote it. Ostensibly it referred only to the case which The Bodley Head had instituted against Pearson, but the word 'miscreant' could be applied with equal force to Allen; all the partners were warming themselves with pleasing thoughts of bringing Allen to justice.

They were thwarted on every count. Pearson was exonerated on the ground that he had not intended a fraud. (From this time on he abandoned the stage for a full-time career as a biographer, with later Allen as his publisher.) Allen received his first national publicity, a newspaper headline which announced 'Allen Lane in Witness Box', and circumstances set him out of reach of the punishment which Willett and the rest longed to mete out – if not beyond the effects of their justifiable suspicion that he was not to be trusted to act on his own. A few weeks after the verdict in *The Bodley Head* versus *Hesketh Pearson* Annie Lane died and Allen inherited the majority shareholding in The Bodley Head. The defaulter had become in everything but name company commander. Three months later Willett retired and Allen succeeded him as Managing Director. He was only twenty-four years old.

In the last six months of Annie Lane's life London had begun to experience the Seidlitz powder effects that the schoolmaster at Telesford House had suffered many years before. Two Lane brothers were together.

After leaving Bristol Grammar School Richard worked for a while on an agricultural research station. He then spent some time as a jackaroo in Australia and returned to England at the time of the General Strike. He persuaded Allen to find him a job in a Finchley Road bookshop, and Annie Lane to take him in at Lancaster Gate Terrace. His salary was derisory but he lived in luxury. Equipped with a new dinner-jacket and a new set of tails, he was ready and eager to join Allen wherever he went, be it to literary cocktail-parties, smart house-parties, or on less reputable but no less enjoyable drinking marathons.

Allen, for his part, was never so happy as when in the company of his brothers. He and Richard goaded each other to ever more elaborate feats of social endurance, but he was also able to share with Richard as with nobody else his more serious professional dreams.

In her will Annie Lane left to Allen the bulk of Bodley Head shares; she had thought it equitable to bequeath most of her money to be divided between Richard, John and Nora. Therefore Richard could afford to give up his menial job in the Finchley Road and devote most of his time to Allen's company.

8 Lancaster Gate Terrace was a leasehold property. For six months, whilst the executors were arranging the sale of the lease, Allen and Richard had the large house, a butler, a cook and two other servants to themselves, and all their domestic expenses paid by the estate. In such benevolent circumstances it was not surprising that Allen and Richard should organize a frantic social life. They were both handsome, both convivial. Richard had money to spare and Allen had power. Their patronage was worth acquiring and their parties lavish. Those who had been frequent visitors to the house in the days when Annie Lane was hostess continued to come. There were also new faces in the fifty-foot-long reception room, the faces of publishers, printers, booksellers and authors of their own generation, among them not infrequently another Bristolian, Beverley Nichols (who had just demonstrated his opinion of his literary significance by publishing an autobiographical account of the first twenty-five years of his life), and almost invariably a bold, pretty girl who was regarded by some critics as a major novelist, cruel, caustic and wise.

Ethel Mannin had been married in 1919 when she was only nineteen years old. Once she launched herself upon the literary world she had not allowed her married state to inhibit her overt intention to prove herself a leading representative of emancipated womanhood. Allen was fascinated by her seemingly complex personality, by her intelligence so much more obvious than his, by the eagerness with which she espoused novel and often outrageous ideas, and not a little by the fact that she was thought to be shocking. For her part, she was not unwilling to prove her emancipation by exercising it, in public in the company of a pleasingly noticeable and already notable young man, and in private with a man who listened to her opinions with respect, who had convinced himself that like her, he had come up the hard way – as she expressed it 'from kippers to caviare'. Allen could match her mischievous disrespect for the poses of the 'lions on Parnassus' with whom they both mixed. Already he knew enough about women so that he did not waste all their time together discussing opinions, background, ambitions or literary acquaintances. Some among Allen's close acquaintances thought that Ethel Mannin might be preparing to consign Mr Porteous for all time to the oblivion from which he had seldom emerged: she would become, even in the most respectable sense of the word, the mistress of The Bodley Head. So it might have been, had not Allen's concern for his independence and his still-powerful provincialism over-ridden the infatuation of the moment. Though the company of Mrs Porteous enhanced his reputation as a leader of the bright young men of London's book world, she was too flamboyant and her flamboyance too well known to be acceptable to his parents. Once, when taking her to a literary dinner, he warned her to wear quiet clothes because his mother would be present.

There were many other girls to court and many willing to be courted. He was then, as perhaps for the rest of his life, quintessentially a bachelor who regarded the company of women as an enthralling pastime but never a career.

The comforts of 8 Lancaster Gate Terrace came to an end, but not the hectic social life. With Richard, Allen moved to the house of a friend who worked for the rival publishing house, Chapman and Hall, but so many were their evening engagements that they found inconvenient even the four-mile journey to Hampstead. As tenants in Albany The Bodley Head had the right to use two servants' rooms on the upper floors. At their own expense Allen and Richard had built in a lavatory, and so acquired for themselves a *pied-à-terre* in London's most distinguished chambers, and for Allen a base only a staircase-climb away from his office.

Living centrally made possible social activity on an even more frantic scale, and the Lanes were willing to go to extraordinary lengths in search of gaiety and free drinks. One evening, when visiting an actor friend in his dressing-room after a show, they heard that a new night-club was opening that night and was offering champagne *gratis* to any who appeared in tails. The Lanes hurried back to their rooms, changed into full evening dress, walked the few yards to Regent Street and for several hours did their best to make sure that the Silver Slipper would not make a profit for many months.

But, despite all his gallivanting, Allen somehow managed to sustain a professional life that was no less strenuous. To some degree, though certainly not to the same extent as Uncle John, Allen did not distinguish between the two parts of his existence. Even in the midst of the most uproarious party, and even after he had taken in more than his fair share of alcohol, he was forever on the alert for a hint that might be elaborated into an addition to The Bodley Head list. He was assiduous in attending more decorous and more obviously cultural occasions, a frequent visitor to the Eccentrics and the Titchmarsh Club; so it came about that he began to develop a reputation for snapping-up the offerings of one-book authors – politicians, explorers and leading hostesses. His readiness to publish this kind of book became public knowledge; he was in truth merely building upon credit in this kind already acquired for The Bodley Head by John Lane. Aspiring authors of memoirs came to look to Allen as the obvious publisher for their one book.

As the benefits enlarged that accrued to The Bodley Head from this specialized activity and, consequently, the volume of work imposed upon Allen and his colleagues, he did not slacken his attention to the more patently professional authors on the list. At this time, even more than had his Uncle John, he aspired to be friend as well as publisher to his authors; Allen was forever entertaining, dining-out with writers, or visiting them in their country cottages.

He had his favourites. The one that he liked best of all was fourteen years his senior and utterly unlike the wild, Michael Arlen heroines who accompanied him to literary parties and night-clubs. Agatha Christie detested crowds, did not drink, played tennis, and was a skilled and enthusiastic needlewoman. Even when she came up to London, which she thought inferior to Torquay, she liked to go to classical concerts and to earnest plays. Despite his early training in Bristol church choirs, Allen could hardly distinguish Bach from Sullivan, his mental and physical restlessness made the long stillnesses of the concert-hall for him unendurable, the snatched champagne-drinking in the intervals was not his idea of conviviality, there was no time for gossip and no chance to pick up the scent of a bestseller. Though it suffered from some of the same disadvantages, theatre-going was more to his taste, but his likes did not coincide with those of the future author of *The Mousetrap*. His taste in live entertainment was unsophisticated. Above all other plays he liked the farces written by his old friend Ben Travers, he enjoyed Noël Coward's plays, Ivor Novello's saccharine musicals and the sharper pleasures served up in intimate revue. He seldom missed a new Shaw play and became remarkably knowledgeable about the Shaw canon, but this apparent exception to the habitual frothiness of his theatrical appreciation was caused originally by his sense of commitment – the *soi-disant* Socialist attending dutifully at the rites performed by the high priest of the cult – and became a permanent part of his critical equipment only when he discovered that Shaw's didacticism could be ignored and that his intellectualism did not prevent his plays from being hugely entertaining. There was also in Allen some highly personalized instinct which encouraged him to enjoy above all else the works of those whose faces and voices he knew.

Agatha Christie's devotion to *avant-garde* dramatists Allen could not share. Nevertheless, when she came to town Allen squired her nobly.

He had come to regard himself as the custodian of The Bodley Head tradition. The finances of the firm were far from secure, despite yet another transfusion of £10,000 provided by yet another new partner, Lindsay Drummond. Allen was alive to the fact that they could not afford to lose one of their richest properties, an author who added to her world-wide popularity and to Bodley Head resources with a new book each year.

Allen's care for Agatha Christie was heightened by nightmare recollection of events in his apprentice days when The Bodley Head – and indeed the world at large – had almost lost Agatha Christie before ever she had been discovered. The manuscript of *The Mysterious Affair at Styles* had brought only rejection slips from several publishers before the author tried Vigo Street, where it disappeared for almost a year before an office-boy unearthed the manuscript. In that time Agatha Christie had made no effort to extract herself or her manuscript from damnation caused by the firm's habitually nonchalant administration.

Allen's loyalty to Agatha Christie was at first heavily loaded with commercial self-interest and entirely free from the overt sexuality which was common to most of his relationships with women, however casual; yet Allen's affection for Agatha Christie was genuine, and it survived even the frustration of his publishing ambitions for her. Agatha Christie deserted The Bodley

Head and published one book, *Road of Dreams* with Geoffrey Bles; then, in 1927, she moved to Collins and remained with them for the rest of her many days and many books. Allen was granted his tiny consolation: a cheap edition of the 1923 book *Murder on the Links* came from The Bodley Head in 1925 and later, as a far more substantial return for his attentions, a score of Christies were in Penguins. The friendship with Agatha Christie survived her break with The Bodley Head. With her he was never arrogant and seldom malicious or mischievous, it was as if he saw himself as a dutiful, loving nephew cosseting a character already well on her way to creating in herself a fair imitation of her own Miss Marple.

Allen's reluctant attention to the theatre was on occasion overborne not only by Agatha Christie but also by the former Bodley Head editor, J. Lewis May, who lured him into at least one hilarious excursion into amateur dramatics at Mill Hill School. Then and ever after, though his acquaintance was varied and wide, Allen seldom sought the company of actors; though his opportunities were many and his susceptibility quick, the long roll of his girl friends, which took in so many attractive women, included only two actresses. The glutinous affability of the Green Room made him uncomfortable; he was equally embarrassed by the profundities of those more intellectual actors who assumed that a publisher must be as familiar as were they with every line, situation and character in the plays of Eugene O'Neill or Karel Čapek.

His brother Richard, in so many respects a younger model of Allen, was in this quite different. He enjoyed play-going and the company of actors. He had at times considered using his good looks and fine presence to make for himself in the theatre the career which he had not yet found in any other trade or profession. Even so he was as amazed as any of his friends when he actually found himself on a ship to Egypt as a member of a touring company which included Ernest Milton, Marie Ney and Philip Harben.

To Allen the departure of Dick was not just a surprise but a severe shock. For all his vast array of acquaintances he had few close friends. Only with Dick could he be entirely open, his gossip uninhibited and his confessions unfettered. Above all he missed Dick because to his brother alone could he reveal what was in truth the most romantic trait in his nature: his idealistic views about his own future as a publisher. Circumstances – his virtual adoption by John Lane, Lane's weakening grasp on the affairs of The Bodley Head in the last years of his life, and his death – had catapulted Allen at a very early age to a position of authority, to leadership in the book trade, and to a sparkling social existence. All these roles he performed with bravura and no lack of confidence, but he was still amazed to find himself at the centre of so much activity. His amazement, and his inherent shyness, impelled him to thrust himself forward, to justify his good fortune and to prove by some public flutterings of unorthodoxy that he was not only worthy of John Lane's mantle but was also an Elisha far greater than his Elijah.

Dick had enjoyed some of the benefits of the patronage of John and Annie Lane, but mostly at second hand because Allen had been selected to enjoy them all. Dick had money, which Allen had not. Allen was ambitious, Dick not mightily concerned for the future. Allen had power and Dick had none, but neither was he compelled to prove himself to himself and to the world. Allen was volatile, Dick seemingly cautious, slow of thought and speech. Already Allen knew himself well enough to recognize that he needed among his courtiers at least one person to head him off from the worst effects of his own impetuosity. Because Dick was his closest friend, his brother and – not least important – because Dick was in no way dependent upon him, Allen was prepared to listen to his advice even if not always to act upon it.

In the months before Dick took to a theatrical career his disagreements with Allen had been substantial and on two issues fruitless.

Allen had convinced himself that he was a Socialist; with unusually warm support from Ronald Boswell he had begun to infiltrate into the Bodley Head list numbers of left-wing books. Dick was not convinced by Allen's protestations of his new political allegiance, nor was he persuaded by Socialist dogma, but he was certain that any publisher who burdened his list with political propaganda was bound to sink in the quagmire of bankruptcy. (This belief was soon to be proved false. The Managing Director of Ernest Benn Ltd was at that moment preparing to move out to establish in his own name the firm of Victor

Gollancz. With its Left Book Club he would make his fame and a not inconsiderable fortune.)

The second issue on which Dick had dared to question Allen's wisdom was more technical. The argument between the two brothers over the niceties of costing (a subject in which Allen was supposed already to be an expert and Dick no more than an interfering neophyte) revealed for the first time the theme of collaboration by opposition which was central to their relationship in the years to come.

Allen had just made his first visit to New York and had brought back with him a series of illustrated children's books. Dick had listened often, patiently and generally with approval as Allen developed his by no means novel doctrine that publishers could help themselves to profits and success by helping the public with low prices; but when Allen announced that he intended to prove the efficacy of this theory by retailing these American children's books at two shillings Dick raised first a sceptical eyebrow and then indignant and carefully argued objections. The successful implementation of Allen's theory, he argued, depended upon mass production, and Allen was proposing only comparatively short runs for these books: they could or would not be bestsellers. What was worse the production cost, 1s 2½d, was so high that it allowed to the publisher only 1½d profit even on sales to smaller bookshops – not enough to cover overheads; it gave him the certainty of absolute loss on every copy sold through the wholesalers or to the chain booksellers who demanded a higher discount than the minimal 33⅓ per cent.

Allen listened carefully, put on his naughty-boy grin, gave no other answer but went off to over-rule similar objections from his sulky fellow-directors. Dick sailed for Egypt. The books sold well and The Bodley Head added another loss to its growing deficit.

It would be an exaggeration to say that Allen had learnt his lesson for the reports that came back from booksellers strengthened his conviction that his instincts had been right. The books, they said, would undoubtedly be dead stock on their shelves had they been priced any higher than two shillings. All that he would admit was that he had under-estimated the potential demand.

However, the experience contributed to his sense of deprivation at the absence of the leader and only member of his loyal

Christmas card sent by Allen, Dick and John Lane from Talbot Square in 1934. The architectural details are based on Edmund H. New's drawing of John Lane The Bodley Head, Vigo Street, in 1895

opposition. He was much relieved when Dick's theatrical career and overseas journeyings came to an end.

By this time it would have been easy for Allen to give Dick a job at The Bodley Head. After his liberated experiences in Australia and Egypt Dick did not favour the drudgery of an office, and both he and Allen were shrewdly aware that it would court disaster to tie both adult Lanes to the faltering fortunes of the firm. Instead Dick, whose knowledge of shorthand was non-existent and whose skill as a typist was concentrated in one finger on each hand, became secretary to A. J. A. Symons, the founder of the First Edition Club and later, with Desmond Flower, of the *Book Collector's Quarterly* and, with André Simon, of the Wine and Food Society.

The Lane brothers were almost religious in their devotion to baths and bathrooms. The absence of a shrine suitable for worship, conferences and ablutions drove them at last from the servants' quarters at Albany, in other ways so convenient for their purposes. They moved to the top floor of a house in Southwark Street where they had two bedrooms, one of them with no electric light. In addition they were allowed the use of a combined sitting- and dining-room on a lower floor and were provided with breakfast – all for one pound a week. There was also a bathroom ('the scruffiest I ever used', Dick called it almost fifty years later) with a geyser worked by putting a penny in the slot. As the coin-collecting box was without a lock the Lanes used the same penny over and over again until the exasperated landlord fixed a padlock. Dick, whose frugal habits included a useful mania for retaining old keys, sorted patiently through his substantial horde until he found the means whereby he and Allen could continue regular bathing without burdening their budget.

At Southwark Street what later came to be called the 'totter of Lanes' was completed when John came to town to work for the London and Lancashire Insurance Company. Allen and Dick shared the larger of the two bedrooms; because the smaller room had no light, they knocked a hole in the wall and passed through it a flex and bulb. The landlord protested, and the Lanes decided that they loathed him and his house. They would find for themselves a self-contained flat – with a good bathroom. Their choice fell on 16 Talbot Square, an address which merits its place in the history of English letters alongside Dickens's 48 Doughty Street and T. S. Eliot's 19 Carlyle Mansions.

The coming together of the three Lane brothers in one residence was decisive and is chronologically identifiable. Their conjunction at The Bodley Head was gradual and its progress ill-defined. Though it took more than four years to accomplish, there can be no doubt that the eventual conclusion was planned almost from the moment when John came to London. It was engineered by Allen with the collusion of his brothers in such a way that what they had intended for so long was nevertheless sprung upon his Bodley Head partners as a surprise. Had Allen suggested to Boswell and Lindsay Drummond that they employ full-time two more Lanes they would have suspected that his prime motive was to increase what was already, by their reckoning, the overweening influence he exerted in the firm: two other echoing voices would blast forth with all the authority that came with the family name. But the Bodley Head partners could hardly object when Allen suggested that a manuscript be sent to Dick for his opinion or that he be asked to read proofs, particularly as he was a careful and competent worker and was paid only five shillings for each job. Nor could they find good cause to resist when, after three years with the London and Lancashire, John decided to set off on a world tour and Allen proposed that, as a favour to the firm, he might call upon publishers, agents and booksellers. John was prepared to pay his own way and The Bodley Head had no possibility of despatching any other plentipotentiary.

So Dick, from being an occasional underpaid reader, moved on to travelling for the firm, first in the London suburbs, then on the East Coast – 'the traveller's graveyard' – and finally, by way of the more comfortable provincial cities, to the rich territory in central London. Thereafter, having added to his editorial experience the undeniable qualifications that he had by that time called on every bookseller in the United Kingdom, it was not possible to block his way to the board-room table even though he owned no shares in the firm.

John's route to a directorship was similar if on a grander scale. His world tour had been a hectic success even before it started. A week before he sailed the Lanes indulged themselves in a series of farewell parties, beginning with a luncheon at Simpson's-in-the-Strand for all his friends at the London and Lancashire. After one evening session at Talbot Square seventeen guests stayed for the night. There were only four beds in the flat.

On the day when John was due to sail several friends joined the Lanes at Drivers Oyster Bar. They had not finished lunch or drinks when someone noticed that there was less than thirty minutes before the boat-train was due to leave for Tilbury. John had not yet completed his packing so the whole party set off in a fleet of taxis for Talbot Square and the docks.

Allen and Dick sailed with John aboard the *Carthage* from Tilbury to Southampton. There the ship tied up alongside a Canadian Pacific liner, the *Montcalm*, which included in its complement of officers several of their friends. Although it was mid-morning their sense of social obligation demanded that the Lanes accept wholeheartedly the Canadians' invitations to drink with them for the hour before the *Montcalm* sailed. Back on the *Carthage* and aware that this must be the last celebration of the trinity for two years, the drinking took on desperate intensity. It should have ended at four o'clock, but two announcements of postponed sailing-time prolonged the session; when at last Dick and Allen obeyed the call for visitors to go ashore Dick walked down the gangway carrying two glasses full of brandy. A uniformed busybody accused him of attempting to steal property belonging to the Peninsular and Orient Steamship Company. His dignity outraged, Dick drank the spirits and, with an elaborate gesture which almost overbalanced him into the sleazy water of the dock, handed the two glasses to his accuser.

John, at the ship's railing, was not even then content to end the party. As the *Carthage* cast off he was still attempting to lower a bottle of brandy to his brothers.

Back at Southampton railway station the hardships of that day and the preceding week at last took their toll. When they approached the ticket-window they discovered that Allen could still speak but had no money; Dick had money but could neither speak nor hear.

Next day both brothers vowed that they would never drink again, a pledge they kept for almost twenty-four hours.

John's world tour was successful for reasons not all of his own contriving. Because he had inherited the name of the famous founder of a famous publishing house many in Australia, New Zealand and South Africa believed that he had inherited also Uncle John's status in the firm and in the British book world. In more remote places some, whose eagerness to catch a literary lion was greater than their knowledge of literary history even believed that this John Lane, who promised to come their way and who announced himself as 'of The Bodley Head', was in fact the publisher of Oscar Wilde and *The Yellow Book*. John saw no reason to disillusion his prospective hosts, and so he was inundated with invitations to address literary societies and to speak on radio. Wherever he went he was met by reporters. Booksellers and publishers' agents, though fully aware of his limited authority, were nonetheless delighted to welcome an itinerant from Britain who could attract for himself and for books so much more publicity than was commonly given to visiting publishers. In the manner of their kind, at once generous and shrewd, they passed him on with warm letters of introduction to professional acquaintances in other cities and other countries. By the time he arrived back in London there were very few booksellers, wholesalers or publishers' agents in the British Empire with whom John was not on friendly terms. Without having as yet spent so much as one whole day working in the office in Vigo Street he had become, in terms of knowledge of distant places and acquaintances with overseas customers, the best-qualified export manager in the British book trade.

Meanwhile, by increasing the frequency of his trips to the United States, France and Germany and by making himself available to entertain publisher visitors from those countries when they came to London, Allen had strengthened his association with the foreign book trade. He was already the firm's principal print-buyer and the most effective of its scouts. By virtue of his personality and majority share-holding, he was acknowledged by the public and by contemporaries in other firms as the head of the house. Now he could claim with justice that he was also expert as none other in Vigo Street in all matters connected with the purchase or sale of foreign rights. With Dick by Allen's side to look after home sales and publicity and John to take care of exports the Lanes had achieved in practice what was not theirs by right of investment: control of almost every major function in The Bodley Head. The other directors might not relish their omniscience and omnipotence but they could do little to disrupt or diminish their power.

Together once more in Talbot Square the three brothers began to plan new ventures which would make their hegemony entire and successful. Allen, who had most to gain and most to lose from a *putsch* in Vigo Street, decided that there could be no sensational advance in their joint professional life until they had made a visible change in that area of living where public and private existence coincided.

The Talbot Square flat was convenient and comfortable for two or three bachelors who spent most of their waking hours either working or amusing themselves at other people's houses. It was no bad place to which to bring back roistering friends of their own generation for day-long and night-long parties such as those which had preceded John's departure for his world tour. But, said Allen with a suddenness and pomposity which amazed his younger brothers, it lacked the dignity appropriate to the residence of the most distinguished family in British publishing. These sleazy rooms were in no way the palace to which the spirit of Uncle John had migrated from Lancaster Gate Terrace, in no way suitable to house a salon to which the great of British letters could be invited. Unless Dick and John would agree to a complete re-vamping and re-decoration of the flat, he would set up for himself elsewhere.

Dick and John conceded his point, not because of his threat but because they had never before noticed their surroundings.

The decision once made, Allen's rare pomposity evaporated. For the first time he had a chance to release his enthusiasm for altering buildings and for interior decoration; he busied himself happily with drawings and with conferences with the builder, whose name, to the delight of all three brothers, was Coffin. Dick and John assisted with ribald comments. That apart, they interfered very little except to insist that each must have entire jurisdiction over the decoration of his own bedroom and that all three be involved in the most vital decisions of all: the design and furnishings of the bathroom.

The project as eventually conceived by Allen was both elaborate and expensive. A bathroom was converted into a kitchen, complete with what was, for those days, a comparatively rare feature, a huge gas refrigerator. A combined kitchen and dining-space became a comfortable dining-room. A passage-way was converted into a walk-in clothing closet with space for fifty suits. A parquet-floor was laid in the sitting-room and, an innovation second in importance only to the bathroom, a cupboard was turned into a bar. Dick's old bedroom was chosen as the chapel of the Lanes, the bathroom; the brothers trooped off to the showrooms in Charing Cross Road to choose the altars and ikons.

Each in turn took off his shoes and climbed into the various baths to test them for length and comfort, all uncaring that the showroom windows faced into a busy street. The nervous sales-man foresaw what must happen next, and he had the blinds drawn just moments before the brothers began a series of similar trials on the water-closets.

The reconstruction of Talbot Square took almost a year to complete; a year during which the Lanes lived in a fantasy of disappearing walls, builders' ladders and paint-pots. It cost them well over £1000, a sum which would have bought a sizeable suburban house, but they had not lost their communal business heads; in return for the improvements which they had financed they wrung from the landlord a five-year extension of their lease at a fixed rent.

When all was finished only John's bedroom was in any sense conventional; he had ordered little more than a coat of paint. Dick, at that time indulging himself as a handyman, had installed in his room a six-foot work-bench complete with vice and lathe. But Allen's room was marvellously eccentric: green walls, green curtains, green sheets, green eiderdown and even a green telephone.

Dick and John for once remained silent on what they regarded as an aberration in their brother, usually for all his social pecca-dillos so conventional in the manner in which he presented himself to the world; so orthodox for example, in dress. He was happy and because what he did with and in his bedroom was no concern of theirs, they were content. They were impatient to return to the old, amiable way of living, which could now be continued and enlarged in a setting more elegant than anything that Allen and Dick had known since the Lancaster Gate Terrace house had been sold up, more spacious than John had ever known.

But Allen was not yet satisfied. Three bachelors of their social standing must have a gentleman's gentleman to wait upon them. They hired an ex-Royal Marine named Knight, a tall, distinguished-looking man, who never forgot his training at Deal, standing firmly at attention, thumbs down the seams of his trousers, back ramrod-stiff, eyes unmoving, whenever he was spoken to, but who soon forgot that he had told his future employers that he was both teetotal and a non-smoker.

Because there was in the flat no spare bedroom a room was taken for Knight over a chemist's shop in near-by Praed Street. His duties began with the making of early morning tea. He would then lay out clothes, run a bath and cook breakfast. When all the Lanes had gone off to work he tidied the flat and then idled the hours away until the time came to prepare dinner for any Lane who was not going out for the evening, to lay out dinner-jacket or tails for whichever was socializing, and to run another bath.

Dick and John were not yet regulars on the book world invitation-list, but even they seldom stayed at home to enjoy Knight's excellent steak-and-kidney pies. Why should they when a superb dinner with sherry and a bottle of wine at the Lord Belgrave or the Diner Français or Simpson's-in-the-Strand cost little more than five shillings a head, when a dozen oysters at Drivers or Wheelers sold for half-a-crown, and when they could take a box at the Metropolitan Music Hall in Edgware Road for six shillings? If he was in London, Allen was usually out on almost every weekday evening. He was by now making six or eight business trips to the Continent each year, one business trip to the United States and at least one holiday motoring in Spain or the south of France with the printer Raymond Hazell and his wife, as well as several trips in Britain. He was away from London almost as much as he was at home, and his brothers began to wonder when all the sufferings they had endured while Mr Coffin was spending their £1000 would bring forth the more formal entertainment which they had been promised.

At last Allen agreed to test Knight's capacity with a dinner-party. The arrangements were explained to Knight with military exactitude and carried out by him with Royal Marine precision. Pre-dinner drinks were served by the hosts; Knight then announced dinner. Whilst the Lanes and their guests were eating his excellent four courses he cleared the sitting-room. At the end of the meal the party moved back into the sitting-room for coffee and brandy. Having collected the coffee-cups and cleaned the dining-room, Knight was ready to obey the last of his instructions before going off to Praed Street. He marched into the sitting-room and bellowed: 'Anything else required, sir?' Allen denied the possibility, thanked Knight for his efforts and wished him good-night, but the manservant stood immobile as the Rock of Gibraltar. Conversation died as guests and hosts alike riveted their attention upon him. 'Sir,' he barked in the uninflected, unemotional voice he had learnt in long years of military service, 'beg to report, one coffee-spoon missing.'

This was by no means the last dinner-party at Talbot Square but Allen had recovered quickly from his fit of grandiloquence. The idea of using the flat as a successor to Lancaster Gate Terrace evaporated almost as soon as it was enunciated. Allen did most of his more dignified entertaining at his clubs or in expensive restaurants. Because it was close to the City offices of the major exporters, John made Sheriffs Wine Bar at the bottom of Ludgate Hill into an unofficial extension of the Vigo Street offices. Dick, who had begun to take over some of Allen's scouting responsibilities and particularly his contacts with the comparatively new but growing breed of literary agents, spread his favours widely and generally wisely around London's better oyster-bars. If the flat was used at all for business purposes, it was most often for spontaneously gathered parties of young writers of both sexes and publishers, booksellers and printers of their own generation; exactly the same kind of people that had come together in Talbot Square in its raffish days before the reconstruction.

Just such a party was put on at two hours' notice to celebrate the first occasion when a London newspaper devoted a full-length article to Allen. On that evening it took Dick and John only a few minutes to invent for the pleasure of their guests a new cocktail, the Allyp, so called because the *Evening Standard* had headed its article 'Allen Lane, London's Youngest Publisher'.

There was nothing contrived in this Lane spontaneity, though undoubtedly it brought them a reputation for unorthodoxy, convenient for publishers. It was, however, a characteristic which was seldom apparent when any one brother was operating solo. Once, it is true, John disappeared for a week without warning either his brothers or his other colleagues at The Bodley Head. When he returned he explained only that he had been drinking at Sheriffs with the London manager of Hachette when M. Joubat complained that he had not seen his family in Paris for two years – so the two of them had caught the night ferry. But usually it needed two or more Lanes for the chemistry to work an explosion.

Spontaneity, however engendered and however useful, was not likely to induce confidence in the minds of their more orthodox business-partners who felt themselves to be, and indeed were, excluded from the Lane mysteries. Generally uncomfortable relationships at The Bodley Head were made even more tense by the Lane habit of using the firm's accounts with publishers, wholesalers and booksellers all over Britain and all over the world as convenient sources for the petty cash which they needed when they travelled. And by now not only Allen but also Dick and John were travelling regularly, widely and often with no purpose other than amusement.

Paradoxically it was not Lane spontaneity or casualness that should have given their partners most cause for alarm but rather the care which the brothers were giving to plans that might make them as independent of their colleagues in reality as in behaviour they liked to appear. It was not the Lanes' cavalier manner with office discipline and the firm's petty cash that should have aroused suspicion so much as their determination, not yet suspected by the others, to build for themselves an empire. Had they but known it the Bodley Head board could have allowed to Allen – the only Lane with a direct financial interest in the firm – without complaint his frequent holidays in Switzerland, France and Spain, his winter sports and his zest for bull-fights, and to Dick and John their lesser but no less expensive whims, if only they could have breached the door of the Talbot Square bathroom. It was there that the Lanes plotted the two *coups* that were to give them their independence from any sort of interference by all who had the misfortune to be born outside the family, that relieved Allen of the irksome burden that had come with the inheritance of Bodley Head shares, that made all the Lanes prosperous, and that ultimately deprived

The Bodley Head of leadership which, for all that it was eccentric and infuriating, was also undoubtedly more alert and progressive than anything that the other directors could contrive.

Thus it is that a description of the bathroom ritual at Talbot Square becomes an essential part of the history of publishing in the twentieth century.

Allen was always first into the morning bath. It was his custom to soak in it whilst Dick shaved and John perched on the lavatory seat. Dick followed Allen, John shaved, Allen took Dick's place, and finally John bathed and the other two stayed with him. Generally the whole process lasted for anything up to an hour. In that time each of the three gave a suitably unbuttoned account of the events of the preceding evening; they exchanged information about plans for the coming day; and often one of the brothers – most often the bather, who looked for any excuse to delay quitting the comforts of hot water – expounded some hopeful if fantastic scheme for engineering their liberation from the busybodies in Vigo Street.

After careful bathroom maturation Allen put to the board on behalf of himself and his brothers the notion that the Lanes be allowed to back their own publishing fancies at no expense to the firm but without actually setting up on their own.

It was a proposal not easy to refuse. Allen was not only the majority share-holder but he was also the one member of the firm with wide connections, especially in the United States (where he had negotiated among other things a seemingly beneficial arrangement for an exchange of titles with Dodd, Mead). Furthermore the board collectively considered that such an agreement might relieve it of some of the dangers inherent in Lane impetuosity: all the wilder Lane projects would be financed by Lane capital. Allen would be freed to give the rest of his time and his indisputable talents to fostering those more substantial projects on which all the directors could agree. It might even remove the tensions which had persisted in the board-room for more than a decade.

Allen's energy and skills had done much to restore to The Bodley Head the reputation for daring which it had achieved in its first decade, but his erratic and sometimes perverse view of publishing economics had produced no equivalent improvement in the financial situation of a firm which, from the first, had never been noted for stability. From its very early days, it had depended for its future health upon frequent transfusions of capital rather than upon turnover and profits. Even Dick and John, who had no doubts about Allen's flair and who shared his zest for uninhibited editorial policies, were nevertheless puzzled by what they took to be his wilful disregard for economic reality. The other directors were terrified when they saw that the renaissance of editorial success was not synonymous with profitability; they were, not unnaturally, incensed when they considered that he was gambling with their money and their careers. Their fury was in no way diminished by his habit of playing his cards always close to his chest.

Allen, for his part, who had taken over so eagerly the role that Uncle John had played a few decades earlier as the bold spirit of London publishing, was by this sense of inheritance and by his own nature made resistant to the frequent calls for caution which came from the newer share-holders and from the old hands in Vigo Street.

The Whispering Gallery case had not helped relations in Vigo Street. There were abroad nasty rumours about Allen's integrity; although none of his fellow-directors suspected him of dishonesty, those outside the family had no doubts that he was not ready to exercise the prim caution that the firm's parlous condition demanded. It was only too easy for his colleagues to complain that he had neither the maturity nor the stability to lead a distinguished house out of the difficulties with which it was beset; his actions made it easy for them to assert that many of these difficulties were of his own making.

It was plain, however, that there was no curbing Allen. To hedge themselves against some of the dangers which they suspected he created for them, the Bodley Head directors conceded this new arrangement which would allow to Allen – and to his brothers – a private kingdom within the Bodley Head empire. If titles titillated the publishing fancy of the Lanes which their partners could not support, then the Lanes could use the Bodley Head imprint and Bodley Head services – for an appropriate payment – but not Bodley Head funds. The brothers would reap any profits that accrued, but they must also bear all losses.

The first venture of this kind was bold but by no means nerve-shattering. The very fact that their fellow-directors were not prepared to publish a collection of Peter Arno's cartoons without a guarantee from the Lanes can be seen as proof that Allen was yoked into a team which could not match his bustling energy.

Shrewdness, and not timidity, informed the reluctance with which the rest of the board regarded another book sponsored by the Lanes: James Joyce's *Ulysses*. Common sense insisted that they guard themselves against the punitive consequences that might follow upon the publication of this explosive title; both precedent and the opinion of men wiser and more experienced than Allen, his brothers and their partners, seemed to insist that those consequences were not just possible but well-nigh certain.

Ulysses had suffered, more even than the rest of Joyce's work, from the fears of printers and publishers on both sides of the Atlantic, from the persecution of postal and customs authorities and the self-appointed guardians of public virtue. In sixteen years it had been suppressed, burnt and successfully prosecuted. That brave woman, Harriet Weaver – whose name should be written far larger than it is in the history of modern English literature – as editor of the *Egoist*, had been the first to accept the book for publication in serial form, but she had been unable to find a printer willing to risk more than a few chapters. The American *Little Review* began publication but, though the text had been minimally bowdlerized by, of all people, the book's most ardent champion, Ezra Pound, the United States proved even less hospitable than Britain to Joyce's genius. The journal was brought to court, fined and the offending numbers suppressed. First Sylvia Beach, from Shakespeare and Company, and then again Harriet Weaver, from the Egoist Press, published the book in full with the aid of a Dijon printer, only to have their copies zealously destroyed by postal and customs authorities all over the English-speaking world.

The task of defending the morals of the public against the assaults of an innovative genius is almost as difficult as the task of those who champion a new and provocative voice. By 1930 there were thousands of copies of *Ulysses* in circulation – the severities to which the book had been subjected, as Joyce himself said, 'have given my book a life of its own' – but most of these copies came either from the Odyssey Press in Hamburg, which had taken over Sylvia Beach's rights, or from the pirated and fraudulent editions which, despite an injunction won by Joyce in the United States courts, were put out in America by Samuel Roth. As yet, James Joyce had earned not one penny from the publication of his masterpiece in the language in which it had been written.

Those who had the right to judge such things, among whom customs, postal officers and the secretaries of anti-vice societies are seldom numbered, had come to regard *Ulysses* as a classic for this century. Inspired by their praise, several publishers in the United States made offers for the book, but, until February 1932, when Bennet Cerf made a bid on behalf of the newly formed firm of Random House, the offers were all hesitant, their validity much reduced by the publisher's insistence that Joyce bear all legal costs consequent upon its publication.

Cerf decided to damn both consequences and costs. He invited a test case, which was brilliantly fought before a United States district attorney by Morris L. Ernst (soon to become a close friend of Allen Lane and eventually a Penguin author). On appeal the judges upheld the lower court, though in the process they delivered themselves of some *obiter dicta* which must make one wonder if judges have the qualification to speak for posterity:

> One may discount the laudation of *Ulysses* by some of its admirers and reject the view that it will permanently stand among the great works of literature ... that Joyce, in the words of *Paradise Lost*, has dealt with 'things unattempted in prose or rime', with things that very likely might better have remained 'unattempted', but this book shows originality and is a work of symmetry and excellent craftsmanship of a sort.

'Shows originality ... craftsmanship of a sort ...': this grudging school-report majority opinion was, even so, more perspicacious than the dissenting view of Justice Manton, who insisted that 'masterpieces have never been produced by men given to obscenity or lustful force – men who have no Master'.

Triumph before the American courts was an encouragement to British publishers, but offered no surety against British puritans or the busybodies of British officialdom. Even the immediate commercial success of the Random House edition – it had sold more than 30,000 copies before ever it came to the Appeal Court – wrested only one offer from a British house: from Allen Lane (who was in New York when the case was heard) on behalf of the Lane syndicate within The Bodley Head.

Joyce himself would have preferred Faber and Faber. He was certain that T. S. Eliot, who had been clamorous in his support, would accept the lead of his fatherland and publish *Ulysses*, but the great high priest faltered. Eliot was prepared to be a champion but not eager to be a martyr. He was convinced that the decision of the American courts was not firm enough to reduce the chances of prosecution if the book was published in Britain. Cerf knew that the moment was ripe for a British publication and that Allen was the man to produce it: if this chance was not taken while Allen was in New York, it might never occur again. Mischievously he conspired with Allen. A cable was sent to Eliot offering him a five-day option. There was no answer. The Bodley Head had *Ulysses*, whether its directors liked it or not.

Other than the Lane brothers they did not like it; in their opinion Allen was once more at the potentially expensive and always dangerous game of tempting the judiciary to act as his publicity managers. They insisted upon a further guarantee from the Lanes: £20,000 as bond against legal costs. Somehow the Lanes found the money, but even so the Bodley Head directors dragged their feet for two years; the delays occasioned by their circumspection were compounded by the circumstance that in the meanwhile the Lanes had become frenetically involved in the beginnings of Penguin. When finally, on 3 October 1936, the first British edition was published – 1000 copies, 100 signed by the author – the imprint was The Bodley Head, the profits were immediate and much went to the Lanes, but the Lanes were no longer in Vigo Street. Nevertheless a year later, when the first popular British edition appeared, the imprint was still that of The Bodley Head. For many years thereafter the reorganized firm was able to recoup some not inconsiderable part of its shattered fortunes from the charges made for distributing the book that it would not have dared publish without the licensed impetuosity of its former managing director.

Just as Uncle John had earlier flouted puritanical opposition and the opinion of the courts by including in his edition of Sudermann's *Song of Songs* the enthusiastic views of distinguished critics, and just as later, in the case of *Lady Chatterley's Lover*, Penguin would indulge in the profitable impertinence of publishing an account of the trial, so now Allen arranged for all the Bodley Head editions of *Ulysses* to carry as appendices an account of the misfortunes that the book had suffered, together with transcripts of the opinions handed down by American judges.

For this one act, for purchasing the British rights of *Ulysses*, Allen must have earned himself a place in literary history, but it is unlikely that he would have merited a biography for that alone, or for anything else he had done or for anything else that he was likely to do had it not been for the coincidental invention of Penguin. Unlikely, but not inconceivable. Perhaps because so many come to the trade as to a haven from the hazards of a career in literature, perhaps because a few years in publishing awakens any shrewd practitioner to the knowledge that the public is forever curious about the inner workings of a profession that seems to the uninformed more romantic than it is in reality, and perhaps because publishers are better placed than most to set their life-stories between covers, into the bookshops and on to the library shelves, there is no scarcity of publishing biographies and autobiographies. Even failed publishers can usually find a more fortunate colleague ready for the book about why they failed and how nearly they succeeded. Allen Lane, at the moment when Penguin was launched, was close to being a failed publisher – and on a sensational scale. He was the head of what had been one of London's leading firms, a firm in its day unrivalled for literary and artistic influence. Admittedly he had come to that position in a time of decline, but a firm that owned the copyrights of such authors as Anatole France, and that now almost owned *Ulysses*, could not yet be described as defunct. Nevertheless, despite the transfusions of capital brought to the firm, Allen was in danger of going down in publishing history as the man who had marched the publishers of the *Yellow Book* into Carey Street. Had this happened it is unthinkable that he would have stayed for long disconsolate among the ruins. His ebullience, his width of contacts and his undoubted ability must have brought him to some new beginning. Because he knew only the book trade but was in that trade already well known it is more than likely that he would have made a new start in some other publishing house and so might have come eventually to a respectable biography. That he would ever have written an autobiography is as inconceivable as the possibility of total failure. He could dictate a vigorous memorandum (if on rare occasions), his letters revealed more of himself than he ever allowed in social relationships, but he lacked the will and the patience to sustain literary effort beyond two or three pages.

In a sense Allen dreamed up Penguin to save The Bodley Head. The Bodley Head refused to be saved – and Allen came eventually to deserve a biography more than any other publisher of his generation or this century.

The evidence of his later career makes credible the mythology about the birth of Penguin. Those who knew him when he was at the height of his success have no difficulty in accepting as history that Penguin was the child of necessity and impulse, conceived on a railway platform and, like the Lane syndicate within The Bodley Head, born in the bathroom at Talbot Square.

CHAPTER  THREE

ALLEN had spent a week-end with Agatha Christie and her second husband, the archaeologist Max Mallowan. On the way back from Devon he found himself in a situation that is for a publisher rare, frustrating and almost humiliating: he had nothing to read. An hour's wait at Exeter station gave him the chance to scour the railway book-stalls but there was little to his liking among the piles of glossy magazines, the expensive new titles, the remainders and the shabby reprints of shoddy novels. The long, bookless journey back to London would have been unbearable had it not set him to mulling over notions that had been present, if vague, in his mind for several years.

Next morning, during the bathroom session, he elaborated his scheme for the benefit of Dick and John. The Bodley Head would publish a new series, reprints of quality fiction and non-fiction, the books to be produced in attractive paper-covers and sold to the public at the unbelievably low price of sixpence – the price of ten cigarettes.

His brothers were sceptical. This, they suspected, was yet another of Allen's formulae for bankruptcy. In turn they quizzed him. Why would authors and rival publishers concede their best titles to a venture of this kind? How could the price be kept down? Given that authors, publishers, printers, wholesalers and retail booksellers must all take a share out of sixpence, would anything be left for The Bodley Head?

His answers were decisive, and all could be summed up in the terms mass-production and mass-distribution. Time and time again he repeated the mystical name Woolworth. What Woolworths had achieved for a variety of goods the Lanes would do for books.

The inquisition stopped and soon Dick and John were adding their refinements to Allen's plans. The export market was wide open. Bright covers must enhance the possibilities of effective displays. Surely authors would welcome the chance to present themselves to a vast audience.

Allen had hit upon the paperback. Had he been less sybaritic – and had he known even that one word of Greek – the aptness of the setting must have prompted him to leap from his bath and to run out into Talbot Square shrieking, '*Eureka*.'

Yet, paradoxically, the principle that he had discovered was in no sense novel. The prospect was exciting for it gave them something new to plan, something that might breathe life back into the tired body corporate of The Bodley Head, but at the time Allen did not know, did not intend and could not foresee that he was about to begin a career as a pioneer; he had no glimmer of a thought that within four years he would be claiming for himself (and others accepting for him) that he had planned and wrought a social revolution as significant as the invention of radio. But even so the will to make book-ownership accessible to the public at large was centuries old, almost as old as printing; it is not extravagant to trace the ancestry of Penguins back to the Aldine editions of classical texts printed in Venice from 1501. In Britain two centuries later John Bell published 109 volumes in his series *British Poets*, selling at one shilling and sixpence. In the 1830s Constable launched the Miscellany series and Murray the Family Library; both held the price down to six shillings a volume by printing on the newly-invented machine-made wood-pulp paper and by binding in paper-boards. At that time the standard price of a work by a popular writer was 31s 6d, so both could boast that they were truly public benefactors.

The prices that prevailed both for cheap and standard editions until the last few decades of the nineteenth century emphasized the restricted nature of the market for books, made dramatic the implications of the publication of the first Penguins at sixpence – and even today may stifle the complaint that books are too expensive. Writing only a few years before the advent of the Constable and Murray series Charles Lamb, an avid book-collector, described himself as 'comfortably placed' on a pension of £241 a year. For him, therefore, and for his middle-class kind over the next fifty years, the purchase of a volume in a standard edition involved handing over to the bookseller two days' income and, for a popular edition, in money terms all that he had to keep him for some ten hours. Weighed in similar if necessarily approximate scales, when Allen worked his magic his first Penguin cost a middle-aged bank clerk no more than his pay for twenty minutes' work. Today, by this same rough but revealing measure, the 1979 successor to that bank clerk and to Lamb would have to hand over a half-day's take-home pay for a first novel and the income from less than one hour for a fiction paperback.

Admittedly, as the growth of literacy enlarged the market in the second half of the nineteenth century so were publishers encouraged to reduce substantially the retail price of popular works, a process furthered not a little by the bursting desire for self-improvement and by the rapid growth of railway travel. Most of the cheap series which appeared after 1850 were directed overtly either at the acolytes of Samuel Smiles or at the beneficiaries of George Stephenson, and often at both. The Irish Parlour Library, Routledge's Railway Library and Bohn's Shilling Library produced for the most part popular reprints of fiction selling at one shilling. Routledge published also the Universal Library, and in 1886 Cassell started the National Library which within four years issued at weekly intervals 214 volumes at 3d. each paper-bound or 6d. cloth-bound. Early in the new century John Lane himself produced his Keynotes series and at about the same time the first titles appeared in series which have survived and held the respect and affection of the public even to this generation: Nelson's New Century Library (founded in 1900 and in 1905 renamed Nelson's Classics), Grant Richards' World's Classics (started in 1901 and taken over by the Oxford University Press in 1905), Collins's Pocket Classics (which began to appear in 1903), and Dent's Everyman Library (1906).

Most, but not all, these series concentrated on re-publishing 'classics', a term open to wide interpretation. Under the provisions of the prevailing Act of 1842 copyright was vested in the author or his estate only for forty-two years after publication or seven years after the author's death, whichever should be the longer period. All the major nations except the United States, Russia and China subscribed to the Berne Convention of 1908; to carry out the articles of the convention Parliament passed in

1911 a new Copyright Act which granted protection for fifty years after publication or the death of the author whichever was the later date.)

The success of all these reprint-series was phenomenal, though none equalled the singular success of a Continental rival, Reclam's *Universal Bibliothek*, which between 1867 and 1942 distributed over six million copies of Ibsen's plays and more than a million copies of Schopenhauer – an author who in his lifetime sold only 140 copies of his first book. Virtually all the later British series introduced history, biography, theology and philosophy to their lists, with an appeal, as J. M. Dent of Everyman put it, 'to every kind of reader: the worker, the student, the cultured man, the child, the man and the woman'. There was, however, an aggressive earnestness and an element of intellectual proselytizing in the editorial policies behind many of these publishing projects which held them from being acceptable as a panacea for the book starvation prevalent in the vast new readership of the thirties. In Britain literacy was by then virtually universal, secondary education was widespread, and to the substantial growth in higher education the universities themselves, with their extra-mural programmes, and movements such as the Workers Education Association, had added an escape route for many who in earlier years had been trapped, their access to both enlightenment and entertainment blocked by their limited educational achievements.

The public library movement, in which Britain led the world, had by that time reached out into every part of the nation. The facility with which books of all kinds were available on loan, far from satisfying the book needs of the people, instead strengthened the impulse towards book-ownership.

All these influences, and the development of radio, produced in the public an eagerness (of which most members of the public were unaware until it had been satisfied) to put upon their own shelves books that were not all earnest nor all pap, but that represented the essentially middle-brow taste which was by that time commonplace.

Several publishers came near to sensing the mood and the commercial possibilities but most of the new developments of the time, Benn's Ninepennies, Collins's Crime Club and Hodder and Stoughton's yellow paperback reprints, either continued the didacticism of the previous generation or settled for an extension by price-reduction of the sales potential of the lighter reading in their own lists. Such exquisitely produced series as the Phoenix Library from Chatto and Windus were not likely to win a mass market: they were unashamedly representative of high literature and, at 3s 6d, could not be classed as truly cheap editions.

That Allen Lane was the founder of the modern paperback is a claim made by many advocates over many years. It has been disputed by authorities from countries other than Britain who have chosen variously the founders of Tauchnitz and Albatross, or Charles Boni who, in America in the twenties, produced a series of cheap reprints. The French, who invented the word *chauvinisme*, are also eager to boast that they invented the paperback, using the undeniable assertion that, so long as there have been French books, those books have had paper covers. Even in Britain there are those who would wish to honour, in the place of Allen Lane, the directors of Hodder and Stoughton for their yellow-covered cheap editions or Victor Gollancz for the work that he did as Managing Director of Ernest Benn Ltd before he founded his own house. Indeed it can well be argued that the commonly-accepted and current definition of a paperback as a 'mass-produced, mass-distributed and low-priced book generally bound in paper' was devised by a former colleague of Allen's specifically – or so it is implied – to give to him the glory. Once Penguin was established, Allen initiated policies which breached one or more conditions of this definition and also produced Penguins which were, no less than the series published by Reclam, Routledge or Nelson, outside the paperback pale. There were to be Penguins that were not mass-produced, not mass-distributed, not cheap, and not paper-bound. Many were earnest and didactic and, almost from the outset, Penguin editors had an inclination to lead public taste that transcended all commercial considerations. In fact, in Allen's lifetime Penguins became the least typical members of the genus he was said to have created.

Yet, for all the objections and all the objectors, the primacy of Penguin can be and perhaps must be accepted, primarily because it was accepted by most of those in Britain and abroad who attempted to imitate Allen's innovative genius. There had been other paperback series before 1935; there had never been a paperback movement. From 1935 to the present day the paperback has taken over world-wide as the principal vehicle for communicating literature of all kinds to the reading public. It has transformed the economics of authorship; it has invaded the classroom; it has changed out of all recognition the commercial style and even the appearance of bookshops.

As he lingered in his bath on that morning in 1934 Allen had no thought for all this. Even the one flash of inspiration that above all others impressed Dick and John led him to a conclusion that Allen himself, but not his imitators, would abandon almost as soon as he had established Penguin. Publishers, he argued, must find outlets beyond the range of conventional bookshops and railway bookstalls: in department stores, tobacconists, tea shops – in any place where the public could be persuaded to impulse-buying.

From this precept, and from the dedication to good design which he had inherited from Uncle John, he developed the thesis that his series must be not only marvellously inexpensive but also, as a kind of compensation lest their economic presentation be regarded as expressing disdain, his books must be produced attractively, with dignity but in cheerful, eye-catching format. He did not use the word 'packaging', which had not yet become a cliché, but the production doctrines which he was urging were significant far beyond the limits of book-publishing.

Dick and John were enthusiastic. A week or so later, Allen came to put his ideas to the rest of the Bodley Head board, but his reception was icy. This, they argued, was just one more example of Lane impetuosity and prodigality. However, if somewhat grudgingly, they conceded that the Lanes could go ahead with preparations for a cheap paperback series to be published under the Bodley Head imprint, that they could negotiate with Bodley Head authors or their agents for the reprint rights of selected titles as also (an integral part of Allen's scheme) with authors on the lists of other publishers, and that they could use Bodley Head staff and facilities – providing always that there was no interruption of *normal* Bodley Head business. This last condition was palpably ludicrous. It was promptly ignored by the Lanes, who turned most of their abundant energy to their new project.

The iciness of their senior colleagues was paralleled and even exceeded by the frigidity with which Allen was received when he called upon his fellow-publishers to seek their immediate and long-term support.

The wise old men of publishing had listened to many another bright young spark with his bright new ideas. They mumbled platitudes to Allen, polite if they liked him, more brutal if they did not; to each other they promised and prophesied damnation for his heretical scheme. Two seemingly contradictory arguments were often used against Allen by one pundit in the space of a single conversation. It was urged that precedent showed the scheme was doomed, because the public was not large enough to support by regular purchase the long runs which alone would make economically viable a series of this kind. Further (and in this the paradox) they argued that if the new series succeeded it would undermine orthodox publishing: who would buy a book at 7s 6d if by waiting a while he could acquire it for sixpence? It must follow that the greater the initial success of the Lanes the more certain and catastrophic would be their eventual downfall: there would be nothing left for them to reprint. They would achieve only disaster for themselves, for their fellow-publishers, and for literature.

Having tried private persuasion and achieved almost nothing, Allen next attempted mass missionary work. As a salesman dealing face-to-face he was most persuasive but he was no orator and knew he was deficient in the demagogic skills which must be used to carry a large audience. The Lanes were impatient to test their confidence by experiment, and Allen realized that the business of seeking converts by personal interview must exhaust not only their own enthusiasm but also the zeal of the few younger members of the Bodley Head staff who were now excited by the novelty and increasingly dedicated to the paperback. Therefore he sought and was granted opportunities to explain his venture to influential gatherings of bookmen.

When he spoke to the booksellers' annual conference he was greeted with hostility that was not disguised by conventional politeness. Some members of the audience conversed with each other ostentatiously throughout his speech, others heckled; when the time came for comment, even the gentler and more genteel faced Allen with questions which they thought unanswerable enshrining all the customary objections to paperbacks. Why should booksellers give up shelf-space to goods that at best would yield only tiny item-profit? Would not paperback stock disintegrate when handled by the inquisitive public? Would not the pocketable format, one of the postulated virtues of his proposed series, merely encourage pilfering, already a bookseller's nightmare? Then, like the publishers before them, the booksellers turned somersault: if the series which could not succeed proved successful it would ruin the trade.

The battering of objection and opposition from all sides convinced Allen that he must be right and goaded all three Lanes into a frenzy of activity. The case that could not be proved by argument must be demonstrated by action.

It is a precept of publishing, and one that goes far beyond mere semantics, that two or three titles do not make a series; the Lanes, as yet unblessed by even a single contract, decided that they would launch their venture with ten titles. But even the initial ten would be little more than an exploratory probe; they must have successors ready to take advantage of the publicity they expected, and of the demand the first list would create.

The search for titles continued. First to give way was Jonathan Cape, one of the most hard-headed publishers of them all. Later, when Allen had proved himself, Cape took none of the credit to himself, nor claimed any greater perspicacity than any of his rivals. Instead, he dismissed his support in tones that were habitually gruff. He had decided from the outset that Lane was bound to fail but the project could in no way harm either the trade as a whole or Jonathan Cape in particular; so he had made up his mind to get what little was coming from Lane for himself and his authors before nemesis struck.

This explanation allowed Cape to retain his reputation for shrewdness and lack of sentimentality, but it is not convincing. Cape liked Allen, he shared Allen's zest for experiment, and he himself had suffered from the orthodox certainties of publishing world theologians. He enjoyed assisting Allen to thumb his nose at the establishment – a pleasure increased because it cost him nothing. Whatever his motives, Jonathan Cape merits a place among the early saints of the paperback movement.

A series is more than titles. It must have a uniform and immediately identifiable format. It must have a name.

Between them the Lanes possessed most of the skills essential for publishing, but not one of them had the competence to design a book. Like any experienced publisher Allen could talk glibly about Caslon or Baskerville but unlike most publishers his eyes were not blinkered by the conventions of book-printing. The innovations of such as Ashley Havinden in advertising and Frank Pick at London Transport had weaned the public from the pretentious elaboration of nineteenth-century typography which still influenced most book-designers. Allen knew instinctively that, if the new series was to be free from all suspicion of being patronizing, if it was to be, in the term that he and his brothers always used, 'friendly', it must be packaged simply, in bold and bright colours, and titled in clear and unpretentious lettering.

The resolution of these precepts as it appeared eventually was so untrammelled by decoration, so gloriously unsophisticated, as to be almost perfect. It intruded nothing of deliberate art between the book and the prospective purchaser: two bands of bright colour – orange for novels, green for detective stories and blue for non-fiction – and a white band of equal size carrying the book title in brave and uncomplicated lettering.

Implicit also was the need for a good series name. In the Vigo Street offices and in the bathroom at Talbot Square suggestions were many and varied. Again the brothers were certain that it must be something that rang friendliness in the ear of the public: not formidable like World Classics, not somehow patronizing like Everyman. It must also be transferable into visual terms and easily reproduced in black and white as a recognizable and cheerful colophon.

The first choice was Dolphin, an animal represented in the Bristol coat of arms, but the name was already pre-empted. Faber and Faber were already using Porpoise, next on the list of preferences, for a series they had taken over from a small Scottish publisher. From Porpoise to Penguin was no great step. Who first made it may never be established as almost anyone who was in any way involved has claimed the conclusive inspiration as his own. What is certain is that, once the name was suggested, it seemed to them all that Penguin was what they had intended from the very beginning.

Edward Young, a twenty-one-year-old amateur artist who was working for The Bodley Head as a junior, was sent off to the

Zoo to sketch penguins. He came back with the drawing* which, with increasingly sophisticated amendment, has survived as the colophon to this day.

Dick was given the task of dealing with authors and their agents. The first contracts were simple; not more than one page long. The Lanes offered to take a licence to sell reprints at sixpence a copy on terms that were not so plush as to cause even the most impecunious writer to regard Penguins as a new philanthropic institution. Wherever possible Dick was to hold the advance to £25 against royalties of one pound for every thousand copies sold; if pressed he could go to £50 as an advance against royalties of one farthing a copy (or about 4% of the published price). The brothers had calculated that the break-even point was somewhere between 17,000 and 18,000 copies per title. They planned to print only 20,000 copies, so no author could hope to earn more than his advance – not even those who were initially paid only £25 – unless his book went into a second Penguin edition, a possibility which seemed unlikely. Those obtaining an advance of £50 would not earn a penny more unless their books sold 48,000 copies – an eventuality which even Allen's most optimistic forecasts did not sustain.

Nevertheless, contracts were signed for the first seismic ten titles and, inevitably if blithely, for many that were to follow after as reinforcements to success. Of these ten as originally planned only two came initially from The Bodley Head, *The Mysterious Affair at Styles* by Allen's friend Agatha Christie and *Ariel* by André Maurois, both authors who had long since deserted to other firms. Compton Mackenzie's *Carnival* had been published more than twenty years earlier by Martin Secker, to whom it was dedicated, but Mackenzie was by now a Chatto and Windus author. Six titles were from Cape: Ernest Hemingway's *A Farewell to Arms*, Eric Linklater's *Poet's Pub*, Susan Ertz's *Madame Claire*, Beverley Nichols's *Twenty-five*, E. H. Young's *William* and Mary Webb's *Gone to Earth*. (Cape had also captured Maurois.)

To complete his ten Allen secured Dorothy L. Sayers's *The Unpleasantness at the Bellona Club*. For reasons both literary and personal, this acquisition gave him more pleasure than the other nine added together. It was one of his cherished affectations to announce that he seldom read a book and this he repeated in

*It appears as the chapter decoration on page 80.

public and in private on many occasions throughout his life (sometimes he would alter his tune and satisfy some gullible interviewer with the tale that he had set himself to compensating for his attentuated formal education by working rigorously through the classics of English and foreign literature). As with most busy but intelligent men the truth lay between the two extremes: he read widely, unsystematically and, above all, quickly. But he also judged what he read with the shrewdness of a professional. He had identified and welcomed the changing mood of the leading English mystery-writers which, in the late twenties and early thirties, was moving them away from the *roman policier*, from the puerilities of contrived detection and two-dimensional characterization, and placing them closer to their 'legitimate' novelist colleagues. Much later in his life, in a letter to his eventual biographer, he listed Nicholas Blake, Michael Innes and 'first and foremost Marge' [Margery Allingham] with Aldous Huxley, Graham Greene and Joyce Cary as 'the best and most enjoyable English novelists of our time'. Already in 1934 he was admitting, though he knew it to be disloyal, that he 'regarded Dorothy Sayers as an important novelist and Agatha as no more than a skilful entertainer'. Even so his especial delight in Penguin number 5 was prompted less by this satisfaction as by the knowledge that the Penguin edition of *The Unpleasantness at the Bellona Club* was likely to infuriate a man who had spurned and insulted him.

Dorothy L. Sayers was a Gollancz author.

Allen had not been surprised by the antipathy of most of his fellow-publishers but he had assumed that Gollancz would not go with the mob. If only as a salute from one rebel to another, Gollancz would make some cooperative gesture. Instead, when the acknowledged nobility of the trade replied to Allen's request for paperback rights with polite if glacial rejections, Gollancz merely ignored his letters. At last and in desperation Allen sent off a self-addressed and stamped postcard. On it he had typed the simple questionnaire:

> I shall be happy to negotiate/I am sorry but I cannot consider leasing to Penguins the following titles. . . . Please delete whichever phrase is inappropriate.

Back came the postcard with everything struck out up to and including the words 'I am sorry'.

Gollancz was not yet Miss Sayers's exclusive publisher. Allen discovered that he was at that very moment preparing to take over from Ernest Benn some of her early books. Allen bustled round to see Benn, a publisher of the older generation but also a man who mistrusted orthodoxies, and persuaded him to release the paperback rights in *The Unpleasantness at the Bellona Club*.

His revenge was sweetened when Gollancz failed to produce his reprint of the book until some months after it had appeared as a Penguin. Gollancz for his part sustained his antagonism to Penguins and to all paperbacks for twenty years. In October 1955 at last he fell victim to flattery and paperback royalties and appeared in the Penguin list – as an author.

With their first ten titles contracted, it was now imperative that the Lanes should test the market. So that they might have something to show booksellers they had Hazell Watson and Viney prepare a 256-page dummy comprising eight sets of a signature from Penguin number 3, Linklater's *Poet's Pub*. Allen went out into the provinces and Dick concentrated on his old stamping-ground, London and the suburbs. John did not move from the office; with consummate impudence he wrote off to all the booksellers he had met during his world tour announcing he would send them the number of copies of each title that he had decided that they were capable of selling.

John's method was marvellously successful; not one of his overseas contacts protested and his only disappointment was that he had not committed more copies to every one of his export outlets. Allen, however, came back from his travels through England and Scotland, his spirit racked by miserable arithmetic: the orders that he had written up were insufficient to meet the expenses of his journey. Dick, too, had been poorly received by most booksellers, but he had two successes which, because of the importance of the individuals involved, went some way to lightening the prevailing gloom. J. G. Wilson of Bumpus had not only ordered well but had also promised to raise his much-respected voice in support of Penguins, and Elliot, the book-buyer at Selfridges, had offered a window on Oxford Street for a Penguin display.

When all orders were added together, John's triumph, Dick's occasional successes and Allen's almost entire failure produced orders averaging only 7000 copies a title, not half-way to the break-even point. The Penguin, it seemed, was dead in the egg.

There followed an episode which has become with the years central to Penguin mythology. Only ten years after the event the author of the first history of the firm wrote of Mrs Prescott as if she were the instrument of Divine Providence. The story of her intervention on behalf of the desperate and despairing Lanes has been repeated so often, and with so many embellishments, that it has been made to seem that without her fortuitious appearance in the office of her husband, the senior buyer for Woolworth, the whole venture must have been still-born.

Allen himself described the circumstances after this fashion. Disappointed by the reception he and Dick had faced from conventional booksellers but unwilling to accept the humiliation of failure, he had revived an idea that had fallen into desuetude in the months when he and Dick had been tramping round the bookshops. He would try to sell his books outside the customary boundaries of the book trade and, with that in mind, looked to Woolworth as a potential customer.

For many years books had been included in the variety of goods which Woolworth marketed at sixpence a time. Hitherto Woolworth had published on its own account a sixpenny reprint series. These books it had sold, exclusively in its own stores, to customers most of whom would never have risked exposing themselves to the patronizing airs of bookshop assistants.

Allen argued that his new Penguins were priced consistently with the Woolworth formula and presented in a manner that must make them suitable for display on the large open counters. They were patently goods that Woolworth could sell.

The firm's senior buyer did not agree. The dummy Linklater Penguin that Allen had thrust into his hand he compared unfavourably with books from Woolworth's own Readers Library; its paper cover and its severe design (the adjective amazed Allen) would not attract customers used to the brilliant pictorial wrappers and the elaborate if pseudo-William Morris embossed paper-board bindings of the Readers Library.

Prescott's rejection, so runs the story, was unhesitating but because he was an old friend, he asked Allen to wait in his office to meet his wife who was expected at any moment. Mrs Prescott arrived, was shown the dummy Penguin, and unlike her husband, pronounced it delightful. Eagerly Allen offered her the list of prospective publications. She had not read one, she said, but she had no doubt that at sixpence a time she would risk buying the lot.

Grudgingly Prescott gave way to his wife's wisdom; he would take a few dozen of each title to try out in the principal Woolworth stores in London.

It was something, but it was not enough to save Penguin.

A few days later Prescott telephoned Allen. Would The Bodley Head accept a consignment order for Penguins? Allen agreed without hesitation and then rang up Sydney Goldsack, the sales manager at Collins, to ask him what Woolworth's meant by a consignment order. Goldsack explained that it involved sending stocks to every Woolworth store. 'What sort of numbers would this mean?' Allen asked. 'Hard to say,' replied Goldsack, 'but certainly not less than 50,000 and could be 100,000.'

Less than a fortnight after the meeting in Prescott's office, the Woolworth consignment order was confirmed at 63,500 copies. Mrs Prescott's intervention had been responsible for a sale that virtually matched all other pre-publication sales achieved hitherto in Britain and abroad. This one order brought Penguin within sight of the break-even point.

There is no denying the importance of the Woolworth order, but certain incidentals have been amended to improve the fable. In the first place Allen had always intended approaching Woolworth. His meeting with Prescott had been arranged some weeks before he and his brother had calculated the disappointing results of their calls on booksellers. Secondly, if Prescott's own evidence can be believed, he was impressed from the first with the potentialities of Penguins; he consulted his wife only as a sociable gesture and made his first order small only because he wanted time to calculate the full possibilities before committing himself to something more generous. Thirdly, Allen knew full well what was implied by the term consignment order, even if he did not at first appreciate the scale of one from Woolworth. Most important of all in reducing myth to history, even before the Woolworth order was secured, rumours of impending success were abroad in the book trade. Consequently those who had been faint-hearted were already sending in unsolicited orders. Booksellers who only a few weeks earlier had resisted were now climbing on the Penguin bandwagon.

But the possibility of success did not silence the Jeremiahs. To coincide with the 1935 booksellers conference, Allen took three pages in the trade press to publicize the publication of the pioneer Penguins, the first page showed penguins in flight and was captioned 'Penguins are coming', and the next two pages gave details of the books on the list. Some book-trade jester quipped acidly that he should have taken a fourth page to announce that 'Penguins have gone'.

With more solemnity Stanley Unwin, the acknowledged master of all truths about publishing, explained to the many who would listen that, though young Lane might have momentary success, he had condemned himself to eventual failure by committing himself to selling his books at sixpence – and not a penny more. The price of paper was bound to increase. When it did Lane's flimsy financial structure would collapse.

Neither ridicule nor stolid reason could any more dispel the euphoria in Vigo Street and Talbot Square. The Lanes and their young and energetic collaborators knew that they were home, and if they were not yet dry there were before them few problems that could not be solved by bustle and sleight of hand. 20,000 copies of ten titles must be printed, packed, delivered and invoiced by publication date, 30 July 1935. By that time another ten must be ready to succeed to success.

At this stage, the Penguin series had earned not one penny and had spent prodigally from the insubstantial resources of The Bodley Head. Fortunately for Allen printers are accustomed to acting as bankers to the publishing trade and, although the credit of The Bodley Head was far from good, several printers were prepared to accept reports from Vigo Street as forecasts of an affluent future.

There were set-backs and tribulations. Agatha Christie's *The Murder on the Links* had to be postponed, and her *The Mysterious Affair at Styles* hurriedly took its place in the first ten. Slipshod investigation of the copyright situation of *Carnival*, compounded by Compton Mackenzie's change of publisher, failed to reveal that the author had in all innocence already dispossessed himself of the sixpenny rights in the novel. *Carnival* appeared in the first ten (eventually listed as number 10) but it had to be withdrawn.

It was twenty-two years before another Mackenzie title, *Whisky Galore*, appeared as number 1220. 'I have always regretted that long exile,' wrote Mackenzie in 1960. 'The escorting penguin on its orange background has shrunk; the 6d. is seven times the size that it was; the picture of myself looks like the father of the author of *Carnival*.' But despite these difficulties, the first Penguins were somehow made ready.

On the Friday before publication Allen spent some time with Ben Huebsch, the most anglophil and one of the finest of American publishers. On Saturday morning, he, Dick and John took off for Gloucestershire, where their parents were now living. It was for them all a regular pilgrimage and the routine had been fixed for some years. First, at Paddington Station, where not so long ago Allen had looked wistfully and hopelessly down the line to Bristol, they enquired if anyone had booked a stop at Badminton, the most convenient station for the family home. If no one had been so obliging (Badminton was a request stop available only to first-class passengers), the Lanes acquired that privilege by buying one first-class ticket and two seconds. They then spent most of the journey in the restaurant car, insisting that they be served the outside of whatever joint was on the menu, and an un-opened tin of Huntley and Palmer biscuits so that they might take out all the digestives. A couple of drinks before lunch, the meal, a bottle of wine and liqueurs saw them comfortably to Badminton where Nora was waiting to drive them to the family home, seventeen miles away.

In earlier years these week-ends had been familiar and, in both senses of the word, bucolic; country walks, huge meals washed down with home-made wine and sloe gin. As the excitement over the new publishing venture built up, though Allen continued to go through the motions and though he never ceased to show affection for his parents and his sister such as he could seldom spare for others, his part in family reunions became more and more transcendental. On this last week-end of the pre-Penguin era he acted according to a pattern which he was to follow for many years to come. The train journey was as it always had been, but once in the house Allen went straight to the telephone and began a series of calls, tracking down astonished booksellers, agents and authors in their homes. Everything must be right for next week, for the second list, for next year's publications; so that this could be assured the conventions of the English week-end must be destroyed.

At Vigo Street during the last week of July 1935 the division of The Bodley Head into two camps – a division imminent and inescapable for some years – became a reality. The Lanes and their young allies bustled about confident that they were on the verge of success. Originally the Lanes had ordered 20,000 copies of each title but prudence had persuaded them to limit the binding to 10,000. This cautious decision was almost immediately overturned; all the remaining sheets were rushed to the binders and, within weeks, reprints of almost every title were in hand. The conservative relicts of an older regime watched helplessly. They had been given no part in this new venture and were tempted to wish it ill but their money, their reputations and the very future of their firm was at stake.

When the first ten Penguins appeared, success was immediate. Many commentators, both panegyrists and confounded Cassandras, have constructed elaborate sociological explanations to account for the avid response to those first Penguins. Their portentous theses relate the unique achievement to the Depression, to the explosion of working-class literacy and to the growth of the adult education movements, even to the falling-off in the availability of domestic service which made small houses desirable and large private libraries inconvenient. All this sophisticated rationalization collapses unless it is supported by knowledge of the subsequent history of Penguin, the firm's proud record of innovation and its corporate skill in making synonymous the public interest and profit. On 30 July 1935, if any of this was visible to Allen it was through a champagne-glass darkly. There was as yet no great originality in concept, editorial policy, marketing technique or price. Like many another publisher before him and like many of his contemporaries, he had realized that there was a market for quality books at low prices. He had gone a little beyond his rivals when he looked to those very rivals to provide him with titles for his list; he had gone beyond most of his predecessors when his reprint list included no out-of-copyright works; but he had as yet no clear idea of what he meant by a 'quality' book, unless it be a book by a reputable and successful author from a reputable publishing house which was prepared to lease it to Penguin.

Allen had been obstinate in the face of opposition and disappointment – an ungenerous way of saying that he had been brave – but in one respect he had discovered an original philosophy of publishing. It was this beyond all else to which the public responded as never before to any other reprint series. Allen articulated this philosophy as 'friendliness' or as 'elegant flippancy'.

Many before him, prominent among them Uncle John, had proselytized for good book design; Allen favoured good design that was direct and cheerful, that proclaimed an end to the piety and pretentiousness which hitherto had built a barrier between the generality of readers and the mandarins of literature. The bold lines, gay colours and, not least, Edward Young's perky penguin, with its beak cocked and its one visible eye opened wide upon an exciting world, nudged the public into a sudden realization: book-ownership in all its variety was no longer a privilege peculiar to the aristocracy and the more prosperous members of the middle-class whilst the rest of society must limit its pleasure to possessing austere reprints of the classics or to borrowing from the public library, whose custodians dressed Baroness Orczy in the same dreary uniform which they put on Aldous Huxley, who made Wodehouse look no different from Sassoon, and both without doubt melancholy. As objects and for what they contained, Penguins pricked the bubble of pomposity and added to the sum of gaiety. Almost as the first ten appeared, Penguins became collectors' items for thousands who had never before done more than dream of building up a library of their own. Many who had not been quick enough to seize the first ten begged booksellers to re-order (and for the most part still received a cool answer). Others who had been wiser, sharper or more fortunate waited eagerly for the second list.

Already, though he was not yet even dimly aware of the significance of the achievement, Allen had contrived something which remains a considerable part of the Penguin ethos. Trades other than the book trade would call it selling by the mark, persuading the public to buy on the manufacturer's reputation; the book trade uses no such term because publishers have seldom managed to impress their individual identities upon the book-buying public. At high tables and in Senior Common Rooms dons might mumble their respect for the Oxford University Press; in its heyday the zealots for a certain kind of precocity had looked to John Lane; so too at about the same time as the birth of Penguin, poetry addicts waited upon the benefits offered by Faber and Faber, and left-wing intellectuals upon the gifts of Victor Gollancz; but no other publisher before Penguin – and few since – had convinced a public beyond the limits of the *cognoscenti* that books on a varied list were worth collecting just because they came from a particular house.

As any sensible manufacturer will testify, the many commercial advantages of selling by the mark are qualified by the nagging necessity to maintain the quality of the products bearing the firm's name. Let Heinz produce a fifty-eighth product which is despised by shoppers, and sales of the original fifty-seven will slip. The customary anonymity of publishers has generally liberated them from this burden. Booksellers, sophisticated in the ways of the trade, may shy away from a publisher who consistently issues books destined for the remainder market, but to the public at large imprint passes unnoticed. If a publisher such as Collins, Murray or Macmillan made a dozen consecutive editorial howlers the sequence of error would not deter readers from buying the thirteenth book.

Allen was no theoretician; even, he was inclined to suspect theory as the province of the unpractical. Most of many affirmations of Penguin philosophy made during his life-time (like most of the rationalizations of the initial Penguin success) were evolved by others to suit the evidence which flowed from circumstances already created by his instinctive judgement. Certainly in late 1935 he neither knew that he was creating a precedent by persuading the public to buy Penguins just because they were Penguins, nor considered either the advantages or disadvantages of selling by the mark. What he knew, what any experienced publisher would have known, was that he must keep the books coming. Even before the initial success was assured, when all others involved were frenetically engaged with the immediate and never tempted to imagine that the first publication might mark the birthday of an institution, Allen was already casting forward into 1936 and 1937.

It would be folly to pretend that 1935, the year that saw Penguins established and the paperback revolution begun, left him by

December a personality utterly unlike the Allen Lane who had celebrated the previous New Year's Eve by throwing an hilarious and almost schoolboy party at Talbot Square. Yet undoubtedly the events of that year erased in him all traces of hesitation or dependence and strengthened in him many of the traits, both virtuous and disagreeable, which had long been discernible; traits which would make him one of the most detested and one of the most admired men in publishing and, to his colleagues, a leader at once exciting and infuriating.

At last he had emerged from the shadow of John Lane. He had created something for himself. He knew that he could depend upon his brothers but on few outside the family; even his brothers and other loyal helpers must be prepared to play the game of follow-my-leader according to Allen's rules. He demanded that his subordinates keep him informed about every detail of current activity, but detail bored him. What was current to others was to him already ancient history. He was so much away from the office weaving his plans for the future that in moments of crisis he was seldom accessible to make the decisions that he insisted were his to make.

This obsession with the future and disassociation with the immediate was apparent even in his private and social life. One evening in October 1935 he took Ethel Mannin to dinner. The lobster was about to be served when Miss Mannin mentioned that her American publisher was in London and leaving next day for the Continent. Without apology or explanation Allen rose from the table and went to the telephone. He did not return to the lobster or to Miss Mannin.

Allen's genius for putting on a bravura performance was evident throughout those seminal months of 1935. Whenever Dick, John or one of the others who was sufficiently involved to hope but well-informed enough to doubt expressed pessimism, Allen's eyes flashed but his answer came coolly: 'Penguins will succeed.' No explanation; no supporting calculations; when his prophecy was fulfilled this act to reassure the timid became real, entire and was from then on for many years virtually unshakeable. He had won; against all sensible opinion and despite the opposition of those who, by his reckoning, should have been his allies.

For this initial and immediate success he owed very little to his fellow-publishers, and henceforth he showed very little interest in courting the communal good will of the book trade.

Nor had he been much helped by the press. The absence of the trumpetings in the advertising columns which conventionally herald a new commercial venture had been taken for stern financial reasons. Buying even a few inches in all the literary papers would have bitten so deeply into the firm's exiguous resources that it must have made it impossible to sustain the sixpenny retail price. But, once the public was seen to buy without prodding from advertisements this too was rationalized and enshrined as a tenet in Penguin doctrine: the Penguin audience, it was argued, was more widespread and substantially different in kind from the readership of *The Times Literary Supplement*, the *Spectator*, the *New Statesman* and the book pages of the *Sunday Times* and *Observer*. Penguin must survive and prosper without advertising (except in the trade press); for publicity it would depend on word-of-mouth recommendation, on book reviews, and on comment in the editorial pages. As so often, by allowing his instinct to respond to *force majeure* Allen was pioneering a novel technique. 'Public relations' was as yet seldom mentioned in the larger world of commerce; though many publishers in some limited degree practised what they did not know to exist, none before Allen had dared to depend upon public relations without advertising. Even for him it was ten years before he institutionalized his instinct by appointing the first Public Relations Manager ever employed by a publishing-firm (and, it is believed, the last!).

At the outset, and indeed for the first year of Penguin, there was very little evidence that could have given Allen justification for his faith in public relations. True, the public bought on a scale that not even Allen had predicted, but the press disregarded for the most part the bright little books that had appeared in their midst. *The Times Literary Supplement* treated the first Penguins to a dismissive sentence; no soothsaying journalist foretold a revolution in book-buying habits; and when the literary editors did deign to give space to Penguin, their reviewers chose to seize upon this as a pleasing opportunity to write bright re-appraisals of individual titles or parrotted the sentence of death for Penguins pronounced by the reviewers' own publishers. George Orwell, for example, held views which might have led him to welcome a series which was intended to offer the joys of book-collecting to the masses; at very least, he should have noticed the decent austerity of Penguin design, so very different from the 'beastly Rackhamesque' book jackets which he detested for their 'elvish children tripping Wendily through a bluebell glade'. Instead he floundered, first considering the list book by book and then, if for somewhat eccentric reasons, calling upon the gods to damn the whole project. Reviewing the third Penguin publication in the *New English Weekly* on 5 March 1936 (admittedly a journal which would not much influence sales) Orwell could find very little to say for any of the ten titles. Only George Moore's *Esther Waters* and Helen Ashton's *Dr Serocold* won his approval; even *Esther Waters*, 'far and away the best' of the ten, he described as one of those 'books which are stuffed full of literary faults but which are not likely to drop out of favour'. Crosbie Garstin (*The Owls' House*) and Donn Byrne (*Hangman's House*) Orwell confessed he could 'not do with'; W. W. Jacobs he conceded to be 'on his low level ... as good a short-story writer as we have had', but his book *Odd Craft* (Penguin number 26) Orwell found 'ideologically poisonous'. He began his paragraph on Bartimeus with the grudging admission: 'I suppose I ought not to be rude to *Naval Occasions*, which I greatly enjoyed when I was a little boy' and a couple of sentences later was as rude as he could be. A few good words about the central character were not enough to compensate P. G. Wodehouse or Penguin for Orwell's proclaimed conviction that 'it was a pity not to choose a better ... book than *My Man Jeeves*'. In similar terms and for similar reasons, he castigated the selection of Sinclair Lewis's *Our Mr Wrenn*, 'a weak early work which hardly seems worth reprinting'. But the full force of Orwell's disdain he reserved for the two volumes of Margot Asquith's *Autobiography*. These, he admitted, he had never read *in toto*, but, he wrote, 'if you are born into one of our governing families and spend your life in political circles, you are bound to meet interesting people, but you don't, it seems, necessarily learn to write decent English.' Time has proved Orwell an indifferent soothsayer even about the one book to which he gave his qualified approval: *Esther Waters* has fallen from favour.

For all his aggressive waspishness Orwell's literary opinion of the list was generally sound. With this one possible exception not a single book in that third list could be regarded as a contribution to the elevation of public taste. Indeed, there was in these terms already visible some falling-off from the high standards of the second set of ten, which had included Norman Douglas's *South Wind*, W. H. Hudson's *The Purple Land*, Dashiell Hammett's *The Thin Man*, Liam O'Flaherty's *The Informer*, V. Sackville-West's *The Edwardians* and Samuel Butler's *Erewhon*. This bag of plump pheasants was something of a fluke. In the first hundred Penguins there are not more than a dozen other books which would merit reprinting forty years later.

Orwell had glimpsed some of the practical difficulties which faced Allen as he cajoled and bullied publishers to lease titles; writing of *Our Mr Wrenn* he said 'presumably it was chosen because the copyright of *Babbitt* or *Elmer Gantry* would have been too expensive'. But he failed to appreciate that, even in what might be called loosely 'educational' terms, Penguins must be considered as a whole. Unlike the editors of Everyman or World Classics, Allen had no thought of bringing to the new buying public, at prices which they could afford, the eternal masterpieces of world literature. All he intended was the dissemination of good and entertaining reading materials at prices so low that the public would be encouraged to buy more. Allen did not judge, did not presume to judge, and did not pretend to have the capacity to judge the potential for survival in a work of literature; he would not have been much perturbed had the ephemeral nature of most of the books he was publishing been revealed to him.

Nevertheless, even if one allows to Orwell critical standards which were sound if misplaced, no similar courtesy can be granted to the generalizations about cheap paperbacks with which he surrounded his more particular literary criticism. A grudging nod to the courage of the publishers 'The Penguin Books are splendid value for sixpence' and then:

> It is, of course, a great mistake to imagine that cheap books are good for the book trade. Actually it is just the other way about. If you have, for instance, five shillings to spend and the normal price of a book is half-a-crown, you are quite likely to spend your whole five shillings on two books. But if books are sixpence each you are not going to buy ten of them, because you don't want as many as ten. . . . Probably you will buy three sixpence books and spend the rest of your five shillings on seats at the 'movies'. Hence the cheaper books become, the less money is spent on books.

Another grudging bow, 'In my capacity as reader I applaud the Penguin Books', and then the curse: 'as writer I pronounce them anathema'. 'And,' Orwell insisted, 'for the publisher, the compositor, the author and the bookseller it is a disaster.' If the other publishers had any sense they would combine against Penguins 'and suppress them'.

This mish-mash of patronizing benevolence and phony economics had as little impact upon the public as the more austere but no less damning pronouncements of the wise men of the booktrade, but in those first months of Penguin history and for all Allen's imperturbable optimism, it seemed possible that Penguins would suppress themselves, suffocated by success, by the need to find finance and credit to extend the list, by the weight of orders and by the problems of acquiring, holding and distributing stock.

Even against the poor record for credit-worthiness of The Bodley Head, Allen persuaded his printers to hold back demands for payment. Soon he had negotiated a small loan from Martins Bank, approved by a manager who was either remarkably far-sighted or else gullible beyond most of his kind, but the arduous business of handling the torrent of orders Allen left almost entirely to his brothers and to those other members of the Bodley Head staff whom he conscripted for this purpose. Not for nothing did he claim *Tom Sawyer* as his favourite book and as his favourite episode in all literature that moment when Tom 'from being a poor poverty-stricken boy' comes quickly to wealth by persuading others to pay for the privilege of white-washing his aunt's fence.

No sooner were the first Penguins published than the logistics of successful paperback publishing created demands for space on a scale quite unlike anything known in a comparatively small firm like The Bodley Head. For that initial publication there were 200,000 books to be received from the printers, to be stored, sorted, packed, invoiced and distributed to booksellers and wholesalers. By the end of the year, though the number of books despatched had exceeded all predictions, space had to be found for reprints of the first and second publications (some ordered hastily from other printers because Hazell's could not find machine-time). Space had to be found for titles on the January 1936 list, and already the printers were delivering some of the books that were announced for March 1936. There were close to a million Penguins in stock.

For some years The Bodley Head had used the crypt of Holy Trinity Church, Marylebone Road, as a store. This Allen took over entirely and made it into the Penguin base. The division of forces which followed presaged the inevitable break from the parent company; for the moment it added also to confusion over shared and divided responsibilities.

There was no office space, the authorities refused to permit the employment of female labour in the crypt, and, because Allen was still Managing Director of The Bodley Head, he kept himself and his secretary at Vigo Street. Dick and John (who was still doubling as an insurance salesman) spent most of their time in the crypt; so did S. H. Olney, in charge of stock control, Ashton Allen, Jack Summers and the new invoice-clerk, R. W. Maynard, twenty-one years old and lured from Chatto and Windus by rumours of excitement and a reduction of five shillings in his weekly salary. Another invoice clerk, Eric Norris, stayed in Vigo Street, where he worked both on the Penguin series and on the Bodley Head list, and so also did Edward Young. Peter Kite, seconded from the Bodley Head, organized and set up the Accounts Department, working extremely long and varied hours, and Bill Rapley, the London representative, was soon carrying only Penguins on his visits to booksellers.

The Crypt – over the years it has taken on the capital letter of a unique, immediately identifiable proper noun – has entered the mythology of Penguins and of publishing. The knowledge that they were taking part in a pioneering adventure informed all who worked there and inspired them to feats of activity and endurance which, had they been reported to a trade union, must have brought down upon Allen the wrath of organized labour. Bob Maynard began work sometimes at 8 a.m., invoiced through the day and on into the night, broke off at dawn to join Dick and John, who had been packing for anything up to eighteen hours, for breakfast at Lyons and, in the summer months, for a row on the lake in Regent's Park, and then began invoicing again. Nor was there any clear demarcation between the duties of one employee and those of another; it was part of the excitement, part of Allen's policy – and remained for many years an integral part of the Penguin mystique – that any member of the staff could be called upon to do any job and, if he thought it necessary, would generally start upon it before he was called.

Fortunately it was a young staff, most of its members under thirty, and many of them little more than twenty years old. Perhaps even more important, almost all were bachelors with no private obligations to disrupt their total commitment to the success of their adventure. As so often happens in an all-male society, and as many of those involved were to discover in far grimmer circumstances five or six years later, the extraordinary and uncomfortable circumstances in which they worked heightened their sense of community and, far from creating discontent, became instead the occasion for perverse pride and for outbursts of hilarity which relieved the tensions of long hours and overwork.

The Crypt was Penguin's Agincourt. Not one of those who worked there was ever after able to resist telling tales of what deeds had been done there – with embellishments.

There is, for example, the incident of the wedding. Holy Trinity was still in use as a church and the packers' bench in the Crypt was directly under a heating grill by the altar-rail. One afternoon just as the priest was asking a bride: 'Wilt thou take this man . . . ?', almost beneath his feet, a packer hit his thumb with a beatle (the wooden mallet used to square the end of parcels). The bride's response was articulate, delivered in an indubitably male voice, and conveyed to the whole congregation a request that had a real but, in the context of the Solemnization of Matrimony, somewhat shattering relevance.

Or there is the story of Bill Rapley, a devout Catholic who crossed himself every time he entered the Crypt. There were stored against the walls the coffins of the dear departed, many of them in their temporal state distinguished participants in Britain's exercise of imperial power. There was also, in the centre of the Crypt, a bricked-in section, some six or seven feet high, containing another stack of coffins. As the number of Penguins in stock increased, the top of this lesser necropolis was commandeered for books. One day when Rapley was looking out titles on this funereal platform high above the heads of his colleagues, the brickwork gave way; he crashed through on to a two-centuries-old coffin, shattered the wood and found himself embracing a skeleton.

The hoist which lowered book supplies had been constructed originally as a coffin-lift. The ledgers and invoice books were filed in spaces created by shifting coffins. These musty appurtenances of death contributed much to the high spirits of the small staff; but if the eschatological is often the basis for good humour in an all-male community as such it cannot compete with the scatological. Not one of the Crypt veterans ever forgets to tell willing and unwilling listeners that there were no toilets in Holy Trinity; for simpler purposes a bucket was kept behind the organ which was emptied each night over the graveyard. In lieu of other provision each worker was given each week in addition to his wages six pennies for use in the men's lavatory at Great Portland Street Underground station.

John was the moving spirit of that small band in the Crypt; by command, good humour and example he kept them going when exhaustion seemed inevitable. Once in that first winter he and Dick worked for forty-eight hours without a break, and always John seemed to be physically tireless.

It was Allen who broke first. He was little involved with the energetic efforts in the Crypt and went there, only a curious observer of a scene which could have inspired Hogarth to illustrate Dante, to hand out wage-packets and the quintessential six pennies; but Allen was also deprived of the release which comes with concentrated physical effort and with communal endeavour. He was also for the most part deprived of the company of his brothers in Talbot Square. Instead, morning, afternoon and evening for six days a week he had to deal not only with the future problems of Penguin but also with the rapidly deteriorating situation of The Bodley Head and with the increasingly open hostility of his fellow-directors.

He decided that he must take time off, and chose to recover his zest and strength on a health farm. By his own account on the first day he was given two salads; on the second one fruit dish; for the next seventeen days he was starved; on the twentieth day again a fruit dish; and then, on the last day, to prepare him for his return to the world, two salads. He came back twenty-one pounds lighter, too weak to last a full day at the office, but with his appetite and his appetite for work revived. It was a process which he repeated almost every year for the rest of his life.

The formal break with The Bodley Head came on New Year's

Day 1936 when the firm of Penguin Books Ltd was formed with a capital of £100 and three directors, Allen, Richard and John Lane. Thereafter the name of The Bodley Head no longer appeared on the face of Penguins, but Allen stayed on for some months as Managing Director and throughout that time kept his office in Vigo Street. Then Penguin took a lease on two offices above a motor sales-room in Great Portland Street, Allen resigned from The Bodley Head, and early in 1937 The Bodley Head went into voluntary liquidation. For all that he was battling with the liquidity problem created by the public response to Penguins, Allen knew that he could not afford to sacrifice the goodwill of printers. To maintain the flow of reprints and additions to the series he had added Purnell's to Hazell's as printers of Penguins; both were owed money by The Bodley Head. If his series developed and the momentum of orders continued, as from all the signs seemed likely, he would have to look for more printers. Because the printers he knew best were those he had courted for The Bodley Head, all the firms that he could go to were those he had earlier persuaded to extend credit to The Bodley Head. His decision as far as was possible to satisfy The Bodley Head's printer-creditors out of Penguin profits had in it an element of the quixotic, for Penguin profits were tiny and the future unsure; it was certainly informed by conscience, but it was also far-sighted.

Later in 1937 Allen made an unsuccessful bid to recover a controlling interest in The Bodley Head. It was not his first attempt; already in January 1936 he had persuaded Jonathan Cape to lend him £10,000 to buy out Boswell and his other uncooperative colleagues. Then, when Penguin was only an incipient tail to The Bodley Head dog, the logic of his intention was clear; so clear that it was resisted by his fellow-directors. Now, eighteen months later, the tail had outgrown the dog, broken off and taken on a life of its own. Indeed, ironically, by the summer of 1937, the biggest trade creditor of The Bodley Head was Penguin Books Ltd. Looking back, it is difficult to assess Allen's motives in seeking to acquire a firm which had few assets and many liabilities. It could be that the move was one of those impulsive gestures, a salute to his own past, to which he was from time to time susceptible, but more likely he was indulging a typically mischievous whim. He knew that there were others in the market for The Bodley Head; a consortium of publishers, many of whom had been vocal and active in their opposition to Penguin. By entering the auction he raised the price that they had to pay for his shares and for control of a firm for which he had once cared a great deal but which was no longer of any use to him. Certainly, he showed no signs of disappointment or frustration when he was outbid.

The Brahmins of publishing persisted with their predictions of disaster for Penguin though, by the summer of 1936, men like Stanley Unwin and Harold Raymond of Chatto and Windus were no longer quite sure whether they should describe Allen as a lunatic bent on suicide or as a wild man with murder in his heart, whether the destruction which he was bound to bring about would be his own or that of the whole trade as they knew it. But publishers could no longer afford to ignore Penguin.

The doubts of the experts about the financial viability of mass-market paperback publishing were largely justified – and would have been strengthened had any of them been able to inspect closely Penguin accounts. In the first two years when overheads were miraculously low and, by the standards of later years, borrowing from the bank comparatively cheap, the profit on each book sold never exceeded one farthing – and many made no profit at all – but the sight of Penguins in every bookshop, on every railway bookstall and, it seemed, on the bookshelves of every acquaintance tempted even the most cautious publisher to reconsider.

This reconsideration was hastened by pressures from authors who, for all that they are the prime producers of books, are not often capable of exercising any substantial influence on the policies of publishers. Few authors are sophisticated students of book trade economics (Orwell's indoctrination when he served his time as a bookseller's assistant may account for his following the conventional wisdom of the trade, as did few of his more innocent contemporaries); on the other hand most writers are also avid readers and many are both bibliomaniacs and poor. As front-line book collectors authors were quick to seize upon the sixpenny Penguins; even Bernard Shaw – assuredly no garret-author – bought for himself most of the early Penguins. And, because most authors write as much because they believe that they have something to communicate as in the hope of gathering to themselves great riches, the benefits that might come to them by way of Penguin were to authors inescapable. Just as their publishers, they saw Penguins all round them; immediately they recognized that here was the way to an audience far larger than anything that had hitherto been available to any but the most popular writers.

Authors began to break down the prejudices of their own publishers. Some publishers decided to launch paperback series of their own, but none as yet had learnt the lessons that Penguin was beginning to teach. These early attempts at imitation, though intended by their publishers as competition to Penguins, were in every case limited to reprints of titles on the producing publisher's own list. As such they were in truth modelled not on Penguin but on long-established series such as Hodder and Stoughton's crime list in its yellow paper-binding. (Even so, mimicry was so blatant that Edmond Segrave, the Editor of the trade paper the *Bookseller* and from the outset a devotee of Penguins, wrote of the first ostensible rival, Jackdaw Books, that its publisher should have called it Parrot Books.)

By mid 1936, however, many publishers were ready to react positively to the pleas of their authors and to the inescapable evidence that Penguins were selling. Belatedly, perhaps, but nonetheless energetically they followed the example of Jonathan Cape. Still by no means certain that Allen could flout the laws of publishing economics, they were nevertheless prepared to let him take risks for them. Within a year of the first Penguin publication few publishers were ready to resist an invitation from Allen to lease a title to Penguin. Before 1937 was out, the problem for Penguins was no longer that they must find enough titles in all kinds to keep the list going; by then publishers, authors and authors' agents were bombarding the firm with suggestions. Now the prime concern was selection.

Experience at The Bodley Head, the successful independent publishing ventures of the Lane brothers, and Allen's sharp editorial instinct had taught him that 'quality' books in all kinds would serve his avowedly commercial purposes far better than more obviously popular ephemera. Only by maintaining high standards could Penguin establish a reputation at once unique and acceptable to the kind of readership which would follow wherever Penguin led, but thus far he had been forced to be largely an opportunist and he had never attempted to analyse what he meant by 'quality'. Now, with a vast range of possibility open to him, editorial policies must be crystallized if Penguin was to maintain an individual and recognizable personality.

Still, as for many years to come, this process remained largely pragmatic; it was not in Allen's nature or within the limits of his capacities to verbalize or to intellectualize; but somehow he communicated his purpose to all his more intimate collaborators. When the senior Penguin staff was small and the exercise of editorial prowess limited to a very few (a period which lasted for at least fifteen years), all those who worked closely with Allen, no less than Allen himself, recognized without much difficulty which titles were suitable and which unsuitable for Penguin.

By the end of 1936 there were seventy titles on the Penguin list (Penguin number 71 was Ethel Mannin's *Confessions and Impressions*), and over-crowding in the Crypt was taking on such proportions as to make effective operations well-nigh impossible even for the unflagging staff. Some minimal improvements had been made: the most useful a wooden slipway down which parcels of books could be slid from an entry-hatch in the graveyard. This served also a secondary but scarcely less useful purpose: when any member of the staff sensed that he was about to be overcome by exhaustion and the fetid atmosphere in the Crypt he could seek respite by attempting to run up the slippery incline. The premises suffered also from a plague of mice, and booksellers complained frequently that Penguins were impregnated with a peculiar, fusty mouse perfume. (Even today, some forty years later, there are those who own early Penguins who insist that they can recognize them as much by smell as by sight.) But it was not the practical difficulties nor yet the mice, but the absence of toilet facilities which at last persuaded Allen that he must find a new base. An application had been made to Marylebone Town Hall for a permit to install a lavatory. An official arrived, edged his way round the stacks of books, spoke to several employees, and then announced to Allen that, because the staff seemed happy he was content to ignore the application, to forget that he had ever visited Holy Trinity or ever heard of Penguin; but his memory would be restored within weeks if he did not soon pick up well-authenticated rumours that preparations were in hand for the evacuation of the crypt-dwellers to more appropriate and more salubrious surroundings.

The inspector's advice was inescapable but it spelt disaster. The renting of suitable space in central London would so increase overheads as to endanger the sacrosanct sixpenny selling-price, which was, even then, being maintained only by courtesy of Martins Bank and by the exercise of the most frugal domestic economy. Royalty payments could not be reduced. As the Jeremiahs had foretold, the price of paper and printing was increasing monthly. The staff was underpaid: the juniors would have fared better as Calcutta coolies; Dick and John drew no salary for the first two years of Penguin; Nora was brought in from time to time, also as an unpaid supernumerary, to work at Great Portland Street; even Allen paid himself only £1000 a year; and it was obvious that, if extra help was not taken on soon, the whole organization would collapse under the weight of achievement.

Dilemma was Allen's favourite stimulant: he became even more boisterous than usual, more optimistic and more ambitious. By projecting the scale of current success into the future he proved beyond doubt, or at least beyond any doubt that he could allow, that in less than two years Penguin would be truly profitable. If the volume of publication could be increased the firm could not only move comfortably into the black but it could also manage to finance a loan, much more substantial and more long term than anything so far wrung out of Martins. It followed that Penguin could afford to buy freehold land and to build upon it a headquarters tailor-made for its purposes and prospects.

Allen's decision to look for a site beyond the districts generally inhabited by publishers and even outside metropolitan London was characteristic. Faced with the inevitable, he responded in a manner which was at once solidly practical and yet tempered by romanticism. The outcome was always unorthodox and often, as in this case, innovative.

Tradition and, more powerful than tradition, the need to keep themselves readily accessible to authors, confined most publishers to Bloomsbury and the West End of London. Allen, who was determined that in the parade of publishers he would be the only man to march in step, was more reasonably convinced that the paperback business on which he was engaged, because it was involved entirely with reprints, was therefore largely freed from dealing face to face with authors. He assessed his priorities and found them unlike those of any other publisher. The considerations that weighed were those which would influence any large-scale wholesaler of industrial products. He needed immediately ample warehouse space and convenient facilities for receiving and despatching goods in bulk; he needed also room for expansion. Vacant sites of this kind were not often available in central London or the inner suburbs; even could one be located, the price would be prohibitive and the mortgage would place a burden on Penguin finances so formidable as to inhibit progress, not only immediately but for all foreseeable future and however successful the enterprise.

This line of argument he presented cogently to his brothers and eventually to his bankers, but other if no less compulsive reasons for wishing to move his centre of operations out of London he revealed to no one for many years. Although he had become so much part of London life, he nourished the conviction that he was at heart a yeoman. He was determined to make a home for himself away from the pressures of urban existence. This he felt he could achieve most satisfactorily if his work-place was close to his bucolic residence. That same benefit he intended to confer on all his staff, even upon those who preferred the smell of petrol fumes to the scent of fresh-mown grass. He had no knowledge of Robert Owen, but he had visited Port Sunlight and Bourneville and, more appropriate to his purposes, he had been a guest of the *Reader's Digest*, whose staff lived in an ostensibly happy community around the plant in New York State. Allen's notions were less elaborate, if perhaps only because he knew that Penguin could not afford to build a Pleasantville in England's green and pleasant land, but he had it in mind that by establishing Penguin in some cheerful rural or semi-rural area where houses were cheap and rents low, the staff would welcome the chance to make their homes within easy reach of their work. How much more comfortable would be their lives if they were not forced to suffer trains in the rush hour. And how much more convenient for their employer if he could call for his staff to work overtime without any employee protesting that the last bus was about to depart and supper shrivelling in the oven.

The task of reconnoitring on Allen's guide-lines for a suitable site was given to Dick, who drove thousands of miles in the Lanes' Morris Cowley before selecting a three-and-a-half acre plot at Harmondsworth in Middlesex. The situation fulfilled almost every requirement. Only fifteen miles west of Hyde Park Corner, it was nevertheless just outside the limits of sprawling suburban development; both westwards and immediately across the Bath Road, which it faced, there were open fields. Only two miles from the end of the London Underground, it was within easy reach of a main-line railway depot at West Drayton and was convenient for main roads to the west, north and south.

The plot was on the market for £2000, but the vendors asked for another £200 for their fine crop of cabbages. Allen agreed the purchase, Martins Bank advanced the money, and Dick was given a new responsibility: the sale of cabbages.

On his birthday, 4 August 1937, Allen's father laid the foundation stone of the main Penguin building.

The fields across the Bath Road were not yet world-famous as Heathrow Airport (which only began commercial operations after the war).

Already, even before the silver trowel and the champagne had been ordered for the foundation-stone ceremony, there had been a slight, if ultimately significant, change in Penguin editorial policy and in that process some reduction in the force of Allen's arguments in favour of abandoning central London.

At the end of April 1937 there arrived in the bookshops six Shakespeare plays, edited for Penguin by G. B. Harrison. Intrinsically this was not an original venture; indeed the reissue of prime classics of English literature could represent a return to the traditions of the old-established reprint series. However, though no one knew it at the time – not even Allen – the Penguin Shakespeare pointed the way to a golden future for the firm as a major producer of standard texts for the classroom.

Like all else coming from Penguin, the Shakespeares were thought to be quality books for general readers who would buy at sixpence but not at a shilling. At the launching-party on Shakespeare's birthday, the first in a long line of similar fabulous occasions which Penguin used to encourage the press coverage which must substitute for paid advertising, there were crammed into the Talbot Square flat almost every leading actor and actress who could be persuaded to come, but not one representative of the universities or the schools except the series editor.

Because of his experience as an aspirant to a theatrical career, Dick saw himself as more qualified than Allen and John to act as host to the great. For once both of his brothers conceded the role. Generally more modest than his brothers, in this company he could not resist letting all who would listen and some who listened only to themselves that he too had once been a Shakespearean actor. A guest who expressed disbelief was taken to Robert Atkins, leader of the Egyptian tour in which Dick had participated. Asked for confirmation of Dick's thespian achievements, Atkins boomed back in the voice that had allowed him to compete with Martin Harvey, Frank Benson and Forbes Robertson, the voice that would soon be heard even above the rain in Regent's Park: 'In my time I have seen many actors and actresses, from stars to people just walking on, but in the whole of my stage career never have I seen an actor better than Richard Lane at walking off.'

Only the historian can identify the first Shakespeare as a change in Penguin policy and as a negation of the case for moving out of London. If he felt called upon to do so, William Shakespeare could visit Harmondsworth with no greater difficulty than if he chose to call at Vigo Street or Marylebone Road; most of the liaison with Shakespeare's editor could be conducted by post. In the next month, however, a new series was initiated which, from the outset, signalled a drastic shift in emphasis. Until that time Allen's aim had been limited. He had revealed no compelling missionary enthusiasm, only a determination to prove that commercial success could be secured without undervaluing the public appetite for good writing of all kinds. The criterion for selection in the Pelican series (launched in May 1937) was not, as hitherto for all Penguins, the author's capacity to entertain but rather his power to enlighten.

It is a nice paradox and one that must have pleased that apostle of contrariness that it was Bernard Shaw, the man who said that 'few books . . . are worth reading. People read to kill time,' who by his uninvited intervention in the Penguin selection process nudged Allen towards the establishment of Pelicans. It was

Shaw, the writer who had persuaded the world to consider a thousand truths by making them worth a joke, who was the first author to appear under the new colophon when the earnest Pelican joined the cheerful Penguin.

CHAPTER FOUR

IN August 1936 Allen had received one of Shaw's famous postcards. His Penguins were good and the list could be made even better if he would add Apsley Cherry-Garrard's *The Worst Journey in the World*. Allen was worried; those of Allen's colleagues who had read the book considered it entirely appropriate as a Penguin, but it was a long work which could not possibly be produced at sixpence and there was much to be said against publishing in two volumes, a practice which booksellers resented and which the public might misinterpret as an underhand way of raising prices. Nevertheless Penguin was even then planning an experiment of this kind (C. A. W. Monkhouse's *Some Experiences of a New Guinea Resident Magistrate* was published in two volumes in November 1936), and so Allen wrote back to Shaw that he would try to buy the paperback rights in *The Worst Journey in the World*. But, he added in a fine burst of opportunism and optimism, the book that he really wanted was Shaw's own *Intelligent Woman's Guide to Socialism, Capitalism and Sovietism*. Shaw never employed an agent but conducted all his own business affairs with a shrewdness which no agent could match. His reply was little more than a terse 'How much?' This in its turn was the cause for misgiving and argument at Penguin, for Shaw was known to be grasping and arrogant in his dealings with publishers. Indeed he consistently refused to accept that Constable were, in the conventional sense, his publishers at all, insisting that they put out the editions of his plays under licence from him. The suggestion was made that Shaw be offered celebrity rates but Allen, too, was gifted with wise obstinancy. Shaw, like every other author, must be given no more than customary Penguin terms.

Shaw not only accepted but, without prompting, offered to write a new section to explain Bolshevism and Fascism to his Intelligent Woman.

To have Bernard Shaw in the list at all was an accolade but to have him in the list with material which had never before appeared in print was a triumph which merited blaring trumpets and banging drums. No sooner had Shaw's acquiescent post-card reached Allen than he was spreading the news among his acquaintances in Fleet Street. Only then did it occur to him that the fanfares could herald a new era in Penguin history. Hurriedly he looked around for other titles that might be suitable as supports to Shaw in a series that would be deliberately didactic.

The selection, like the selection of the first ten Penguins, was both pragmatic and arbitrary. H. G. Wells, that other apostle of new truths, had already appeared in Penguins; now his florid *A Short History of the World* was transferred from the Penguin list and prepared for re-publication alongside Shaw in the new series. Julian Huxley, Sir James Jeans, G. D. H. Cole and Leonard Woolley were corralled; all of them distinguished scholars but all of them possessed also of a public reputation which guaranteed that their scholarship would not intimidate the bookbuyers who had responded so eagerly to the Penguin list. To complete the proposed first publication Penguin added two titles, admirable in themselves and yet somehow out of step with the rest: Olaf Stapledon's *Last and First Men*, and *The Floating Republic* by G. E. Manwaring and Bonamy Dobrée. Both books might just as well have appeared as conventional Penguins; their selection for the new list indicated an uncertainty about the boundary-lines between the two lists which, though not surprising in the experimental period, has persisted to this day.

The choice of titles once made, and negotiations with authors, agents and originating publishers being completed, it remained to name the series. Not the least pleasing if among the more time-consuming consequence of representing the Penguin operation to the public as, in some very real if indefinable sense, a venture in which they were participants was that, from the very beginning, readers in large numbers wrote to the firm. Prominently displayed in early Penguins was a bold invitation: 'If you have any suggestions to make for future books, please don't hesitate to send them in.' The public did not hesitate; they inundated the staff with suggestions, criticisms, comments and not a little Wonderland lunacy. (One letter, more lunatic than most, dates from a later period. Addressed to Allen Lane it asked: 'Are you the Allen Lane which runs from Harmondsworth to West Drayton?') For reasons which defy explanation many correspondents, including even several authors, fall into a common error when spelling the firm's name, a solecism not eradicated by more than forty years of ever-increasing fame; many thousands of letters have been addressed to Penquin Books. In the first eighteen months, for reasons that are no less mysterious, dozens of correspondents insisted on writing to Pelican Books. Fearing that some wily competitor might take over the misnomer and use the confusion to his own advantage the Lanes decided to pre-empt it for themselves. Thus Pelican Books for the new series and thus the subsequent alliterative aviary Puffin, Ptarmigan, Peregrine, and the one intruder to the aviary if not to the alliteration, Porpoise Books.

The two volumes of Bernard Shaw's *Intelligent Woman's Guide* duly appeared, as Pelican A1 and A2, with a characteristic Author's Note:

> As several newspapers have announced this Pelican edition of the Guide as re-written, implying either that the original work was ill-written, or that the present issue is an abridged or cheapened version, I must assure its readers that they have in their hands the authentic original text in full, word for word, but with the addition of two new chapters dealing with events that have occurred since its first publication in 1928. The present edition is in fact a better bargain than the first edition was, though the price is so much more modest.

The undeniable prestige that came with Shaw as the first Pelican author was enhanced by his considering it appropriate to publish in his Pelicans his own views on the two hideous threats which were lowering over Europe. Another book published in the same month signed the way to a future which would give, not only to Pelicans but to Penguin as a whole, a character virtually unique among paperback publishing houses. G. D. H. Cole's *Practical Economics* was not a reprint at all but a book contracted by Allen for exclusive publication.

It was part of Allen's skill as a publisher that he was so often capable of turning accidents into policy. It was also a not inconsiderable element in his genius that he knew the limitations of his own abilities and was quick to recognize in others the capacities which he himself lacked. The experience of his small staff was, for the time being, sufficient to manage wisely the seeking out from other publishers books for a series that was almost entirely dedicated to entertainment but that he had stumbled into producing books of a sterner sort and almost into commissioning them for himself, he knew that he must find advisers better qualified than he, his brothers or any of the young staff in the Crypt to guide him through the academic minefield and the intellectual jungle. He turned to Krishna Menon.

V. K. Krishna Menon was a few years older than Allen and in upbringing, personality and aspiration so unlike him as to make it seem inconceivable that the two could work together in amity. An Indian from Malabar, he had come to London with already two degrees from Madras University. He had then worked his way earnestly to three more degrees, in Arts, Science and Law. He had been called to the Bar and had established some reputation as an advocate in cases involving immigrants and the unemployed. He was, as Bernard Shaw had been, a Labour Councillor in St Pancras and he was hoping to find a parliamentary seat. He despised commerce, social frivolities and light reading; the only passion admitted into his ascetic existence was his enthusiasm for the twin causes of Socialism in Britain and independence for India. On occasion he had reported on manuscripts for The Bodley Head and Allen had learnt to respect his austere judgement and, as a publisher if not as a cheerful and sybaritic human being, to covet his large acquaintanceship among intellectuals. He invited Krishna Menon to take on the editorial direction of Pelicans.

To support Krishna Menon there was set up a panel of three advisory editors: Peter Chalmers-Mitchell, H. L. Beales and W. E. Williams.

Science stood first in the categories of books proclaimed as within the Pelican territory and the name, career, honours and reputation of the scientific editor guaranteed to the scientific community that the pelican was no fly-by-night bird. Sir Peter Chalmers-Mitchell CBE, FRS, FZS, DSC., Lit.D had been Secretary to the Zoological Society from 1903 to 1935. He was a good administrator who recognized that his Pelican responsibility involved him with an audience which was inevitably larger than the respectable, introverted and highly specialized academic world. He was also himself a clear and cogent writer, possessed of knowledge and interests which ranged far beyond his own subject. Not the least of his enthusiasms was a passion for good food and good drink and not the least useful of his skills – and the one which endeared him immediately to the Lanes – was his capacity for mixing and drinking cocktails. He was said to make the best Dry Martini in London; in Allen's opinion at this art he outshone even the bar-tender at New York's Twenty-One.

H. L. Beales, Reader in Economic History at the London School of Economics, was a friend of Krishna Menon's, warmer, less puritanical but nevertheless closer in spirit to him than to Chalmers-Mitchell or to Allen, and like Krishna Menon a devout Socialist.

The third Editorial Adviser had been introduced to Allen by Krishna Menon. By the bland, unrevealing measure of the reference books he seemed to come from the same mould which had shaped both Krishna Menon and Beales. Williams was just forty when he helped to initiate Pelicans. A product of Manchester elementary and secondary schools and of the University of Manchester, he had spent several years as a schoolteacher before becoming a Staff Tutor in the University of London Extra-Mural Department and then, in 1934, Secretary of the British Institute of Adult Education. Like Krishna Menon and Beales, he was a Socialist, committed to the view that the masses would never reach the Socialist Nirvana unless their road was paved with solid reading-material. But there the similarity ended. William Emrys Williams was a Welshman to every letter of his unmistakably Welsh name; even if he did come from Manchester. The rich rhythms of his Welsh voice, cunningly modulated by a controlled stammer, freed him from the suspicion of patronizing the audience that hung over so many of the Oxonian and metropolitan popular educators of that era. He was mercurial, as eager to make friends as he was quick to find enemies, and his earnest political opinions, like his devout concern for public understanding, was tempered by commercial shrewdness. Unlike Krishna Menon or Beales, he was essentially a polymath. Although his career had been so studiously dedicated to the earnest and generally left-of-centre adult education movement, his enthusiasm for the political, social and economic theorizing that was the staple diet of that movement did not match his zest for the arts. (Eventually almost all of his own contributions to the list were in *belles-lettres*.) He also shared with the Lanes and with Chalmers-Mitchell, but not with the other Pelican editors, an unfettered capacity for hedonism.

Nevertheless, by choosing three of his four editors from the vanguard of missionary radicalism, Allen committed Pelicans to predominantly Leftish policies, a bias which has never been abandoned entirely and was most marked in the first two years. Because many of the books were originals and the audience for the high intellectualism of Pelicans smaller than for Penguin reprints – and the public response more timid – the Pelican programme developed more slowly. In the two years between the first Pelican and the Second War fifty Pelicans were published but almost three times as many Penguins.

The political predilections of the editors were obvious in the Pelican list; of that first fifty more than half were by men whose dedication to Socialism was well known. This emphasis was the occasion for some suspicion that Penguin Books was an extension of the Labour Party propaganda-machine or even of the Third International. In the next years this suspicion was to take on the quality of hysteria; during Allen's life it was never entirely quelled – and since his death suspicion has erupted at times into ferocious public denunciations of the supposedly Marxist bias in Penguin books.

In the early days of Pelicans Allen indulged the political inclinations of his editors, but he did so with his eyes wide open to the commercial advantages of adherence to the Left. He was himself not much interested in politics, and in the abstraction of political theory not at all. Whenever he was called upon to vote he marked his paper dutifully for the Labour candidate but rather because he found the Conservatives dull and the Liberals ineffectual than because he was persuaded of the rightness of the Left; he felt no compulsion to assist in the overthrow of the capitalist system, from which he was already profiting and which he intended to exploit to its limits. He professed admiration for the trade union movement – the father and arch-patron of the Labour Party – but then, and for many years thereafter, he refused to allow any union to insinuate into the affairs of Penguin Books. Nevertheless he did not need his editors to show him that in the thirties the exponents of radical doctrines owned most of the best stalls in the market-place where he had to sell Pelicans. Britain was dragging itself slowly out of the Depression; The General Strike of 1926 and the Great Crash of 1929 were still open sores on the national memory. Mussolini, Hitler and Franco were strutting around Europe, their distorted shadows looming threateningly over Britain and the whole western world. The young, the less affluent among their seniors, the intellectuals and the aspirants to intellectualism – all those who were likely to acquire wisdom at sixpence a package – looked Leftwards for salvation.

Allen's old adversary, Victor Gollancz, had proved with his Left Book Club that in this political climate a publisher could be both prophet and profiteer; not least because Allen had been lucky enough to win Shaw's support he had the advantage over Gollancz, and over all other publishers, that he could lure into the Pelican list radical writers who, like Shaw, had achieved the respectability of bestsellerdom without sacrificing their Socialist ideology. Included in those first fifty Pelicans were books by many successful pontiffs of the Left, among them Laski, Cole, Haldane, Wells, Tawney and the Webbs.

But Allen had no wish to identify himself with the Left quite so blatantly as did Gollancz. He insisted that the prime consideration for inclusion in the Pelican list must be scholarly excellence; however fervent and however apposite the theorizing Pelicans, they must also be entertaining. And, with warm and knowledgeable assistance from Williams and Chalmers-Mitchell, he made the Pelican list balance politics, economics and the social sciences with books on literature, the natural sciences and the visual arts.

Except for Williams, none of those responsible for the creation of Pelicans was entirely aware of the historical context in which they were working. Chalmers-Mitchell's role was limited almost exclusively to advice about the natural sciences; Krishna Menon sought to use Pelicans to further the Socialist cause; Dick and John looked upon Pelicans as a useful and exciting addition to the commercial strength of their new firm. Allen's own place in the early Pelican story is more complex. Ever a pragmatist and not much given to rationalizing, he was nevertheless so quick to seize a hint that it seemed often to come from his own mind, so urgent and energetic in manipulating an opportunity that he was often so far ahead of his advisers as to make their advice appear superfluous. Williams almost certainly pointed out to Allen that the adult education movement was a major, outward and practical response to the torments of the time and Williams may well have brought him to realize that the movement – and particularly its most influential organization was in danger of becoming ossified. The WEA had drawn its students largely from the mass of blue-collar workers whose formal schooling had ended at fourteen and most of its tutors from among bright young men who had been over-educated in the ancient universities. As Williams recognized, literacy and a desire for further education had reached millions not prepared to undergo the rigours of a three-year WEA course; many even among those who had enjoyed an extended schooling still hankered after more education; and, even among the highly educated, many looked for relaxation to intellectual disciplines from which they had been cut off by the highly specialized curricula of British schools and universities. Pelicans could be the next development in adult education, a new Birkbeck or Ruskin College for tens of thousands of students, the only entrance qualification the willingness to pay the sixpenny fee, the only time-table that which suited the individual, the tutors, all of them, the most eminent authorities on their subjects – and the liveliest. Allen saw the logic of extending the Penguin doctrine to Pelicans but, even more than Williams, he was intent that scholarship for a large audience, no less than literature for an even larger audience, could not afford to be pompous. Just as Penguins, so also must Pelicans be lively, provocative and (again his own favourite word) 'cheerful'.

Allen's editorial rapport with Williams developed rapidly into friendship and before long Williams's influence spread also to the Penguin list. The frontier between the two lists was not easy to define. Penguins included no originals (except anthologies) but many Pelicans were also reprints; some subjects, notably history and biography, were placed sometimes in the one list and sometimes in the other for no reason, it seemed, beyond the whim of the moment. (For example, Liddell Hart's biography of Marshal Foch was a Penguin; the Hammonds's life of Lord Shaftesbury a Pelican.) Neither Allen nor Williams had any great enthusiasm for rigorous definition; Allen was disinclined to give more time than was absolutely necessary to the bureaucratic and administrative processes, to the inter-departmental memoranda and series meetings that customarily support clear-cut divisions of editorial purpose. Before long, although the editors' names still appeared on the half-title of all Pelicans and although their advice was still sought, the selection of Pelicans was for all practical purposes merged with Penguin selection, undertaken by a cabal of the Lane brothers, Williams and, sometimes, Beales.

One of the most pleasing paradoxes in Penguin history, and one which has its roots in the fact that, whatever his faults, Allen was never pompous, is that this cabal came together to deliver those editorial judgements which would shape the future of the firm in the comfort of a good Spanish restaurant, the Barcelona in Beak Street, and sharpened their collective wisdom with plentiful supplies of sherry and *tinto*. The firm's one van brought from Great Portland Street (and later from Harmondsworth) the books proposed for reprinting, manuscripts, letters with suggestions, and editorial notes; all these were piled under the table and brought up one after another for consideration. (A few years later, when some other editors were admitted to the ritual, the more cunning learnt to hide away their favoured candidates until they could join the port and brandy on the table.) It was all far removed from the cocoa and biscuits of the Workers' Educational Association.

The rise of Bill Williams, the relaxation in dedication to Socialism and, perhaps not least, the seemingly casual and certainly amiable mode of conducting editorial meetings led to a decline in the influence of Krishna Menon, and soon to his removal. There was no overt act of dismissal; instead he was eliminated by being ignored, his notes unanswered, his editorial suggestions disdained.

The brief history of Allen's relations with the first editor of Pelicans followed a pattern which was repeated many times in the next three decades. For a while Allen had been impressed and even overawed by the Indian lawyer's ability and connections and had thought him the answer to the prayers of an ambitious publisher. Whilst this honeymoon period lasted Allen made all manner of promises, if only Krishna Menon would devote himself without reserve to the Pelican cause. Then, as should have been obvious from the outset to both of them, the incompatibility of the two began to erode respect and all semblance of amiability; it needed only the sudden recognition of an alternative messiah to persuade Allen to turn his back on Krishna Menon, without apology, without reparation and with none of the promises fulfilled.

As so often in the future when he rid himself of temporary favourites, Allen offered no explanation even to those who retained his confidence; on those few later occasions when he did account for his actions, too often his reasons for dissatisfaction were founded upon some insubstantial or imagined grievance which no one else could credit as sufficient cause for his erratic and callous behaviour. With Krishna Menon, as again so often in years to come, Allen's essential judgement was as sound as his methods were unprincipled. He flourished upon experiment and argued that people, like publishing ventures, could be tested only in action. Krishna Menon had missed his chance to move Pelican away from the direction which Allen wished to follow. Menon's fiery politics were fast becoming a liability and his dedicated asceticism a bore, whereas Williams, like Allen, never allowed his social conscience to interfere with his social pleasures and was disinclined to hoist the Red Flag if it would write red figures on the Penguin balance-sheet. So, out with Krishna Menon and in with Bill Williams!

Many years later, Victor Weybright, another who had suffered from Allen's capriciousness, wrote of his treatment of Krishna Menon that ever afterwards the aggrieved editor refused to trust any British or American publisher. Stretching psychological analysis beyond the bounds of credulity, Weybright went on to insinuate that Allen's actions were a prime cause of Krishna Menon's advanced Anglophobia. Weybright's sense of grievance against Allen was well-founded, as indeed was Krishna Menon's, but against his inferences stands the evidence of most of the other men who were turned away from Allen's court through no fault of their own. A surprising conclusion that must be drawn from Allen's life history is that the majority of his unrelenting enemies (and he made many) had no experience of working with him and had suffered little at his hands. The rest, his one-time colleagues and the victims of his machinations, look back through disagreement and disaffection; like old

Desert Rats who forget the harshness of battle and the wounds in cheerful reminiscence of hearty nights in Cairo, they remember only the excitement of serving Penguin and the ebullience and charm of Allen Lane. Even Krishna Menon, who in the thirty years after he broke with Allen rose to be one of the world's leading statesmen and Foreign Minister of India, lists proudly in all the reference books 'First Editor of Pelicans'.

At about the time when Krishna Menon was discovering that in relationships with Allen Lane there could be no convenient dispassion, that the favourites of today were by tomorrow discarded and ignored, there entered into Penguin a personality who was to contribute enormously to the firm and who, more than most of her colleagues, was to prove capable of handling the erratic leader. In the first months of the Penguin adventure Allen had continued to use for all Penguin secretarial work his Bodley Head secretary, Joan Coles. Immediately thereafter, once he set up his Great Portland Street office and thus was freed from the prohibition on employing women which held in the Crypt, Allen had taken on as a Penguin secretary Joan Skipsie, the first woman hired by Penguin, who was within months lured away to work for the Editor of the Penguin Shakespeares. Early in 1937 Allen advertised for a replacement. There was no great rush of applicants. Allen called for interview a young woman then employed by the Chelsea Arts Club.

Eunice Frost arrived in Great Portland Street dressed as if for Ascot, on her head an enormous cartwheel hat. The chaos in the small office was discommoding; Allen, his jacket off, sat behind a desk which seemed to carry most of the firm's files and half of the total output of British publishing. He was talking on the telephone but he waved Eunice Frost to the one uncluttered chair. She listened, at first nervously and then with growing excitement as she realized that the man on the other end was called Seagrave. Through her mind went visions of herself, notebook in hand, in the pits at Brooklands and standing by the timing-device on Daytona Beach in Florida. Allen put down the telephone: 'Edmond Segrave of the *Bookseller*,' he explained, and though the information meant little, it did serve to erase from Eunice's mind the image of Sir Malcolm Seagrave.

Allen asked a few trivial questions, had her type a simple letter, brushed aside her offer of references, and then enquired if she could start work on the next Monday.

It is symptomatic both of the zest and of the glorious amateurishness that prevailed in the organization then and for many years thereafter that, with no previous relevant experience and with no training except by performing a multiplicity of functions which a more orthodox house would have regarded as beyond her years or competence, within twelve months Eunice Frost had become an essential and influential member of the team, devoted to Allen and dedicated to the Penguin cause. Already before the outbreak of war she was recognized within the trade, and more particularly by authors, as a superb editor. Still in September 1939 she was nominally Allen's secretary but her role was set; in her own words, she had become Penguins' 'principal literary midwife'.

Back in 1937, even after two years of almost continuous success, there were publishers who still looked with suspicion upon Penguin and others who watched hopefully for the fulfilment of their gloomy prophecies, but the trade generally had come to accept Lane's folly as an unescapable feature of the publishing scene. Most hardback firms were willing and even eager to offer paperback rights to Allen, recognizing that publication as Penguins or Pelicans gave an author a new and enlarged audience which heightened his reputation and increased the market for his next hardback. Lane, they conceded, was adding minimally to their profits but, more important, he was providing publicity for books in general and for their own authors in particular – all at no cost to the original publisher. The authors, too, impressed by such as Bernard Shaw, H. G. Wells and Aldous Huxley, were quick to recognize that publication by Penguin was not a condescending gesture but a privilege which conferred an accolade upon the writer.

These fundamental shifts in prejudice coupled with the liberalizing influence of Williams were reflected in the catholicity of the list. No longer largely beholden to the goodwill of Jonathan Cape, by the end of 1937 the Penguin–Pelican editorial board had selected and published works by several of the most distinguished authors writing in English, among them William Faulkner, Evelyn Waugh, G. K. Chesterton, Sinclair Lewis and Richard Aldington, and by many of the most popular, including Ian Hay,

Francis Brett Young, Michael Arlen, W. W. Jacobs, E. W. Hornung and Angela Thirkell.

Jealous observers might have suffered less from this flaunting success had they known that progress was as yet more obvious than real; all that Allen had achieved could still fall apart if Martins Bank withdrew its enlightened charity. Month after month Dick called at the Cocks Biddulph branch of the Bank, in his hand a completed version of that morning's *Times* crossword puzzle to serve as conversational preface to the awkward moment when he must ask for an extension of overdraft facilities so that Penguin could cover its immediate and growing expenses.

Early in 1937 the firm was threatened with another and different financial crisis – and was saved, not by Martins Bank but by a burglar. The auditor pointed out that the nominal capital had never been paid in. Allen and John both swore that they could not find £100; Dick's insurance company had just paid on a claim for items stolen by a thief who had broken into his room in Talbot Square. With this he met the brothers' legal obligations – and was never repaid.

Despite these problems the burgeoning of Penguin Books Ltd was undeniable. Allen, always most contented when pioneering and most restless when novelty became routine, began to show signs of boredom. Conferences with the architects and the builders preparatory to the move to Harmondsworth amused him for a while; when the building was completed and the logistic planning passed inevitably to others lower in the Penguin hierarchy, he began to cast around for other beginnings.

Like Uncle John before him and like every successful British publisher, he found tantalizing the knowledge that a huge section of the English-language market was virtually closed to him. He considered carefully establishing an American company. He would himself go out to New York to sound out publishers, to look for capital and to employ staff. Letters were written to all his old American contacts, tickets bought, and hotel rooms booked. Then Allen had second and more sensible thoughts. In his Bodley Head days he had become as expert as any of his British colleagues in the ways of transatlantic publishing but most of his knowledge was editorial, gathered in buying and selling rights; the little that he knew about American sales techniques persuaded him just in time that the American market was beyond his competence. Even to try it might so stretch Penguin's limited resources as to endanger the parent company. Dick was sent off to New York in Allen's place with a brief limited to reconnaissance, to improving relations with American publishers and to attempting to find some way round the United States' law which limited to 1500 copies the import of any foreign book. Allen turned instead to two quite different ventures, less obviously imperial than the conquest of the United States, but nevertheless innovations of consequence.

The first Penguin Special, *Germany Puts the Clock Back*, by the outspoken American foreign correspondent Edgar Mowrer, and the first number of *Penguin Parade*, edited by Denys Kilham Roberts, both appeared in November 1937. Both were in effect ventures into journalism.

Fourteen numbers of *Penguin Parade* were published between 1937 and 1948. For all that it was a consistently lively attempt to present original short stories, articles and poems to the general run of Penguin and Pelican readers, neither its first nor its second editor established it with an unmistakable and compelling identity. *Penguin Parade* was not a failure but it was certainly not one of Penguin's major triumphs. It would pass little noticed in the history of the firm and the biography of Allen Lane were it not that it was the first attempt to break Penguin out from the confines of book publishing into the periodical market. There followed the highly influential *Penguin New Writing*, *New Biology*, *Russian Review*, *Science News*, *Film Review* and *Music Magazine*, all occasionals; and from September 1943 to June 1946 Penguins produced monthly *Transatlantic*, a magazine devoted exclusively to American and Anglo-American affairs.

Book publishers have fallen often to the lure of periodical publishing and some have prospered from temptation. 'Maga' has kept their name alive long after the house of Blackwood has slipped into decent obscurity. Murray's, though still as alert as when they published Byron and Conan Doyle, persisted with *Cornhill* until it was swept out of existence by the intractable economics of the last decade. Heinemann produced *Windmill* and Chambers their *Journal*, but the motive that persuaded most of these firms to indulge in these expensive and uncertain activities was irrelevant to Penguins and to Allen. A book publisher puts on the disguise of a periodical publisher for two reasons above all others: because he hopes to entice prospective authors of books or because, by publishing extracts from work in progress already contracted for publication in book form, he thinks to arouse in the reading public eager expectation.

Allen's firm took its fiction at second hand; it had neither the intention nor the possibility of persuading even the authors of non-fiction to commit themselves to exclusive devotion, and therefore had no need and virtually no use for periodicals. The distribution of magazines, which are generally sold either by subscription or on a sale-or-return basis (a formula which for Penguin as a whole Allen detested and resisted), necessitates an organization dissimilar to that required for the marketing of books. This organization at first Allen could not afford and later refused to authorize. Yet for almost twenty years he persisted, gulled by the past, by a half-understood memory of *The Yellow Book*, and by some dim glimpse of a future in which he was the master of every mode of disseminating the printed word. With the exception of *New Writing* and the two scientific periodicals, he never came near to his ambitions.

Penguin Specials, on the other hand, were from the outset entirely appropriate to the Penguin formula. Probably no other publisher in Britain could have matched Allen's capacity for supervising their production; certainly there was none who would have so revelled in the complicated, bustling business that went into the making of a Special.

Launched originally upon a world that was living through the nightmare prelude to war, the Specials were in a sense an alternative to the politically-committed Pelicans that Krishna Menon had planned, satisfying Allen's undoubted desire to inform readers about the events that were shaping their lives all too drastically, but more than any missionary exercise he was invigorated by the sense of being under pressure that went with all stages in the preparation of Specials.

First, it was necessary to identify a subject that was of immediate concern to the public, and to avoid confusing the topical with the merely ephemeral. Next, a writer must be found whose authority was undeniable, who could write quickly without losing cogency or falling into cliché, and had to be cajoled into maintaining a severe schedule. All the functions common to book production and editing had to be performed at three or four times the customary pace of book publishing, even in those days when the machinery of publication ground just as surely but at much greater speed than today. Printers were held to time-tables that demanded superhuman efforts – one Special was in the bookshops only four weeks after the delivery of the typescript – and Penguin travellers were not infrequently writing up orders for a book before the author had typed its first line.

There were aberrations in the classification of Specials, as there were in the division between Penguins and Pelicans. (In those early days there was even an anomalous category of Pelican Specials.) There is no ready explanation for the appearance of Arnold Bennett's *Literary Taste* as a Special; some selections such as Hašek's *The Good Soldier Schweik*, published in October 1939, seem to have been thrust into the Special list because this could heighten a sense of immediacy and take advantage of current publicity. Others, such as Arnold Haskell's *Ballet*, were later transferred to the appropriate orthodox list, in this case Pelican.

Generally the selection of Specials was a superb example of editorial perspicacity and shrewd timing. A recital of some of the thirty-six titles produced between November 1937 and the outbreak of war brings back to anyone who lived through these two years all their miserable realities and could serve to a later generation as chaste headings for the prelude to battle: *Blackmail or War?*, *China Struggles for Unity*, *The Air Defence of Britain*, *Europe and the Czechs*, *Between Two Wars?*, *The New German Empire*, *Poland* (this published two months before Hitler's invasion), *Our Food Problem*, *The Attack from Within*.

The Specials were topical, authoritative and justifiably successful, but the choice of subjects and authors strengthened the case of those who suspected Allen's political stability. Soon London was listening to whispers that Lane was a cunning participant in a Soviet plot, Specials just one more demonstration of his willingness to brain-wash the innocent British public.

Undoubtedly, by any arithmetical analysis, the Specials did tilt leftwards what was already a left-of-centre bias, but this weighting could have been defended on perfectly rational grounds. In those years any series devoted to current affairs was bound to deal substantially with the threat from Fascism and with the means whereby Fascism could be destroyed; because so many who had early come to realize that Britain must be alerted to the sinister implications of what was going on in Europe were men of the Left, it was inevitable that Penguin must look to the Left for the authorship of Specials.

It was, however, an article of faith for Allen that he would never explain or excuse to the public his editorial policies. When at last, in the summer of 1938, there reached his ears a rumour that had been passed among his enemies with much delight for many months, his first reaction was bewilderment and his second, spluttering protests addressed only to his closest friends.

The *canard* that Penguins were designed as propaganda for the Soviet Union and Allen himself a paid-up member of the Communist Party was repeated frequently in the next thirty years (and is not yet a dead duck) but at its first appearance the malice was supported by some half-truths and some full-blown lies.

There was, for example, the tale that Allen was about to launch a current affairs journal, overtly Communist and edited by a prominent member of the Party. This was founded upon two unrelated possibilities that Allen had been canvassing for some months. His new enthusiasm for periodical publishing had set him to contemplate a Penguin magazine which would deal, briefly and on a regular basis, with the kind of topics handled at greater length, but occasionally, in Specials; it was said that he intended to appoint James Maxton as the magazine's editor. In truth, he was seeking from Maxton a book to go into the Special series and had not for one moment thought of Maxton as editor of his periodical; almost from the outset he had agreed (as he had written to Ethel Mannin) that 'it would be best to have someone with no obvious party affiliations'. But whether as editor or as author, the leader of the Independent Labour Party, like many another British Socialist, was as virulent as any member of the Cliveden Set in his opposition to Soviet Communism.

It added to Allen's fury that some of his closest friends seemed unable or unwilling to differentiate between Specials and the proposed periodical. Even Ethel Mannin, who saw herself in the role of a wise adviser to Penguin, whose advice he sometimes took, and who was his link with the Scottish MP, consistently misunderstood the scope of his intentions for Maxton. To Allen's comment that 'it would be good to have something from Maxton' she replied with an almost verbatim repetition of Allen's own disclaimer, 'better have an editor whose party affiliation is less obvious'. She went on to point out, in a manner that was shrewd but scarcely apposite, that Maxton's puritanism was so intense that it was inconceivable that he could work congenially with Allen. ('Jimmy doesn't drink.')

When, to Miss Mannin as to other close acquaintances, Allen voiced his resentment of the slander that he was a missionary for Communism he found her less sympathetic than he had hoped. Perhaps he should have known. As one who, only two years earlier, in *South to Samarkand* had proclaimed her 'final disillusionment with the USSR', she would be likely to respond to any hint of Communist infiltration with all the fervour of a recent convert. But he could not have expected that, to his obstinate assertion that 'I'm damned if I'll supply any evidence except the Penguin list against such fool accusations,' she replied with a severe, schoolmarmish lesson in the doctrine of guilt by association. It did not surprise her to hear that his 'name was linked with the CP' because so many of his Bodley Head cronies 'among them Krishna Menon and John Lehmann are Communists'. And she went on to scatter similar allegations with glorious abandon: 'Then again in the Penguins you have published a Communist writer's novel of the Spanish struggle – Ralph Bates' *Lean Men*. In the Pelican list you publish Harold Laski, another Communist . . .'. There followed a sly thrust: 'if a Communist edits your paper, whether you like it or not you'll be lined up with Gollancz . . .'.

This should have been enough to persuade Allen to look again at Penguin editorial policy; it was not enough for Miss Mannin. He must take some positive steps to redress the balance in his list. If he intended to rest his case on the record of Penguin publications he must add to the list some books that would make it obvious, even to the most unsophisticated, that he was not exclusively well disposed to the disciples of a faith that had its cathedral in Moscow. 'Having done Ralph Bates' extremely unfair book' about the Spanish Civil War he should now publish as counter-weight Ramon Sender's *Seven Red Sundays*, a book by a writer who, for all that he had been a brigade-commander in the army of the Republic, had been forced into exile by the Spanish Communists. As even more extreme corrective to the many Penguins, Pelicans and Specials which seemed to justify the suspicion that Allen was a fellow-traveller, Miss Mannin suggested that he acquire the reprint rights for I. A. R. Wylie's *To the Vanquished*:

> It's not a propaganda novel in any sense – it's just the story of how the Nazi movement got going in Germany ... probably the most impartial thing ever published because it shows both sides as human beings, equally sincere. ...

Gratuitously, and it could be irrelevantly, she offered to persuade W. B. Yeats to become a Penguin author.

Allen replied huffily that *Seven Red Sundays* had been published by Penguins that spring, only four months after *Lean Men*. He did not mention Miss Wylie or Yeats and made no move to secure either author for Penguin, but from this time on his friendship with Ethel Mannin was noticeably less warm. Three of her novels had appeared as Penguins in the first three years of the firm's existence. She had to wait for almost four years before Allen accepted another of her books – and that was the last. She herself seems to have recognized that she had offended; henceforth her interventions in Penguin policy were limited to reports such as that 'there are no Penguins on sale in Davos'.

Allen never again showed any inclination to publish a current affairs periodical.

The move to Harmondsworth in November 1937 coincided with the realization that the Penguin reprint list was now firmly established with publishers, booksellers and the public, and Pelicans safely launched on a similar course. It might well have diminished or even erased that sense of co-operative adventure which had united the staff from the beginning, which had been heightened by the intimate discomforts of the Crypt and by the knowledge that they were working together to overcome prejudice, outright opposition and the dangers of innovation. But the frenzied activity which went into the creation and dissemination of Specials removed all possibility that anyone involved, from Allen himself to the most junior packer, could slip into complacency or into the belief that working for Penguin could ever be conventional drudgery. Almost before his colleagues had time to notice the comparative luxury of their new surroundings and before Allen sensed the deprivation from the ending of this pleasurable association with architects and builders, the whole team was infected with the delicious delirium of Specials. For Allen Specials became, for the moment, an obsession. The fiction list, he argued, could take care of itself and Williams could take care of Pelicans. John, Dick, William and the others did not accept his theses as proven but all fell to the excitement of an experiment which was, in its way, even more innovative than the original conception of Penguins: high-class topical comment and information produced in book form and, most important to Allen, selling undisguisedly as books.

In the twenty-two months of uneasy peace left to the world after the publication of that first Special with its sinister title *Germany Puts the Clock Back*, there were published thirty-five Specials. In that same period only some twenty Pelicans were added and not more than a hundred conventional Penguin reprints.

The sales figures were no less sensational and to Allen conclusive proof of the rightness of his judgement in over-riding all cautious advice. By 1939 Penguins were selling on average 40,000 copies, the most popular selling out in three or four months, and Pelicans too were doing well, most of them reaching a similar figure in less than a year, but almost every political Special sold 100,000 in a matter of weeks and the most successful achieved a phenomenal quarter of a million sales in less than four weeks.

This rate of sale placed a new burden upon the staff, and only the logistical skill of John averted a breakdown in distribution early in 1939. But the rapidity of turnover cured for the first time the cash-flow problem which had plagued Penguin for three years; Dick's early morning tussles with the *Times* crossword puzzle on his way to the bank became less frequent; he and John were at last added to the payroll and, though Allen rejected any suggestion that he might raise the general level of salaries and wages, he did concede a system of annual bonuses.

Their working headquarters having been moved fifteen miles from Talbot Square, the three brothers began to discuss transferring also their domestic base. The decision was not easy to make: in some ways the move of the office made it more imperative than ever before to maintain a foothold in central London, as much for their professional as for their multifarious social activities. Dick's enthusiasm for the theatre, for good food and better drink was unabated. John liked to be readily accessible to his many friends and to business acquaintances visiting from overseas, and Allen was not ignorant of the fact that his greatest service to the firm was his alert ear and his ready capacity for perceiving the professional advantage that could be found in social occasions. In addition, a trait that had been apparent in Allen's character from his earliest days was by this time becoming almost an obsession: he could not abide loneliness. He feared that once removed from the metropolitan life he might remove himself also from the easy opportunities for companionship which went with life in London.

The dread of solitariness was compounded by his awareness that he was now middle aged and that, though he had added the advantages of prosperity and success to his undeniable charm, he was still a bachelor. He had always liked girls and, more important to him, most girls he met liked him. If his conquests had been often more vocal than physical, the number of women who let it be known that they had shared a bed with him was at least one-quarter as many as the number of those who, by public reputation supported by his mischievously ambiguous twinkle whenever their names were spoken, were thought to have given their all for Penguin. His search after female companionship was becoming frantic. As in so many things, he complicated the issue because he was constitutionally incapable of settling upon one candidate in preference to all others and perversely enthralled by the delights of letting each and everyone suffer from the knowledge that there were others. (His sister Nora, fresh from a Quaker school and left to man the phone at Talbot Square, was given instructions to find out which of four girls called Phyllis was calling: Phyllis from the North, Phyllis from the South, Phyllis from the West, or Phyllis from the East?)

Against all the arguments for staying in Talbot Square the two most cogent reasons for moving were the objection to travelling to work which all three shared and, particularly strong in Allen and Dick, their romantic ideal of rural life. All three Lanes, though children of a city, were romantically certain that moving to the country would restore the delights of boyhood. They seldom paused to consider that as all three had also developed an enthusiasm for yachting – in Dick and John, a passion – the amount of time that they could give to enjoying a country home must be severely limited.

One new and heretical consideration did enter into the developing debate: should they move from Talbot Square but to separate establishments? Part of the reasoning behind this sensational speculation was not voiced at the time by Allen, by Dick or by John; even many years later when it came to the surface in conversation with friends, it was spoken only to be dismissed as insubstantial or the invention of enemies. Nevertheless, and if only in afterthought, most of those who knew them well at that time are convinced that the Three Musketeers act was beginning to wear thin; notably between Allen and John, tension was growing that must have presaged an explosion had not Hitler intervened. The two brothers were remarkably alike, even in appearance, but Allen lacked John's stamina, his zeal for detail and his range of overseas contacts. On the other hand John was not, like Allen, well known to the book world aristocracy of London and New York; his experience was limited; and he was short on those two indefinable qualities, charm and flair, which Allen possessed in inordinate measure. John was also the younger brother and in a close-knit family such as the Lanes the habit of looking to the eldest as the leader persisted even into early middle age, so John was reluctant to assail Allen's supremacy, even if he thought that he had anything to gain by asserting himself or any chance of winning an open struggle. In reality John was a superb lieutenant, far better equipped than Allen to handle the minutiae of Penguin operations, but Allen was an inspired general, a daring strategist whose mind was always filled with preparations for future campaigns. The two, with Dick as a versatile *aide-de-camp*, made a team that had at that time few equals in British publishing. Even so John was inclined to resent his subordinate role. He was, unlike Allen, in close contact with the rest of the staff, and in those pioneering days it was still possible to assert that the tactician was more useful than the strategist. His resentment persuaded many to share his belief that his was the achievement and Allen's only the glory. So the myth grew up which persisted for several years among those who had come early into Penguin and was passed on by them to the next generation, the myth that John's was the brain behind Penguin.

Allen was not unaware of John's resentment and in his turn resented it, but he was alive to John's ability and was at all events not yet ready to treat his family in a ruthless manner. The temptation to reduce the tension of continuous association by setting up separate households was short-lived and overridden by his distaste for solitude and by his shrewd determination to get the most out of all his staff, even his brothers, by extending the office day into the sociable night whenever it was convenient to him.

The search began for a house within easy reach of Harmondsworth which could serve as a home for all three brothers.

Silverbeck was a solid William IV house standing in nine acres of garden and meadow in the hamlet of Stanwell Moor, two miles from the office and a surprisingly rural oasis in the desert of ribbon development and light industrial estates which, in the first forty years of the century, had been allowed to sprawl all over Middlesex. In the house there were seven bedrooms, a sitting-room, dining-room, library and billiard-room, a large farm-house kitchen, ample cellars and two bathrooms. The grounds were littered with potting-sheds, mushroom beds, an aviary and workshops, and the estate included half a mile of river frontage on the River Colne. Obsessed as always by building projects, the Lanes planned extensive alterations to both house and grounds – including an extra bathroom.

In ordinary circumstances the unassailable position of Penguin coupled with the acquisition of a country gentleman's residence and with the immediate delight of redesigning Silverbeck would have quelled even the habitual restlessness of the Lanes, but in 1938 there were no ordinary circumstances. The lunatic rampaging of Franco, Mussolini and Hitler pressed omens upon men and women in Britain which could not be erased by Neville Chamberlain's hopeful promises. Like thousands of their contemporaries John and Dick decided that, as sooner or later they were bound to be called to active service, they might just as well make it sooner than later. Both joined the Naval Reserve. Several other members of the staff went with them to the Navy or into the Territorial Army. (Edward Young left for full-time service some months before the outbreak of war and was eventually the first Volunteer Reserve officer to command a submarine.)

Allen decided to take a long holiday, but first sent John off to the States to take up and further Dick's half-hearted attempt to establish a Penguin subsidiary.

Allen's covetous intentions upon the American market had been sharpened by the arrival upon the New York scene in 1937 of the first full-blooded emulator of Penguin, Robert de Graff's Pocket Books, but the renewed Penguin invasion of the United States was occasioned as much by the shadows looming over Europe as by publishing practicalities. Peering into the future, Allen could but accept the possibility that Britain at war might be no place for him or for Penguin. He needed an alternative base.

John's mission was moderately successful. Penguin Books Incorporated was established with as yet no major responsibilities beyond marketing home-produced Penguins and acting as an outpost of Harmondsworth convenient for forays into the literary world of the United States.

At the time Allen did not know that all the legal documents relating to the new subsidiary had been signed by John baldly with his own signature, just 'John Lane' instead of 'John Lane for Penguin Books Ltd'. It was an error, if error it was, that would cause much difficulty in the not-too-distant future.

There was sound logic behind the organization of an American outlet. By contrast Allen's decision to absent himself from England for all of six months seems in retrospect well-nigh lunatic. True, Penguins, Pelicans and Specials were selling well and establishment in the carefully planned order of Harmondsworth when compared to the inconvenience and chaos of the Crypt and Great Portland Street gave all involved, including Allen, the feeling that the total operation had settled into a comfortable routine. Allen knew that several of the essential cogs in his efficient machine might be removed by the whim of the Armed Services of the Crown, and several new publishing projects, still very much in the planning stage, demanded his attention, as did the substantial alterations to Silverbeck. Despite these seemingly inescapable reasons for staying close to his command-post, he decided to disappear into Asia. Convinced of the coming of

Armageddon, certain of doom and consequently determined to use the money at last available to finance one superlatively self-indulgent jaunt, he travelled the world without any obligation to excuse his pleasure by pretending that it was business.

From time to time in the summer of 1938 he announced his intentions to his family and friends but with each telling the proposed itinerary changed. Those who knew best came to believe that this highly publicized vacation was no more than a daydream, or a threat held over his colleagues to persuade them that he was indispensable. Then, through Sir Sydney Barton, the father of one of his dancing partners, he met the Governor of Aden and, having set before him hints that could be resisted only by outright rudeness, received the invitation that he coveted: to attend as the Governor's guest the celebrations of the centenary of the British occupation of the colony.

This achieved, Allen began to worry about travelling alone. He could hardly take Dick or John with him, for that would leave Penguin with only one director. Protocol made impossible the company of any female friend; even if His Excellency was prepared to condone what might seem to be an illicit relationship, Allen himself was not ready to make any move that could be interpreted as committing him to one from the safety of many.

Indecision was only momentary: Nora would make an admirable travelling companion; she shared many of his enthusiasms and yet was still sufficiently the dutiful and adoring young sister that she would not question his more extravagant whims. The Governor courteously added Nora to his invitation and, almost before she had time to find Aden on the map, they were on their way.

They were expected back at the end of January 1939, but Allen was enjoying his taste of life among the proconsuls. To Nora he announced that, as Aden was half-way to India, they might just as well add the sub-continent to their travels. 'It may be our last chance,' he told her, 'in another year or two I doubt that we will be able to get to these places.' A cable, the first of many, was sent to Dick demanding that a draft to Allen's credit be wired to a bank in India, and the Governor of Aden obligingly commended his guests to his brother satrap in Bombay.

In this fashion Allen and Nora made their progress, from

Bombay up to Delhi, on to Lahore, Peshawar and the Khyber, back to Darjeeling, down to Cochin and by ship to Ceylon, staying always with senior officials, with military commanders, with nawabs, rajahs and maharajahs. After twenty years in publishing Allen could have found his way without difficulty into India's literary and journalistic circles; though his relations with Krishna Menon were by now decidedly frigid, he had in the days of their collaboration met many of the leading Indian expatriates and could have acquired introductions to any of India's notable politicians but he was bent upon emptying his conscience of all thought for Penguin; he kept away from any contact that might remind him of his duty to seek authors, to secure sales or to contrive publicity.

Paradoxically this Indian journey aroused in Allen for the only time in his life an ambition to write a book himself. As preparation he sent home long, meticulously drafted letters recording his impressions of India – adding to each letter a strict injunction that it be kept for use in the proposed work.

The book was never written and the letters have long since disappeared, but those who read them all report that they were deftly constructed, witty, perspicacious and sensitive. All agree that, even if the notepaper was uniformly embellished with engraved insignia, their prevailing recollection of the tone of the letters is that Allen's first experience of India aroused a sense of shock at the hideous poverty, the disease and the degradation of the mass of the people, and a deep sympathy for Indians of all classes.

In Ceylon Allen was taken ill. The return home had to be postponed – and Dick was ordered to cable more money. Allen and Nora arrived back in England early in July 1939 bringing with them trunk-loads of lavish presents and handsome Indian carpets to replace the cheap rush mats which Dick and John had bought to cover the floors of Silverbeck.

Dick and John had been in residence for just over two months when Allen returned and the alterations and additions – including that essential extra bathroom – were already completed, though they were still engaged upon an enthralling battle with the antique ram which controlled the water level on the Colne. They had also hired a cook, two maids, a gardener and an odd-job boy to take the place of Marine Knight. From the moment of their first occupation they pretended to themselves and to their friends that the spirit of Talbot Square had moved with them to rural Middlesex; on the very first night after they moved in they gave a large dinner-party. Once back Allen collaborated in the charade so that throughout the summer of 1939 Silverbeck was the setting for innumerable cocktail-parties, receptions, dinners and week-end gatherings of friends. Charade it undoubtedly was. Not only was it no longer possible to indulge in impulsive hospitality when some twenty miles from London and accessible only by car or by a branch railway line which decanted passengers at a tiny halt impressively named 'Poyle for Stanwell Moor', but also the growth of their business had forced all three into more artful, deliberate and selective sociability. Above all, like most thinking men in those months, the Lanes could no longer avoid the awesome realization: Europe was on the brink of war; all gaieties were forced, and both personal and professional life must be accommodated to an uncertain future.

Although he discussed the subject with all who would listen, and with many who preferred to live for the day without burdening their minds about what was to come, not even Allen could foresee the implications of world war for his firm. His instinct was to build upon success, to enlarge upon growth, and to let the years ahead take care of themselves.

Already before he had left for India he had sanctioned preliminary plans for two new series, the Penguin Guides and King Penguins; most of the early work on these series was completed by Dick and John whilst Allen was away, but conferences continued at Harmondsworth and at Silverbeck throughout that last summer of peace.

The Guides were no great novelty. In all respects but their price they followed rather lamely the model of the Blue Guides with which they shared an editor, L. Russell Muirhead. King Penguins, on the other hand, were for Britain and for Penguin an innovation in concept and as revolutionary as anything that Allen had initiated.

Earlier, in May 1938, Penguin had made one substantial attempt to enter the field of illustrated books. The Illustrated Classics went some way to satisfying Allen's wish to emulate a mode of book presentation which The Bodley Head in its heyday had indulged with great effect. They gave an opportunity to test the out-of-copyright market which had been so thoroughly exploited by World's Classics and Everyman but the choice of title was almost too obvious; their newly created British audience expected from Penguin something more original than Jane Austen, Swift, Sterne and Defoe. The American booksellers, who seem to have been a particular target for this series, were not yet convinced of the saleability of the quaint little paperbacks from Britain; they too would have needed something more unconventional than books by Melville and Poe or Thoreau's inescapable *Walden* to entice them away from the well-established reprints of the classics. But the venture was damned as much by its technical inadequacies as by any failure in editorial judgement or by indifferent perception of the market potential. The charming wood engravings commissioned for the series, some by artists of high repute such as Gwen Raverat and Robert Gibbings, had about them all an outmoded refinement, as if they had been prepared by tired disciples of the old John Lane school of book illustrators. Their extravagant elegance did not match either the bustling, youthful vigour of Penguin or the starkness of a world hurtling towards war. The weaknesses of illustration were exacerbated by the indifferent paper and by the Penguin format, seemingly too cramped to carry illustration. The series was discontinued after the first ten.

This had been Penguin's one disaster. It might have dented Allen's growing reputation for infallibility had he not buried the series in the month of its birth.

Despite this experience, and despite his dedication to the tenet that failure reinforced is failure compounded, Allen remained devoted to the idea that somehow he must enlarge the Penguin range to include illustrated books. Thus he came eventually to King Penguins.

Kings were in concept, scope and appearance unashamedly modelled upon the successful monograph series produced in Germany by Insel Verlag. For Britain they were something entirely novel, in their way no less revolutionary than Pelicans or Specials and far more notably innovative than the early 'orange wrapper' Penguins. Within the totality of Penguin production Kings represented a break with tradition, or perhaps an explicit assertion of a purpose that in all previous series had been subordinated to the principal intention of informing or entertaining. King Penguins were essentially books for the collector, designed to please the eye and satisfy the gloating instinct which exists in most bibliomaniacs. Only the bargain price, originally one shilling, was entirely consistent with Penguin philosophy.

Hitherto one of the most remarkable aspects of the Penguin story had been the rapidity with which each new scheme had been developed from the hint of an idea to full-blown achievement. Allen had begun to talk seriously about his reprint series only eighteen months before the first Penguin titles appeared in the book-shops; Pelicans were just under a year in gestation, Specials even less; for all that their production time was necessarily extended to allow for the collaboration of artists, even the aborted Illustrated Classics appeared just fourteen months after they were first discussed. King Penguins – though not yet under that title – were mooted in the spring of 1937 but none was published until November 1939 – and even then only two books appeared.

What might seem to be, after the event, untypical dilatoriness was in reality caused by the necessity to investigate and to experiment in techniques with which none in Penguin was familiar and to find among British printers one who was prepared to join them in investigation and experiment. The editorial and marketing problems involved with the publication of Penguins, Pelicans and Specials had been considerable but, except that the runs were longer than usual, the printing was entirely conventional. Kings made demands upon the printer that seemed superhuman. The printer must somehow use mass-production to provide for the public a fair reconstruction of some of the most expensive and esoteric colour printing of the past.

As editor for King Penguins, Allen chose Elizabeth Senior, a young scholar on the staff of the British Museum, and for their production he went to Adprint. (Though they did not continue for long their association with King Penguins, Adprint soon made their mark as producers of another and not dissimilar illustrated series, *Britain in Pictures*, published by Collins and edited by the music critic and Georgian poet, W. J. Turner.)

By the time that Allen took ship for the Middle East he had proved to his own satisfaction that the technical problems could be overcome. Because most of his closer collaborators were by now so indoctrinated with the conviction that Allen's intuitions were justified by results, not one of them noticed that his faith was supported largely by bold assertion and far less by experiment or demonstrable evidence. Consequently, he had left them with a plethora of minor and major technical problems still to be solved. Their gullibility, however, was not so intense that they could be persuaded that the ability to mass-produce monographs illustrated in colour was sufficient to ensure the success of the series. One after another the privileged sceptics put to Allen their more substantial doubts about the future of Kings. To each in turn Allen replied with bland assurance that it could be done and would be done.

The doubts in the minds of his advisers were in essence not so very different from the objections that had been raised by so many critics when first the idea of Penguins had been mooted; but, they argued, these doubts were strengthened by the esoteric nature of Kings. The peculiarities of the series meant that the success of Penguins, Pelicans and Specials could not be used to prove that they would be wrong about Kings.

Like all manufacturers, publishers are forever seeking a formula relating price to volumes of sales and are forever discovering only a circular argument: set the price too high, and sales will not justify a price low enough to achieve a volume of sales sufficient to justify the price ... and so on. When he had launched Penguins Allen had started from the premise that in this elusive formula the x for price must be sixpence; he had then calculated that the y representing break-even sales would be 17,500. With these figures before him he had dared the assumption that at a price of sixpence he could contrive sales of 17,500 and more. His boldness had been rewarded – and more comfortably than even he had hoped. Now for King Penguins he plucked another x out of the air, made it one shilling and calculated the y at 20,000. But, said Dick, John, Bill Williams and the rest, though the accuracy of the calculation is undeniable (and would remain undeniable if both x and y were altered, provided always that they remained in a constant relationship), the calculation was in truth valueless because a break-even point represents not a promise but an aspiration; they could see no reason for believing that Kings would sell 20,000 copies of each title and many reasons why they would not.

Above all other objections and following received doctrines, they raised the possibility of bookseller resistance. Kings would be unnoticeable and unidentifiable if displayed spine-forward on a bookseller's shelves. Even if they were noticed by the public the attempt to identify one title from another by pulling it out of the shelf must put the insubstantial, paper-bound book at constant risk of damage, something no bookseller could tolerate. Allen countered with the obvious suggestion that Kings be displayed face forward; to this the others replied with the comment, no less obvious but far more devastating, that no bookseller would give up so much space for the meagre returns on a one-shilling book. Allen shifted his ground: the same objections had been raised against Penguins, Pelicans and Specials. But, came the answer, the books in these other series were mammoths when compared to Kings. Even spine forward and even shelved in small numbers, the books in earlier series were colourful and, more important, most were by authors or on topics known to be of interest to the public. Why would British buyers be ready to buy pretty little books, more picture than text and with text by unknown writers? Allen shrugged, reiterated that he was sure that Kings would succeed, and went off to Aden.

Almost every decision was still to be made by those who stayed behind in the overcast winter of 1938 and the unhopeful spring of 1939. There remained with them, however, the recollection of Allen's confidence and of his two commands. The King Penguin experiment must be limited in the first instance to two or three books. The titles chosen must be of a kind that, given the novelty of the series, would nevertheless come as close as was possible to being familiar to the prospective audience.

The tenor of both these instructions might seem to indicate that Allen's confidence in the success of King Penguin was not as firm as he pretended. Undoubtedly the first breached a major article of faith which Allen held in common with most publishers: a new series cannot succeed unless it be introduced in strength, and, conversely, evidence drawn from two or three titles is not significant for the future of similar titles, even if the initial publications are closely related in subject-matter and format. The second instruction, however, was consistent with principles which Allen had held throughout his previous publishing career and to which he was to remain faithful. It was again little more than a statement of the obvious, but the obvious passes frequently unnoticed by those who seek a reputation as innovators. Boldness, he insisted, is not synonymous with bravado and it is folly to lengthen the odds in the preliminary heats by burdening oneself with weights that need not be carried until your reputation is secured by victory in the final – if then.

In meetings at the British Museum, at Harmondsworth, at the printers and at Silverbeck, the plans for King Penguins were laboriously and sometimes vehemently debated by Dick, John, Eunice Frost and Elizabeth Senior, with an occasional pungent interpolation from Bill Williams. Allen's letters contributed nothing to the discussion and very little to the control of more general policies. Passing his days in careful and sympathetic observation of the social, political and economic predicaments of Asian life and his evenings and nights in the lavish and flattering conditions created for him by surrogates of the Imperial power, he seldom noticed the ambivalence in his experience of the East. Everything he saw in Asia was enthralling, everything he did uniformly exciting, so that he had no mental energy left to contemplate the inevitability of war, and neither time nor patience to give to the insignificant predicaments which he had left for others to resolve at Harmondsworth or to his responsibility for the development of his own tiny empire. For several months he seemed to have erased publishing from his mind, and his only interventions in the business came in those not-infrequent cables demanding that drafts on Penguin for three, four or five hundred pounds be wired to some bank in an Indian city.

Stumbling their way through the problems bequeathed by Allen, those he had left in charge came, with some suddenness, to realization that hitherto not one of them had quizzed him about the target for the Kings or the effect that the production of the series on what would now be called the 'image' of Penguin. By concentrating upon such practical issues as colour printing and marketing, he had diverted their attention from the more metaphysical objection to Kings: that a series of this kind seemed destined for an audience quite different from that which, in only three years, had developed a fervent loyalty to Penguin. The staple reprint series, the Pelicans and Specials, varied widely in subject matter, but all had in common an attraction for a wide range of readers who looked for entertainment or information presented in a manner that would never offend their intelligence. Penguins, Pelicans and Specials were invariably sold at bargain prices but the purchasers were never allowed to feel that they were being patronized by author or publisher. Now, with King Penguin, Allen was planning to invade territory that had always been the stronghold of the privileged and, even among the privileged, of a recherché minority that doted on books as visual objects. There was no evidence that readers hitherto resistant could be infected with the disease of bibliophilia (a circumstance that had been discussed with Allen, and one that he had shrugged off); also, more insidious and yet more difficult to ignore, the attempt might destroy the firm's reputation for understanding the needs of readers, might cast doubt on the authority of the other successful series, and might suggest that Penguins were acting in a condescending manner.

With these thoughts in mind, and also Allen's instruction to be bold but not foolhardy, the unofficial editorial committee looked around for pioneer Kings that would bridge the gap between collectors and readers, for titles that would be immediately recognizable even to that majority of Penguin devotees which had never before thought of buying a book because it was exquisite. Unanimously they decided for Redouté's *Roses*.

Pierre-Joseph Redouté's *Roses* had been published originally between 1817 and 1824. From the first it had been a collector's item, and with time complete sets changed hands at prices that could be paid only by national libraries and covetous millionaires, but reproductions of individual plates became if not exactly commonplace then certainly not rarities; in the 1920s and 1930s, a Redouté rose blossomed on the walls in many a bedroom in many a hotel whose proprietor had decided to show that his taste was discreet and immaculate.

The restraint of Redouté's presentation, the almost puritanical manner in which he concentrated the eye upon the refined drawing and exquisite colouring of the rose without permitting the luxury of incidental embellishment or irrelevant diversion, made his work an ideal model for his successors at Penguin and at Adprint. Reducing the page size to fit the format planned for King Penguins was not a formidable task, as it might have been with so many of the best-known picture-books of the past.

In addition, the editors felt that they could place some reliance on the British addiction for horticulture and particularly for roses.

Similar considerations led to the choice of the companion volume, *British Birds on Lake, River and Stream*, based upon the 1873 edition of John Gould's *Birds of Britain*.

Allen had been back home for six months, and Britain at war with Germany for two, before these two Kings appeared in the bookshops. (Almost the first public demonstration of Penguin's war-time activity was, then, an overt imitation of a German series; the very first was a generally enthusiastic biography of a man who, in the league table of Britain's favourite enemies, came close behind Hitler and Mussolini, Sean o'Faolain's life of De Valera.) When set alongside subsequent additions to the series *A Book of Roses* and *British Birds* are humble productions. The standard of the colour printing is low and the binding shabby. Under the technical supervision of R. B. Fishenden, unquestionably the leading British authority on colour printing, the quality of production was advanced consistently despite the restrictions enforced by the austerity regulations of war-time and of the immediate post-war period.

In 1941, just after she had added to King Penguins her own selection of portraits of Christ, Elizabeth Senior was killed in an air-raid; her place as series editor was taken by Nikolaus Pevsner. This addition to the outer ranks of Penguin advisers of a scholar of substance continued the policy which had started with the appointment of G. B. Harrison to edit the Shakespeares, a policy which Allen would perpetuate in the years to come; it goes some way towards explaining the growth and consistency of Penguin's reputation as provider of authoritative works and also the willingness – even the eagerness – of reputable scholars to write for the various specialist series. Already before the end of the war, in a way that had never been true for any other popular imprint, the public was prepared to believe that a book commissioned by Penguin was likely to be just as scholarly as any book from a university press – and almost certainly more readable. Even more surprising: in pious academic circles where publication is an imperative for promotion and where hitherto 'popularization' had generally been regarded as disreputable, the addition to a colleague's *curriculum vitae* of a book published by Penguin came to be respected and even to be envied.

In the pursuit of illustrious scholarship Penguin held an advantage over almost all other publishers. It is a principle of conventional publishing that the strength of a house is based largely on those authors who stay with the list for book after book; the one-book author must be regarded as an exception. Penguin were essentially publishers concerned to produce the right book by the appropriate author, whether or not he would ever again appear in their list. This distinction allowed the firm to free itself of many of the inhibitions against 'poaching' that affected rivals; indeed, it allowed Penguin editors the comfortable illusion that they had no rivals and intended no competition. As the firm's academic reputation increased so also did the Penguin thesis of its uniqueness become increasingly persuasive upon scholars who saw no disloyalty to their regular publishers in a single or occasional excursion into the Penguin list.

The prevalence in the list of *the* one book on a particular subject by an eminent authority and the fact that the editor of the series into which that book had been commissioned was himself so often the most eminent, and therefore the most obvious, authority on the range of subjects in the series gave cause for the only serious and adverse criticism of Penguin academic policies. Remarkably adventurous in the choice of topics and consistently demonstrating that readers were both eager to try and competent to accept standards of erudition even in the most esoteric disciplines, nevertheless Penguin did less to encourage new work by promising but unknown scholars. When, in response to a whim, Allen entrusted a major series to an editor who had no standing in the academic world – because that editor knew no better and had no brief except to edit a history series – the editor looked instinctively among the still-to-be recognized scholars of his own generation. The consequence for Penguin was without exception advantageous and for some of the authors well-nigh miraculous. Several historians made their reputation by contributing books to the Penguin Histories; in almost every case the promise apparent when first they were published by Penguin has been fulfilled. But more often than not and it could be too often, books in Penguin specialist series – and even many commissioned Pelicans – though not in fact reprints, were in spirit distillations of the author's earlier, well-established work.

For this inherent conservatism and implicit timidity the fault, if fault there be, must be marked against Allen and W. E. Williams, neither of them inclined or competent to look for Field-Marshal's batons hidden in the knapsacks of the Other Ranks of scholarship. But Nikolaus Pevsner, within the limits that were set for him, performed a magnificent service for Penguin and, by way of Penguin, has done more than any of his contemporaries to enlarge the knowledge of a world-wide public in the plastic arts and architecture; more than any other scholar, he has persistently encouraged in readers an understanding of their visual heritage.

Pevsner is one example of the benefits gifted to Britain by the malevolence of Hitler. He is also a distinguished member of that rare and remarkable group of men who learnt English as a second language but write and speak it better than most Englishmen. Born in Germany and educated at four German universities, he had begun his professional career at the Dresden Gallery; before he was driven from Germany by Nazi persecution he had been lecturer in the history of art and architecture at the University of Göttingen. Already when he took Elizabeth Senior's place the catalogue of his works, in German and in English, was almost as long as the list of his public and academic honours has since become. In the year after he settled into the King Penguin editorial chair he contributed to Pelican *An Outline of European Architecture*; a book that has seldom been out of print from that day to this, it is in almost every sense an archetype of the best in Penguin non-fiction, comprehensive but comprehensible, scholarly but not pedantic. Generally his authority and energy as editor, first of King Penguins and subsequently of *The Buildings of England* and of the monumental *Pelican History of Art*, added both quality and range to the Penguin list such as no other outside editor (not even E. V. Rieu) has engineered. These ventures more than all else sustained the uniqueness of Penguin when competitors trailed after Allen into the paperback fiction market and when some, made bold by his success, attempted to emulate Pelicans.

In the context of the life and career of Allen Lane, the influence of Pevsner is almost as significant as the influence of those closer associates, his brothers, W. E. Williams, Eunice Frost and, later Kaye Webb. Pevsner's unassailable eminence and his somewhat austere personality aroused in Allen a sentiment that he seldom felt when dealing with collaborators, colleagues or employees: a sense of awe. In consequence Pevsner was not often subjected to those sudden withdrawals of favour which almost all others experienced and which not a few suffered without justification and so dramatically that Allen's whim ruined their careers. But Allen's persistent confidence in Pevsner was not entirely the product of the least lovable of his traits; in melodramatic terms the unease of the bully in the presence of one too big to be bullied; there were, too, in Allen's make-up some admirable instincts which hitherto he had not often been able to release, some worthy ambitions which he had seldom been able to fulfil. Pevsner was not only a catalyst, he was also an agent – a highly professional and almost always a gratifyingly commercial agent – through whom Allen could satisfy his intrinsically laical aesthetic sensitivity.

From Uncle John, Allen had inherited the conviction that books must please the eye no less than they satisfy the mind; this conviction, despite the limitations of format and price, he had made part of the Penguin creed. His zest for the visual had launched the unsuccessful and unsatisfactory Illustrated Classics and the successful and satisfying King Penguins. Allen had also shown in the Talbot Square reconstruction and, above all, in his energetic interventions in the building of the Harmondsworth headquarters, as he was to show frequently in other similar exercises, that his understanding of architectural problems was shrewd and sometimes inspired. (In later years, against all documentary evidence and the recollection of his contemporaries, he claimed that his early debut in publishing had thwarted the one stirring ambition of his young life, to qualify as an architect.)

Since his young manhood Allen's uninstructed infatuation with the visual arts had found some additional outlets in collecting. With the years and a burgeoning bank-balance he played the part of connoisseur more often, more effectively and with the additional advantage that he could justify his self-indulgence as shrewd investment. Perversely he showed very little interest in collecting rare or beautiful books but, on advice that was generally sound, he gathered in a fine collection of fine paintings – and a few that were not as good as he thought. Also with guidance he built up an excellent cellar, but the more endearing side of his character was most often revealed when he ventured alone into the auction-rooms and acquired some extraordinary bargain. Then, as Allen's eyes sparkled with boyish pleasure whilst he rehearsed the story of how he had tricked all rivals, even the most sceptical members of his audience were apt to hold back their opinion that, for example, Ribbentrop's overstuffed armchairs from the German Embassy or the bridge furniture from the Royal yacht might be extraordinary but could hardly qualify as bargains.

Collecting and amateur building could not alone fulfil what was undoubtedly an artistic strain in a nature that was generally hampered by artistic inarticulacy; even his concern for the design quality of his books was little more than a palliative for frustrated aspiration. But once he found Pevsner Allen discovered his role. With Pevsner as both guide and principal executant Allen could involve himself wholeheartedly as a creative patron. Freed from the inhibitions hitherto imposed by his ineptitude, by his lack of knowledge and by his inability to use the grammar appropriate to the task, he was now able to provide for readers an aesthetic education.

At first, in his limited capacity as Editor of King Penguins, Pevsner worked slowly. In those early years he held the series close to its original preference for classic illustrations of natural history: gradually, with Allen's entire support, the editorial policy became more adventurous and the publications more obviously influenced by Pevsner's particular expertise and Allen's especial enthusiasm. Kings took on the formidable difficulties of producing, in necessarily attentuated format, a selection from Rowlandson and Pugin's *The Microcosm of London* and selections also from Ackermann's *Oxford* and *Cambridge*. Occasionally, too, Pevsner moved closer to the Pelican concept, publishing titles such as Leonard Woolley's *Ur: The First Phase*, and *A Book of Scripts* by that exquisite calligrapher and notable authority on calligraphy, Alfred Fairbank, books which, without departing from the King Penguin formula of attractive illustration in small space, nevertheless added an undeniably didactic intention.

Allen was inordinately proud of King Penguins and not a little smug. The immediate success of Kings he regarded as a personal triumph – over the sceptics in the firm. For the next fourteen years, until the series was finally extinguished by intractable economics, above all by the soaring cost of colour printing, he seldom missed an opportunity to celebrate comfortable sales records with a self-congratulatory smirk and a blatant 'I told you so' – even when he was addressing colleagues innocent of the doubts that had attended the birth of the series. Nevertheless, he never allowed his pride to out-run his caution. The King Penguin programme was severely limited; the series, he accepted, was as much an indulgence for those who produced it as it was a luxury for those who bought their products. It made money almost to the end, but not much. It added to the prestige of the firm, but not extravagantly, and prestige was a commodity which came to Penguin in comfortable quantity in those years. Twenty King Penguins appeared during the war and when the last King was published (as late as 1959) it was only the seventy-sixth in the series.

But by 1955 Pevsner was well-launched on Penguin programmes far more magnificent than pretty little illustrated books for sale to collectors.

CHAPTER FIVE

THE publication list for July 1939, the last of peace, was obstinately cheerful. Except for two Specials, W. J. Rose's *Poland* and *The Attack from Within* by Elwyn Jones, it was made up entirely of books for holiday reading: Ian Hay's already old-fashioned *Pip*, Stephen Leacock's never-to-be outmoded *Literary Lapses*, and several deliciously escapist novels by J. C. Masterman, Henry Wade and Margery Allingham. (Nine years would pass before Penguin could again follow this comfortable precedent but thereafter a summer list predominantly in green covers became an annual and useful convention.) By the summer of 1940 two young men but recently members of the Penguin staff had been killed in France and several were in the Services; all who remained at Harmondsworth, like all others in Britain, were facing problems far more sinister than bodies in locked rooms, murders in country vicarages or criminal intrigues in Oxford colleges.

The outbreak of war brought many relief: at last the uncertainty seemed over and the hideous tension passed which had bedevilled a whole generation. There was in the last months of 1939 and the first of 1940 none of that romantic exhilaration which had possessed the young men of Britain in 1914 but rather a sad acceptance of the inevitable. Now, at last, the canker of Fascism could be cut from the body international. When nothing happened, no battles, no air-raids, no assaults upon Germany and Italy, the unreality was unnerving and frustrating, as if the miserable hesitations of the previous two decades were being perpetuated even in the uniformed charade. After this disappointment, and in a sense that has seldom been recognized by historians, the débâcle in Flanders, the miracle at Dunkirk, the first severe air-raids and the heroic but expensive victory snatched by the Royal Air Force in the skies above Britain reiterated the sense of release that had first come to many on 3 September 1939 only to be thwarted by the phony war. The false start was over; Britain was back on its tracks. (At the end of 1941 many Americans experienced similar feelings when the attack on Pearl Harbor put an end to national hesitancy.)

Even so, few men or women in Britain looked upon the advent of war – phony or real – with any pleasure. Only armaments-manufacturers, black marketeers and a few half-crazed adventurers could face the prospect of Armageddon with enthusiasm. Allen was none of these, but the heightened excitement of a nation at war suited his personality. His chance had come; no less than twenty-five-pounder shells or anti-submarine devices Penguins could be useful to the war effort and to him potentially far more profitable than in peace-time. A public deprived of easy access to entertainment must turn to reading. Service men and women, removed from familiar surroundings, often lonely and frequently subjected to long periods of idleness, must find in books respite from both boredom and danger. Allen silenced the occasional nagging at his conscience which came from the awareness that he was still young enough to serve in some more overtly bellicose capacity, from the knowledge that he had held a commission and from seeing his brothers and many of his staff in uniform. Only much later, when the war was already won, did he so much as hint that he felt in any way deprived by being just too young for active service in the First War and too important to join in the more obviously military activities of the Second; and even then such unease as there was in his conscience he revealed only by sulky silences when in the company of old soldiers and forced to listen to their reminiscences.

Allen's belief that Penguin must prosper in times of war was justified by events, and even more gloriously than he had expected because all manner of circumstances conspired to its advantage.

From the beginning Penguin, in item-terms and as a matter of precept, had used paper more sparingly than conventional publishers with comparatively expensive formats. When paper rationing was introduced the quantity allowed to each publisher was calculated not on item-use – the amount of paper required to produce a single book – but on bulk use – the amount of paper required for the publisher's total output. The measure used was the individual publisher's production in the year immediately before the war, the year of the phenomenal runs of Specials. Penguin found themselves plush beyond the wildest dreams of any aspiring competitor. A number of hardback publishers, recognizing that paperbacks had come to stay (at least for the duration of the war), banded together to establish Guild Books in the hope of diverting sales from Penguin to their own firms, but found themselves hopelessly handicapped by a meagre paper ration.

A widespread sense of time suspended and the access of seriousness as a concomitant of war made comparatively earnest literature congenial to many who had hitherto left it for politicians, parsons and other professional pundits. Life in the Services and travel sharpened the curiosity and widened the educational possibilities for thousands of men and women. Allen, already well established as a provider of just the kind of books that were required for this audience, soon reaped the benefit of having his principal adviser, W. E. Williams, firmly ensconced high up in the directorate of Army Education.

Other incidental and even coincidental advantages came to Allen and to Penguin by way of war. Penguins were uniform in size and therefore ideal library books for military units at home and abroad. They were inexpensive to buy and inexpensive to post, a convenient addition to the innumerable parcels of cigarettes, socks and balaclava helmets sent out to soldiers, sailors and airmen by wives, girl friends, parents and charities. The service gas-mask haversack had a compartment into which a Penguin fitted as precisely as if it had been tailored for the purpose. When eventually the new battledress was devised, there above the knee was a pocket, intended ostensibly for an entrenching tool, which, like the haversack, conformed exactly to the shape of a Penguin.

The success of Penguin publishing had been assured before 1939. By 1945 Penguin Books had become a national and even an international institution.

Though much of this development came Allen's way accidentally, by benefit of the extraordinary circumstances of war, from the beginning he envisaged something of what would happen, planned for it and schemed to make the most of every accident that might present opportunities to his creation. Yet what he did not see – or feared to recognize – was the possibility, the near-certainty, that the cost of professional and commercial triumph must be high and paid in the currency of loneliness and tragedy. In September 1939 simple men everywhere allowed themselves no illusions; Allen, sharp, sophisticated, alert to the trends of taste and to economic auguries, nonetheless persuaded himself that, somehow despite the apocalypse, his own life would go on as before, cheerful, sociable and easy.

When war came John was in New York, organizing the distribution of Penguins in North America. Allen wanted him back and so bombarded him with cables as if in ignorance of the fact that the moment he arrived in England John was likely to be summoned to duty in the Navy. Nora was with John in America; she too was summoned with ever-increasing asperity both because Allen liked to have her around and because he expected her to replace some of the younger members of the Penguin staff who had already been called up. He seemed to be oblivious to the other demands upon Nora's presence in England more powerful than his; she was engaged to be married. When John and Nora stayed on in New York Allen refused to accept that it was because they could not get a ship. There they were, idling in comfort, whilst he worked day and night to gear Penguin for war. His cables took on tones at once self-pitying and abusive.

And when eventually the two did get back still Allen refused to accept that other agencies had jurisdiction over his collaborators more potent than his. The work in New York was not yet completed; Dick must go to the States to finish what John had started. Allen had his way, even with their Lordships of the Admiralty; Dick, by now accepted for a commission in the RNVR, was granted leave; before ever he put on a uniform he sailed for America to do the duty that Allen expected.

Nevertheless Allen's shrewdness was evident even in the minutest details of his preparation for war. On 1 September 1939 he announced to Dick that petrol rationing was inevitable. They must buy bicycles.

Undoubtedly Allen was working harder than ever before, but also he was playing harder than he had for several years. No less than contemporaries and immediate juniors who faced a grimmer and briefer future, he seemed to be obsessed by the need to live every day as if it was his last. Every week there were parties at Silverbeck, some carefully planned and some spontaneous but all hilarious, and few invitations were refused to socialize at the expense of others. On one occasion, still in September 1939, Allen and Dick, neither of them by inclination port-drinkers, were invited to lunch and a wine-tasting by the directors of Croft's. Disdaining the conventions of wine-sampling both Lanes drank hugely from each bottle that was presented for their inspection: Allen passed most of that night asleep in his car outside Silverbeck; Dick spent part of it in the house trying to telephone to himself; and the two maids left, frightened away by the peculiar behaviour.

Yet nothing in those hysterical months was quite so peculiar – nor quite so symptomatic of the phonyness of the phony war – as the decision taken by Allen and John to go to Switzerland for the winter sports. They crossed the Channel by ferry, went sight-seeing in the Maginot Line and were entertained at Allied Headquarters in Arras before going off to Chamonix.

Self-indulgence of this kind ended when Hitler's armies invaded Belgium and France; Dunkirk and the Battle of Britain could not be ignored. For Allen, coincidentally, the national predicament was made immediate and personal because Dick and John, after months passed in the uneasy status of civilians susceptible to naval orders, were at last commanded to join a ship. Nora had married and gone to live in Newcastle-upon-Tyne. For the first time since his apprentice days at The Bodley Head, Allen was left alone, with no member of his family to share his amusements or to serve as foil and ally in his professional life.

There was little time for self-pity. Not only his brothers but also many other staff had left, were planning to volunteer or knew that conscription must catch them soon. The duties of the more senior members of the organization had to be shared out among the survivors – for the most part between Allen himself and Eunice Frost – and it was by no means easy to replace even the humblest employee. At the very time when the capacity for initiative was being reduced, when the sum of experience was declining and when even the number of staff was falling, the amount and complexity of the work was increasing. The ambitious programme planned in 1939 was coming to maturity, the world-wide sales of Penguins in all kinds were booming and Allen knew that he must take advantage of war-time circumstances to ensure even larger sales. But war had brought with it a plethora of controls and it fell largely to Allen himself to deal with the new and often intrusive bureaucracy.

To most men this would have been exhausting and exasperating but to Allen, though it was time-consuming it was also wonderfully satisfying. Few things pleased him more than reading the rules so that the game would be played his way; he seldom enjoyed himself more than when he was using his charm and persuasion to gull some stony-faced official into believing that it was he who had first dreamed up a gracious concession which would allow to Penguin an advantage that had at first seemed unwarrantable.

Although in dealings with individuals Allen was often casual and sometimes ruthless, his commercial integrity was generally beyond question. He acted sometimes in ways that others found intolerably devious not because he was by nature dishonest but because his view of ethical problems was astigmatic, directed always to what he genuinely considered to be the greater good of the greatest number, which to him meant the greatest benefit to Penguin. He believed his divinely imposed responsibility was to avoid the more sinister consequences of man-made regulations, to use or to bend the rules to his own purpose, but he seldom attempted to break them. Thus, though he must have been frequently tempted to slip the most severe of all war-time inhibitions to the advance of Penguin, paper rationing, by going into the black market, there seems to have been only one occasion when he moved in that direction, and even that was half-hearted.

For all that the paper allocation to Penguin was, by the accounting of rivals, exorbitant, it never satisfied the firm's appetite or Allen's ambitions. Maynard, who had taken over as production manager when Young joined the Navy, instituted all manner of economies, abandoning the wrappers which had hitherto been a feature of Penguins, reducing margins, and using lighter weight paper; but still there was never enough paper for all the books that Penguin wished to print and were certain that they could sell. Littlewoods put to Allen a proposition which would set in motion their huge printing plant rendered idle by the closing down of football pools; because the plan included an offer of paper, Allen seized upon it avidly, only to find that the small supply of paper envisaged in the deal did not allow Penguin to fulfil their part of the agreement. Allen confessed the shortfall to Littlewoods; then, in a manner not uncommon in those times, someone slipped him a card with on it the address of a paper merchant.

Allen went immediately to see the black-marketeer but, as if he expected opposition from his senior colleagues, made no deal. And the opposition came, firmly from S. H. Olney, the Company Secretary, and most cogently from Maynard who pointed out that, if the authorities discovered Penguin in a breach of the rationing regulations, not only would the firm be liable to prosecution but it could no longer expect to be treated charitably by the Paper Controller.

The last chapter of this episode was dictated by Allen in a manner that was very much his own. He took himself off for a holiday and left it to Olney and Maynard to extricate Penguin from the contract with Littlewoods.

The generally good relations with those responsible for paper rationing became almost idyllic when other Governmental agencies, in Britain and elsewhere, began to appreciate the part that Penguin could play in the war effort. Propaganda at home and in Occupied Europe, information for the civilian population and, increasingly, entertainment and education for the Forces: all these desirable objectives could be secured with the aid of Penguin. No official in Paper Control was likely to look severely upon a publisher who was ready to produce, in comfortably recognizable format, books for France, Norway, Italy, and for the home market (eventually in the phenomenal quantity of three million copies – at that time the bestseller in the Penguin list) a handbook on aircraft recognition.

The Canadian Government had invited Penguin to produce run-on editions for the particular use of its Armed Services; it was not Allen but Dick who had conducted the negotiations with Ottawa. Whether by error, luck or sleight of hand, the deal brought benefits to the firm which the Lanes had no right to expect. The Canadian authorities had agreed to a barter scheme whereby Penguin would be paid for their services with shipments of paper. The original calculations had been made in North American tons, but the Penguin account was submitted, and met, in Imperial tons, giving Penguin an unmerited bonus of 10 per cent.

The British Government followed the Canadian example more expansively but without equivalent gullibility. Allen shared the popular belief that bureaucrats are leaden-footed and much of his early correspondence with the War Office about the establishment of the Forces Book Club is tinged with impatient asperity; yet an author in the later seventies who has become accustomed to a year or more passing between presentation of a manuscript and publication, can but marvel that in the war years, when all manner of official bodies had to be consulted, the gestation period of the Forces Book Club was just ten months. Allen put the idea to the War Office in November 1941; it was approved in July 1942; and by early October parcels were on their way to units overseas and at home.

One factor in the negotiating process goes far towards explaining the remarkable speed of progress from conception to birth: there was never any sign nor ever any possibility of friction between the front-line negotiators. The idea of a Forces Book Club was almost certainly Allen's and it found immediate sympathy from General Willans, the Director of Army Welfare; once the principle was agreed, Allen left the details to his chief adviser, W. E. Williams, who had no difficulty in making a sound working relationship with the General's nominee, the Director of the Army Bureau of Current Affairs, W. E. Williams. Allen put to the War Office the proposition that Penguin should look exclusively to their own list for titles for the Club and argued that all the difficulties of renegotiation with the original publishers could be avoided and the service to the Forces begun in conscionable time if the Penguin imprint was used even on Club books. Williams it was who persuaded his War Office masters that his Penguin master was talking sense, and that the benefits would compensate for any criticism that must be levelled at giving such palpable preference to one entrepreneur.

Williams's diplomatic ingenuity was tested most severely in April 1942 when the Publishers Association got wind of the proposals that were being discussed between Penguin and the

Services and piously announced that 'sooner or later the Services will have to do something to make the publication of such books possible if they really feel the troops must have light reading...'. The Association was inclined to join in a venture of this kind by way of its co-operative paperback series, Guild Books, though naturally it could not act until the whole matter had been thoroughly investigated and discussed by its Council.

In an obvious attempt to conquer by dividing, the Publishers Association addressed itself, not to the War Office, but to the Naval Branch of the Services Welfare Committee; yet two days after the letter had been signed by Walter Harrap, the President of the Association, a copy was on its way from Bill Williams to Allen. Next day Allen's characteristic if confidential comment was cheerfully passed on to General Willans: 'If I know anything of the PA,' he wrote, 'I think we may well be in for a protracted correspondence and at the end of it get nowhere.'

W. E. Williams, whose opinion of the Publishers Association was then, as later, no more enthusiastic, continued to do all in his power to prevent the intrusion of Guild Books into the Forces Book Club. His firm, if somewhat devious report, prepared for General Willans in August 1942, put an end to any hopes that others might be allowed to break the Penguin monopoly. The opening line of the document reads as follows: 'The Publishers Association (which controls the defunct sixpenny series called Guild Books) will not play with Penguins.' The total implication was undoubtedly accurate but the word 'defunct' was gratuitous and, almost certainly, deliberately misleading. No Guild books appeared for some months but the series was not defunct and did not disappear until some years after the end of the war.

However, even without Williams's eager assistance, the Publishers Association had done its ample best to ensure that it could never establish a comfortable working relationship with the Service authorities. Its officers and officials persistently treated the welfare departments to patronizing lectures on the economics of publishing: 'Quite obviously,' wrote the President, once more to the Secretary of the Naval Branch, 'you have never studied the manufacturing angle,' and again, in a letter which demonstrated also how little the generality of publishers had learnt from the success of Penguin, 'it is not possible ... to produce a book of 256 pages if all the producer gets for it is 5d'. (Even for the unsophisticated amateurs in the Services, Harrap's right to speak *ex cathedra* must have been made additionally dubious because he allowed his secretary to type '7500 coppies' even though the context, his calculations and the thrust of his letter – which like all others in the sequence was on Allen's desk, decorated with Williams's marginal notes, in a matter of days – proves that he knew that Penguins and the War Office were contemplating 75,000 copies of every title for the Forces Book Club.)

So, at the last, Penguin had the field to themselves. Ten titles a month were produced, each in runs of 75,000. For this purpose Paper Control allowed an extra allocation of sixty tons a month; for a book publisher by the standards of the time a huge addition to his ordinary ration but, as Allen was not slow to point out, no more than a national newspaper used in one day. In gross terms the deal was worth almost £200,000 a year but the Forces Book Club and similar schemes which followed – such as that instituted especially for British prisoners of war in German and Italian hands – were, both in the short term and in the long, far more important than could be measured by improvements in the bank balance, in cash flow or even in paper stocks.

In the short term, being guaranteed by the authorities substantial orders for each title, Penguin could write off most of the prime costs of publishing against the subsidized edition and run on, at comparatively low cost, copies for the public market. In the short term, too, the various official contracts negotiated by Allen and W. E. Williams improved the already generally favourable relationship with authors. The certainty of an additional £75 royalty was not to be despised, even by the most affluent writer, but for many an author even more persuasive than money in encouraging him to look kindly upon Penguin was the knowledge, flattering to his pride and to his patriotism, that his books were helping to win the war.

But the cumulative long-term effects of the various official schemes upon the future history of Penguin was beyond measure. For thousands of men and women, books and Penguins became virtually synonymous. Many, who before the war had seldom opened any book but a school book found for the first time, and against the pressures of boredom, loneliness and fear, a world of entertainment and enlightenment theirs to command by the intervention of Penguin. Many others, no less terrified, no less lonely, and even more bored than their less literate companions because Service life seemed to demand a break with their more literate peace-time past, discovered that Penguins allowed them to retain a hold on interests that must otherwise have been put aside.

It was without doubt one of the most successful public relations campaigns of the century: this conditioning of a whole generation to a sense of gratitude for Penguins, to a degree of autobiographical identification with Penguin achievement, and to the conviction that Penguin would neither cheat nor patronize. The reservoir of goodwill was to be of immense value after the war.

Allen foresaw nothing of these eventual benefits as he manoeuvred, argued and hustled the authorities. For the moment his prime concern was with the moment, with ensuring that Penguin would prosper, and with contributing something to national life that would make harsh circumstances just a little less harsh; but it says much for his perspicacity, for the wisdom of W. E. Williams, and not a little for the sense of the Service departments that all were agreed that the standards which Allen had set up for Penguins from the beginning were entirely appropriate for servicemen and women. There were, for example, in the choice made for the Forces Book Club several titles that suited precisely the categorization 'light reading' which Harrap condescendingly allowed as suitable and essential for the Services, but there was much more: the list included a shrewd sampling of Penguins, Pelicans and Specials covering literature, the arts, the sciences, politics and religion, and offering in its totality a salute in acknowledgement of the vast change that had come to Britain and to its armies since the First World War.

Service to the Service departments did not protect Allen or Penguin from inconvenience caused by the actions of those very ministries. Already in September 1939 officials from Whitehall had visited Harmondsworth with a polite but unchallengeable requisition order for the buildings. For more than a year nothing further was heard; then, just at the moment when the Forces Book Club negotiations were beginning, the Air Ministry gave Penguin six weeks' notice to quit Harmondsworth. Allen moved most of the offices to Silverbeck and the rest of the organization to a warehouse in West Drayton.

As if he still feared that life made easy might also become too real to be borne, Allen drove himself to take on extra responsibilities. He joined the Home Guard and, more out of character, he accepted innumerable invitations to speak in public.

Hitherto, despite occasional press publicity and despite the vast popularity of Penguins, the name of Allen Lane was little known outside the book world. Now the peculiar conditions of war-time opened to Allen the opportunity to make himself into a truly public figure, one of that new class of entertainers which had been developed by radio, the purveyors of seemingly expert and always 'instant' opinion delivered for enlightenment and amusement. He became a frequent participant in discussion programmes staged on aerodromes, at army bases, naval stations and factory canteens up and down the country and in accessible centres abroad. Superficially these personal appearances in performances that combined education with entertainment fitted well the image of Penguin that Allen was intending to project. Even yet the firm was not buying advertising space outside the trade papers; it was vital that he seize every possible occasion to communicate directly with the potential Penguin audience. It was tempting but also dangerous to accept the possibilities created by these intellectual charades; the public, observing the creator and master of Penguin playing the role of a slick and supercilious communicator, might come to believe that this was the level of Penguin editorial intentions. Allen was eventually saved from the temptation and Penguin held from the danger because he had the sense to realize that he was not well-qualified to compete with the intellectuals and self-styled intellectuals who entranced audiences with their verbal wizardry. He had travelled widely and observed closely, he held strong opinions, he had read more than he pretended, but he was expert in nothing except the techniques of publishing; though he could be pungent in private conversation and persuasive in public when speaking from a prepared brief, he was not easy on a platform and he lacked the two weapons that are essential to the armament of the successful panellist: the capacity for sharp repartee and the ability to strike off, at a moment's notice, an original, memorable and seemingly decisive phrase. (Examples in both kinds are not unusual in the Lane legend but many, and perhaps most, of Allen's best impromptus were most carefully rehearsed.)

By the end of 1941 the pattern of Allen's private life had changed; from then well into 1942 he used this change as reason for refusing to continue his brief career as a performer. In truth he was never inclined to return to it; though later in life he was interviewed frequently on radio and on television and though he would do his duty – if grudgingly – at any Penguin function, he seldom allowed himself to be cast as star on a public platform.

For the head of a young, bustling enterprise many activities were more important in those early war years than public speaking or serving in the Home Guard. As one after the other his brothers, his senior male employees and several of his outer ring of part-time advisers were called to the Services or committed to other war work, more and more responsibility fell upon Allen. All decisions must now be made by him alone, all plans instigated by him and the whole complex machinery of the rapidly growing organization supervised by him, with only Eunice Frost and S. H. Olney as senior aides. Bureaucratic regulation increased and enemy bombing caused frequent dislocations to transport arrangements.

Disadvantage and unusual perplexities combined to create an atmosphere in which Allen blossomed. He had devoted so much care to the planning of the Harmondsworth headquarters, and Penguin had occupied the premises for such a very short spell, that he would have been justified had he felt resentment for the high-handedness of the authorities but he showed no anger at the disruption of his private and professional routine; instead, immediately and enthusiastically, he set about improvisation. As ever he was more content when planning than he could find it in him to be when plans were realized; his attitude towards the bureaucrats who drove him from Harmondsworth was almost one of gratitude – their *fiat* had saved him once more from the boredom of an ordered existence. When the Government instituted a crippling profits tax Allen not only refused to be crippled but even looked with affection upon the inspectors responsible for enforcing the provisions of the legislation, honoured opponents who had challenged him in a game he loved. The very least he could do was to offer the finest champagne whenever they called; and the cost of the best champagne was only one minute entry in his big and ever-growing list of essential business expenses, no more than an infinitesimal contribution to this well-organized, comforting and comfortable counter to Excess Profits Tax.

Allen's family loyalty had persuaded him that he enjoyed working with his brothers. He had undoubtedly relished the companionable days in Talbot Square and the romantic team effort in the Crypt and Great Portland Street, but he was now close to forty, unwavering in his certainty about his own ability and, as never before, free to use his gifts not as the first among three equals but as the omnipotent head. Since first he had taken over The Bodley Head, Allen had demonstrated his publishing genius most often and most obviously by his readiness to build schemes from the dreams that others dreamt. Except in the one truly seismic decision, the founding of Penguin, he was not so much an innovator as an impresario to other men's innovations, and even then he had always had to reckon with the countervailing reasonableness of Dick and John. Once the triumvirate was dispersed and Allen freed from his brothers' prophylactic sanity, there were occasional signs that he might fall victim to the headiness of dictatorial powers, but either his zest for eccentric adventure was largely satisfied by collaborating and duelling with the authorities or else in the solitariness of responsibility he discovered a reservoir of sagacity. The incipient wildness was stifled; Allen contributed most to the strength of the empire he had founded in these years when he ruled without challenge.

There was, it is true, in the early war years a not untypical wilfulness behind many of his major decisions. Stolid commercial sense demanded that in uncertain times Penguin should concentrate upon certainty; even if for diplomatic and economic reasons Allen directed some energy to such esoteric schemes as the Forces Book Club, he must nevertheless concentrate on the proven series, the Penguin reprints, Pelicans and Specials, for which there seemed to be no limits to growth except those imposed by paper shortage and by the capacity of the reduced staff to handle increased business. Allen closed his ears to this dreary wisdom. When Specials were conceived, he had argued that the fiction list and Pelicans were healthily established, their growth virtually inevitable – and Penguin must never rest on its achievements. Again, even in war-time, he insisted that the Penguin ideal must and could be adapted to readers not yet captured by Penguins, Pelicans, Specials or Kings. So, although the future was impenetrable, there were added to the complement three forward-looking influential series: *Penguin New Writing*, Puffin Picture Books and Puffin Story Books.

Penguin New Writing was launched in November 1940, the first four Puffin Picture Books appeared that December, and a year later came the first four Puffin Story Books. All this, and also the first Penguins in French and the first Penguin Poet, was largely planned and brought into being in the most unpropitious eighteen months in modern British history, the grim period between Dunkirk and Pearl Harbor.

Such ebullience at such a time, like his readiness to add further to his work-load, must have led to disaster for Allen or for some or all of his schemes had he been intensely committed to their intellectual or artistic purposes; but it was part of Allen's strength that he felt no compulsion to pry beyond the limits of his vision. His concern was to widen the Penguin range. Once a project was instituted he left the addition of depth to width almost entirely to his editors.

He found a new willingness to delegate, the product as much of necessity as of wisdom – engendered more by impatience for the next innovation than by an abashed appraisal of his technical or literary limitations – which contributed much to the catholicity of the total Penguin list. This is the almost entire explanation of a paradox otherwise beyond resolution: Allen, apt to suspect his more able subordinates, who at some time came to blows with each one of his intimate colleagues, nevertheless managed to live, often for many years, in productive and disarming neutrality with outside editors, among them those who, by the measure of public fame and intellectual ability, were undeniably his superiors and even with some for whom his empathy was dubious.

The teaming of Allen Lane and John Lehmann was in many respects incongruous. Lehmann belonged to a world which, for all his experience at The Bodley Head and for all the confidence given by increasing Penguin success, Allen could never regard as his own: the world of old-established artistic families, of the Bloomsbury set, of left-wing elegance. In that world Lehmann was a leading figure, a poet to be considered with Auden, Day Lewis and MacNeice and an observer of contemporary Europe to be measured with Orwell or Isherwood. He was, it is true, also a publisher, but as a partner of Leonard and Virginia Woolf in the Hogarth Press Lehmann's experience of publishing was inconsequential to any association with Allen. Yet the collaboration of the two men, without roots in personal affection or shared background, bore rich fruit; the progress and influence exerted by *Penguin New Writing* was made possible almost as much by Allen's abdication of any over-riding control (and, in this case, by his careful smothering of Williams's more credible literary pretensions) as by Lehmann's undoubted genius as an editor.

The connection between Allen and Lehmann was not new. Already in Allen's last days at The Bodley Head Lehmann had come to him with a prospectus for a 'book-periodical' dedicated to two gods, literary elegance and anti-Fascism. Allen was prepared to offer devotion to both deities. As from his earliest days he had lived with the fame of *The Yellow Book* as spur, so his eagerness to fall in with Lehmann's plans was inevitable. The chance came in 1940 when Lehmann suggested developing his *New Writing* into *Penguin New Writing*. Allen did not hesitate. Lehmann offered no concession to populism, and Allen demanded none. Only price, format and frequency of publication differentiated *Penguin New Writing* from its parent publication; the élite corps of regular contributors was intrinsically unaltered and Lehmann's discoveries were, most of them, heirs to that élite. Allen had his own *Yellow Book* at last, and when *Penguin New Writing* was at its peak it sold, as no other 'high-brow' journal in the history of publishing, more than 100,000 copies an issue.

Even so *Penguin New Writing* was essentially not Allen's achievement but Lehmann's, for Allen never came to understand, and perhaps never wished to accept, the literary *haut-monde* in which Lehmann was both a central and a typical figure. Artistic and intellectual versatility was beyond Allen's competence; he could not aspire to the cosmopolitanism that was natural to Lehmann; and, for all his worldly success, he was never comfortable in a rarified society led by Old Etonian aesthetes. The relationship between publisher and editor remained remote and cool, yet this uncomfortable collaboration held together for a decade. *Penguin New Writing* must be numbered among the most significant of all Penguin ventures, the voice of a literature at war, a platform for distinguished writers of the middle generation, a source of hope to their neophyte juniors, and a link between writers and artists and their dispersed audience.

Ambitious as he was to take Penguin into all corners of the literary market-place it is perhaps surprising that Allen took so long to establish a children's list. This was to him strange territory, something about which he knew even less than he knew about the *belles-lettres* of *New Writing* and for which he had none of the instinctive appreciation that guided him towards the creation of Specials or King Penguins. His brothers, Bill Williams and Eunice Frost were in this sense no more competent and no more enthusiastic. They shared the disability of being without children of their own to offer instant and frequent reminders of the necessity for good, inexpensive children's books. But almost every publisher glimpses from time to time a delectable vision in which he plays the part of a Santa Claus for all seasons whilst an attendant host of doting parents and benevolent aunts or uncles refills his emptied book bag with bank-notes, and grateful young readers assure him of their life-long dedication to his list and of more bank-notes to come when they are themselves doting parents and benevolent aunts or uncles. Allen was familiar with this vision, but it had always been crowded out by other, more compelling dreams and it is doubtful that it would have been roused had the prompting come from one of those desiccated spinsters who were at that time generally responsible for editing series for children.

Noel Carrington, the instigator of Puffin Picture Books, was not in any sense an expert on children's books but he was a much respected authority on printing and design. It was to him that Allen had gone early in 1938 when he was looking for an author for a Special on design. Carrington had refused the commission (and advised him to ask Anthony Bertram). Instead he suggested a project which 'he had had in mind ever since I saw the first Soviet books for children ... produced by the million on very cheap paper, but the drawings ... vigorous and the colour delightful'. Penguin should produce under his editorship a series of books for children on 'nature, mechanics and farming'.

sixteen pages of colour and sixteen of black and white illustration 'with limited but authoritative text'. By using lithography and planning long runs the books could be retailed at sixpence. Carrington was confident because he had costed the whole venture most carefully for his employers, the Newnes Group, and though his masters had refused to support him, this could be no reason for Allen to reject a proposition so appropriate to Penguin.

All this Carrington put before Allen over lunch in Allen's favourite Spanish restaurant, and Allen's answer was immediate and enthusiastic. Then he went away and for a year ignored or evaded all Carrington's efforts to bring him to negotiate terms. Just when Carrington had decided that Allen was no longer interested and that, at all events, the new circumstances of war made the whole project inconceivable, a note came from Allen. Children, he wrote, were being evacuated from their city homes to an unfamiliar countryside; they needed books that would teach them something of rural life. No less than adults, the young were caught up in the nation at war; they must be given some means of understanding what was happening to them, to their fathers and brothers. With the air of a man who has just dreamed up something which, for all that he knows it to be original, he nonetheless recognizes as likely to match the tastes of an acquaintance, he asked Carrington if it was not the case that he had shown some interest in a children's series which might be adapted to the purposes which Allen had in mind. He knew that he could trust Carrington to oversee the printing as well as the editorial policies – but they must waste no time!

The first Puffin Picture Books were notably bellicose, *War on Land*, *War at Sea* and *War in the Air*, but thereafter the war was not often noticed, the series concerning itself pre-eminently with natural history, with crafts, technologies and history.

The success of Puffin Picture Books sprang largely from a combination of good design, bold colour printing, unashamedly didactic intention and low price. It was in the Penguin stud-book the progeny of distinguished parents, Pelicans and King Penguins. When the inhibitions of war-time had disappeared, Puffin Picture Books would serve as inspiration and model for a new generation of books for the young – cheerful, elegant and yet overtly educational. The immediate succession was within Penguin, and obvious: there must be a juvenile version of the firm's central series, a fiction list for the young to match the Penguin reprints; and so Puffin Story Books.

Already before 1939 Allen's life had been hectic; with the advent of war and his access of authority it became frenetic. He had long maintained the habit, which he never abandoned, of regarding cocktail-parties and dinners as opportunities for prospecting for authors, for books or for ideas for series. (He never used a notebook, and the exquisite cut of his jackets was often ruined by pockets bulging with old envelopes, menu-cards and scraps of paper on which he scribbled names, addresses and memoranda.) The austerities of war made little impact upon his social life but now, still revelling in the excitement of discovery, he savoured also every moment of his new unchallenged authority. As he proved to himself and to the world that Penguin could be made to flourish even in the uncongenial climate, so did his experience of uninterrupted success add to the sum of his confidence and to his capacity for offering a public image of untrammelled assurance. At forty he was an outstanding success; no other publisher of his generation and nation had to his credit a major innovation to equal the institution of Penguin and few innovators of any kind, any place or any time had themselves profited so much or so rapidly from their own innovations. Yet perversely he was still lonely. Miserably aware that he had many acquaintances but few intimate friends, with his brothers off in the Navy, now there was no one to whom he could air his wilder schemes or reveal his deepest ambitions, no one to oppose his impulsive liking for a newly discovered acquaintance, or to question his just-as-sudden distaste for a recently acquired favourite. He missed Dick and John, for they were both family and friends. They were colleagues, too, but they were also rivals and as such he was glad to be rid of them. Nora, on the other hand, was the adoring younger sister, a companion, a mirror in which he could see reflected his own glory. She had never questioned his hegemony nor attempted to brake his impulsiveness. Her marriage just when he was set to become the unchallenged and unchallengeable ruler of the Penguin empire he took almost as a defection; more even than the enlistment of Dick and John, it contributed to the destruction of that intense inwardness which had existed since childhood between all the Lanes. It was as if there was now nothing left that could keep him from becoming all-visible, all public personality, a book world genius who did not smile or speak or breathe unless he sniffed printers' ink.

Given Allen's circumstances at this period, no novelist would have any difficulty in writing the next chapter. Here is a man close to middle age, successful, untroubled by financial worries, suddenly faced with loneliness such as he has never experienced in his adult life but simultaneously with the compensating knowledge that at last he can make decisions by himself about his personal and his professional life. The story must go on to marriage, and so it was with Allen; yet he had been for so many years one of the book world's most eligible bachelors that many had come to consider that he would hold that title for the rest of his days. Even his closest colleagues were amazed when he produced Lettice Orr as his fiancée.

Members of the family were also surprised, even shocked. It was an unspoken but accepted tenet of family faith that not one of them would ever take a major step without first consulting all the others, and what step could be considered more important than bringing in a stranger to be a Lane? Allen knew full well that his engagement must be regarded as a kind of treachery; he did not announce his intentions to Dick or John until the very last moment and thereafter brazened it out like a naughty child who has done something irrevocable which pleases him but must displease others.

Lettice Orr was a pretty, articulate and earnest young woman from a background utterly unlike Allen's. Her father was a distinguished member of the Colonial Service who ended his career as Governor of the Bahamas. Lettice had spent much of her childhood in official residences in the colonies, but in her late teens she had rebelled against the stolid conservatism of her parents and replaced it with a suitably high-toned Socialism. At first she had thought of a career in politics, but then took a social science diploma and trained as a psychiatric social worker.

Behind her first meeting with Allen lay a series of events, coincidences and accidents which gave to that occasion an almost comic inevitability. It began in Lettice's student days at Bedford College, London University, where she was taught

Economics by Gertrude Williams and much influenced by her tutor's fiery radicalism. Early in the war the London School of Economics was evacuated to Cambridge and with it the Reader in Economic History and member of the Pelican Advisory Board, H. L. Beales. Lettice also moved to Cambridge, to Addenbrooke's Hospital; there she made friends with a couple who were friends of the Beales. It was they who told her that the Pelican editors had taken to meeting at Beales's home, away from the London blitz, and it was through them she had herself invited to a party given by Beales in honour of his Pelican colleagues. She wanted to meet W. E. Williams, the husband of her former teacher, but once arrived in the Beales's sitting-room she noticed immediately a 'short powerful-looking man in country gentleman's tweeds ... standing apart from the crowd who were mostly dancing'. Instinctively she knew that 'this was not Bill Williams', but it seemed inconceivable that, as her friends whispered, this silent, withdrawn, almost forlorn man was Allen Lane, the creator of Penguin.

She went up to him. 'You're looking sad.' It was a bold gambit and it produced an amazing response. Yes, he admitted, he was sad ... and there followed a recitation of his sorrows, how his brothers were in the Navy, how his sister had married and gone, of all places, to Newcastle, how now he was left without a companion.

Lettice persuaded him to dance. He was light on his feet and performed with carefully schooled precision all the more conventional dances. It was never his custom to attempt in public anything which he knew he could not do well and so he avoided the more exotic dances, the rhumbas and the tangos; sitting them out in Lettice's company, he continued to pour out his woes. She would have preferred talk of his publishing ventures or his travels but she was at once captivated by his personality and professionally fascinated by what she took to be a psychologist's case-book study.

Allen, for his part, was always ready to talk to a good-looking girl; here was one who was not only prepared to listen but also seemed to know how to prompt. As he spoke he became ever more fluent about his misery, and ever more certain that the fates – and Nora – had treated him cruelly.

Then foolishly – as she judged it immediately she had spoken –

Lettice's professionalism got the better of her social sense. 'It all sounds a bit suspicious to me,' she said. Allen's reply was extraordinary: 'It is strange, I can tell you.'

She was disappointed but not surprised when he said good-bye without suggesting another meeting. She was surprised but elated when a few weeks later he wrote inviting her to spend a week-end at Silverbeck. She had measles and had to refuse. Back came his courteous response: she must come to Silverbeck to recuperate.

They had known each other for less than six months when they were married at Harmondsworth on 28 June 1941. The honeymoon was cut short by a telegram from John announcing that he and Dick had shore-leave and were on their way home to Silverbeck.

It was Lettice's first meeting with her brothers-in-law and it was not a happy experience. Dick and, more particularly, John made it clear that they looked upon her as an inconsequential interloper who had acquired the name Lane by subterfuge; though Allen was affectionate and generally courteous when they were together in private, he did not seem to resent the rarity of the opportunities for privacy. John objected to the manner in which, as he saw it, Allen had taken advantage of his absence to take undisputed control of Penguin; he made no secret of his conviction that Allen's marriage was sufficient proof of his incompetence to make important decisions on his own account. Allen, unwilling to cede one iota of his new-found authority, was nonetheless touched by a sense of guilt and occasionally by a genuine and not unnatural desire to recover the fraternal spirit of Talbot Square – at least for the duration of John's leave. The tensions created by these contradictory sentiments led to continuous bickering and to occasional outbursts of anger. To all of this Lettice was a witness, but even Allen made it clear that none of it was her business.

The scenes were sometimes farcical and the issues between Allen and John trivial, as if neither was willing to recognize the two unrelated realities of their situation: Allen's omnipotence was now unshakeable; no sea-going naval officer could look to the future with any confidence. Early in the morning John would burst into Allen's bedroom claiming that he had some important matter of business to discuss. Allen, he demanded, must come to his room to talk. Allen insisted that if anything was so important that it must be discussed before breakfast then discussed it must be, but here in his room. And so they would argue, sometimes for a half-an-hour on end, about protocol, without once coming to the issue that John wished to raise and without once deferring to Lettice.

She hardly dared admit to herself and she dared not admit to Allen her relief when his brothers went back to sea. For a while thereafter Allen seemed to settle down to something approaching a conventional domestic existence, but if he was to maintain the growth of the Penguin empire the calls on his time and energy were many. The unease which he felt because he was safe and his brothers in danger, combined with his determination to prove that he was right to rule alone, drove him on to greater and ever greater efforts. More practically, the establishment of Silverbeck as office as well as home contributed to make impossible that division between working and domestic life which is for most men and women essential to sanity and marital amity.

It is possible to speculate that if Allen had married when he was younger, before his success was assured, or even if he had married in peace-time, he might have been able to resolve the conflict between career and ease. As it was he set his marriage on the wrong track almost from the beginning; he paid comparatively little attention to it whilst perversely maintaining the ancient fiction that business and family life must be kept separate. Thus, though the Penguin offices were at Silverbeck and though, for long periods, members of the staff were actually living in the house, Lettice was but rarely admitted to editorial discussions or asked, even informally, by Allen for any opinion on Penguin policy. Graciously he conceded to her the responsibility for catering for the staff working at Silverbeck.

The deterioration in Allen's relationship with his brothers was accelerated by his isolation from the experiences that they were sharing. Both served as watch-keeping officers on ships escorting convoys and somehow managed to come together frequently. Though Dick was considerably older than most lieutenants, and even John somewhat above the average age, their sybaritic shore excursions emphasized and attenuated the age-gap between the two of them and Allen, setting them a generation apart from him. It was as if, whilst Allen had moved on into harassed, public-spirited – and married – middle age, Dick and John had found in war the means to make the spirit of Talbot Square everlasting. Then John's ship was sunk. John spent most of his survivor's leave with his parents but Allen was miserable, his conscience battered by his inability to comprehend what John had experienced and by his concern that somehow he had wronged his brother. This confusion of sentiment was repeated and its intensity doubled when Dick and John, having by some Lane magic persuaded the Admiralty to let them go to sea *in tandem*, were together when their ship was torpedoed.

It was a grim experience, but not grim enough to prevent Dick and John from turning a trick against the authorities. When they heard the order to abandon ship they hurried back to their cabins, changed into their best (and most expensive) uniforms, ready to claim for the loss by enemy action of uniforms that had in fact survived with their owners.

It was Allen who seized upon this story and made it part of Penguin mythology. The anecdote, as he told it over and over again with embellishments, was not so much about disasters at sea as about Lane shrewdness and Lane effrontery in the face of bureaucracy; he showed his audience that he saw the episode as a parable extolling the impudent spirit of the Lanes and of Penguin. But no public posturing could dull his private awareness that Dick and John, drawn together by danger, hardship and frivolity, were closer than they had ever been even in the heady decade before the war, nor could he free himself from the suspicion that their intimacy not only excluded him but was in some sense directed against him and threatening to his interests.

The old camaraderie was not entirely suppressed, and there were still times when the brothers acted as if they were back in the bathroom at Talbot Square. John came to Silverbeck for part of a leave; one evening, when unusually there were no guests present, Allen kept him sitting long after dinner whilst he elaborated a theme which had been in his mind for months. They must buy a farm. Dick was on sea-duty out of Gibraltar but the others knew that he would fall in with the plan; like Allen he had come to accept as whole truth the half lie that they had been brought up in a tradition inherited from a long line of yeoman farmers. It was not quite so easy to convince John that some clarion call from the past summoned them all to a future in agriculture – if only part time – but he was alert to the necessity to diversify and he agreed that there is no better protection against hard times than the ownership of land. Once his last doubts were removed by Allen's demonstration of tax advantages to come, he was as enthusiastic as Allen and, because he must soon go back to sea, far more urgent. They would look for a farm easily accessible from Silverbeck and from Harmondsworth so that eventually all three could run it as a hobby and as a second business.

Within days they had found some properties that seemed appropriate, and together they started attending auctions. If the auction was held during the afternoon it was imperative to lunch first and to lunch well. So it was that, after lunch at the Hinds Head at Bray and attendance at an auction room in Reading, Allen despatched a cable to Dick:

WENT TO FARM SALE IN READING STOP JOHN SLEEPILY NODDED STOP LETTING BANK MANAGER KNOW TOMORROW

There is extant a cruder version of the story of how the Lanes acquired Priory Farm. It is said that John habitually picked his nose and that the auctioneer took each exploration of John's nostrils as a bid.

Priory Farm belonged to all three Lanes, but immediately and for the duration of the war the control of their farming interests, like their publishing, must remain virtually exclusively Allen's. That responsibility he exercised with zest; no matter whether the family connection with agriculture was real or imagined, Allen's feeling for the land was genuine and deep. From the first at Priory Farm and for ever after, as his holdings grew so did his enthusiasm. He studied hard, read every book on farming that was recommended to him and badgered experts for advice. It was not in his nature to be patient or conventional. If he had a fault as a land-owner it was of a kind not so very different from what was both his greatest virtue and his greatest failing as a publisher: he could never let well alone. He was forever experimenting, amending, re-casting his intentions so that, according to one well-qualified observer, 'he beat the life out of the land'.

The situation of Priory Farm, close to Reading and less than an hour's drive from Silverbeck, was in most senses ideal for Allen who hoped that somehow he could fit part-time farming into a more than ordinarily full life in publishing. Yet because the area was conveniently placed for Reading and even for London it did not and could never satisfy one part of his essentially romantic dream as the heir to a long line of farmers: returned from making his fortune in the city to serve as benevolent and well-loved squire. Later, in North Devon, he found what he wanted. The personality who is remembered at Iddesleigh – generous, modest, eager, involved with the community – is almost unrecognizable to those who knew him only in London or New York, but at Priory Farm, and above all during the war years, however hard he tried he had little hope of being anything but a businessman in gumboots.

For the moment farming and even marriage were no more than diversions. He was convinced that in commerce there can be no standing still, that a business which is not growing must be slipping. In its turnover and editorial range, he had no reason for concern about the present health or future strength of his enterprise, yet always nagging at his pride and at his publisher's sensibilities was his failure to make an impact on America. Each in his turn John and Dick had done what he could in the United States, but the small American subsidiary was incapable of matching such bustling indigenous rivals as Pocket Books. The problems were intensified by paper shortages in Britain and by the difficulties of transportation across the Atlantic. Ian Ballantine, who was in charge in New York, was comparatively inexperienced. He was, in Allen's opinion, not qualified to settle the foundations from which Penguin Books Incorporated could challenge the Americans. The times were not ripe for expansion in America and Treasury regulations forbade the transfer of working capital, but New York had no black-out, no bombs and no rationing. Allen's will to escape for a few weeks from the claustrophobia of life in Britain bolstered his habitual confidence that when he himself took a hand in affairs previously insurmountable obstacles were magicked out of existence.

He enjoyed his 1941 visit to the United States more even than his earlier visits. There was apparent in the generally anglophil publishing-circle a sense of guilt about American neutrality which found compensation by offering extraordinary hospitality to any visitor from Britain; but neither guilt nor friendship for an old colleague was sufficiently compelling to force concessions from hard-headed American publishers. Nevertheless when Allen boarded the ship for the return passage he knew he had made provision for Penguin Books Inc. that would ensure its immediate survival and prepare for its eventual rise to a position among the paperback firms of America which would not shame the British parent house. This he had achieved, he thought, by bringing in Kurt Enoch as a Vice-President.

In Allen's career as a tycoon – and by 1941 he could fairly be called one – it was no infrequent occurrence that he made appointments on impulse, thinking often, and often erroneously, that personality and experience could overcome all difficulties. Because he saw himself as an innovator, his artfulness when faced with opposition sometimes deserted him when he had to choose collaborators; he was inclined to favour men or women he thought were in his image. Most of his many disastrous selections had their origins in this elementary error. Because there was no room in the Allen Lane empire for any potential usurper, the men and women he had chosen in this way, once he had secured their collaboration, either incurred his suspicion or else rebelled against the reduction in status to which they were almost immediately subjected. It would be an exaggeration, and unfair, to number the appointment of Kurt Enoch among the disasters, but the history of Penguin in America might have been less tempestuous and more successful had Allen recognized from the first that he could never allow Enoch to be an equal and that Enoch would not for long submit to being a subordinate.

The similarities between the two were real. Both were ebullient, energetic, individualistic and innovative, but it would have been surprising if Enoch had not felt some resentment at Allen's success for he could persuade himself, as later he was to attempt to persuade others, that some years before the birth of Penguin he had launched from Germany an English-language paperback series which was substantially the model for Penguin. In truth his Albatross Modern Continental Library, established in 1932 with the aid of a consortium of British publishers, was no more than a modern version of the century-old Tauchnitz series. It sold, like Tauchnitz exclusively in non-English speaking countries, low-priced paperback editions of books by modern and classic British and American authors. Within these limitations Albatross had enjoyed for a while a great vogue. When Enoch negotiated a merger with Tauchnitz, at that time their only rival, it seemed that the future was bright for a firm which had several thousand active titles and which could add fifteen or twenty new titles each month.

It had been Allen who had first disturbed Enoch's rosy dreams; almost from the beginning Penguin had succeeded in negotiating with the originating publishers Continental as well as British Empire rights. Once he launched Pelicans and therefore a programme which favoured commissioned works, all markets were open to Penguin and to Penguin exclusively. The runs of Penguins and Pelicans were often ten times as great as Albatross could manage and so Penguin undercut Albatross–Tauchnitz even in their traditional market. Enoch's venture was already foundering when an enemy more sinister than Allen Lane brought it to an end. The Nazis forced Kurt Enoch out of Germany.

Many years later, when relations between the two men had been soured by collaboration, Enoch claimed that Allen had derived most of his publishing philosophy from Albatross and Tauchnitz. Such assertions, based on abstractions, are difficult to sustain or disprove; the evidence of Allen's colleagues in The Bodley Head tends to deny Enoch's associated accusation that the format and typographical manner of the early Penguins (and therefore, essentially, of all Penguins produced before the end of the war) were unashamedly and deliberately borrowed from the designs produced for Albatross by Hans Mardersteig. If these reservations about Allen's originality and even about his integrity were already in Enoch's mind when he fled from Germany and set up in Paris and London they did not prevent him from having even that early, several meetings with Allen to discuss collaboration in a new scheme of Enoch's, the production of mass-circulation editions of French classics.

At that time, the summer of 1938, Enoch's future depended entirely on the success of this scheme, but to Allen it was only one of a hundred proposals he was contemplating. By the time war came, he had forgotten that he had not answered Enoch's requests for a decision, nor did he think to go back to Enoch when Penguin began to plan publishing in French. Although he must have known that Enoch could not stay in Paris once the city was in the hands of the Nazis, the news of Enoch's move to New York seems to have come to Allen quite by chance at a cocktail-party given in his honour two or three days after his arrival in America. Nevertheless, it was Allen who approached Enoch, though, as was his habit in situations like this, his negotiating technique was speculative, elusive and non-committal. At their first New York meeting he made no reference to their pre-war dealings but poured out his sorrows as if seeking the sympathy of an old friend. The miraculous success of Penguin in Britain, he suggested, must justify his dream of triumph in the United States, yet here he was, frustrated by war-time regulations and shortage of capital, with no one to turn to for advice and help except the inexperienced Ballantine. Soon he was duty-bound to return to England. There was nothing for it, he must close down Penguin Books Inc.

Thus abbreviated and paraphrased the recitation seems simple and the purpose too obvious to deceive an experienced protagonist but Allen knew his man: Enoch was ambitious; as yet he had not established himself in American publishing and he considered himself to be, at very least, Allen's equal as an operator in the paperback market. Almost before Allen had finished his *misericordium*, Enoch was suggesting that as Penguin's American subsidiary was unable to import large quantities of Harmondsworth titles it should print on its own account. He, eager to be involved, would do what he could to raise the necessary capital in the United States. Enoch foresaw some difficulty with Ballantine but Allen shrugged off the possibility; he was, he said, so sure that Ballantine would welcome Enoch that he proposed that Enoch raise the issue with him without a word from Allen. He was, of course, correct in this assumption, for Ballantine had no choice but to keep his real feelings to himself lest Allen would get rid of him or of the American subsidiary.

Enoch raised a loan. Allen made him a Vice-President of Penguin Books Inc., promised him 5 per cent of the company's shares – as soon as the Treasury relaxed the regulation forbidding the transfer overseas of British-owned shares – and sailed for England. By December 1941 the first genuinely American Penguins were at the distributors.

On 7 December 1941 the Japanese bombed Pearl Harbor.

Allen had never felt the need – so imperative to most men – to separate his private from his professional life. He had grown to adulthood working in Uncle John's office and living in Uncle John's house. John Lane brought the triumphs and difficulties of Vigo Street home with him to Lancaster Gate Terrace and organized the pompous sociability at his dining-table and in his drawing-room to enhance the name and prosperity of The Bodley Head. Allen had come early to the belief that this was the way to success. Later, when success came and with it independence, still he was only rarely tempted to separate his domestic from his professional existence, his social from his business life. His brothers were his partners and his flat-mates; most of his more intimate acquaintances were men or women who shared his professional interests; many were writers, publishers or printers with whom he had commercial dealings; and almost all of them shared his conviction that the professional day lasted for eighteen or twenty hours, that it did not end when the centre of activity moved from the office to the club or the cocktail-bar. For him and most of his associates 'shop' and book world gossip were the only truly fascinating topics, discussed anywhere at any time.

Allen was in no way disconcerted by the need to set up his office at Silverbeck. To him the move was only a rational development of the state of affairs which had existed, as it were emotionally, when office and home were a mile or so apart. Indeed his attitude was not merely acquiescent but positively hopeful, for he saw in it the means to ameliorate the damage done to his lifestyle by the war. He had been miserably aware that his employees and even those of his book trade cronies who had not gone off to join the Forces were no longer willing to continue the business of the day into the evening. Dusk, which in the past had signalled a move from office to bar, club or restaurant but no shift in the professionalism of the conversation, was now greeted with glances at watches, more or less furtive according to the seniority of the glancer, for all had in mind the need to get home before the black-out, before dark brought fire-watching or Home Guard duties, air-raid sirens and bombs. But, thought Allen, if Silverbeck was office, bar, club, restaurant and, when need be, also dormitory, some at least might abandon time-wasting, pleasure-wasting and, as he saw it, treasonable habits and return to the sensible practices of pre-war days.

For a while it worked as Allen hoped that it would. The house was always full and if much time was taken up by conviviality most of it was given to preparing the greater glory of Penguin. Then, in April 1942 Lettice gave birth to their first child, a daughter.

Allen was as proud of himself as if he had launched successfully a new Penguin series but at first, just as he might have been with a series, his pride and his pleasure were somewhat tempered by his incompetence to do much more for daughter Clare than he had done already. He belonged to a generation of men which was never called on to assist in the care of small babies and he had even less experience of tiny children than most of his contemporaries. He admired, he petted, he preened himself and he was very pleased with Lettice, but he was impatient for the day when Clare would talk, would play with him and would respond to his eagerness to show all the world that his daughter was the best-looking, best-dressed girl in Britain. Meanwhile, for one so small, she did take up rather a lot of Silverbeck space and the attention paid to her even by visitors was apt to disrupt the worship of the Penguin gods.

Dick came home on leave again in November 1942. It was he who received over the telephone at Silverbeck the clipped but spirit-shattering message: 'The Admiralty regrets to inform you that Lieutenant Commander John Lane is missing, presumed killed.'

Still hoping for the impossible, next day Dick went to Whitehall and there was told the entire and inescapable truth. John's ship, HMS *Avenger*, had been sunk on the morning of 15 November whilst covering troop convoys approaching the North African beach-heads. Of her complement of 800 officers and ratings only four had been picked up. John was not one of the four.

The impact of this tragedy upon the surviving brothers was profound. In the lives of both of them thereafter it is possible to detect traits which indicate that neither ever recovered entirely from the shock. There was from then on in Dick a quantum of reserve, an almost impenetrable sanctuary, which seemed out of place in a man generally so open and convivial unless it could be explained by John's death. For his part Allen erased from his mind the suspicions and animosities which he had felt for John in the last two or three years of his life, persuaded himself that theirs had been a perfect relationship, and encased himself in a spiritual armour which he hoped would keep him free from similarly generous relationships and from the consequent danger of suffering hurt.

Immediately, however, though the matter was not discussed between them, both men knew that in the years of the war Dick and John had come closer together in an amity which excluded Allen. It followed, perhaps not surprisingly, that Allen's grief, compounded with guilt and with jealousy, was much more public and much more hysterical than Dick's. Calmly Dick asked the Admiralty to give him a temporary shore appointment so that he might have time to sort out John's affairs. It was Dick who discovered that John's will was invalid because it had only one witness (a detail which would not have mattered had not the will been drawn up before the war when the exemption for servicemen was not yet in force); therefore, because he had signed the deeds establishing Penguin Books Inc. in his own name without appending the phrase 'for Penguin Books Ltd', the American subsidiary now passed to his next-of-kin, his father. It was Dick who explained the situation to their parents, and he who guided them through the legal procedures necessary for returning the firm to its surviving founders, their surviving sons, Allen and Dick.

Meanwhile Allen took to solitary drinking, ate very little and did his best to avoid looking at his daughter Clare because, he said, she reminded him of John as a baby. And at night he cried himself to sleep.

Allen's need to demonstrate the intensity of his grief vanished when Dick returned to duty, as he had requested, to a shore-appointment in the Orkneys. There followed a period, brief but halcyon, when Allen seemed to be for the first and only time in his life entirely content, and entirely content because he had discovered a balance between the excitements of business and the more placid pleasures of domesticity. As energetic as ever in furthering Penguin prosperity, he was nevertheless at this time as quick to look at his watch as any man, not because he worried about black-out or air-raid alerts but because he was eager to see his daughter before she was put to bed. Next summer, when the Lanes went holidaying in the Scillies, although many members of the party which accompanied them had some connection with publishing, Allen spent most of his days on the beach, endlessly building sand-castles for Clare to destroy.

This idyllic interregnum could not last. Even had he not become disenchanted with orderliness and ordinariness, Allen could not have resisted for more than a few months the excitement of command. The war had brought a tragedy into his family, but he knew very little about warfare as it had shattered his seniors and was even now scorching his immediate juniors. For all that he had served as a Territorial, guns, torpedoes, tracer bullets, the whole hideous paraphernalia of tactical warfare, meant nothing to him. He paid little attention to the great strategical movements except as it was necessary for him to consider the implications for the marketing of Penguins, but for many years he had been aware of himself as a leader – and had delighted in the role. Now, with most of his equals removed from the scene and faced with demands for leadership and decision from all over the world, he knew that he was a commander.

Of the men who had joined the Penguin staff before the war only S. H. Olney was left. When Allen decided that he needed a plenipotentiary to work with Enoch and Ballantine in New York he sent out his only senior female colleague, Eunice Frost. He could trust her to guard his interests but her departure left him, virtually single-handed, in charge of editorial, sales, publicity, responsible both for the immediate and for the long-term future of Penguin.

It would seem that Allen never doubted, and it could be that he never considered, the eventual outcome of the war. This unnatural remoteness from the matters which concerned most of his countrymen, both the great and the insignificant, gave him the confidence to continue the expansion of Penguin even beyond the scale granted by the circumstances of war. It was enterprising but not particularly courageous when Allen took advantage of the fact that during 1942 and 1943 Cairo was an additional capital for the English-speaking world; he licensed Schindler to produce Egyptian Penguins for the hundreds of thousands of English reading men and women who were forced to regard the Middle East as home from home. It was enterprising but not particularly courageous when, in September 1943, with his friend Tom Fairley as editor (and with US government backing) he launched a monthly journal, *Transatlantic*, dedicated to informing the British about the culture, politics and social mores of their American allies. But at a time when the news from Italy was grim, when the battle of the Atlantic was in full spate and the battle of the Pacific just beginning, only a man gifted with superhuman confidence or protected by extraordinary insensitivity would prepare a new series of books designed to introduce modern painting to a huge audience. Only Allen Lane would have dared to launch the first four volumes of Modern Painters (*Henry Moore, Graham Sutherland, Duncan Grant* and *Paul Nash*) in the month when the Japanese were invading Imphal, when as yet no one could be certain that they could be held from breaking into the heartlands of India, and when the Allied invasion of Europe which must come soon might end in victory or disaster.

The birth of a second daughter, Christine, revived briefly Allen's zeal for family life but his pride in his children and the pleasure that he found in playing with them acted as a kind of convalescence which left him more eager than ever for the excitements of publishing. By the middle months of 1944 he had returned wholeheartedly to his old routine; week-days, evenings and week-ends were all taken up with the Penguin affairs, and sociability was again business garnished with food and drink.

Still there were not many among Allen's acquaintances who were ready to accept with him that business as usual meant socializing as in pre-war days, but among those who were prepared to follow there were even a few who could match his energy. There was Roger Manvell from the Ministry of Information, Victor Weybright from the American Embassy, Edmond Segrave of the *Bookseller*, Robert Lusty, a director of the publishing firm of Michael Joseph, and, more and more as the war progressed, there was W. E. Williams.

Before 1939 Allen and Bill had been much in each other's company but despite their mutually-held pleasure in good food and good wine their intimacy had depended to a considerable degree upon an exchange of professional benefits, an exchange in which Allen conferred far more than he received. True, he profited from Williams's editorial acumen and used Williams's contacts but there were available to him other editorial advisers; once the reputation of Penguins and Pelicans was fairly established, there was always battering at the doors a host of acquaintances speaking for themselves and for their friends as putative Penguin authors. Williams for his part, though in one sense more deliberately altruistic than Allen because more aware of the educational advantages that the growth of Penguin must bring to the nation, was also at that time much more than Allen committed to the continuance of their collaboration and dependent upon its success for the advance of his own ambitions. Only on Allen's shoulders could he climb out of the comparative obscurity of adult education. Either his timing was impeccable or else he was remarkably lucky: war broke out just when Williams's work with Allen had brought him sufficient public reputation to separate him from his anonymous colleagues in educational administration. Directing the Army Bureau of Current Affairs he had worked hard and even with brilliance, but he had not been content to stay within the sphere allotted him by authority. With Mary Glasgow he laid the foundations for what was to be the Arts Council. He began a new career as a journalist, contributing regularly to national newspapers. He accepted every invitation to serve on committees and, if he thought the committee useful to his purposes and was not invited to be a member, he somehow let it be known that he was indispensable.

Williams's new prominence and ubiquity changed the balance in his relations with Allen. Now that he was virtually independent and certainly more useful than he had been in the past Allen was prepared to accept that he was irreplaceable in the Penguin hierarchy. This enhanced respect took on more personal characteristics as Allen was distanced from his brothers; in the numbness that followed between him and Dick after the death of John, Allen began to believe that Bill Williams was the surrogate to whom he could turn for that conjunction of camaraderie and business partnership once found only with his brothers.

Nevertheless the relationship between the two was ambivalent; though their association continued in some form until Allen's death its quality puzzled many observers and to this day remains enigmatic even to those who knew both men. Williams's editorial contribution was for many years considerable and Allen was aware that his taste and sensitivity was of inestimable value to Penguin. Yet, even when he had become Secretary-General of the Arts Council, had found his way on to almost every influential committee in the arts and had become the arch-manipulator of patronage, Williams never shook off some sense of inferiority to Allen which prevented him from checking Allen's more monstrous decisions. Allen was aware of this; he used Williams as his executioner and Williams allowed himself to be used.

During the war years Allen's many gifts and considerable advantages came together to establish him, it seemed without challenge, exactly where he had wanted to be since first he took over from Uncle John: at the forefront of the book world. In publishing everything that he touched prospered; he had his elegant house, his farm, his talented and attractive wife, his two pretty little daughters; despite the tragedy of John's death he could count himself as one of the luckiest of men and did so frequently and boldly. Not then nor, it must be said, at any time in later years, did he notice that he suffered one hideous misfortune from which many simpler and less successful men are spared: there was within the circle of his intimates not one person who was prepared to warn him of the dangers that he was creating for himself both in his private affairs and at Penguin. Then and for the rest of his life he was seldom blessed with a friend who had the competence to criticize and the independence, confidence and force to persist with criticism against Allen's disconcerting habit of accepting rebuke, caution or adverse comment with a naughty-boy smirk which made it clear that whatever he had in mind was most certainly not contrition.

True, given the benefit of hindsight, some familiarity with the personalities of those most closely involved and the supporting evidence of other knowledgeable observers, it is impossible not to conclude that the chances for long-term stability in Allen's marriage were never good. Not all the advice of the saints and sages could have prevented eventual disaster. The situation in Penguin was very different. Allen had always thrived on opposition; whether it was the overt and jealous antagonism of the book trade or the generally amiable argumentativeness of Dick and John, the knowledge of struggle made him think more

clearly. He seldom admitted to being converted by his opponents
– not even by his brothers – but, once forced to hesitate, quite
frequently he would then come up with an idea not so very
different but now all-powerful in that it was all his own. But in
the last years of the war, when the excitement of the moment
seemed to presage a future of incessant bustle, continuously
stimulating tension and unhindered success, it was virtually
impossible for Allen to stem his obsession with the immediate so
that he might give himself pause for serious consideration of
Penguin a decade later. The war made Penguin, but it is no less
true that many difficulties which later troubled Allen had their
origins in the war years. They were created largely because
Allen had no time to contemplate the vulnerability implicit in
Penguin's virtual monopoly of the British paperback market and
no inclination to ponder the dangers that must accrue if he
continued forever as the unique and unchallengeable sovereign
of the Penguin Kingdom.

Such captiousness, like the comments about his marriage, is
strengthened by the smugness of after-knowledge, but no
miserly retrospective calculation can reduce the stupendous
record of the war years, nor can the most stringent consideration
of Allen's qualities as a leader destroy the admiration due for all
that he did between 1939 and 1945. One statistic can represent the
record: between September 1939 and August 1945 Penguin produced in England more than 700 titles, almost half of them
originals. And another statistic illustrates just how much of the
Penguin organization was Allen Lane: in all those years the
number of full-time staff – directors, editors, production men,
packers, drivers, travellers, secretaries – never exceeded forty.
After 1942 only six of these had pre-war experience with the firm.
When Eunice Frost went to New York, of the pre-war staff in the
front office only Allen himself and S. H. Olney survived.

There were many reasons why Allen did not rebuild the staff:
the noblest of these was that he was loath to fill the shoes of men
who at any time might come back expecting to put them on
themselves; the meanest that he was making up the pay of
employees who had gone to fight and hated the idea of paying
twice over for one job. Generally Allen was content because the
company worked and because he enjoyed the total commitment
which made it work. In fact in those years Allen added to the

permanent staff only one employee who was to have any noticeable influence on Penguin.

Alan Glover's place in the hierarchy was always ambiguous. His erudition made him extraordinarily useful to a firm which had acquired many of the intellectual characteristics of a university press; throughout his Penguin career he was more often than not the only member of the senior staff competent to conduct informed discussion with the authors of the many abstruse books on the list. The range of his knowledge – from Greek and Hebrew literatures to *Wisden*, from London Transport time-tables to psycho-analysis – and his quick and accurate eye qualified him also for the role to which he was generally relegated, as the head of a copy-editing department so tiny that it seldom numbered more than two, Glover and his secretary-assistant. Glover had the ability and the background that could have made him the guardian of the Penguin conscience, but Williams was too canny to allow a rival behind the throne and Glover himself showed no enthusiasm for power.

There lingers on in the recollections of those who knew him an elusive reference to a novel whose central character is modelled on Glover. It would seem appropriate that his memorial is an unidentifiable work of fiction, for when he was alive not even his most vigilant acquaintances could ever establish with any certainty the details of his *curriculum vitae*. When on occasion his closest friends asked him direct questions about his past his answers were at once disarmingly frank and yet disconcertingly incompatible with some hitherto incontrovertible item in his record. The certainties are that his name was not Glover, that under another name he had married a lady who was not the Mrs Glover known to his Penguin colleagues, that, again not as Glover, he had published a distinguished translation of medieval Latin hymns, that during the First World War he had gone to gaol as a conscientious objector, and that he had worked for a while in the circulation department of the *Daily Herald* and later in the London office of the *Reader's Digest*.

This latter experience, inserting the 'u' into 'color' for the United Kingdom edition of the world's largest circulation magazine, served as a prelude to his entry into Penguin. An avid collector of books (as also of gramophone records) he had bought every Penguin from *Ariel* onwards and, irritated by the slipshod copy-

The Williams family c. 1912. The children are (*left to right*) Allen, John, Nora and Richard

Allen Lane. A photograph taken in New York when he was about 30

Richard (*left*) and Allen Williams as choirboys in Bristol

Allen Lane at the time he came to London, 1919

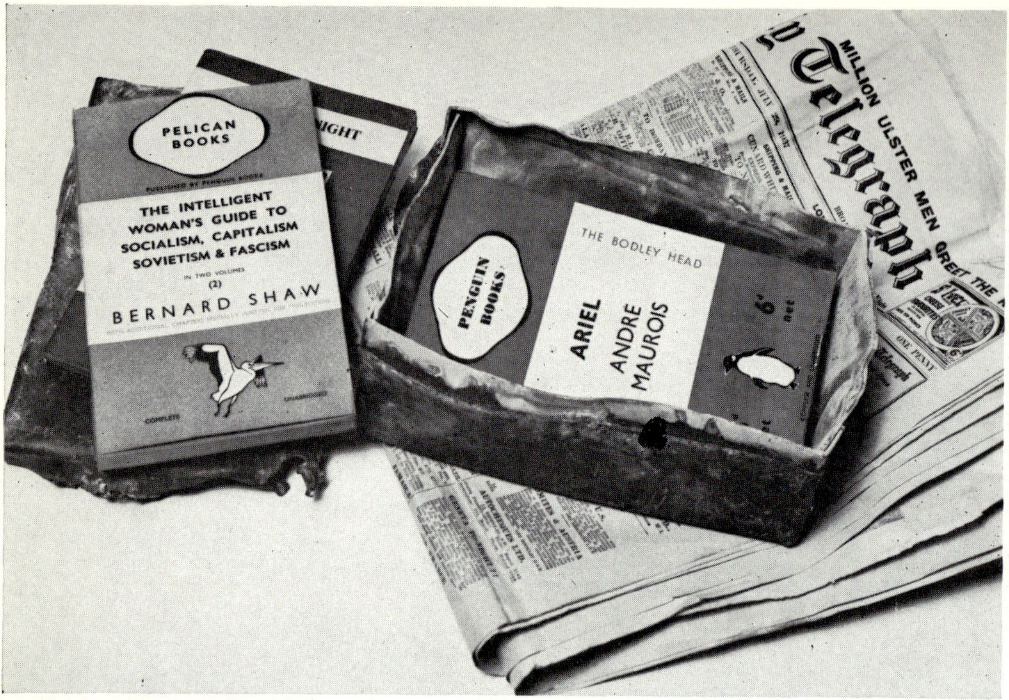
PELICAN BOOKS
THE INTELLIGENT WOMAN'S GUIDE TO SOCIALISM, CAPITALISM SOVIETISM & FASCISM
IN TWO VOLUMES
(2)
BERNARD SHAW
PENGUIN BOOKS
THE BODLEY HEAD
ARIEL
ANDRE MAUROIS

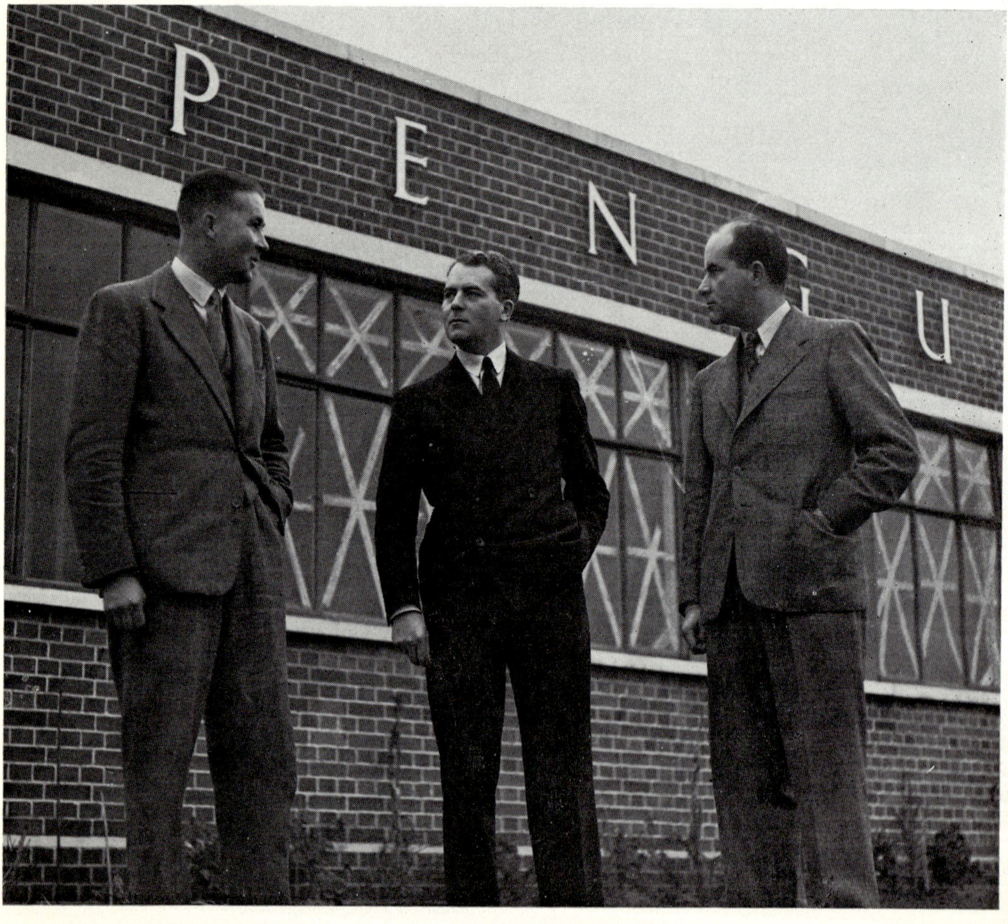

Allen Lane at work, Harmondsworth, 1940

Lead box and contents (Penguin 1; Pelican A1 and A2; Penguin Shakespeare B1; *Daily Telegraph* for 29 July 1937) found under the foundation stone of the original Harmondsworth building during its demolition in 1970

The Lane brothers at Harmondsworth, 1940: *(left to right)* Richard, Allen and John

John Lane at work, Harmondsworth, 1940: exports to Ceylon, the West Indies and Australia

Richard Lane at work, Harmondsworth, 1940: cheques and contracts

E. V. Rieu at the time of his retirement as Penguin Classics editor, 1964

Allen and Lettice Lane after their wedding in 1941

'After the Conference' by Rodrigo Moynihan RA, 1955 or 1956:
(*left to right*) E. V. Rieu, Sir Allen Lane, J. E. Morpurgo, R. B. Fishenden, Sir William Emrys Williams, Richard Lane, Noel Carrington, Eunice Frost, A. W. Haslett, A. S. B. Glover, C. A. Mace, Michael Abercrombie, Sir Nikolaus Pevsner, Gordon Jacob, Sir Alfred Ayer, M. L. Johnson Eleanor Graham, Sir Max Mallowan, John Lehmann

Sir William Emrys Williams

Sir Allen Lane after the *Lady Chatterley* verdict, 1960

editing and proof-correcting of the war-time production, he had taken to sending in long lists of misprints and factual errors. There was nothing for it but to invite him to join Penguin's team.

Allen could never establish a comfortable relationship with Glover. As with Pevsner, so with Glover he was awed by the other man's learning. Unlike Pevsner, Glover had no proud university title to substantiate his scholarship; he was instead almost entirely dependent on Allen for such dignities as might be granted him. Awed, suspicious, embarrassed, uncomprehending: the confusion of contradictory sentiments set Allen apart from Glover, but the democratic organization at Harmondsworth, though largely illusory, allowed to him the convenient excuse that, as there was no severe hierarchy at Penguin, it was not necessary to clarify Glover's status.

Partly because Allen was so reluctant to push him forward as a representative of the firm and partly because he himself preserved his anonymity behind his highly-coloured disguise, Glover remains to this day an unsung hero of the Penguin story. In the wider world of publishing he was known to very few; he is mentioned in none of the histories and the innumerable autobiographies which the trade publishes in its own honour. Similarly there is no record of his name (nor of any of his names) in the printed annals of scholarship, though his place could be justified not only by his all-important contribution to the scholarly quality of Pelicans but also by his translations, by his scrupulous editing of the leading journal of psycho-analysis, and by his Nonesuch editions of Shelley and Rousseau.

It is tempting (and perhaps too easy for one who was for many years Glover's most intimate colleague) to resent on his behalf the deprecating manner in which he was treated by Penguin and particularly by Allen. Yet at the last it must be admitted that Glover was never heard to express discontent with his situation. Glover was older and more experienced than any other member of the upper echelon of the Penguin staff; Allen was prepared to offer grudging recognition to his seniority when it suited him, but he never treated him to that easy sociability which was the demonstration of his confidence. Newcomers and newcomers to Allen's favour, men who even in the ill-defined Penguin battle-order were palpably junior to Glover, found themselves at the end of the working day coralled by Allen into drinking-parties at the Peggy Bedford or at Silverbeck, but Glover was seldom of the company. Yet it was he who was always the first to encourage the upstart ambitions of his younger colleagues and it was he who, without stooping to disloyalty, somehow contrived to warn aspirants that life at the top alongside Allen was unpredictable. Folk memory holds the fame of Alan Glover for the unique dexterity which allowed him to read and correct galley-proofs whilst strap-hanging in a crowded Tube train. Those who worked with him in the bank-less, shop-less wilderness of Harmondsworth can add reminiscences of his regular service as money-lender to his colleagues, always ready to provide a pound or two – without usury – and always providing pristine notes, as if he had run them off each morning in his West Hampstead flat. But Glover has his place in the biography of Allen Lane not for his eccentricities, not for his kindliness, not for his versatility, nor yet for his undeniable part in the development of Penguin. Glover's long career with the firm is the most extravagant example of reaction to Allen, which was to some degree common among his employees and collaborators. He stands in memory as the representative of many who, for all that they were not blind to Allen's faults, nevertheless allowed themselves to be caught up in the excitement which he engendered, who for all that they knew that he who offers his shoulder as a mounting-block risks being kicked in the teeth, nevertheless were so certain of Allen's unique capacity for leadership and of the idealism of the Penguin philosophy that they allowed him to use their skills, their energy and their experience, to use – and sometimes to abuse – their loyalty.

CHAPTER SIX

IN the last week of July 1945 Allen received from all over the world messages of congratulation on the tenth birthday of Penguin. Anniversaries of this kind he celebrated with zest: here was an excuse for a party, an occasion for much publicity (most of it free), and an opportunity for jabbing a malicious elbow into the ribs of those who had either tried to ensure that his Penguins would be still-born or else had prophesied for them death in infancy. But, at the time of the tenth birthday, other matters were competing for public attention. On 26 July, after a delay of three weeks for the counting of ballot papers from the Armed Services overseas, the British people discovered that they had elected to government the Labour Party, for the first time with an overall majority in the House of Commons. On 6 August the atom bomb was dropped on Hiroshima, and eight days later Japan surrendered. Nevertheless, Allen managed his own celebrations with an indifference to history that is now almost inconceivable.

The centrepiece of the birthday tribute was a series of articles written by Edmond Segrave, ostensibly for publication in the *Bookseller* but from conception intended both by the author and by Allen for reissue to a much wider and less professional audience than that which subscribed to the trade paper. *Ten Years of Penguins* (as the articles were entitled when they appeared in pamphlet-form) was written in such a manner that three decades later a reader not gifted with a sense of chronology might well miss the fact that six of those ten years had been years of war. Perhaps even more surprising except to those who know that Segrave, from his early association with G. K.

Chesterton might have rebelled had he been asked to draw attention to the coincidence of Penguin achievement and the Labour Party's success, the pamphlet made no reference to the powerful and growing political influence of the Penguin list.

Later – almost twenty years later – Allen was apt to preen himself on his part in the General Election of 1945. By the 1960s it had become fashionable to comment upon the sociological significance of Penguin, and Allen had learnt to believe much of what he read about himself and his work. By then, too, it had become received Harmondsworth mythology that there was a causal connection between the advance of Penguin during their first decade and the triumph of the Labour Party at the end of that decade – no less a person than Clement Attlee had first suggested that his road to Downing Street had been paved with Penguin Specials. Attlee's remark, as it was passed to Allen by one of his senior colleagues in the summer of 1963, ran something like this: 'After the WEA, it was Lane and his Penguins which did most to get us into office at the end of the war.' Allen was not unnaturally flattered by the comment. He did not trouble to notice that it had been made to a Penguin editor who was escorting the eighty-year-old Attlee from a Penguin party to his home in King's Bench Walk nor did he choose to remember that, only a month or so earlier, W. E. Williams had reported a recent conversation with Attlee; similar in tone, in detail very different in that it was the Army Bureau of Current Affairs and not Penguin that followed the WEA as midwife to the Labour Government.

Ten Years of Penguins was unassuming, bland and not particularly informative. Only once in an essay some 5000 words long did the author's long-standing loyalty to Allen push him into a splutter of acid directed against those who had tried to frustrate Penguin:

> The publication of new books ... now form four-fifths of the entire Penguin Books output. This development, which is continuously increasing liberates Penguins from the danger, always hovering over the reprint publisher, that he may ... be deprived of access to his sources of supply. Not all publishers have been willing to see their best books published in a cheap reprint series controlled by another firm. For Penguin Books, nowadays, a publisher's unfavourable attitude to cheap reprints is a question of publishing theory ...; it is no longer, as it used to be, a matter of urgent practical significance....

The statistics were exact but the inference was both dubious and potentially dangerous, the more so because Segrave was merely articulating Allen's twin convictions that he could maintain the Penguin preponderance of commissioned books and also that, by emphasizing the publication of new books, he had liberated himself for all foreseeable time from dependence on other publishers. The Penguin fiction list, he assumed, would be sustained, partly because already it enjoyed a prestige of its own among publishers, authors, booksellers and readers, and partly because in the eyes of those same groups it must always thrive in the light reflected from Pelicans, Kings and Specials. For all his acuteness Allen – and with him Segrave, that most experienced observer of the book trade – did not take into account the probability that, now that the war was over, there would be a surge of imitation and competition. He had been right to disregard Guild Books; as a threat to Penguin a collaborative venture run by a committee of competing publishers was as effective as a platoon of cyclists against a Panzer division. Pan Books was the one British paperback house founded after Penguin that had established itself as seemingly a permanent fixture in the trade; but to Allen's way of thinking – and to Segrave's – Pan was so clearly committed to editorial policies utterly unlike those of Penguin, to books that were perhaps more obviously 'popular' but certainly more ephemeral, as to be in reality no more in competition with Penguin than fish-paste is competitive with caviare. It had not as yet entered Allen's mind that ultimately he must fight a war on several fronts: against a horde of new entrants for paperback rights, against all paperback publishers for a share of the limited rack-space in bookshops sufficient to continue the volume of sales essential to support the Penguin economy and against all other commodities for an appropriate share of the limited funds available to the public.

Segrave's *Ten Years of Penguins* ended with a tribute and a flourish of optimism:

> Allen Lane is very much the head of Penguin Books Ltd. He is its principal source of inspiration and invention as well as its presiding genius. He has a pretty clear idea of what he wants Penguin Books to become, but it would require a whole Penguin Special to accommodate all the details of his plans. Compressed into a sentence the Penguin programme still remains, in essentials, what it was ten years ago: to supply something good for all needs and moods. The operative word is good.

Segrave was no sycophant; he believed in Allen, he believed in Penguin and he believed what he wrote was true. So did Allen believe in Allen, in Penguin and in the veracity of Segrave's assessment; but his vision was not as pellucid as Segrave suggested. Since 1940 he had been so busy with negotiations, projects and expansion that he had had no time to consider what would happen to Penguin when the war was over; nor had he found time or intellectual capacity to consider the new Britain that must come with peace and the place in it that Penguin must fill. The plans that, according to Segrave, would have filled a Penguin Special would have left space to spare if written down on one of Allen's envelopes; though the sentence which Segrave used as synthesis of the Penguin programme was accurate so far as it went, the future as Allen saw it might be expressed more cogently as 'more and more of the same and more and more of all that can legitimately be contained within the Penguin province'. Though his autocracy was real and had been exercised shrewdly and successfully for almost five years, Allen could not, or perhaps would not, accept that the continuing enlargement of Penguin demanded not merely delegation of authority but also, in some instances, abdication and the handing over of entire responsibility to others.

There was so much to do: reorganization on a grand scale and picayune problems of administration to settle. Allen had no intention of doing everything himself but he was accustomed to being involved in everything. He could not easily discard the habit.

That Dick would soon return from the Navy should have given Allen some comfort – there were tasks that he could entrust to his brother as to no one else – but Dick was the one man who must threaten his hegemony, and there was between him and Dick the shadow of John.

Several other members of the pre-war staff were due for demobilization. Allen's loyalty to the Penguin pioneers was intense to the edge of sentimentality. Whenever His Majesty dispensed with their services, then in that moment, he insisted, they could return to Penguin. There was, indeed, work enough and more for all, but slowly it was borne in upon Allen that it was not possible to pretend that 1945 was 1939. Penguin had changed and four, five or six years in the Services had changed the men who had gone away; they could not be shuffled back into their old jobs. Here was a new set of problems; as Allen became aware of it so also once again did all signs of boredom evaporate. The market-place, he realized, would soon be filled with young men eager for employment. Add some of these to his returning warriors and he could build a staff that would extend the line of Penguin success. Move the operational headquarters back to Harmondsworth, where the War Department had obligingly promised to leave behind the temporary buildings that it had added to the original Penguin office-block. From there, relieved of war-time frustrations, he and his eager subordinates could range out all over the world.

Once aroused to the need to reorganize and redeploy, Allen bustled into action with enthusiasm. It is doubtful if ever again he was as certain of his vocation or as content in his rule as he was in the eighteen months or so after VJ Day. It was as if he was founding Penguin all over again, this time with the assurance of successful precedent and the blessed comfort of money in the bank. Perhaps because his actions at that time were not inhibited by doubts, those months are rich with examples of Allen's idiosyncratic style of command. There had been and there would be again times when he showed himself to be mercurial, perverse, generous, malicious, a genius, a coward, a prevaricator or a man capable of bold and precise decision; in 1946 and 1947 he was all of these things virtually coincidentally.

Because Allen's conscience was never bruised by inconsistency, there is no neat or logical explanation for his motives and methods; yet linking all his professional decisions was an element of instinct, not easy to describe and impossible even for himself to define, that can be called the Penguin factor. It had influenced his actions almost from the days in the Crypt; though with diminishing force, it continued to affect him, sometimes disastrously until the very last days of his supreme power; but it was never so insistent as in those months of reconstruction and in nothing was it quite so compulsive or so obvious as in his manner of making appointments.

The presence of the Penguin factor in an aspirant to employment was not susceptible to measurement. Not even Allen could be certain that he could identify its existence in a single brief interview. To improve his chances of arriving eventually at the right selection Allen kept in a state of hopefulness many more men than he needed. Some were held by promises, and some were actually taken on to the staff, either to posts that did not exist or to posts that existed but were already held by someone else. Considered long after the event it is not easy to absolve Allen of callousness, but this was a time when hundreds of able young men were jockeying for jobs. Allen would have been irresponsible had he not taken advantage of the affection and respect which in a decade had come to surround Penguin, colouring the ambitions of many and making working for Allen one of the most coveted of all possibilities. Allen experimented on a scale that in other circumstances would have been considered vicious, and his experiments were undoubtedly, by all conventional measures, ludicrously expensive not only in human but also by simpler and cruder financial measure. He believed that he had every right to spend past profits to secure future development; to Allen's way of thinking risking his future was just one of the ordeals that a candidate for employment or advancement had to endure to prove that he was rich in the Penguin factor.

Years later, when discussing life at Penguin before the war, Eunice Frost commented on the 'amateurishness' of the staff, on the lack of inhibiting professionalism which melded a collection of youthful and inexperienced individuals into an effective team and which explained the zest, freshness and devotion of those who worked for Penguin. Allen's manner of conducting his experiments in the great days of post-war reconstruction would seem to indicate not only that Eunice Frost's assessment is justified but also that Allen was conscious of the advantages that had come with dedicated dilettantism. He had every intention of continuing and extending them into the next era. Of those who came new to Penguin – even of those who were given to understand by Allen that they might be allowed to come – very few had what the Posts Vacant columns describe as 'relevant experience'. Then, as for some years to come, it was Allen's view that most publishers engendered in their employees narrowness, timidity and dedication to the drearier conventions of the trade; service with some other publishing house was generally a disqualification to employment by Penguin. Even when he looked within the established Penguin staff before filling a post of novel or heightened responsibilities, still he made his decisions by some instinctive process which avoided consideration of professional qualifications or demonstrated skills.

Allen's friendship with Victor Weybright had ripened in the last two years of the war; as was his way with close acquaintances, he had from time to time discussed the possibility that Weybright might become associated with Penguin. Nothing had been decided and nothing communicated to Kurt Enoch in New York. Then, in the early summer of 1945, Weybright told Allen that he was about to leave the American Embassy and would soon be returning to the States. It suited Allen to be vague with Weybright and secretive with Enoch; though he was convinced that Weybright's knowledge of the American literary scene might be useful to Penguin Books Inc., he knew also that Weybright had no business experience. He thought it best to leave to Enoch the responsibility for accepting or rejecting his services.

The situation in Penguin Books Inc. was tense. The three leading American paperback houses, Pocket Books, Avon and Dell, were all planning post-war programmes based on long runs of essentially popular titles suitable, as they thought, for distribution through outlets, such as drug-stores, railroad and airport bookstalls and cigar stores, not ordinarily exploited by the book trade. Ballantine had advised Penguin to follow their example; when his advice was rejected, he had gone off to found Bantam Books, taking most of the Penguin staff with him.

So when Weybright arrived in Enoch's office, though as a stranger and though the suggestion that he put forward as from Allen was couched in the vaguest terms – nothing more definite than that he might join Penguin Books Inc. in some executive capacity – his arrival was well-timed. And so, in all probability just as Allen had planned, Enoch and Weybright came to work together.

In April 1946, R. W. Maynard was demobilized. In the early days of the war Maynard had taken on responsibilities that a conventional employer must have thought beyond the range of his age and experience; in those few months he had developed an intimacy with Allen such as was enjoyed by very few members of the staff. But all that was four years past; four years in which Maynard had served in many parts of the world as a naval officer but patently without adding to his knowledge of the book trade.

Yet Allen could not push him back to clerking and would not be rid of him. Within weeks of his return to civilian life Maynard was on a ship bound for Australia, to serve as Allen's representative there.

Hitherto Penguin's business in Australasia had been in the hands of an agent, and Allen was convinced that the poor results were due to the agent's indolence. Even so, he did not see Australia and New Zealand as significant for the future of Penguin. He might have allowed the agent to muddle on had he not felt compelled to find something for Maynard consonant with his ten-year association with Penguin and which provided a suitable return on Allen's hitherto unproductive investment in him, the salary paid throughout his naval career. If he thought fit, Maynard was to sack the agent and thereafter look into the possibility of establishing in Australia a full-scale Penguin operation, with himself at its head.

Once he had proposed a solution Allen could believe that he had disposed of a problem. Having sent both Eunice Frost and Weybright to join Enoch in New York and having despatched Maynard to Melbourne, Allen was ready to assume that he had settled the shape of the Penguin organization in North America and in Australia, his intentions already Penguin achievements. Now he could leave distant places to these plenipotentiaries and, at least for the moment, concentrate his attention upon enlarging and reorganizing Harmondsworth.

Then, and only then, did he become fully aware of the weakness of his headquarters staff and of the gaps that needed to be filled. Although even now it was not his intention to set up the severely compartmentalized structure common to most publishers, he could but accept that all the functions that were in other publishing houses performed by departmental heads must be covered somehow at Penguin. Looked at thus, he had Olney as Company Secretary; the only other department that might be adequately staffed was Editorial, with Eunice Frost (once she returned from New York) and Alan Glover. He had no obvious candidate to take the place of John as Home and Export Sales Manager. During the war Edward Young had added a DSO, a DSC and the distinction of being the first Volunteer Reserve officer to command a submarine to his pre-war glory as the artist who had drawn the original Penguin device; but Young had decided not to return to Penguin and Allen saw no one to take his place as a potential Production Manager. Before the war the firm had distributed a free news-sheet, *Penguins Progress*, but more publicity had come to Penguin either because of the adventurousness and novelty of the firm's editorial and pricing policies or because Allen had himself cornered some journalist of his acquaintance and charmed or bribed him into writing about Penguin. The shortage of paper during the war years put a premium on casual publicity and made impossible the production of the publicity leaflet, but as the firm sold everything that it published with no great difficulty the absence of publicity was insignificant. It was, however, obvious to Allen that amid increasing competition Penguin needed something more aggressive than the lackadaisical publicity arrangements which had sufficed in war-time and more deliberate than the opportunism which had served well enough before September 1939. It was still intrinsic to his publishing theology that a paperback house could neither afford nor profit from press advertising; what Penguin needed, in addition to comment in the editorial columns coveted by all manufacturers, were direct links with book buyers all over the world. Put in terms appropriate to the conventional organizations of a conventional publisher, Allen was looking for a Publicity Manager, but there was more in his mind than could be implied by this title. When, late in 1945, he drafted a memorandum to Williams on the subject of staff reorganization he labelled the vacancy in a fashion never before used in publishing: Public Relations Manager. For that job, he said, which would 'subsume the editorship of *Penguins Progress*', there was no obvious candidate at Harmondsworth.

Precise definition of the posts that must be filled could give the impression that Allen was himself aware of precision in his *desiderata*, an impression that may be strengthened by the quotation from his note to Williams (the only record of its kind which survives). However, the drawing of demarcation lines was not consistent with his nature. The experience of most of those who came to Penguin in the post-war reconstruction period supports the view that he wished to create a team which in its totality would handle all the jobs that needed to be performed. Except in the more technical departments, he had no intention of preventing the overlapping of skills and functions; rather, because he considered competition healthy and insecurity a spur to energy, he did his best to make certain that no senior Penguin employee could ever be an island.

In terms of total manpower Penguin was still a tiny firm. It would still be tiny even if Allen doubled the size of his staff – and Allen had no wish to be that expansive – but there was a danger, which he recognized, that if he added a few bright newcomers to his promoted returning servicemen he would find himself supported by a council of chiefs, but of chiefs without Indians. There was, as Allen saw it, no certain way out, but again it helped if the hierarchical order was undefined and the boundaries of responsibility blurred. He who possessed the Penguin factor would carve out his own principality within the Penguin empire; the weaker sort would leave or stay on as subordinates.

Among those who came into Penguin at this period were several who played an important part in the future of the firm and some who did not stay long at Harmondsworth but who nevertheless achieved distinction elsewhere. Ruari McLean, Hans Schmoller, Harry Paroissien, Jack Morpurgo, Tatyana Kent (later Tatyana Schmoller), Peter Messer, Peter Wyld: all were newcomers, and there were of the pre-war staff returning from the Services, in addition to Dick Lane and Bob Maynard, Peter Kite, Jack Summers and Ron Blass. Allen made several half-hearted attempts to find someone for the role which in other houses would belong to the Sales Manager but, perhaps because he could never resist the temptation to interfere in sales matters, not one appointee survived more than a few months. Only with the arrival of Paroissien in February 1947 did Penguin have a Sales Manager who had the experience and the personality which persuaded Allen to grant him authority.

The situation in Production was similarly indeterminate; because here Allen's enthusiasm was genuine but erratic and unprofessional, the seniority in this vital department was for several years a matter of dispute. Though after the appointment of Schmoller as typographer it was immediately obvious that his influence over design must be powerful, it was still some time before he appeared as the unchallenged and unchallengeable chief of Production.

Although it was a novel creation, and just because of its

novelty of especial interest to Allen, the office of Public Relations Manager did not have such significance for the future of Penguin, but, for reasons that will become obvious, the short history of this unique post is in all its details known to Allen's biographer. For this reason and because it contains almost every element of Allen's characteristic behaviour in selection, negotiations and administrative practice, it merits re-telling.

On several occasions in 1943 and 1944 Allen had hinted to Edmond Segrave that either a place could be found for him within the Penguin organization or else that he could be given a retainer as adviser on publicity. Segrave's reply was unvaried: he was fond of Allen, he admired Penguin and he would do all that in decency he could do to further the Penguin cause, but he preferred the solid security, the independence and the authority of the editorial chair at the *Bookseller* to the uncertainties of the Penguin heaven. When at last Allen was convinced that Segrave meant what he said, he also persuaded himself that it was not Segrave that he wanted: he had not devised the post to fit the man, but truly needed someone to direct Penguin publicity.

His friend Tom Fairley had suggested that he might join Penguin once the war was over. Fairley had proved himself as an editor with *Transatlantic*, and at first Allen promised him no more than that he could edit *Penguins Progress*, if and when it was revived, but in the course of many conversations there developed between them a much more elaborate vision of Fairley's post-war role.

Fairley had experience of the new-fangled profession of public relations consultant and was able to convince Allen that he could build upon the success which Penguin had always had in reaching the public without advertising. Almost from the beginning Penguin readers had ascribed to the firm a personality which drew from them a body of correspondence, of praise, complaint and suggestion, such as came to no other publishing house. Answering this correspondence in a manner that would not seem routine or superior was by no means easy, but Fairley could manage it better than most.

As they talked, Allen added to Fairley's brief another function which could not be regarded as within the ordinary province of a publicity manager, even of a publicity manager beginning to acquire the titular dignity of Public Relations Manager. Despite his dislike for Gollancz Allen had been much impressed by the success of the Left Book Club; he had measured with envious eyes the prosperity of American book clubs; and, when he had sampled the letters coming to Penguin from the public, he had noticed as a recurring theme a suggestion which, though it was couched in a variety of ways, was always close to the proposal that Penguin should establish its own book club. Some correspondents asked that Penguin post to them all Pelicans in a subject area, all novels, all detective stories, or all Puffins. Some offered to send cheques – for sums up to £100 – as payment in advance for all Penguins. To create a service of this kind in wartime had been unnecessary and impossible; if after the war it could be systematized and publicized, above all to readers in the outposts of Empire, the benefit to Penguin could be enormous. Allen shrugged off the objection that direct selling was anathema to the Publishers Association with the undeniable comment that the Publishers Association was anathema to him; to the more cogent criticism that successful direct selling must antagonize booksellers and might therefore explode in his face he replied that booksellers needed Penguin as much as he needed booksellers.

There was no written agreement between Allen and Fairley nor even an explicit promise that Fairley would be employed by Penguin, but the probability was conveyed to him frequently, not least by the amount of time that Allen spent in his company discussing the tasks that would be given to the Public Relations Manager. All that stood between Fairley and Penguin – or so it was implied – were the Axis Powers. Once they were defeated and Fairley released from the Ministry his place in Penguin was assured.

Two days after VE Day Jack Morpurgo* returned to England. He was then a few days over twenty-seven, he had been in the Army since September 1939 and he had served overseas – 'in twenty-six countries, two major campaigns and four little wars' – since the winter of 1940. He had no intention of abandoning a career as a writer and historian which had been interrupted by

*From this point on I write of myself in the third person, not from any unnatural coyness but because I sense that one first person singular would be intrusive among the many third persons of the narrative. I cannot pretend to dispassion about events in which I played some part or about persons who have influenced my life, but I can assure readers that the passages in which I appear are not written as autobiography. Wherever possible I have checked my recollection against written evidence and on occasion I have abandoned long-held convictions in favour of the opinions of others better qualified than I to judge. J.E.M.

service in the Army but could not afford to live entirely in the shadowy suburbs of academe. Yet no sooner was he back in England than he was offered a post as an extra-mural tutor by Oxford University.

God and the Military Secretary, both of them given to quirky decisions, then took a hand. Morpurgo was categorized 'demobilization deferred indefinitely' given a large room overlooking Whitehall, a pompous title and an ATS secretary. The Public Relations Directorate of the War Office was not at that time overworked and Morpurgo found himself admirably placed to make contacts which might help him escape a life of evenings teaching American History to earnest trade unionists in Staffordshire. From the Middle East, from Greece and Italy he had sent back to England short stories, articles and poems which had been published in various anthologies and journals, among them *Penguin New Writing*. From his War Office desk and with the skilful if unauthorized support of his War Office secretary he launched himself into literary journalism and (at first in breach of King's Regulations) into broadcasting. He was fortunate in his mentors; later it transpired that both John Lehmann and George Orwell mentioned his name to Allen, but it was Fairley who eventually brought the two together.

Morpurgo had been made a Fellow by his American college before the war and that prestigious title he still held (and its duties he was to continue for many years to come). He was, therefore, a useful contributor to *Transatlantic*. In a comparatively short time Fairley and Morpurgo had come to like each other and, without telling Morpurgo, Fairley had suggested to Allen that when he (Fairley) joined Penguin Morpurgo might take over the editorship of *Transatlantic*.

Allen was not in the least excited by the suggestion; though he had not revealed his intentions to Fairley, he was already planning to abandon *Transatlantic*. Perhaps because he had heard this young man's name three times in as many weeks from three seemingly irreproachable sources, and more probably because he was prepared to look at anyone who might be worth a place in the Harmondsworth hierarchy, Allen summoned Morpurgo to meet him in London. By the end of their first exchange Morpurgo believed that he had been offered a place in Penguin but, when no confirmation came from Allen – even after much prompting – he shut out his rosy dreams. Then, suddenly and as if nothing had passed between them previously, he was invited to Silverbeck. He could not credit that he was to be inspected all over again.

Morpurgo accepted the invitation. There was no reason for him to refuse; but he had no idea that he was being inspected and indeed during lunch Allen divided his time between his food, the telephone and three other guests. However, when the party broke up and just as Morpurgo was offering his thanks to Lettice Lane, Allen interrupted and demanded that he come for a tour of the gardens.

It was an activity which ordinarily Morpurgo abominated. He was also miserably aware that he had used his dubious authority to sign out a War Office car and driver for his trip to Silverbeck. But he could hardly refuse Allen's invitation, and for the next hour they wandered through the grounds in the hot sun. As Morpurgo remembered it later, Allen did most of the talking. Much of it was about farming, a subject in which Morpurgo was both ignorant and uninterested, and the only direct questions which he was asked were about his years at universities in Canada and the United States and his spell (briefer than he admitted) as drama critic of the *Egyptian Mail*. For a few minutes they stopped to talk to Allen's two small daughters who, stark naked, were splashing in and out of the ornamental pond.

They were approaching Morpurgo's car and the blowsy ATS driver was doing her poor best to wake up, to button her tunic and to get out of the back seat in one move when suddenly Allen stopped and said, 'Come and work for me.'

To this day Morpurgo believes that he was so taken aback that he did not reply but the pause may have been shorter than he imagined. He is aware that his driver was standing by, her hand on the door handle, while Allen offered him the job of Public Relations Manager, explained its various functions and dismissed as irrelevant Morpurgo's reservation that, dearly as he would like to work for Penguin, he was still a soldier and might still be a soldier in 1984. 'Come to us when you get out,' Allen replied, 'or come to us while you're in; you can't have all that much to do these days.'

Morpurgo agreed and drove off, elated and dazed. It was not until he was half-way back to London that he realized that Allen had not mentioned money and that he had not told Allen that he knew nothing about public relations. His job in the Public Relations Directorate of the War Office was almost entirely writing and editing war histories.

There followed months of typical Lane vacillation. At Allen's invitation, in War Office time and in uniform, Morpurgo attended all Penguin editorial meetings, in those days held at the offices at 117 Piccadilly which Williams had taken for his putative successor to the Army Bureau of Current Affairs, the civilian Bureau of Current Affairs, but Allen had gone off to South America to attempt to set up yet another Penguin subsidiary. When he came back he greeted Morpurgo as a friend but sidestepped all suggestions that they formalize the agreement made in the Silverbeck driveway. When, in March 1946, Morpurgo announced that he was to be released by the Army in April and must know if indeed he was to be employed by Penguin Allen grinned, promised him a contractual letter in the next post and that evening telephoned to say that, though he still wanted him as Public Relations Manager, it would be three or four months before space could be found at Harmondsworth for the new department.

Morpurgo lacked the courage to tell Allen that he did not intend to spend his gratuity on reserving himself for Penguin. He was about to take a job with the BBC when Williams intervened and offered him employment with the Bureau of Current Affairs until Allen was ready to use him. Two months later he was working at Harmondsworth; so also were two other ex-servicemen who, like Morpurgo, had been given to understand that they were to head a Public Relations Department.

It was several years before Morpurgo discovered that he had taken over the chair that had been promised to Fairley.

The struggle for power which Allen had contrived for his new department never materialized. One of the three contenders left almost immediately; another was obviously destined to be an also-ran; and Morpurgo himself soon became an ancillary editor, reviving unsuccessfully *Penguin Parade* and launching the very successful Penguin Histories. The Public Relations Department disintegrated. Letters from the public were once again answered by whosoever had time to deal with them; Glover, Morpurgo and (when she returned from New York) Eunice

Frost between them edited *Penguins Progress* and wrote most of it themselves; the mail-order business collapsed, not because of any pressure from the Publishers Association but because, once he gave it careful consideration, Allen realized that its costs were exorbitant. By 1950, when Morpurgo left Harmondsworth to take over another publishing firm (but remaining History Editor to Penguin), the only visible vestige of the Public Relations Department was the continuing service of the department's secretary, Irene Pierions, as the firm's principal (and best) blurb-writer. Whether it be called vacillation, selection by survival or bold experiment, the methods which Allen used to find himself a Public Relations Manager were in one detail or another, and sometimes in all, repeated by him as he sought to fill other posts.

Rare among Allen's appointments at that time, Paroissien was much more than a promising neophyte. He had behind him many years of service with the book-wholesaler, Simpkin Marshall and had toured the Middle East and North Africa as Commercial Books Officer for the British Council. At the time when Allen began to seek him out, he was Managing Director of the Book Export Scheme. Even so when, after months of Allen's habitually bonhomous courtship and a succession of not-quite-explicit promises, Paroissien finally agreed to join Penguin as Sales Manager, he was not unnaturally surprised by the sudden change in Allen's manner. Now Allen was no longer the pursuer but the pursued. Sulkily he admitted that before he could give Paroissien full responsibility for the Sales Department he would have to find alternative employment for the two men who then controlled sales in the United Kingdom market, but, when he saw Paroissien's enthusiasm for the whole venture vanishing, Allen's determination revived. His brother John, he said, had performed miracles with exports. Until the sales organization could be totally reshaped with Paroissien at its head, he could busy himself as Export Manager in the place left vacant by John's death. And there were hints – but no more – that this was the route to a directorship.

Paroissien was persuaded. When he arrived at Harmondsworth he discovered that the Export Department was a poetic fiction created by Allen out of distant recollections of pre-war days and of John's idiosyncratic but highly successful manner with overseas customers. During the war, though Penguins had been printed in many countries and though large stocks of British-produced Penguins had been sent abroad, most of this activity had necessarily been organized through official or quasi-official intermediaries. Such conventional export business as had been maintained had been loosely controlled by whichever member of the firm had the time and zeal to spare – often Allen himself. This deliberately unsystematic system had not been altered in the eighteen months between VJ Day and the advent of Paroissien. So he discovered that he could not be Export Manager until he constructed an Export Department, and that before he could construct an Export Department he must drag assistants out of other sections. But his first priorities were to find himself an office and to buy himself a desk.

Judged even by the harshest standards of commerce or industry it must seem that Allen was both casual and callous in his selection, manipulation and rejection of employees. A recital without embellishment of the case histories of some of his appointments must make a stranger to Allen and to Penguin wonder how it was that so many men and women – all of them able and most of them shrewd – allowed Allen to gamble with their lives and careers. The explanation is assuredly not financial: publishers pay badly, pay at Penguin was lower than at other publishing houses, and everybody who worked for Penguin knew it. There was undoubtedly common among the men who had survived the dangers and the boredom of war a fear of the future which made them seize any job lest they find none. For these who had behind them years of experience that was not easily negotiable in terms of peace-time utility, Allen's readiness to discount conventional qualifications was particularly convenient as was his promise of independence and excitement notably attractive to men who dreaded nothing so much as they dreaded routine.

Exegesis of this kind could explain the eagerness of McLean (from the Navy), Morpurgo and Wyld (from the Army) and Messer (from the United States Army). Tatyana Kent, half-British and half-Russian but born and reared in Uruguay, was in part attracted to Penguin because she was attracted to Britain. Her future husband, Hans Schmoller (who came to Penguin at the very end of the post-war reconstruction period), was a refugee from Nazi Germany who had spent nine years running a press in Basutoland, to whom working for one of the world's leading publishers in London was a delight. Even Paroissien, the most seasoned professional of the new entry, moved to Penguin in part because he had doubts about the future of the Book Export Scheme.

But all these rational motives added together do not come close to building a satisfactory explanation of the magnetic force which worked upon so many disparate personalities and compelled them to contract themselves to the confusing, erratic and insecure world of Penguin.

A mature bookman like Paroissien, who had watched the progress of Penguin from a well-placed observation post within the trade, was confident that the firm must prosper in the postwar world and was eager to be part of that prosperity. But Paroissien, and most of those who joined the firm at this time, condemned themselves willingly to the gamble of life with Penguin because they were essentially romantics, convinced that Penguin was in some vital but indefinable way outside the frontiers of publishing, more useful, more exciting and even more noble.

Then, as in earlier years and for a few years yet to come, the romantics on the staff believed that the most romantic of them all was Allen, and their assumption was by this time generally justified. Having succeeded initially by refusing to subject his impulses to the weight of other men's reason and experience, Allen had come to believe in the sovereignty of instinct. It was part of his charm and of his genius that he allowed to his subordinates what he claimed for himself – at least until their impulses collided with his own.

This sense of freedom, of licensed spontaneity, as much as the shortage of patently useful experience or obvious qualifications among the senior staff, justified Eunice Frost when she used the word 'amateurish' to describe activities at Penguin in the early days, and there was no great change in the atmosphere until the mid fifties. Yet Eunice Frost's description merits refinement: those who worked for Allen soon developed an intense professionalism but a professionalism that was only superficially similar to that of their contemporaries in other publishing houses. Versatility was at Penguin more treasured than expertise, a capacity for dour and sensible planning was less highly regarded than deftness or opportunism.

Those who worked at Harmondsworth in the late forties and early fifties are apt to look back nostalgically to that period. Even those among them who either failed to make their mark at Penguin or else, through no fault of their own, were treated by Allen in a way that was less than just, are ready to boast that they were part of Penguin's golden epoch. Their intimate opinion is shared by many informed observers. That was the period which saw the custom launched of issuing on one day one million volumes by a single author, which saw the beginnings of *Science News* and *New Biology* and the inauguration of several major Penguin series, the Histories, the Archaeologies, *The Buildings of England* and *The Pelican History of Art*. Allen was in some way or another responsible for instigating almost every one of these projects.

Looking back over the pioneering ventures of the post-war decade, it is easy to see how Penguins (the word is used generically) invaded the classroom and in time came close to making the old-fashioned textbook redundant in the upper forms of secondary schools and in higher education; only those who experienced from the inside the casual nature of Penguin planning can accept without question that the invasion was accidental. There is nice irony in the fact that Allen, who seldom lost a chance to remind his friends that he had left school at sixteen and who pretended to despise university graduates, can be numbered among the few men who have influenced teaching methods, not only in Britain but elsewhere in the world. And the irony is compounded when it is realized that Penguin made no deliberate attempt upon the educational market until long after this period and that when they did, in the mid sixties, the effort was comparatively short lived. In those halcyon days after the war, Allen's influence, though all-powerful, was also remarkably erratic. There is justice in the argument that he made his most significant contribution to the re-shaping and re-vivification of the firm, as also to the training of his younger colleagues, by absenting himself so often from Harmondsworth.

Released from the fortress conditions of Britain at war, he was able to make frequent short trips to the Continent and longer journeys to North and South America. He also abandoned, if only for himself, the doctrine of dispersal which had persuaded him to move Penguin headquarters to Harmondsworth. He now believed that he must be at the centre of life and took for himself at various times offices in different parts of central London.

From Silverbeck, from these central London eyries or directly from the airport or station on his return from a Continental trip, he would descend upon Harmondsworth, breeze through the corridors, invade offices and warehouses, read letters, call for the stock-books, chivvy the packers and then, if the time was appropriate, gather up those members of the staff who happened to be in favour that week and take them off to the Peggy Bedford or to Tom Girtin's White Horse at Longford. Harmondsworth then settled back into an atmosphere as near as Harmondsworth could ever manage to calm.

The only concessions to conventional administrative regularity were the 'weekly meetings' of heads of departments at Harmondsworth and the editorial selection sessions at 117 Piccadilly. The 'weekly' meetings were not held every week because Allen was so often absent and, when they were held, the composition of the gathering varied according to Allen's current partiality. The editorial meetings (still called Pelican meetings though their purpose was no longer confined to Pelicans) were summoned only when it was decided, by some process that remained and remains mysterious even to one who took part in them, that the supply of prospective titles was dangerously low.

Allen was still his own senior scout. Though more and more he left the seeking-out of authors and titles to his series editors, to Eunice Frost and to Glover, more often than not it was he, with some assistance from Williams, who sensed the direction of public interest and set Penguin to enlarge the enthusiasm from which he intended to profit.

It is never easy to discover the origins of fashion; it could be argued (as indeed this book has already suggested) that Penguin was ready for any explosion of excitement in a particular subject only because Allen hankered after ubiquity in the list: he did not, for example, foresee that the British public would develop curiosity on a grand scale about archaeology and most certainly did not use Pelicans to produce that curiosity. Rather, archaeology was just one of the many lines explored, and so when archaeology became almost as popular as football (largely through the influence of the BBC programme *Animal, Vegetable and Mineral* and the stellar personality of Mortimer Wheeler) there were the Pelican Archaeologies, edited by Agatha Christie's husband Professor Max Mallowan, already available to enlarge and support understanding.

This theory has a certain resemblance to blanket-bombing: drop enough bombs over a sufficiently wide area and some of them are bound to find targets. In any analysis of Allen's philosophy of management it gathers support from the analogous tendency to take on more staff than he needed in the belief that among the many he would find the few who were his natural collaborators. But some of his initiatives were beyond the frontiers of ubiquity; they would be classed as lunatic had they not proved so successful.

Of these the outstanding example is the translation of *The Odyssey* and the subsequent (and still continuing) series of Penguin Classics. The editors of other houses' reprint series had long since included in their lists translations of the great books of the ancient world. There was, already long before 1946, a tired inevitability about publishers' attempts to make profits out of the adventures of Odysseus so that even those within Penguin who were accustomed to Allen's impulses ('I met a man at a party last night and I think he has a book . . .') were ready to argue when he announced that he intended to commission E. V. Rieu to translate *The Odyssey* as the first Penguin Classic. They pointed out that between the wars there had been eight different versions of *The Odyssey* circulating in Britain; five were newly published, and of these five only two had sold more than 3000 copies.

Allen did not flinch and the devil's advocates passed on to their next argument. If Penguin must move into this difficult and over-crowded field would it not be wise to seek out either a distinguished scholar or a well-known writer? Rieu was neither; he was a retired publisher, and even in that capacity not entirely respectable, for he had spent most of his life editing and selling school textbooks. His only claim to literary reputation depended upon a volume of light verse published by his own firm in 1933.

Dick did not enter the argument but he was known to favour a general lightening of the Penguin list. *The Odyssey* was hardly a suitable ingredient for the recipe that he had in mind. Glover was a formidable classical scholar and expressed doubts about the accuracy of Rieu's translation. Williams knew no Greek but he was a sound judge of English style; when he saw the specimen chapters he conceded cheerfully that Rieu had 'made a good story better' and that *The Odyssey* might sell. Even so, he was far from certain about a series; a Penguin section devoted entirely to translations of the classics would succeed only if it included early in its development some authors 'more obviously popular' than Homer: 'Balzac, Maupassant or Chekhov for example'. Morpurgo, who was shown the complete typescript a few days after his first meeting with Allen (and, he discovered later, months after the decision to publish had been taken) reported that 'he liked the vigour of the translation but missed the poetry'.

Allen, who knew rather less Greek than his chauffeur and who admitted later that he had 'never read *The Odyssey*, only the first two chapters of Rieu's translation', commissioned Rieu and encouraged him to look for other translations of other classics. He pacified his critics with the tale that he intended to use *The Odyssey* as a loss-leader. By the summer of 1978 Penguins had sold 2,255,000 copies of Rieu's *Odyssey*, there were almost 350 titles in the Penguin Classics and translations had been included from almost every literature of the ancient and modern worlds!

Uninformed but prescient decisions such as this – and there are many in the history of Penguin – confirm the view of Allen as a leader whose gifts were largely instinctive. He made no attempt to discourage this opinion, which freed him from the need to rationalize his motives, even to his closest colleagues. Also, because of his disinclination to commit his ideas to paper, it is often difficult for the chronicler to establish any prelude of thought to an explosion of action. Many of the best stories about Allen could serve as parables to his capacity for unpremeditated but superbly consequential decision, and of them all none has been repeated so often by his admirers as the tale of the employment of Jan Tschichold.

One day in 1947 – so runs the story – Allen was lunching with Oliver Simon, one of the greatest of English book-designers. In a way that was undoubtedly typical, he asked a number of direct questions, among them: 'Who do you think is the best typographer in the world?' Answer: Jan Tschichold, a German living and working in Switzerland. 'Can we get him?' Almost before his friend had completed an expressive shrug Allen was at the telephone calling, first, Tschichold in Switzerland and then an air-taxi service. Within twenty-four hours he had contracted Tschichold to come to England.

The story has verisimilitude, even if it is not true in all its details, and it is certainly true that Allen had acted without consulting Dick, his only fellow-director (who was not best pleased when he discovered that the salary offered to Tschichold was more than his and Allen's added together) and without obtaining permission from Exchange Control to employ a foreigner who must remit sterling out of Britain.

Dick was bludgeoned into accepting Allen's decision ('we had long arguments about it but eventually Allen had his way'). Exchange Control was placated. As Allen was conveniently abroad when Tschichold arrived to take up his duties he spared himself the problems caused by the typographer's indifferent command of spoken and written English.

Nevertheless his decision to bring in a renowned and expensive typographer was not as spontaneous as Allen allowed the world to think. His genuine and long-standing interest in good design had been frustrated by the uncomfortable austerities of wartime. Now that more prodigal times seemed imminent he was ready to settle for Penguin a grammar of design that would sustain into the future the advantages of immediate recognition that had been a major premise of his publishing philosophy since 1935. There was, he felt, no individual within the Production Department at Harmondsworth who had the weight to persuade his colleagues to accept his tenets of design.

So, even if Allen did not know it until it was pointed out to him at that famous lunch, his thinking was already leading him towards a typographer of Tschichold's calibre and reputation before ever he heard his name, and one prejudice, strongly held by Allen, made the selection of Tschichold if not inevitable then at very least likely. In Britain and more particularly in the United States, most rival paperback firms used pictorial covers; there were, even at Harmondsworth, occasional murmurs of envy and across the Atlantic the executives of Penguin Books Inc. were strident in their insistence that without pictorial covers Penguin could never hope to compete in a market where sales success depended largely on exposure (in the circumstances a precise word!) in drug-stores, department stores and the new supermarkets. When it was necessary for him to argue his case Allen took to himself a devout puritanism, insisting that he objected to the lubricity and dishonesty of the 'bosoms and bottoms' school of jacket-designers. His revulsion was probably genuine, and certainly he held to it for the rest of his life, but even more persuasive was his determination to ensure that no other paperback could ever be mistaken for a Penguin and that no Penguin could ever be thought to have been produced by some other firm. He believed that he could isolate Penguin from the competition by holding to typographical covers. So for his overall production policy he must go to a man whose fame depended largely upon his skills in manipulating type and design.

The rightness of his choice is proven by the achievement. Tschichold laid down for Penguin certain design rules which continued, though with enhanced elegance, the decent directness of early Penguins and which set patterns which survived for almost twenty years.

As in the Tschichold affair so also in many other issues, good order and sense was most often argued by Dick and rejected by Allen, less often by specific statement than by the simple but crushing method of acting as if Dick's objections had not been uttered. Dick urged that 'we define accurately everyone's position in the firm'; Allen handed out tasks to his subordinates in a manner that even now would seem erratic were it not for its record of achievement. Dick suggested that they spend more time at Harmondsworth; Allen disappeared for weeks on end. Dick passed to Allen an opinion held by Williams 'that pre-war selling conditions will return very shortly' and his own view that 'the home market should have our first priority, with export as a luxury'; Allen busied himself with expansion overseas. There was little friction between the two brothers; they were no longer close enough for friction. 'I dislike people who call themselves directors,' Dick wrote to Allen in August 1947, '[but] as this is our job we should aim to carry it out.' There were two names on Penguin's letter-head, Allen Lane and Richard Lane, but Allen had cut the Penguin cloth to suit his style and the cloak could not cover the two brothers. Dick's admiration for Allen's flair was unabated; whenever it seemed that respect must be shattered by Allen's refusal to pay heed to his sensible advice, Allen restored his confidence by some extraordinary coup.

It was not only Dick who was wrong-footed by Allen's sudden bursts of magnificently creative and original energy. Sometimes in one of the loosely organized departments, and occasionally in all at once, irritability caused by Allen's alternating indifference and bustling interference simmered, boiled and seemed about to explode into mutiny. Then, as if he had his eye forever on the pressure-gauge, Allen stepped in with some novel adventure which persuaded even the most disgruntled to forget his grievances and to remember once again that he was a member of a unique and uniquely privileged team.

There was, for example, the ninetieth-birthday edition of the works of Bernard Shaw. In a suitably breathless and self-indulgent article *Penguins Progress* described this 'great occasion' as a tribute to 'the most celebrated nonagenarian in post-Biblical history'. Almost certainly an author had never before lived to see one million copies of his works published on one day – certainly not at one shilling a volume – but the events of 26 July 1946 were almost as much a tribute from Shaw to Allen, proof of his continuing admiration and support for Penguins; 'The old boy ... has a very great personal regard for you,' Dick wrote to Allen; and that 'personal regard' is apparent in all the dealings between Shaw and Penguin, in his gentle treatment of the inexperienced Penguin editors who had immediate responsibility for preparing the ten-volume edition for the press, and in his frequent assertion that Penguin, his publishers, were in manner and authority different from those other firms which he had from time to time 'authorized to distribute' his works:

> My agreement with Dodd, Mead & Co. [he wrote] is that whilst they have the exclusive right (or license rather) to deal with editions selling at $2.50, or thereabouts, I am left free in regard to cheap editions of 50 or 100 thousand, which they, being old-fashioned, are unable to handle. . . .

Even with Penguin Shaw insisted on his eccentric orthography. William Maxwell of R. & R. Clark of Edinburgh was the only printer in the Kingdom who had experience of the ways of Shaw, so Penguin had to print their edition in Scotland.

On another matter, however, Shaw was remarkably docile. A list of the proposed ten titles was put to Shaw, in Allen's absence, by Glover. Back came a Shaw postcard:

> The ten volume arrangement you suggest is all right except for the titles Pleasant & Unpleasant. The Unpleasant volume has always been a bad seller: the result of crying stinking fish. It may be wiser to call them Three First Plays and Four Popular Plays or something of the sort.

There was consternation at Harmondsworth. It was argued, and with justice, that abandoning the familiar titles must confuse the buying public. Allen came late into the discussions, listened to the opinion of his colleagues, rang Blanche Patch (Shaw's secretary) and within an hour was at Hounslow West station on his way to see Shaw at Whitehall Court. The two collections appeared as *Plays Unpleasant* and *Plays Pleasant*.

Many other millions came from Penguin in the years that followed but, with the possible exception of the Lawrence Million (and that for peculiar reasons), none excited the public as much as the first. Not any other Million nor yet any other occasion in Penguin history is such an exquisite example of Allen's unorthodox leadership. From preliminary negotiation to publication the whole process lasted for a little under eight months, and in that period almost every member of the staff was involved in some way. In the weeks immediately before publication the professional packers worked overtime and at the last were joined by members of the sales and editorial staffs who could be spared from answering calls from the press. Pre-publication orders from booksellers justified the boldness of the venture and at the Blue Diamond Café, that greasy-spoon next to the Harmondsworth offices where senior staff regularly drank nauseating coffee to wash away the appalling taste of the Penguin canteen lunch, a sweepstake was organized on forecasts of the date when the million volumes would be sold out. Nothing extraordinary beyond all that was already out of the ordinary was planned for the publication date, Shaw's birthday. Allen and Williams were to be present at a ninetieth-birthday party given at the National Book League but it was generally believed that Shaw himself would not attend. Morpurgo was to represent Penguin at the midnight matinée at the Arts Theatre when he would give specially bound sets of the ten volumes to Alec Clunes and Jack Hawkins, the leading actors in the Birthday performance of the Don Juan scene from *Man and Superman*. But it was not envisaged that the day would be in any administrative sense sensational. Even so, by eight o'clock on the morning of 26

July there was present at Harmondsworth almost all the Penguin staff. Everyone had a different but equally specious excuse for arriving early, and at 8.45 a.m. the first telephone call made excuses irrelevant.

That first call came from the manager of the W. H. Smith bookshop in Baker Street. He had entered his shop, as usual, by a back door from the Underground station and, looking out casually into the street, he had been surprised by the length of the queue for buses. Surprise had turned to elation when he realized that the orderly line was formed not of morning commuters but of members of the reading public waiting for Smith's to open so that they might make sure of their Penguin Shaw Ten. In all his years as a bookseller he had never seen anything like it; he had to tell someone and so he rang Penguin.

By nine o'clock the news from Baker Street had reached every Penguin office and every corner of the Harmondsworth warehouse. Of itself it was almost enough to make up for muddle, bad pay and cavalier treatment, but more and better was to come. Before noon the switchboard was jammed and the operator was distributing calls indiscriminately to whichever extension happened to be free. Booksellers from all over the country were ringing through orders for replenishment stocks, members of the public calling to complain that their local shop had no Shaws on sale, and reporters to enquire if it was true that Shaw had demanded an advance of £50,000. (It was not; his contract was no different from that of any other Penguin author and his earnings from the Million added eventually to £3750.)

The Million sold out in just over six weeks; after much debate it was decided to award the sweepstake prize to Glover, the most optimistic soothsayer, who had forecast New Year's Eve 1946, and it was benevolently agreed that the Jeremiah who had plumped for 26 July 1948 would not be fined for his gloom.

The stimulation provided by the Shaw Million kept the staff at a high pitch of excitement – and loyalty – for several months and survived even the shock of discovering that one of the titles, *The Black Girl in Search of God*, was banned in Eire. Not only was all the carefully designed packaging and display material of no use for Ireland but also every parcel intended for the Republic had to be unpacked, its contents purified by extracting the one offending title, and then re-packed; a Shaw Ten reduced to a Shaw Nine.

Flurries of sensational activity such as the publication of the Shaw Million were also the occasions which held for Penguin its lead over all other paperback publishers in the affections of journalists. There was, it seemed, always something brewing at Harmondsworth that was worth a paragraph, a column, even a page. Because Penguin was so often in the news, so also was Penguin, more than any other paperback house, familiar to the public – even to that large part of the public which never bought books.

It was at this time, in the years that followed immediately after the war, that the word 'penguin' began to be used by the public as a synonym for a paperbacked book. The habit of the generality was faithfully reproduced by dramatists and script-writers but the grand inquisitors at the BBC refused to condone such blatant advertising; whenever the word 'penguin' appeared in the script of a play or documentary it was excised by a censorious editor and in its place the author was forced to invent some inelegant circumlocution: for example, 'an inexpensive book bound in paper covers'. For several years Penguin staff fought an intermittent battle with the BBC hierarchy and at the last it was conceded that 'penguin' like 'mackintosh' or 'hoover' had entered the language, acceptable as what Gilbert Harding (who joined the campaign on its behalf) called 'an unproper noun'. Years later Morpurgo boasted to Allen that this victory was his one great achievement as Public Relations Manager. He was somewhat taken aback when Allen rounded on him. 'And because of you, now every sleazy production published by shoddy publishers in Warrington is called a Penguin.'

(Twenty and more years later when in the English-speaking world the word 'paperback' has become commonplace usage it may be necessary to indulge in a little parenthetical scholarship. 'Paperback' was rarely used as a noun in the early days of the 'paperback movement'. It does not appear in *Penguins Progress* until 1952 and was rarely used in the British Press before 1946. In the United States, as in Britain, both public and press derived the popular name for the *genus* from the pioneering firm, in America Pocket Books Inc. Although the American language permits another meaning to the noun, pocket-book remained in the American vocabulary as the word most often used to describe all paperbacks until about the same time when in Britain the slipshod use of 'penguin' was abandoned. In 1953 the French who, though they had always bound their books in paper covers, came late into paperbacks, purloined the American term, and gallicized it as 'Le Livre de Poche', the generic title given to the first French series which, by contemporary definition was paperback. *Taschenbuch* has been in the German dictionary since the eighteenth century, but for almost 200 years the word suggested to Germans almost exclusively those miniature editions of the poets which romantic young men carry in their pockets on country walks; and it was not until 1950 that Allen's friend Ernst Rowohlt launched in West Germany the first series which justified the definition of *Taschenbuch* that could be applied to this day: 'a German book akin to those published in English by Penguin Books Ltd and Pocket Books Inc.'.)

Though it is possible to sustain the argument that it was the Shaw Million (and similar, less grandiose occasions) which won the notice of the press and held press, public and even to a considerable extent the Penguin staff to the conviction that Penguin was unique, not just better than its ever-multiplying and utterly different competitors, somehow blessed by the gods of literature and privileged as no other paperback house to pluck the finest fruits of the literary harvest for popular feasting, it is not so easy to be certain of Allen's attitude. His view of public relations as of personnel management was never subtle and seldom intellectualized; though he was not insensitive to the effect of a circus upon the morale of his staff and upon the public attitude to Penguin, his enthusiasm for big events, parties, novelties was engendered not so much by considerations of policy as by the long-standing and incurable disease: his incapacity to tolerate routine. Not all of his ways of fending off boredom were as profitable or as sensible as the decision to publish the Shaw Million. Sometimes indeed his prophylactics were vacuous. Suddenly he would decide to count the books in the warehouse. Sometimes his cure was self-indulgent: a trip to the Continent or Ireland. For almost two years after the war he kept himself amused, as he had before the move to Harmondsworth, by planning a new headquarters, this time at West Drayton, but his elaborate and practical scheme was frustrated by the local authority and his many stimulating discussions with architects and landscape artists came to an end – for the moment.

He could not discover in his home life a panacea against boredom. He was suitably proud of his two attractive daughters, but fatherhood was for him yet another routine activity for which he could find only fitful enthusiasm. In the relationship between Allen and Lettice there were on both sides suspicions and misunderstandings; though in the formal sense the marriage held for several years, there was never any real possibility that the two would find serenity in each other's company once their third daughter was born a mongol. In later years this tragedy exposed in Allen some of his finest and kindlier qualities and he showed to Anna tenderness, patience and protectiveness such as he seldom, if ever, revealed to any other; but immediately his pride was hurt, he refused to admit that he had helped to create something that was less than perfect and he lashed out with accusations that no woman could be expected to forgive.

Because Allen feared boredom above all else, his quest for the opiate of change – though primarily for his own satisfaction – often created excitements for those who worked with him. Thus, early in 1948 Allen shattered the tedium of an uncommonly dreary 'weekly' meeting by suddenly announcing: 'I think we're getting into a rut.' As for the best part of an hour he had been analysing stock-sheets, those present were not inclined to disagree. He ordered, 'Someone must come up with an idea.' Like students demonstrating that their tutor's perplexing question is not addressed to them, all in the room busied themselves with notebooks and cigarette-lighters and then, just as a tutor faced with this elaborate resignation from responsibility must isolate and identify a victim, so also did Allen. Morpurgo was foolish enough to allow his eye to be caught. 'Come on, Jack, something to wake us up.' Some hitherto half-considered idea flashed onto the blank sheet of his mind and immediately Morpurgo blurted out 'pocket scores'. (Later he remembered that he had once discussed the notion casually with Ralph Hill, the Editor of *Penguin Music Magazine*.) Allen's response was not immediate: the words meant nothing to him; but within an hour Morpurgo, who would never describe himself as a musician, was lumbered with finding out about the economics of music publishing.

Four weeks later the distinguished composer Gordon Jacob accepted an invitation to edit a series of scores. With a little assistance from Glover and Morpurgo, but with none from Allen, he selected from among the great works of the great musicians the ten compositions that appear most often in the concert repertoire and in the record catalogues. As was the Penguin custom, the ten would be published simultaneously. First the Production Department and then the sales representatives had to master techniques and practicalities which were for them entirely novel. This they did, the designer, Jan Tschichold, with notable brilliance so that the Penguin Scores are still remembered, by experts and by music-lovers, as the most useful and elegant miniature scores produced in this century.

Unfortunately the plan to engineer yet another Penguin occasion by putting ten scores on the market on one day was disrupted by the unpunctuality of some of the critics who were writing introductions. The first three, Mozart's *Symphony No. 40*, Bach's *Brandenburg No. 3* and Beethoven's *Coriolan and Egmont Overtures*, were in June 1949 received with enthusiasm both by the critics and by the public.

Allen, however, had lost interest. He had followed his instinct by accepting a suggestion which presaged a new adventure and which seemed to lead Penguin further on the way to ubiquity, but it needed very little afterthought to alert him to the realities. The ability to read music is not widespread and even among those who have mastered the skills only a small proportion are competent or willing to follow a score. Therefore, the market for Penguin Music Scores must remain small and, because the sales outlets for scores are necessarily different from those commonly worked for books, there could be little hope that the Scores could be used as a loss-leader or, conversely, could be made to benefit from the impulse-buying which so often overcame book lovers when surrounded in a bookshop by Penguins of various kinds.

Allen's reason for withdrawing his benediction from the Scores were sane and sound; behind them there was also another motive, by no means irrational but far more personal. In all else that Penguin published Allen, even if far from expert, was never so ignorant as to be reduced to inarticulacy. Novels, children's books, illustrated books, art books: on all these he had something to say, generally something that was fresh or illuminating. Even when faced with the most abstruse non-fiction, if the subject matter was outside his intellectual competence, he could always fall back upon discussions of the printing and design. But despite distant recollections of Mendelssohn solos sung in a Bristol church, he knew nothing about music and, from his point of view even more debilitating, he knew nothing about music publishing and nothing about music printing.

He did recognize that the Scores were prestigious; even more to his credit, he not only conceded that work on the Scores gave considerable pleasure to some of his staff but was prepared to allow that this pleasure should continue for as long as the series was, by the most generous interpretation, self-supporting. At the last, after seven years and thirty titles, as with so many of Penguin's most adventurous series, it was mounting costs and not Allen's lack of interest which brought to an end the history of the Penguin Music Scores.

No less than his collaborators Allen had come to believe what others had told him almost from the beginning of Penguin, that he was leading a mission. This expansive view of his role in society was justified for him when Bristol University conferred upon him an honorary degree. Recognition in this kind comes but rarely to commercial publishers; Allen was in many ways a romantic; he, who had boasted so often that he left school at sixteen, was now just as quick to boast that by his work he had achieved academic respectability and he was extravagantly delighted that the tribute had come from his own home city. Some of his friends, more sophisticated than he in the ways of universities, were less pleased: it is symptomatic of the contradictoriness of the loyalty that he inspired and of the peculiar sense of protective care that this often uncaring man aroused in others that it was not fear of his anger but unwillingness to hurt or disappoint him which silenced those who could tell him that an Honorary Master of Arts degree is ordinarily conferred upon a retiring Chief Clerk in the University Registry and that, for the man who had changed the face of publishing, of secondary and university education, an MA is not an honour but almost an insult.

If, for all that it was perverse and erratic, Allen's mode of command was generally effective at Harmondsworth and his personality for the most part compelling even upon those in Britain who suffered most from his fickleness, neither mode of command nor personality were designed to be exported. Not the least of reasons for the inability of Penguin to exploit their presence in the United States was Allen's failure to develop an American persona comprehensible to his American collaborators and the consequent suspicion that somehow he intended to keep Penguin Books Inc. in a state of colonial subservience to the imperial power of Harmondsworth. The very 'amateurism' of the home-based company was anathema in a country where even publishing, that most instinctive and unstructured of all commercial exercises, was in the forties and fifties much more than its British equivalent infected by the highly intellectualized structures of the business schools. Weybright and Enoch soon resolved their own differences and came together in alliance against what they regarded as the indifference of Allen and his collaborators to their reasoned and reasonable statements about the huge potential of the United States market. At the outset to his emissaries, Dick and Eunice Frost, and eventually to Allen himself they set out the facts: 'the statistics on college matriculation, on the ultimate high school increase that would ensue from the baby-boom . . . on compulsory attendance in high schools . . . on the GI Bill of Rights'. At first they hinted, then they suggested, and at the last they demanded: that Penguin Books Inc. be given authority to plan and develop, freed from fear of inhibition or proscription by the parent firm.

Whenever he was pressed Allen conceded the point, but concession was never translated into formal and legal reorganization.

The generalized, constitutional and methodological differences between Allen and his American colleagues were crystallized in disputes over editorial policy and presentation.

The argument over editorial policies found Allen immediately and Weybright eventually in defensive but equally illogical and unjustifiable positions. Early in their association Weybright had recommended that the American house should buy the rights on the Southern novelist, Erskine Caldwell. Allen's response was facetious: Penguin Books Inc. must set up a separate imprint – called perhaps Porno Books. But he did not veto the purchase and, according to Weybright, his chagrin was real when Caldwell's *God's Little Acre* sustained Penguin Books Inc. during a temporary slump in the market late in 1946; it was undoubtedly intensified when Caldwell, having been signed for a British house by a refugee from Harmondsworth, by his fantastic sales figures made possible the future of an upstart and hitherto small London firm. Allen objected also when Weybright took on James M. Cain, James T. Farrell and from William Faulkner the greatest of all American novelists, the least (but undeniably the most pornographic) of his books, *Sanctuary*. All were, according to Weybright, 'too gamey' for Allen's taste. 'He was,' Weybright wrote years later, 'still far from being a convinced general publisher of serious modern literature that might offend the parsons and squeamish readers of the United Kingdom' and, he continued, 'as the years ran on he changed his mind, but too late to keep in step with us in New York'.

It was a comment that cannot be justified by the record: the man who had first published *Ulysses* in Britain could not be accused of timidity; and a list that included Graham Greene, Aldous Huxley, Shaw, Graves, Osbert Sitwell and, as early as January 1938, Faulkner's *Soldiers' Pay*, could scarcely be said to ignore serious modern literature. There was, it is true, in the home-based Penguin list a dearth of serious modern *American* literature but the reasons for this were economic – founded upon the unwillingness of American hardback publishers, authors and their British agents to reduce the advances demanded for paperback rights – rather than either chauvinism or prudishness. Yet, if Weybright's complaint, like his claim to have signposted a way that Allen would not follow until it was too late, cannot stand the test of casual investigation of Penguin catalogues, closer analysis of Allen's correspondence written at the time does indicate that Weybright's wayward arrow somehow found the target – scoring a magpie if not a bull. Over the years Allen and his editors had developed a shrewd idea of just how far they could go – in the British market – and there was among them an unspoken but well-understood and not unjustified conviction that, for the moment, American and British literatures had different standards of frankness. Allen was ready and even eager to march Penguin to the frontiers of British taste but, properly sensitive for the reputation that the firm had established in its first decade, he would not move one step beyond that line until he was convinced that he could take at least a large minority of his readers with him.

Undoubtedly Allen regarded Penguin Books Inc. as no more than an extension of the home firm. His instincts were not tuned to American needs and he was nervous lest excesses in the American programme might waft a bad odour back across the Atlantic. He was not well-informed about recent developments in American fiction, and his British editorial advisers were either too busy or themselves without the interest that would have persuaded them to enlighten him, but anyone who was ever involved in business dealings with Allen would have recognized his procrastination over the formalizing of the status of Penguin Books Inc. as typical of his manner when prompted to a decision that might prove irrevocable and therefore would be willing to swear that it was not, as Weybright suggested in his memoirs, a symptom of inherent anti-Americanism, nor even an omen of ill-will between Penguin Books Ltd and Penguin Books Inc.

Both at the time and forever after when he spoke or wrote of his Penguin experience it was not Allen's editorial timidity which Weybright identified as the prime example of Allen's insensitivity to the needs of the American market and also as the silliest demonstration of Allen's 'vicarage-garden prudery'. These dreary distinctions Weybright conferred upon his implacable opposition to picture covers. Weybright could not know that, even whilst he and Enoch were begging, cajoling and at the last attempting to bully Allen, members of the Harmondsworth staff, including Dick, were presenting many of the same arguments in the hope that he would license pictorial permissiveness for Harmondsworth Penguins. Reports were set before him from Holland and Scandinavia (in Continental Europe the best markets for English-language books) which purported to show that, when offered the same title in its British and American editions, the shameless Dutch and libertine Scandinavians selected the American version even though it was almost twice the price of the British. From Australia Maynard added his voice; it was, he wrote, beyond dispute that Queen Victoria was in her grave. At one of the 'weekly' meetings at Harmondsworth, having first conspired together to create a cabal, colleagues put before Allen what seemed an irrefutable and logical proposition. Penguins, they argued, sold well in Britain and were not unsuccessful in all markets, despite the handicap of typographic covers. It followed, therefore, that prosperity must be transformed into opulence if the books were displayed to the world decked out in the gaieties, the unabashed enticements of picture covers. And, they added with practised cunning, surely this licensed abandon would come closer than the prevailing austerity to Allen's philosophy of the cheerful Penguin.

Allen grinned, muttered, 'Bosoms and bottoms' – by then his routine response to all arguments of this kind – and moved on to the next business.

His Harmondsworth and Melbourne colleagues suspected him of puritanism, but kept their suspicions to themselves; Weybright saw no reason to be circumspect – not then nor ever after. There was justice in their shared opinion for, despite this acquired metropolitan sophistication, Allen never discarded entirely the stolid influence of his provincial up-bringing, but there was in his obstinate opposition to picture covers, as in so many of his seemingly puritanical decisions, a cogency and force which few had the shrewdness to recognize. Just as, for example, he resented the term 'penguin' being applied to all paperbacks because it risked devaluing his own Penguin so also did he fear that, if Penguins looked like their rivals, they must soon become in the minds of book-buyers indistinguishable from their rivals.

Nevertheless Weybright's total *misericordium* had in it strains more compelling than his objections to Allen's imagined editorial, commercial and promotional reserve. Accustomed as Allen was to exercising intimate control over Penguin affairs and aware that distance made impractical those sudden swooping bursts of energy which held his authority even over his most individualistic colleagues at Harmondsworth, Allen set brakes upon the independence of his New York associates. That in so doing he made the breach with Weybright and Enoch inevitable must seem in retrospect one of his major errors. Even a dispassionate historian who considers the subsequent success of the discarded American directors with Signet–Mentor Books and New American Library is tempted to sigh for what-might-have-been; but thoughts of this kind are less than just to Allen's reputation for at the time of the schism he was still at the height of his powers as a schemer. The success of Penguin, like the success of any other business enterprise, could be judged by the balance-sheet, by sales figures and stock in hand, but Allen knew that Penguin had developed also an unquantifiable asset, a personality which set the firm apart from all other publishing houses. Allen had dreams of world-wide influence; like Uncle John, he was ambitious above all to become an American publisher, but to this end his associations, first with Ballantine and later with Enoch and Weybright, were experiments – and by his measure very tentative experiments – to establish if his Penguin could take United States citizenship without being imprisoned in an American strait-jacket. Again by his measure, both experiments failed, the second in a glowering confrontation conducted almost entirely by lawyers in a London hotel room. Allen was fortunate to escape without financial loss and without damage to his personal prestige or the reputation of Penguin. Weybright and Enoch were fortunate in that the dispute laid the foundations of their independent success.

For Allen, too, the American story was not finished. If Americans could not or would not naturalize the Penguin without also changing its personality, then the translation must be contrived by a satrap from Harmondsworth, by an Englishman versed in the peculiarities of the Penguin character. A little over a year after the collapse of the arrangement with Enoch and Weybright Harry Paroissien moved to America to begin a new chapter in the history of Penguin Books Inc.

Notably with New American Library, Weybright continued and enlarged the publishing philosophy that he had derived from the Pelican element in the Penguin list. For many years these two lists were the only major examples of original paperback publishers in the English-speaking world, but there was never again any genuine sympathy between Weybright and Allen. Weybright's fascinating autobiography, written after Allen's death, reveals still a bitterness towards his one-time friend which is not equalled even in the recollections of men who suffered far more than he from Allen's eccentricities and which comes surprisingly from a man who is generally charitable and perceptive. He misunderstood Allen, mistaking perversity for pettiness and misrepresenting care for Penguin prestige as cowardice but in that manifestation of Allen's character which dismayed and surprised him above all others, which he took to be squeamishness, Weybright arrived at a correct conclusion after arguing the wrong evidence. For all his boldness in creating new modes of publishing Allen's venturesomeness was limited not only by those distant recollections of Bristol but also by his awareness that he (and his creation) had become part of what Britain was beginning to call the Establishment; he was determined not to risk that status either for himself or for Penguin by any publicly noticeable immoderate act. Caution did not demand of him that he must be conventional; he knew, as middle-class leaders of the English middle class have always known, that eccentricity is not only permitted but positively expected, but it must be kept within bounds that are not easily defined but that are readily comprehended by their equals. He knew his constituency for he was a member of that constituency. He knew, too, that just as Penguins and Pelicans were enlarging the constituency by bringing into hitherto middle-class cultural preserves large numbers of hitherto working-class constituents, so also must he hold himself and Penguin from any act that might scandalize.

In the post-mortem recriminations across the corpse of the Enoch–Weybright Penguin Books Inc. the spilling of bile was not left entirely to Weybright. In 1956, using Bill Williams as his spokesman, Allen published to the world his version of the 'differences which had developed between Penguin and its American associates'. The names of Weybright and Enoch do not appear in *The Penguin Story* nor in any 'official' Penguin history published in Allen's life-time; like some ancient potentate it was Allen's custom to strike from the chronicle the names of those who had offended him; but the 'American associates' as later just 'the Americans' are patently the two villains. They, wrote Williams, wanted 'quarter million sales or more, for every title'; because sales on that scale could only be reached through magazine outlets 'which had no interest in books as such' and preferred 'a commodity with garish and sensational eye-appeal . . .' the contents of the book were relatively unimportant: what mattered was that its lurid exterior should ambush the customers.

Non sequitur succeeded *non sequitur*, and the account of 'the differences' reached its damning peroration in a passage which, accurate though it undoubtedly was in terms of the total American paperback market, had about as little relevance to the case of Weybright and Enoch as a description of the running bulls of Pamplona to a Test Match commentary:

A good book is one thing, a fast seller is another. The 1954 sales of American paperbacks are said to have totalled 250,000,000. But a further 80,000,000 were left unsold on the news-stands and were returned to their publishers. Most of them could not even be pulped because the adhesive material in their bindings made them unfit for re-manufacture as packing paper – and so they were dumped into the sea or into holes in the ground. Several million paperbacks had to be written off as 'premature returns', a trade euphemism for parcels returned to the publishers without ever being opened in the drug store or the news-stand. This cut-throat competition continues in one segment, and that the largest of the American paperback industry, and will doubtless end with the elimination of the weaker members of the pack and the stabilization of a handful of big operators making a good thing out of a noisome commodity with which, by comparison, the 'horror comic' is as innocuous as a parish magazine.

These floundering irrelevancies are the measure of Williams's pique – and almost certainly of Allen's – at what he took to be the betrayal of the Penguin ideal by Weybright and Enoch.

As Allen managed with remarkable adroitness the professional balancing-act between progress and conservation, between flashiness and convention, so also did he contrive something of the same sort in the public presentation of his private life. A few, a very few, of his chosen acquaintances knew that his marriage was derelict long before it formally ended; others, who liked to pretend to an intimacy that they did not enjoy, extended into the late forties and fifties antique raffish rumours and whispered to each other new but equally lubricious stories about goings-on in the flat that he had taken for himself in Whitehall Court (an address which was for its Shavian connection second only to Albany for literary distinction). When eventually Allen established an extra-marital relationship with Suzanne – a German lady, elegant, charming and a knowledgeable adjutant to his search for antiques – it soon took on a kind of monogamous respectability. If for a while friends were occasionally embarrassed by his unthinking, unapologetic habit of accepting invitations *pour deux* without giving notice whether he would be accompanied by Lettice or by Suzanne, none of this reached the gossip columns.

In matters more mundane, respectable success had become so much part of his public act that he had become himself the most convinced member of his audience. Such zest for self-publicizing as had been his in the Bodley Head days and the early years of Penguin had vanished with middle age and prosperity. Though he did not avoid the centre-stage he seldom thrust himself forward. He knew that his nature was paradoxical, he enjoyed his own amicable perversity, and he liked to have his quirkiness discussed – if only in the comparatively close circle of the book trade. There was at his disposal a car and a chauffeur but he still preferred to move around London by Underground and bus, and he was quick to demonstrate to any companion that his knowledge of fare-stages was infallible. ('Only a half-mile to walk and we will save a penny each.') His suits came from the most expensive tailor in Mayfair, but even the most casual acquaintance was told that his underclothes were by Marks and Spencer. To Silverbeck he added the farm and the flat in Whitehall Court, a plot of land in the South of Spain and there, before he had built on it the holiday home that he planned, he negotiated with the local authorities a profitable exchange of sites – and saw to it that his shrewdness be trumpeted to his friends.

CHAPTER  SEVEN

ALLEN was fifty when he was knighted. A year earlier, at the time of the Festival of Britain, a *Times* leader-writer had commented that Allen Lane had done more for the book trade than any man since Gutenberg. In less than seventeen years he had changed the face of publishing: he had so enlarged the Penguin concept that it now included virtually all disciplines, all modes of entertainment and all methods of enlightenment that could be transmitted to the public in book form; he had produced at precisely the right moment the means whereby the printed word could resist the challenge of radio and television; and he had presented to Britain, again precisely at the right moment, an opportunity, by no means insignificant, for seeking compensation for the loss of empire by using the advantage of the English language and inexpensive books to establish a new form of influence over the minds of millions, no less potent but far less suspect than the old, discredited imperialism. In commercial terms, the pioneering courage of the Lanes and the 'burglar's hundred pounds' paid by Dick had been so nurtured by Allen that the early flutterings over finance, the constant borrowings from Martins Bank and the habitual hesitancy in the payment of printers' bills, were but part of misty Penguin mythology. Now the firm was contributing handsomely to Britain's balance of trade. In every sense, editorial, financial and commercial, Penguin was successful, its reputation unassailable, its pre-eminence among paperback houses – and even among all publishers – virtually unquestioned. In Australasia Penguin was prospering and, despite so many vicissitudes, Penguin Books Inc. had settled under Paroissien's care to the task of capturing a sizeable if specialized segment of the American paperback market.

Allen could afford to be smug. Success in any pioneering endeavour is largely dependent upon timing and – whether by design, accident, the wise selection of shrewd advisers, or a combination of all three factors, it is difficult to assess – his timing had been immaculate, his courage immense. He had set up his stall in the market-place just when in the developed countries the new advanced literacy had brought millions to the wares he offered. Yet the benefit of hindsight provides one reservation. For reasons that are explicable he missed almost entirely an opportunity to enlarge the Penguin doctrine far greater than anything presented to him by the educational explosion in the advanced countries of the English-speaking world. He failed to exploit the huge new readership in the developing countries.

All over the world in the decades that followed the war, especially in Africa and Asia, millions were stumbling out of illiteracy into literacy. 'Nations, new to the excitements and to the responsibilities of independence and eager to establish economic and social health, were attempting to compress into one generation the processes which Western Europe ... achieved after four hundred years of gradual development.' The infant states were determined upon literacy; inspired by motives that were at once altruistic and self-interested, both economic and political, the established countries of the West and the East were all eager to assist, realizing that, despite the attractions of other and more facile methods of communication, the printed word had not yet been displaced as the 'most persuasive, influential and permanent method of mass-communication ... as the way to touching the minds, the hearts – and the pockets of millions'.

To this process the paperback was peculiarly appropriate. The author of the pamphlet *Paperbacks Across Frontiers* wrote in 1959:

> Huge and potentially vital blocks of the world's population are learning the pleasures and profits of reading. Presented suddenly with a skill which connects them for the first time with so many possibilities of decision and relaxation, these are the very people who are just entering upon their economic and political power. But, though their collective capacity is enormous, they are still by the standards of Europe or America desperately poor, so that even the acquisition of an inexpensive paperback is a strain upon the pockets of the majority of the new literates.
>
> But the gap between promise and reality closes with every addition to the literacy figures. In Africa and Asia the huge potential of the market makes paperback production attractive. The circumstances of African or Asian

merchandising are more easily adapted to the possibilities of paperback series publication than to more conventional forms of book distribution, which make far greater demands both on the retail distributor and on the prospective purchaser.

Others took up the challenge; Allen did not. The Russians flooded the Asian market with cheap books both in vernacular languages and in English. The East Germans followed on a more limited scale with an English-language series produced by a state-controlled publishing house. The Americans were just as determined but, if only in degree, more subtle; their intention was not very different but their means of carrying it out less blatantly propagandist and imperialist than the Communists' methods. The United States government gave to American publishers privileged facilities to enable them to export to the developing countries books originally produced for the home market. United States government agencies, notably the United States Information Service, commissioned translations into vernacular language (including, perversely, some translations of appropriate Penguin titles) and distributed the books in developing countries at prices that were unashamedly uneconomic. But the Americans used as their principal weapon in this campaign organizations that were, at least in outward appearance, patently philanthropic. In their turn these organizations, notably the Ford Foundation and Franklin Books, worked sensibly and efficiently through controlling boards and management teams composed entirely of nationals of the individual developing countries. By the mid fifties Franklin Books was producing paperbacks in the Lebanon, Iraq, Iran, the United Arab Republic, Pakistan and Indonesia. (In Indonesia in 1957 the indigenous publisher Pembangunan working 'in cooperation with the Jakarta office of Franklin' produced ten titles and the first printing of each title was 10,000, a run unprecedented in the East.)

Press hand-outs in the United States claimed that in all countries where Franklin operated 'local advisers ... decide what books are most needed. ... The books are selected, edited, translated and published locally.' What a sceptical if anonymous British observer thought of this disingenuous statement he made clear in an article in the *Manchester Guardian*:

The Southern Languages Book Trust established in Madras with aid from the Ford Foundation has among its principal objects the publication of good inexpensive reading material for the growing literate public of Southern India. Some 60 per cent of the books to be published are to be by Indian authors or on Indian subjects, while the remaining 40 per cent should constitute a representative cross-section of worthwhile foreign language books.

Wearing star-spangled spectacles to read the literatures of all time and of the whole world, the selection committee set up in New York has drawn up its first list of some three hundred titles. Greece, Rome, China, Germany, France, Russia, even Thailand and Indonesia are in the race, but way out in front as producer of worthwhile literature is the United States with 122 titles against the fifty-five of the panting runner-up Great Britain.

The classified lists of recommendations demonstrate some remarkable judgements. Gilbert Stuart and Grandma Moses are more suitable for Indians than Turner, Constable, Sutherland or even Rembrandt and Rubens. France and Italy have one book each in the nine books on art. Ceylon scrapes in with a book by the late A. K. Coomaraswamy – of the Museum of Fine Arts, Boston, Massachusetts: the rest of the books are all American, including a history of American art. Britain has produced no art worth writing about and no worthwhile writing about art.

And so the article continues.

British attempts to compete for the emerging markets of the Third World were spasmodic and for the most part pathetically timorous. Britain held advantages not shared by the Communist countries, by the United States or by any western power except, in a limited sense, by France. The educational structure in most of the newly independent countries had been copied from the British model and few showed inclination or intention to make drastic changes even after they had won political sovereignty; indeed, many maintained a fervent devotion to British educational institutions and even to a British-based examination system. There remained in many parts of Africa and Asia a vestigial and often a substantial British-linked book trade organization. The masses, the intellectuals, the social and the political leaders in most of the former colonies continued to demonstrate what was in the circumstances remarkable good will towards their former rulers and a considerable and flattering respect for Britain and all things British. Yet, though naturally and accurately the book trade roared that trade follows the book and though from time to time Members rose in Parliament to point out to Ministers that the book was the means whereby Britain could discover a role, whether because of obsession with Britain's new impecuniosity or from fear that any other course might revive, in Britain and in the Third World, cries of imperialism, government after government paid lip-service to the need to act – and did very little.

This fragile government support and the consequent impracticability of competing with the huge and strenuous efforts made by the Soviet Union and the United States, both in their various ways backed by vast government resources, made Allen doubtful of the wisdom of committing Penguin energies and Penguin resources to the new readers of the developing world. To succeed he must be prepared to venture into vernacular languages with books specially commissioned for the needs of developing countries. Such was the climate of the time, that he knew that national pride and, in many countries, national legislation would demand that he operate through locally established companies managed by nationals. His dominion was already widely dispersed; any enlargement of it must deny him the capacity for personal supervision which he relished and which was, in fact, the only method of command that he understood. In 1953 he did launch a West African series – edited, produced and distributed from Harmondsworth – but generally he was prepared to cede the great new opportunities in Asia and Africa to firms such as Longman, Heinemann, Macmillan and the Oxford University Press, all well established in the educational markets in those continents. He was content to look for advantage among the much smaller, much less rapidly growing audience of comparatively highly educated individuals, to those eager to seize upon the conventional home-produced Penguins and Pelicans and qualified to enjoy them. Even this much he engineered eventually largely, not by establishing Penguin outposts but by using his more committed rivals as his agents.

If this caution seems out of character no such suspicion can be aroused by a further consideration which first came to Allen in the late forties when he had many discussions with Sir Julian Huxley, the Secretary-General of UNESCO. It was strengthened when a few years later, he himself was appointed to UNESCO committees and able to observe the various projects sponsored by the United Nations, by national governments, by quasi-governmental institutions and by commercial organizations, all designed to satisfy the book hunger of the Third World, and was made gospel-truth for him by the end of the fifties when he had seen the miserable fate of most of these schemes. Almost without exception those who had entered the field had been promised by the countries that they proposed to assist freedom from interference in commercial or editorial policies; almost without exception the governments had subjected them to controls, to the shackles of prescription, even to censorship, and in every country, if in some more blatantly than in others, the outside agency had found itself enmeshed in political wrangling, in the debilitating process of waiting upon hesitant decision-makers, and in outright chicanery. It was no comfort to those agencies that their experience was no more devastating than had been endured by indigenous publishers, but Allen's sense of relief was immense – and his smugness not concealed. By his perspicacity he had avoided the trap into which so many others had fallen.

Later in the decade, he was offered a virtual monopoly in providing books for a broadly educational market in the West Indies, a part of the developing world comparatively free of authoritarianism and corruption and surely blessed with high standards of literacy – and in English. Allen refused the blandishment. He negotiated (in business he could resist anything except negotiation); an invitation to haggle under a Caribbean sun was his idea of a pass to Paradise and all the more to be enjoyed because someone else paid the bill for his weeks of luxury; but, though the discussions dragged on for months Allen allowed them to fade into vague promises of future consideration – promises which he did not keep and never intended to keep.

The lure of commercial success, prestige and influence in the Third World was immense but Penguin was still very much Allen's property, his life's work and hobby. The flash of enthusiasm which he had experienced during his pre-war tour of the Indian sub-continent had waned, flickered and almost died. Henceforth, because he knew that it was expected of him, he would make occasional forays into Asia and Africa but for himself as traveller he preferred the Anglo-Saxon countries and Europe, and for Penguin he concentrated on the old Dominions and the United States.

For political reasons South Africa was not easy to conquer. There the Nationalist government, puffed-up by victory over the British which their predecessors had failed to achieve in a century of effort, was not well-disposed to British commercial incursions into their newly independent country. Afrikaners were particularly nervous about a British organization which they knew to be liberal, thought to be libertarian and suspected of being an instrument of propaganda, if not for the British government then certainly for the English language. Allen's agent in South Africa was modestly successful but he was never more than an agent.

Canada was difficult for quite different reasons. As with South Africa, British publishers insisted on holding Canada within their copyright jurisdiction. Though South Africa withdrew from the Commonwealth and Canada remained a member, even the braggart hold over Canadian rights was difficult to sustain and before Allen's death had become a fiction.

For a century and more Canadians had glowed with complacent pride whenever they spoke of the 3000 miles of undefended border between their country and the United States, but this open boundary had drained much of the strength from Canada's cultural and economic life and, at the same time, weakened the links with British and European institutions. In speech, orthography, modes of thought, social and cultural mores English-Canadians (and even, if to a lesser extent, the fiercely chauvinist *Quebecois*) became with time ever more Americans living under a flag that was not the Stars and Stripes. Easy communication between United States manufacturing and distribution centres and all the major Canadian centres of population made Canada into an extension of the American home-market. At primary and secondary levels – and increasingly at the tertiary level – the Canadian educational system distanced itself from the British and moved closer to the American system.

The proximity and the prolixity of American radio and television hastened the 'Americanization' of Canada's culture. To a not inconsiderable extent reading habits are influenced by listening and viewing, so the cross-border bombardment from the American media softened further the Canadian population for an attack from American publishers.

All these developments were particularly galling to British publishers, who still liked to think the Canadian market was theirs, and were particularly seductive to American publishers with imperialist ambitions. Although the cost of producing books in the United States was substantially higher than in Britain, even this potential advantage to the British trade was largely eroded by the expense of transporting books across the Atlantic and, above all for paperback houses, by the prices which American publishers could contrive by their longer runs. For all these reasons it followed that even individual Canadian bookbuyers were apt to buy American books in preference to British (or Canadian); even when they required books originating in Britain they purchased them not infrequently from book stores just across the border in the United States. Because American wholesalers offered more generous terms than their British principals or British publishers' Canadian agents, Canadian institutions which needed books in bulk – above all Canadian education authorities – 'bought around', preferring to meet their requirements from American sources rather than from British or Canadian. In 1960, for example, the British Columbia school-system bought substantial stocks of Penguins, but all from a dealer in Seattle, just across the United States border.

Despite all these inhibiting factors many British publishers refused to resist the temptation of Canada. In the period after the war several established Canadian subsidiaries. Many of these and of others with a longer Canadian history were soon granted virtual autonomy from the parent house and developed a genuinely indigenous character, becoming in most respects, except the vestigial connections provided by name and one or two token British directors on their note-paper, virtually indistinguishable from native-born Canadian houses. Like them they made their reputations, in Canada, by emphasizing in their lists books written by Canadians for Canadians to read. Like them they suffered disadvantages in that, at least until the upsurge in Canadian nationalism in the early sixties, the number of Canadians who wanted to read Canadian books was pitifully few; even thereafter, the population statistics of English-reading Canada denied the likelihood of a thriving Canadian publishing industry.

No less than any of his British contemporaries Allen's determination to build a Canadian base was founded upon a belief that somehow Canada must remain for British publishers part of their imperial heritage. His conviction, probably anachronistic and almost certainly mystic, was compounded by his wish to claim all the English-speaking world for Penguin. There was, however, more sensible inspiration behind his many attempts to open in Canada and it came paradoxically from observing Penguin experience as an American publisher.

When Paroissien took over as chief executive of Penguin Books Inc. he made two changes of substantial significance.

The first was geographical and was made at Allen's command. Just as before the war Allen had moved his British headquarters from the conventionally acceptable districts of central London to the publishing wilderness of Harmondsworth where there was room to spread on low-priced land. Paroissien abandoned Manhattan and set up his headquarters, not in Chicago, Philadelphia or Boston – the cities generally regarded as the only conceivable alternatives to New York – but in the outskirts of Baltimore, still at that time blessed with excellent railway communications, easily accessible by sea and air from Britain and, of course, much cheaper than New York, or even Chicago, Philadelphia and Boston.

The second change was in editorial and commercial philosophy. Penguin had not succeeded in competing – and perhaps were prevented by their own policies from ever competing – with the popular range of titles produced by their American paperback rivals. Not merely because Allen refused to countenance garish covers, nor yet because he was adamantly opposed to the sale-or-return methods that the Americans had borrowed from magazine publishers, but more particularly because much Penguin fiction and almost all else in the various Penguin series was inappropriate to the market, Penguin could never hope to compete with Pocket Books, Dell, Avon and the rest for rack space in drug-stores, station-bookstalls or any of the other outlets which in Britain, even at Harmondsworth, were unconventional but which American paperback houses found the prime roads to commercial success. But in one area of publishing Penguin Books Inc. was ahead of all its American rivals, ahead even of its own discarded offspring, Signet–Mentor. There was no comparable American equivalent of the Pelican list. With the possible exception of the growing New American Library, there was as yet no wholehearted American competition for those elements in other Penguin series which might fairly be described as intellectually and academically respectable. (It was not coincidence but a carefully considered move when, almost as soon as he became independent of Allen, Weybright commissioned for his new firm a translation of *The Odyssey* to counter Penguin's outstanding triumph in the American academic market.) American higher education was burgeoning and, as admittedly Weybright had himself tried to demonstrate to Allen before the schism, many Penguins, Pelicans and Penguin Classics appeared custom-built as set books in this huge and growing college market. So Paroissien made tertiary education his major target and used the rapidly developing college-bookstore system as his principal outlet.

In Britain, too, if on a less sensational scale than in the United States, the number of pupils staying on at school was increasing, the older universities were doubling and trebling their intake, new universities were founded, more were planned, and the benefits of higher education were no longer limited to those whose parents could afford to pay and to those who could win their way by outstanding academic excellence. Bemused by the Penguin legend of service to the individual reader, Allen and his Harmondsworth advisers saw all this as a convenient addition to the number of those blessed by their educational preparation with the will to invade bookshops in the quest for Penguins. Because he was short on understanding of pedagogic processes Allen failed to grasp that British and American educational methods were converging; like their American equivalents, British schools and universities were coming to use Penguins in large numbers as text books. At this time, in the fifties, communication between Baltimore and Harmondsworth was conducted almost exclusively through him and he liked to keep the privileges and pleasures of trips to America for himself; the cue spoken in Baltimore was not heard in Harmondsworth. Consequently events preceded perception; the spectacular prospect of large sales created by the will of schools and universities to use Penguins as classroom-texts was seen only dimly from Harmondsworth even some years after the practice had become commonplace. Only then was applicability to academic use (almost from the beginning an incidental but unspoken Penguin tenet) made explicit in editorial and sales policy.

If Allen was slow to accept for Britain the lessons taught in the United States, his appreciation of their relevance to Canada was both immediate and sensitive. It was, of course, easy to recognize the affinity between Canadian and American institutions. It would have been no less easy to follow the American example and service Canada from the United States. However, Allen's pride in himself and in Penguin was matched by his sympathy for Canadian pride in Canada. He sensed already something which did not become evident for many years: Canadians must grow resentful of American domination of their cultural and economic life. To make Baltimore the Penguin capital of Canada could be disastrous; in terms of prestige and public acceptability it would serve his purpose no better than dealing with Toronto and Moncton, Moose Jaw and Vancouver, from Harmondsworth.

Allen wanted Canada for Penguin and he tried several times to become a Canadian publisher or, at very least, a Canadian-based wholesaler for Penguins originating in Britain. As he had sent Maynard (and later Dick) to Australia so he sent out Harmondsworth-trained executives to Montreal or Toronto – and then recalled them. He gave agencies to friends – and soon came to deny their friendship and their rights as agents. He made deals with Canadian-controlled firms – and almost immediately called into question the agreements that he himself had devised. He contracted a British publisher with a Canadian subsidiary – but removed himself from the concordat because he suspected the other party of using Penguins as loss-leaders. It was not until the mid-sixties that he contrived for Canada an organization that had the appearance of permanence. By then he was too tired and personally too little involved to change his mind. Penguin Books Canada was, as it remains, when compared to Penguin in the United States and in Australia, small-scale both in turnover and in purpose.

The manner in which Allen prosecuted his imperial intentions demonstrates the effects of his complex emotional chemistry on all his activities. In public his assurance was complete and even in the more limited but still detached company of professional associates he seldom revealed any doubts about his infallibility. But those few who were genuinely intimates all speak of his inward uncertainty; all tell of occasions when he confessed to sleepless nights worrying about a decision, sometimes great but often trivial, which he had just promulgated as dogma. It may have been no less than innate malevolence which brought down upon him accusations of uncaring capriciousness and which caused him so often to cause grief to others by his irrational and seemingly treacherous *voltes-faces*. He propounded the doctrine that failure should never be reinforced but, until he was well into middle age, the security that came with success bored him and his restlessness could never be subdued entirely; he was always eager to set aside what was immediate and invulnerable in favour of some novel and seemingly hazardous experiment. Travel was his most effective panacea for both indecision and tedium, and his frequent and energetic interventions in the American and Australian subsidiaries gave him the best of all reasons for purposeful travelling. Abroad, he was liberated from constant demands to handle the day-by-day and largely monotonous business of the British company, and abroad he could escape from the dramatic consequences of some of his own more dubious and impulsive actions. In Baltimore and later in Melbourne he could billet himself in the homes of his representatives, finding companionship among people who knew his ways and were, at very least, prepared to tolerate them, sparing himself not only the miseries of hotel life but also the expense. And from the home of Paroissien or Maynard he could move out into a professional community that was different and yet not uncomfortably foreign to that with which he had long been familiar or into a more widely based society which accepted him and which he understood.

His concentration of effort upon the United States and Australia was, of course, dictated by rational considerations. The American market was full of riches and, despite several false starts and much dissension, Penguin had already gathered in some of them. The Australians with the New Zealanders (who those responsible for Penguin, like most Englishmen, long regarded as no more than the inhabitants of an off-shore island) were, in proportional terms, the most avid users of books in the English-speaking world. Australia was not at that time the target for the expansionist attentions of American publishers, could never suffer as did Canada from the discomfort of a close all powerful neighbour and had no substantial indigenous publishing industry. Yet these impeccable arguments were less persuasive to Allen than more instinctive and more obviously intimate considerations: his long experience of the American publishing scene, his easy acceptance of American and Australian society, and in the case of Australia, most intimately and eventually most powerfully, the fact that his sister Nora had emigrated with her husband to Sydney.

It was, however, seven years after Maynard had established himself in Australia before Allen visited Australia for the first time. The Atlantic crossing was no longer an impediment to regular travel between Britain and the United States, and for Allen was made even easier; Heathrow was within walking distance of Harmondsworth or Silverbeck and Baltimore only an hour's drive from the Washington airport. Allen shuttled across the Atlantic and his frequent appearances in Baltimore did not always give pleasure to Paroissien equal to the pleasure that they provided for Allen. In other ways, too, the psychological and practical contraction of the Atlantic crossing and the consequent conviction, so very real to Allen, that Harmondsworth and Baltimore were next-door neighbours, exercised a strain upon Paroissien's patience and upon his loyalty. For more than a decade he was General Manager in Baltimore, the calls made by Allen for his presence in London becoming increasingly frequent and ever more imperious. A combination of accident and whim had deprived Allen of many close collaborators. A dictator at heart, nevertheless he needed a brother-figure, someone who would on occasion say him nay even though he intended to use their opposition as no more than a debating process to search out the imperfections in his own intentions, no more than a buttress to his determination. John was dead; Dick had been exiled to Australia; Allen's relations with Williams were no longer so close; Paroissien was a convenient brother-substitute, sagacious, knowledgeable, devoted, but no competitor for Allen's suzerainty. Not least important, Paroissien was aware of the personality clashes that were becoming a regular feature of life at Harmondsworth and yet he was generally unsuspected of being partisan.

These summonses from Allen were disruptive to Paroissien's family life and to his control over his huge territory, yet his association with Allen prospered. Perhaps because he never saw himself as a challenger either to Allen's commercial supremacy or to his fame as the public representation of the Penguin personality; perhaps because, though his dedication to the firm was intense, he never had (even in the days before he went to the States) and never did allow himself to become married to Penguin – a trap into which so many others high in the Penguin hierarchy stumbled almost eagerly and which Allen scarcely noticed because he had been the first and most willing victim of the snare that he himself had set; perhaps above all because, despite Allen's regular denials, Paroissien knew that 3000 miles of ocean was still an effective moat. Despite Allen's frequent assaults on his isolation, he was able to act – sometimes even for months on end – as if he were truly master there.

A cursory history of Paroissien's reign in the United States points to the wisdom of that first crucial decision to foster Penguin's rare characteristics rather than compete in a market which the firm could never hope to conquer. The statistics of that period reveal also the scale of the shift in sales technique which Baltimore contrived from this resolution to benefit from Harmondsworth's unique policies.

Paroissien landed in the United States in November 1949. In December he set up the corporation. (For its first year, as a concession to Weybright and Enoch it was called Allen Lane Inc., and thereafter once more Penguin Books Inc.)

In the same month he found the premises in Baltimore – 12,000 square feet on a ten-year lease at the modest rent of $6,000 a year including heat and light – and by January 1951 the operation was fairly launched. The pump-priming stock was all provided 'on consignment' by the parent company. As Paroissien's instinct for the needs of the American market developed, and with it his appreciation of the role that Penguin must play in the United States, he was able to increase the proportion of orders imported on a firm basis. By the end of his time in America books brought to Baltimore in this fashion accounted for almost half of the business of Penguin Books Inc. By then the custom had been established of producing bulk orders destined for the United States, including specially requisitioned reprints on wood-free paper with the dollar price printed on the cover.

It is, however, not only technicalities of this kind but even more emphatically analysis of the Baltimore list and of the subsidiary's customers which demonstrates the scale of the concession to American potential and which reveals how far Penguin Books Inc. had moved from what Allen still thought of as the immovable Penguin ideal. Paroissien himself estimated that after ten years half of Baltimore turnover was made up of orders explicitly for school or college syllabuses and that most of these were purchased as classroom-texts. This estimate is supported by a bestseller list compiled in Baltimore for the year 1960. Of the first 100 titles in that list only a handful were patently outside the educational field (the first of those, Peter Heaton's *Sailing*, which admittedly had only recently returned to the catalogue after an absence of several years, was as low as number 60 in the Baltimore list). The honours go almost exclusively to the Penguin Classics, to Bernard Shaw and to the *Pelican Shakespeare*, before 1960 the only series devised, edited and produced by Penguin Books Inc. The runaway winner was Rieu's *Odyssey* – against direct competition from Signet–Mentor's alternative translation by W. H. D. Rouse – with the phenomenal record of 82,715 copies sold, some 30,000 ahead of the runner-up, Coghill's modern English version of Chaucer's *Canterbury Tales*; next in the frame, but 40,000 copies behind its stablemate, was *The Iliad*, again Rieu and Homer. (Paroissien estimates that in the fifties Baltimore sold more than half a million copies of *The Odyssey*.)

Baltimore's concentration on the educational market led to an agreement with D. C. Heath and Company, probably the largest publisher of elementary and high-school texts in the United States and also a leader in the college field, whereby Heath's many college representatives would urge professors to adopt Penguins for their courses. For most of Paroissien's time in the United States, Baltimore had no full-time salesmen of its own, not even for the general market. Even so an arrangement of the kind made with D. C. Heath was, at that time, still regarded as heresy at Harmondsworth.

No less heretical was the decision to abandon traditional Penguin antagonism to press advertising. In this, as in the concordat with a textbook publisher, Baltimore moved only a few years before Allen conceded that Harmondsworth must abandon this aspect of Penguin theology.

The fifties saw Penguin Books Inc. firmly established in the United States. Paroissien had been sent to America with £3000 for working capital and running expenses. From that time all growth was financed out of earnings. And growth was manifest.

In 1951, Penguin Books Inc. sold something over 600,000 books, in 1960 almost three times as many; in those years turnover rose from some $200,000 to well over $1 million. When Paroissien returned to England Penguin Books Inc. had 1,600,000 books in stock, a substantial quantity of printing-plates and rights, and its net worth was set at $350,000. Most important of all it had never failed to provide for the parent company a profitable and useful overflow into the American market; profitable for the obvious reason that money passed from Baltimore to Harmondsworth, and useful for reasons less obvious but ultimately more significant: orders from Baltimore inserted an element of certainty and predictability into generally psychic calculations which preceded print orders, allowing the decision-makers at Harmondsworth to increase their stake without lengthening the odds and thus giving to Penguin Books Ltd the chance to hold its prices at a time when the potential of the home market was being reduced by the incursions of a number of upstart competitors – most of them, happily for Penguin, not as yet blessed with similar star-spangled advantages.

Allen's part in all this was as ambiguous as was his reaction to the achievement. He meddled but he did not initiate, he proposed but he seldom decided, never prohibited and did not even argue with any conviction against Baltimore's abrogation of traditional Penguin principles. He was, not unnaturally, puffed up by the knowledge that he was at last undeniably an American publisher and that Paroissien had given to this status an air of permanence such as none of his predecessors – nor yet Uncle John – had been able to ensure, and he revelled in the opportunities which this new prestige offered for marching on to the United States stage. But even this glory was dimmed, and dimmed principally by the one decision about the future of Penguin Books Inc. which was irrefutably and uniquely Allen's: because the spotlight on the American publishing scene was focussed on New York. Harmondsworth was out of London but it was a suburb to London. By American standards Baltimore was close to New York but not close enough to allow the immediate access to the intimacy of the book world which was his greatest pleasure and his way of life in London. Consequently Allen was restless in Baltimore, always eager to fly off to New York or to test his fame on some other American city. And, because his nature demanded companionship and a knowledgeable audience, and, in places other than New York, because he either pretended or imagined that he needed to be presented to the natives, he seldom travelled in the United States without insisting that Paroissien accompany him.

Yet, if the story of Penguin Books Inc. in the fifties gives some evidence that Allen's capacity for leadership was already waning, and with it that rare ability to find a new route to success by instinctive processes without the map of precedent or the compass of logic, still in one respect Allen's view of the Baltimore venture was forward-looking. Against all his inclinations he was accepting, even though he neither confessed nor recognized in himself any lessening of energy and ability, that he knew the time must come, and must come soon, when he could no longer act as autarch over an empire whose bounds were set ever wider still and wider, an empire that as it grew mightier became more complex and difficult to rule. Perhaps, for no other reason than that he was too close to Allen's own age, Allen did not see Paroissien as an heir-apparent but, at least in the early years of Paroissien's time in America, Allen's belief in his own immortality was unimpaired and his gestures towards securing the succession hectic but dutiful. What he had in mind for Paroissien, already in the mid-fifties, was the rank to which he was eventually promoted – as Grand Vizier, an able, loyal and unthreatening deputy. As preface to this elevation, the more-or-less independent command of Penguin's strongest, most important and most vulnerable outpost was both trial-by-combat and training-ground.

Paroissien suffered at times from being too accessible to Harmondsworth, from Allen's confidence that he understood American publishing, from Allen's curiosity about the United States and all things American, and from this resolve to be accepted as an American publisher. Maynard in his early days in Australia suffered for reasons that were well-nigh antithetical. Not only geographically but also emotionally Melbourne was a long way from Harmondsworth, so far out of sight that it slipped easily out of mind. Whereas Penguin Books Inc. was treated as a self-governing dominion, Penguin in Australia, when it was considered at all, was no more than a colony. Allen had never visited Australasia; only Dick at Harmondsworth had any conception of the vastness of the Continent or of the difficulties that the distances between Australia's major cities impose upon a centralized commercial operation. This ingenuousness about the facts of Australian life, by no means peculiar to the Penguin staff and indeed far from uncommon among British businessmen, was exemplified by a letter sent to Maynard bidding him to give coffee some morning in Perth to a Western Australian girl who, when holidaying in Britain, had met someone from Harmondsworth at a cocktail-party and again, even more dramatically, when in 1953 Allen at last decided to visit his Australian territories, by his command that Maynard bring his car to Fremantle so that they could drive back together to Melbourne – a round trip of some 4000 miles, much of it across desert!

Nevertheless, Penguin prospered in Australia, quietly but surely. When compared to the vast opportunities in the United States the pickings were small but so also was the competition. For several years, before other paperback houses, both British and American, realized that the possibilities, though limited by the size of the population, justified whole-hearted invasion, Penguin had the upper end of the Australian market virtually to themselves. Just as Paroissien looking out from Baltimore appreciated the consonance between Penguin editorial policies and American academic requirements, so also did Maynard from his vantage-point in Victoria recognize immediately the compatibility of his list with the Australian educational system. British school-teachers defended resolutely their God-given right to select, each according to his own preferences and prejudices, the books for their own classrooms and there were in the profession as many prejudices as there were teachers, and almost as many preferences as there were books. This freedom of choice was generally popular with the trade. It spread the range of educational purchases over many lists and many titles, but it made it difficult and uneconomic for any one publisher to concentrate his sales effort on one title from his list and was notably discouraging to Allen whose concern was entirely with cheap books and narrow profit margins. The disincentive imposed by the fragmentation of the school market was not the least nor by any means the least sensible reason why he delayed for so long before making a deliberate assault on British schools.

When he at last established within Penguin a specifically educational list, he did so not out of prescience, not from any inspiration about the direction that Penguin must take, but because he believed that British teachers had already shown him the way by concentrating their preferences and prejudices so magnanimously upon Penguins and Pelicans.

Australian teachers had surrendered to the State authorities some of these rights of personal selection, not so abjectly as their American nor so completely as their Canadian colleagues, but sufficiently to offer to Maynard a blessed opportunity to sell in bulk. All he had to do was to persuade State prescription committees and committees of the examining bodies that Penguins were ideal for their schools. It was a formidable 'all', but less arduous and more economical than the task Harmondsworth endured of persuading teacher after teacher to adopt Penguin titles. Maynard knew that many of his books had been, in one way or another, by the acquisition of paperback rights or by commissioning, brought into the list as if Harmondsworth editors had the upper forms in Australian secondary schools in their sights. Many – and particularly the originals – were written in a manner that was precisely, if accidentally, tailored to suit Australian taste, at once independent and authoritative, unconventional, not pompous and yet elegant. It was not long before the committees accepted Maynard's knowledge as if they had discovered for themselves the truths which he expounded so patiently but with such fervour. Thereafter the vitality of the Australian business depended to some considerable extent upon requisitions from the States. For example several States ordered in thousands volumes of the *Pelican History of England* and, year after year, continued to order them in thousands; one title in the world history series sold 5000 copies to South Australia alone in every year from 1956, when it was first published, until it went out of print in the early seventies.

Orders in this kind were easy to service and called for no great expansion in Melbourne's staff. They were the best and perhaps the only means of subverting the difficulties of Australian geography. The substantial mark-up which Penguin, in common with all British publishers, added when fixing Australian prices allowed Maynard to make a comfortable profit not only on bulk sales but also on the more orthodox method for Penguin of selling to retail outlets. Allen was content: in those early Australian years he had no wish to give Melbourne even that limited autonomy he allowed Baltimore. It was, to his way of thinking, little more than a wholly-owned agency and if the thought was a paradox then so be it; the manipulation of paradoxes was the logic that he understood best of all. His perception of the world scene and his dreams of having Penguin, like the Royal Regiment of Artillery, fighting in every battle, had taken him to the point of establishing his own subsidiary. Further than that he did not wish to go – as yet. Viewing Australia from the depths of his ignorance and from the far side of the world, he was not roused to action by Maynard's reports. Australia was growing; that he knew, and he knew also that in some senses it was growing away from Britain and away from all external influences; but he measured the potential of the Australian market and, even when he added 3 million New Zealanders to 13 million Australians, he could not accept that Australasia could support an indigenous paperback industry. He had given Penguin an Australian identity and that was enough. Again he had no thought of producing in Australia books by Australian authors for an Australian audience.

Maynard urged Allen to come himself to Australia, to show himself to the Australians, and there was behind his pleadings an imperative but unvoiced motive: Allen might rid himself of his myopia about Australia and all things Australian. Instead Allen sent Dick.

Dick's visit to Australia in 1948 was overtly in response to Maynard's letters but for both brothers there were influences at work that made Maynard's requests coincidentally convenient.

Dick's presence at Harmondsworth unsettled Allen. His grief for John was genuine and undimmed but in it there had always been an element of grievance, almost of anger with the Fates for taking a skilful collaborator. As time and success distanced him from the pioneering days, he came to erase all recollection of their rivalry and to remember only John's virtues and his ability. Dick reminded him of John but Dick, too, he recognized as now the only legitimate challenger to his hegemony, by now entire; without reason, he feared that Dick might be, at worst, the figurehead of a palace revolution or, at best, the agent who divides the loyalties of the staff. Dick, dependable and solid to the edge of stolidity, stood nevertheless as a reminder of a shared, rip-roaring youth; though Allen delighted in telling to his intimates stories of Talbot Square and the Crypt, he liked to be the unquestioned hero of his own anecdotes, even of those that he told against himself, the unique creator and the sole inspiration of the greatness of Penguin. Others who knew them both saw Dick as self-effacing, loyal, efficient within the limitations that he was the first to comprehend. They knew that he questioned some of Allen's decisions but never his right to make them, and that he made no move that might reduce Allen's glory. Allen, too, knew all this, yet that perverse insecurity which he never cast out entirely excited his imagination. He thought that he saw Dick's eye upon him, that Dick's informed scepticism was measuring and reducing the validity of the self-portrait that Allen had drawn for public viewing, of a Prince Hal whose far-off, brash, roistering days, even, had been preparation for the time when the kingdom would be his. Even Dick's most notable professional attributes, once so useful to Penguin and to Allen, his brother now found irksome. He resented Dick's agility with figures which enabled Dick to counter Allen's instincts with statistics. As Allen saw it, Penguin no longer needed to be driven with one foot close to the brake.

In this situation Allen could not help himself; it was not enough to tolerate – and to go his own way. He had to attack and, at first, the manner of his attack was slow, subtle – and, in retrospect, hideously successful. By his actions, by his tone and sometimes even by statement he let it be known that Dick was a director only because he was a Lane, but of the Lanes the least, that members of the staff need not trouble to consult Dick even when Allen was abroad, that Dick's opinion was scarcely worth having.

Yet Dick continued to offer sound advice. Because Allen had the professional competence to know that it was sound, he resented it even more than if he had been able to decry it as foolish, mischievous or self-seeking; even whilst he manipulated Harmondsworth opinion of Dick, Allen's conscience, always most sensitive in matters that touched his family, would not allow him to ignore entirely the need to do something for Dick. Despatching him to Australia was a magnificent expedient, dealing with all his confused feelings about his brother at one stroke. There Dick would be out of the way, handling a job that needed to be done but that Allen had neither the will nor the intention to do himself, in a society that was not yet, by Allen's measure, important to his own success or to the preservation of his own image.

Dick, for his part, seems to have sensed something of Allen's manoeuvrings at Harmondsworth. Though probably either unaware of the full extent of Allen's erosion of his reputation and status or else tolerating it as a mischievous quirk in his mischievous and quirky brother, he was more than willing to go somewhere where his role would be unquestioned, out of the shadow cast by his brother's eminence. He was also, like Allen, a compulsive traveller and he looked back with feelings of nostalgia to his days as a jackaroo.

The plan did not work out as either Allen or Dick had intended, though for Dick personally it had a happy conclusion and for Allen, and indeed for Penguin, considerable consequences. On the ship to Australia Dick discovered, as Allen had done before him at almost exactly the same age, that he was not as he had thought himself to be, an unshakeable bachelor. He arrived in Australia, took himself and Maynard off for an eight-week tour of New Zealand, married his Australian fiancée in Sydney and returned with her, to England, to live at Priory Farm. Inevitably he had had neither the opportunity nor the inclination to advance by much his understanding of Penguin affairs in Australia. Eventually, when Allen was fully apprised of its potential and discontented with the management of Penguin in Australia, Dick was on hand, an obvious and willing replacement.

Meanwhile Maynard persevered in Melbourne, steadily if undramatically, his quiet competence unfluttered by Dick's brief and, in Penguin terms, irrelevant intervention and unfettered by any intrusive concern or passionate approval from Allen. Still unable to persuade Allen to go out to Australia, in 1950 he was authorized to return to England 'for leave and consultations'. It was during this visit that tragedy occurred to Maynard and his wife which touched Allen's sympathy and roused him to a series of acts of generosity of a kind that many who worked for him or knew him well remember and which, for Maynard as for others, led them to hold him in affectionate and grateful memory even against the recollection of acrimony and injustices endured.

Allen was away from the office, laid low by influenza. Maynard was at Harmondsworth trying to work, though his mind was with his only child, a baby daughter, who was under observation in the Great Ormond Street Hospital for Sick Children. He rang the hospital; over the telephone and without any preparatory softening, the sister-in-charge gave him the shattering news that Leander was blind. Maynard turned to Allen, who put aside immediately his own insignificant ailment. Lettice was despatched to bring Maynard back to Silverbeck (this was one of the very few occasions when anyone can remember seeing Lettice in the office) and subsequently, in a manner both practical and unpatronizing, Allen settled on the child a sum of money that was, even for him, not inconsiderable and, for the Maynards, a surety against the financial implications of the distress which money could not lessen but which money and spontaneous benevolence could make more bearable.

In 1953, at last Allen went out to Australia. Maynard met him in Fremantle, but not with the car, and because he did not enjoy train travel he flew back to Adelaide and left Allen to cross the Nullabor by railway. In an interview given to the press at the end of that dour journey Allen made the remark which was used next day as theme for a newspaper-cartoon and which has since entered Australian folk-lore. Asked the question that all interviewers insist on asking visitors, even if they have been in the country for only a few days: 'What do you think of Australia?' Allen replied that his most sensational first impression was of the diamond-studded railway-line and then added, for the benefit of the mystified reporters, 'the track is framed by empty beer-bottles and in the sunlight they glitter like gems. There's 1500 miles of diamonds from Perth to Adelaide.'

Allen enjoyed his first visit to Australia. He was lionized everywhere as the creator of the paperback revolution, interviewed by every major newspaper and at all the important radio stations. Both flattery from others and his own perspicacity, supported at last by the evidence of his own eyes, aroused that sense of anticipation for a new development that was for him more compelling and more delectable than any other motivation.

But not all in Australia were as satisfied by his stay among them as was Allen. In Britain he had for some years indulged himself with outrageous behaviour, accepting invitations to functions that he did not mean to attend, arriving late for appointments and making promises which he did not plan to fulfil. Already in Britain – as probably he knew and intended – his unmannerliness was becoming part of the Lane myth, was expected of him and generally forgiven to him. The Australians were more sensitive to slights, real or imagined, and especially to slights inflicted by a Pommie. They noticed, they were hurt and they did not forgive.

Twenty years later A. D. Hope, the finest of Australia's poets, a distinguished scholar and one of the greatest men in the Commonwealth, still remembered with revulsion the humiliation that he had suffered at Allen's hands. (It must be admitted that the hurt was inflicted during Allen's second and even more tempestuous visit to Australia.) For months editors at Harmondsworth had been in correspondence with Hope about an anthology of Australian poetry which they wanted him to edit. All seemed settled except the practical details, which were to be agreed in a meeting between Hope and the head of the firm. When Hope was summoned from Canberra to meet Allen in Sydney, he travelled up expecting talk about business, and a signed contract. Instead, he found himself hovering awkwardly around the edges of a cocktail-party in a suite at the Hotel Australia, ignored by his host and by most of the large and noisy company. A patient and modest man, he waited until the other guests had gone and then introduced himself to Allen who welcomed him warmly but, it seemed, without recognizing either Hope's name or the reason for his presence. Hope reminded Allen of the proposed anthology. 'Oh that,' said Allen. 'It's all settled; I've commissioned three chaps to do it.' Hope went back to Canberra *sans* apology, *sans* explanation and *sans* contract. Allen had not even offered to meet his expenses. It was no solace that when eventually he received his voucher copy of the *Penguin Book of Australian Verse* he found it contained more poems by A. D. Hope than by any other poet, living or dead, except one of the three editors, Kenneth Slessor.

It was not only the Australians who were disconcerted by some of Allen's antics during that first visit. The Maynards, too, who boarded him in their home for much of his stay, which was inevitably centred upon Melbourne, found that he had become even more erratic than he had been in the past, at times solicitous, always gentle with Leander, but also at times demanding and even rude. His drinking was harder than they remembered (and that placed him in the First Division of topers), but he managed alcohol less discreetly than he had when young. He urged them to invite to the house numbers of Victorians who had supported the development of Penguin, who might be willing to give the firm publicity or who were eager to add Allen Lane to their collection of celebrated names for dropping. When the spirit took him he loosed his charm, was courteous, interested and interesting, but if his mood was black, if the company bored him and especially if the spirits took him, he glowered in a corner, silent and unapproachable. Not infrequently, he disappeared to bed even when a party was at its height, leaving the Maynards to fend off guests who had not yet met the star of the evening and to explain as best they could his disappearance.

Nevertheless, Allen went back to England well satisfied with his Australian excursion. Maynard settled back, not without relief, to the same unsensational routine that had been his before Allen's arrival. No strenuous criticism of his methods had been advanced by Allen, no sensational developments agreed – not even the modest growth proposed by Maynard – and there had been no hint that Allen intended any change in either the status of the subsidiary or in its management, but the magic of experience was at work. Allen's interest had been aroused; he had discovered Australia and he had found it rich with possibility, a new playground for his energy, another market ripe for exploitation. And the airlines were making Australia ever more and more accessible to his personal intervention. There remained unsolved the problem of what to do with Dick, and Dick knew Australia and was married to an Australian. Allen worried and worked towards a conclusion that seems in retrospect inevitable. Penguin Australia must be made more dynamic. He himself would play a leading role in its development and Dick would be his viceroy. But what to do with Maynard? Even before he raised with his brother the notion that Dick might settle in Australia at the head of a vitalized Australian subsidiary Allen had convinced himself that Maynard was not the man for the job that he now wished to have done. In this his judgment was sound. Maynard was hard-working, shrewd, loyal; he had made in Australia a reputation for integrity and competence, but there was no flamboyance in his personality. He was not notably possessed of gifts that would allow him to appear before the Australians in a novel guise, no longer the mere representative of Penguin but the incarnation of Allen himself, a visible, audible and immediately recognizable representation of Allen's genius and vigour. Dick, on the other hand, whose limitations both real and invented, Allen had contrived to publicize, was nonetheless a Lane; even distanced as they had become he was more than anyone else instinctively responsive to Allen's instincts. He was also one of the founders of Penguin, and Allen realized that to have a Lane who was a founding-father in their midst must be for the Australians a powerful demonstration of the earnestness of Penguin's intention to enliven their Australian business. But Allen was fond of Maynard and, in his own way, grateful to all who had been his aides in the fabled days before the war. As so often when necessity, as he saw it, forced upon him action that must damage those he classed as both friends and colleagues, he prepared in advance a rampart against his conscience. It was a technique that he used over and over again, so often but with such blandness that he would have denied that he used it at all. The break must come not from him but from Maynard.

There was no need to hurry. Allen was busy elsewhere in the world and haste would have ruined the plot, but Maynard was steadily subjected to a series of comments, queries, mild criticisms, all perspicacious and each one of them capable of being interpreted as no more than an earnest to Allen's new-found knowledge of Australia and new-found interest in his Australian company. By his own admission Maynard was slow to appreciate what was happening. It was two years after Allen's first visit to Australia before he woke to the knowledge that Allen was acting towards him in a manner which he had observed in his actions towards others.

The incident was not of itself important enough to cause war between the two but it emphasized the nearness of battle. Without cousulting Maynard, Allen took on in London and sent back home to Australia a woman to serve as sales representative in New South Wales. Maynard must buy for her use a panel-van; Allen recommended an Austin and supported his recommendation with the appropriate brochure. Maynard bought the van and the woman arrived in Melbourne. Maynard asked her if she could drive. She had driven, but not for some years. Had she a licence? No. She was given some coaching, passed her test, took off for Sydney and that very day overturned the van and left it, a battered heap, on the Hume Highway. Maynard reported the disaster to Allen and back came an abusive letter. Only an idiot, wrote Allen, would have dreamed of buying a vehicle of that kind, so inappropriate for the roads of Australia.

Still Maynard held back from any irrevocable move but Allen's campaign became rapidly more intense. Maynard had to admit that if, as it seemed, he no longer enjoyed Allen's confidence, then he could no longer be Penguin's Australian manager. He made one last effort; on the telephone from Melbourne to Harmondsworth he told Allen that he would catch a plane next day for England so that they might discuss their differences face to face. Allen would have none of it. Maynard recalls his words, the last that they ever exchanged as colleagues: 'No, no, no,' Allen said, 'don't do that on any account. I won't be here. Don't do that.'

Thereafter, the matter of severance was dealt with by solicitors. Allen, who not long before had admitted to Maynard that he had been underpaid for years, instructed his lawyers to ensure that the handshake was not gold but Britannia metal. Yet on all his subsequent appearances in Australia Allen spoke to Maynard on the telephone, enquiring with concern that was not feigned about Leander, assuring the Maynards of his everlasting friendship and, more than once, admitting that their parting had been a mistake. If so, it was a mistake that he did not attempt to rectify even years later, when Dick had abdicated from all involvement with Penguin and Maynard's long-standing knowledge of Penguin principles and of the Australian scene might have made his return a sensible alternative to the frequent, desperate and sometimes incomprehensible changes in leadership inflicted on Melbourne.

If there were times – as with Maynard – when Allen was prepared to admit that he had acted unwisely or without sufficient thought for others and though he was much given to retrospection, neither reason nor sentimentality could bring him to retrace his steps. There appears to have been only one occasion in all the long history of honeymoons, trials and divorces when Allen reinstated a previously discarded favourite; if his protestations of abiding amity towards those he had exiled from Penguin were probably genuine they were spoken rather to comfort himself than to console others. He liked to be liked; business was a matter of calculation; if one of his employees was by his reckoning no longer a useful digit in the Penguin sum he must be erased from the addition and another digit put in his place. Why should this sensible process arouse antagonism? None came from him and it must be admitted that it was not often that any came from his victims. 'A.L.,' they would say (or, if they knew him more intimately 'Allen'), 'is like that. His favours are ephemeral.' And they would go away, most of them to successful careers elsewhere, certain that they had profited greatly from their time in Penguin (though never financially), ready to proclaim his genius and the uniqueness of Penguin.

Any attempt to assess Allen's activities must involve the man who makes it in an exasperating effort to separate cause from effect. The dog is forever chasing its own tail. So it is with the events in Australia after Maynard had been dethroned. It cannot be said that the Australian business prospered just because Maynard had gone; rather, Maynard went because Allen had at last decided that he would make the Australian business prosper. And prosper it did, despite all those changes at the top.

The manner in which Allen announced one of those changes has become part of the Lane fable. It is told, often inaccurately but always in a spirit of benevolent resignation, reluctant admiration and some affection, even by those who had experienced something similar, half as tribute and half as criticism.

It dates from Allen's third visit, after Dick had been replaced. Allen had spent some weeks in Australia, touring the country in the company of Dick's replacement and the manager's immediate subordinate. He had stayed for days in the home of his Australian manager. Together the three had made plans for future development. There had been comments on past performance but no criticism that might have aroused foreboding. The two Australians took Allen to the airport to catch his plane to England. They shook hands, Allen moved to go, and then Allen turned back, looking, as one of them said years later, 'as if he wanted one last word with old friends'. He pointed at the manager, 'You're out.' He stabbed his finger at the second-in-command, 'You're in,' smiled, said, 'I'm off,' and walked calmly through the door that separates travellers from well-wishers.

It is a good story but untypical. Generally when Allen wished to rid himself of a colleague he either forced the man to hang himself or delegated Williams, Dick or Paroissien to serve as hangman, but there was no surrogate executioner in Australia – and his plane was on the runway.

This was not the last of Allen's dramatic interventions on the Australian scene. Two years later, made suddenly impatient by the arrival on his desk of accounts reporting poor profits for the year, he decided to abandon Australia. Ron Blass was sent out to wind up the company but, once arrived, formed the opinion that much could be achieved by limited surgery. In a series of lengthy telephone calls to London he persuaded Allen to postpone execution. From then on, though still burdened by frequent changes at the top, the story of Penguin Australia is one of almost consistent growth. Ron Blass was authorized to maintain overall supervision, but from Harmondsworth. That apart, Melbourne was granted considerable autonomy and, if a little late then still not too late for success, was allowed also to publish on its own account books intended primarily for the Australian market.

Before Allen died the number of Penguin employees in Australia was greater than the number which had administered the world-wide Penguin business in the halcyon days after the war. It is appropriate to Allen's original intention to make all things Penguin immediately recognizable that the firm's headquarters outside Melbourne is so like his British house that any first-time visitor familiar with Harmondsworth is apt to forget that at Ringwood the sun sets in the wrong quarter.

There were other overseas adventures and Allen's urge to travel was never stilled, but with Baltimore and Melbourne firmly established his imperial pretensions were satisfied.

CHAPTER EIGHT

DURING the period of overseas consolidation, in broad terms the decade of the fifties, Penguin at home was growing in scale and in confidence. The competition was by now intense and yet from the vantage-point of Harmondsworth or Silverbeck it seemed to offer no real threat. Other paperback houses might approach the firm's figures, one at least – the oldest competitor, Pan Books – could on occasion shatter Penguin records for the sales of individual titles, but only Penguin was a national institution, much more than a publishing house, respected, admired, even loved, and none could dispute Penguin's virtual monopoly of the upper end of the paperback market.

The first two volumes of Pevsner's *Buildings of England*, planned as long ago as 1946, appeared in 1951. In 1953, under the direction of the same editor, Allen launched a project which presaged a shift in emphasis which seemed at the time heretical. But *The Pelican History of Art*, cloth-bound, extensively illustrated, in format expansive and (for Penguins) expensive, fulfilled the second part of Allen's aphorism about the two justifiable prices for books, sixpence and six guineas. When Maynard was given advance notice of *The Pelican History of Art* he remembered an exchange with Allen years before. When asked what he meant to do when he had conquered the paperback market, Allen had replied without hesitation: 'Move into hardbacks, and sweep that field clean.' Maynard could not guess that Pevsner's series was anything but a tiny step in that direction; Penguin had previously made half-hearted and not notably successful attempts to market some titles in their original paperback format but with cloth bindings – principally as a counter to the infuriating custom, royalty-stealing, profit-purloining and technically illegal, of some public librarians who provided durability and therefore the possibility of multiple lending by replacing Penguins' paper covers with cloth bindings. Allen alone knew that *The Pelican History of Art* was more than a gesture to the editor he admired above all others, more than a calculated commercial risk, more even than a concession to his preference for large-scale, elaborate and audacious projects. He was testing the water, and he found it pleasurably warm. He hovered on the edge for several years, the temptation nagging at him, before at last he dived in; for all that he had accomplished he had never rid himself entirely of doubts about the status of paperback publishers, could not convince himself that even the founder of the paperback movement was entitled to the glory and respect given without question to more orthodox colleagues; was not yet satisfied that his place was secure alongside Uncle John in the pantheon of British publishing.

For the moment, however, *The Pelican History of Art* was an aberration. Most of the editorial developments of the fifties were in fields which Penguin had been mining since before the war. By 1960 the Penguin catalogue read like a dictionary of English-language literature, plus a sizeable contribution from foreign authors. The distant past was represented by writers as various and as far apart in time as Fielding and Disraeli, the more recent past by, among others, Oscar Wilde, Arnold Bennett, Conrad, Max Beerbohm and Buchan. From the generation whose works had been accepted as classics since the First World War there were T. S. Eliot, E. M. Forster, D. H. Lawrence, John O'Hara, Raymond Chandler, James Joyce, Eric Linklater, George Orwell, Robert Graves, Scott Fitzgerald, Ernest Hemingway, W. H. Auden, Edith and Osbert Sitwell (poor deprived Sacheverell!) and, from a younger but still well-established galaxy, Angus Wilson, C. P. Snow, Pamela Hansford-Johnson, Patrick White, Ivy Compton-Burnett, H. E. Bates, Arnold Wesker, Iris Murdoch, John Wain, William Golding, L. P. Hartley, Nancy Mitford, Denton Welch, Alan Paton, Budd Schulberg, Tennessee Williams and Doris Lessing. Compton Mackenzie came back after his long absence, first with *Whisky Galore* and then, in 1959, wholeheartedly with five titles.

One distinguished and popular author looked at the Penguin

constellation, was surprised by the indifferent showing of his own books and was not too proud to tell Allen that he felt slighted. The virtual omission of J. B. Priestley is cause for raised eyebrows, and not only Priestley's, though he could have found some back-handed consolation in the even more surprising fact that his great predecessor, Thomas Hardy, came to Penguin only as a poet (in truth, because Macmillan refused to release to Penguin rights on his novels). Priestley, who knew full-well that he had earned his place as archetype of the Penguin author by his skill and by his reputation, nicely balanced between the sagacious approval of the literary high-priests and popular acceptance by a vast congregation of readers, was in no way comforted by the publication of his first novel, *Angel Pavement*, in 1948. What hurt was that thereafter, when Penguin was harvesting the works of his peers and his inferiors, no major Priestley novel was gathered in, not even in 1956 when the firm reached its majority and announced that it was celebrating the occasion by 'looking back and doing full justice to the writers of the thirties'. In Priestley's eyes the affront was made all the more vicious because he had known Allen in his neophyte days at The Bodley Head and looked upon 'Billy Williams as a friend of mine'. In 1966, even after his dignity had been assuaged by the publication of *The Good Companions*, still Priestley was not satisfied. 'No attempt was ever made,' he wrote to Allen, 'to publish a number of my books altogether' and he added, he blamed the exclusion upon 'somebody there [at Harmondsworth] who is against me and my work'. He suspected 'one of Dr Leavis's pupils'.

It must be doubted that Allen caught the allusion; certainly he made no reference to it in his conciliatory reply. The bickerings of academic literary critics seldom reached his ears and, had they done so, would have been beyond his comprehension. The controversial Cambridge don, who in his life-time was so little honoured except by those he had taught and by his American disciples, was himself never beatified by the Penguin Congregation of Rites. He made two brief appearances in Penguin history, once in an entirely negative way (as will appear) by his refusal to support the firm in the *Lady Chatterley* case and once as an author, the first to be selected for the Peregrine series, that collection of esoteric, high-priced, high-brow and from the publishers of

Penguins seemingly tautologous titles produced as counter to developing competition from what came to be known as egghead paperbacks. His astringent personality can be seen, if dimly, in the background to *The Penguin Guide to English Literature* which was edited and almost exclusively written by Leavisites. But the bias against Priestley, if it existed at all or is not accountable to some reluctance upon the part of his prime publishers, William Heinemann, to part with any rights in an author who sold in hundreds of thousands even without Penguin assistance, cannot be marked against some quisling from Downing College, Cambridge, lurking unnoticed among the more generous-minded inhabitants of Harmondsworth, for there was none such.

But if this attempt to impeach Leavis can be said not to bear scrutiny, Priestley's undisguised admission of a sense of grievance does emphasize the manner in which writers had come to regard publication by Penguin as an accolade and selection as the author of a 'Penguin Million' – already accorded to George Bernard Shaw, H. G. Wells, Evelyn Waugh, Georges Simenon, Agatha Christie and D. H. Lawrence – as the literary equivalent of elevation to the peerage.

The inclusion of such powerful representatives as Thomas Mann, André Gide, Pierre Daninos, Georges Simenon, Jean-Paul Sartre, Pirandello and Albert Camus would have been testimony enough for Allen's insistence that Penguin editorial policy was international in concept. There were many other translations, both of masterpieces and of popular fiction, and the eighty titles added to the Classics, ranging in time from Plato to Ibsen and in source from the Middle East to Belgium, all add strength to the contention that Penguins were neither linguistically chauvinistic nor historically myopic.

In that decade the non-fiction list burgeoned almost as rapidly (close to 250 Pelicans, most of them commissioned, 15 volumes of *The Buildings of England*, 20 Handbooks, 27 Music Scores, 13 Reference Books, 17 King Penguins, 37 Penguin Poets and 18 volumes of *The Pelican History of Art*, alongside 500 fiction reprints). Almost every topic from soccer to sociology, from homosexuality to horticulture, from philosophy to gambling, was food for Penguin consumption and the non-fiction writers match for fame and variety the fiction list. There was Bertrand

Russell, William Temple, Sherrington, Bronowski, A. J. Ayer, H. J. Eysenck and, a prime example of Penguin lavishness and generosity, in addition to the commissioned volumes in the history of England, reprints of books by some of the greatest living historians: Neale, Trevelyan, Runciman, Huizinga, Churchill, Helen Waddell – and Sellars and Yeatman.

There was, however, in this decade a noticeable tailing-off in interest in politics. Only twenty-four Specials appeared in the fifties, as compared to four times as many in the forties. To a degree the decision to hold back from the pleasures of topical controversy was forced upon Penguin by changed attitudes within the printing industry for it was no longer possible to persuade or bribe operatives to meet seemingly impossible deadlines. There was also a realization that controversy, particularly political controversy, was no longer likely to produce the profits that had come in the heyday of Specials. The public, which in the years of crisis before the war, in the war years, and in the immediate post-war period had been almost obsessively involved with things political, had come to think of politics as a distant and generally boring business conducted in distant and generally boring places by distant and generally boring politicians.

Had Williams continued to wield the power in Penguin and the influence on Allen that he had throughout the forties, he might have persuaded Allen to maintain the flow of political Specials. Though Williams's interest in politics generally had always been subordinate to his interest in the politics of the arts and though his sympathy for the Left had never fired him as it had Krishna Menon, he was at heart a journalist and never so happy nor so acute as when he was dealing with topicalities and excited by pressures. Indeed, as late as 1956 Williams did draft a memorandum for the Penguin editorial board (in itself a symptom of changed circumstances; hitherto most of his advice had been offered less formally) pointing out that Penguin had made its reputation and its unique status by creating public taste, not by bending to the winds of opinion; the firm could and should revive public interest in politics.

This memorandum led to the resuscitation of Specials in the next decade, though the revivification was less real than apparent. The series was no longer dedicated almost exclusively to the immediate nor yet so palpably political as it had been in its vigorous youth but, if still in the fifties each man would have claimed the other as his closest friend, the quality of their intimacy had changed. Williams was now unquestionably Allen's equal, his ability, energy and his genius for being in the right place at the right time (a capacity which he shared with Allen) had marched him to the top of the hill. As Secretary-General of the Arts Council he was Britain's arch-dispenser of patronage, much courted by artists, and consulted day in and day out by civil servants and ministers on issues connected with government support for the arts. These issues British civil servants and ministers of all parties always find particularly embarrassing; they are therefore relieved to find someone who, like Williams, will offer incisive advice and who is willing to accept, as was Williams, that theirs was the glory and his the opprobrium that followed upon their actions. Williams's involvement with the Arts Council reduced the time and energy he could devote to Penguin and reduced also both the self-seeking and the altruistic motives that had inspired his dedication to Penguin. He no longer needed Penguin as the ladder to fame and power; all that he had once done for readers by way of Penguin he was now doing for a larger constituency of artists and a wider and more varied audience by way of the Arts Council. Allen, for his part, never entirely at his ease with equals and above all uncomfortable in the company of equals who had once been in any way dependent upon his beneficence, found cause for offence in Williams's amnesia which allowed him to ignore the part Penguin had played in his rise to power.

Allen, however, had reasons of his own for accepting and even encouraging a reduction in the number of Penguins dedicated to political affairs. He had always resented the imputation that the editorial policies of the firm were inspired by Leftish prejudices representing his own predeliction. As has been seen, this resentment had gripped him even in the pre-war days when it could fairly be argued that vocal opposition to the dictators came most ardently from men of the Left; his courage in providing a platform for the prophets in the wilderness of appeasement and complacency had been misinterpreted, even by some friends, as proof that he was, at very least, a fellow-traveller. In truth Allen had thought very little on political matters and never deeply, but he was thoughtful about the status of Penguin and sensitive to any change in public opinion that might bring it into disrepute. He had visited the Soviet Union and had found it generally depressing. He disliked the drabness of Moscow and was bored by the one diversion arranged for him by his official hosts, a visit to the Bolshoi (later he was pleasantly impressed by China, where the entertainment provided for him was much more lavish). But he was no better prepared than any other unsophisticated reader of British newspapers for the hideous revelations that followed upon the death of Stalin. The Cold War and, more particularly, the revulsion which, after 1953, transmogrified western opinion of Russia, making the so-recent noble ally into yet another hideously oppressive regime, made him realize that if, as was almost certain, moderate radicalism was now misrepresented as virulent Marxism, the consequence for Penguin must be much more dire than before the war. He was by then no longer certain of his commitment even to moderate radicalism. Prosperity, acceptance and middle age had eroded a radicalism which had never been as potent as he had liked to pretend; by nature perverse and having achieved respectability and eminence in a period that coincided almost precisely with the advance of the Labour Party to respectability and to government, he had come to be uneasy about his identification with the new Establishment and sought to recover his youthful reputation for rebellion by demonstrating his independence from the movement that he had helped towards power. Capitalist though he was, he could never lock away in the junkroom of the past the self-portrait of Allen Lane, apostle of egalitarianism. When asked, he continued to insist that his vote went always to a Labour candidate but there were no longer many perfervid Socialists among his advisers or closer acquaintances. In the next years as he searched for a putative successor twice his eye fell upon Conservative Members of Parliament, C. M. Woodhouse and Edward Boyle, both admittedly politicians as unsympathetic to the Monday Club as they were to the Tribune Group, but both inconceivable as partners of Allen Lane in the days of Krishna Menon and Jimmy Maxton.

Nevertheless, prosperity, acceptance and middle age had not blunted Allen's shrewdness as a publisher. This very capacity in time frustrated his intention to free Penguin from the stigma of Marxist leanings. He had made his way and he had established Penguin as an institution by being bold, by taking risks both commercial and editorial, and he knew that if he allowed himself to settle to a walk others would jump as formerly he had jumped, and would jump past him, leaving Penguin as just one more modestly successful and entirely unnoticeable publishing house. But the organization was now too big and too complex for him to jump bearing all on his own back. He must concede to subordinates the right to carry some of the burden. He needed venturesome adjutants, young men who would perpetuate the advanced policies that had helped to impress upon the public the uniqueness of Penguin. Because venturesome young men were more often than not inclined to the Left (though those he employed were not as red as they were subsequently painted by their critics), it was inevitable that they brought to Penguin with their editorial liveliness more than a touch of political bias and thus opened the way in the late sixties and early seventies to a renewed outburst of vilification of Allen and Penguin.

In the fifties, however, Allen looked around at his creation 'and saw that it was good'. There was little cause for qualms: he found none even in the heightened competition; but many reasons for jubilation and several times in ten years Allen ordered fanfares to honour the glories of an institution that could no longer be numbered among the *arrivistes*, an organization with a rich history, aware of its robust present and bustling with unfettered confidence in a future that promised to be as vivid as its past and as prosperous and energetic as its present.

The publication in 1954 as Penguin number 1000 of Edward Young's account of his war-experiences, *One of Our Submarines*, was more intimate than other blasts of self-congratulation. It was, perhaps, a sentimental gesture but sentimentality was an aspect of Allen's character that, above all others and against contrariness on his part, added affection to the admiration felt by all who worked for him and helped to sustain their loyalty, often despite the evidence of their own eyes and of their own experience. The purpose of this gesture towards the man who had designed the first Penguin emblem may not have been understood by many outside the immediate Penguin circle; within that circle it was accepted and appreciated for what it was, a salute to the pioneers and an expression of gratitude to all who had served Allen in the nineteen years of Penguin history. (It was a salute made all the more remarkable because, on this rare occasion, Allen forced himself to suppress his habitual antipathy to war-books.)

The other anniversary celebrations were more public and more blatant. In 1956, to honour its coming of age, the firm published *The Penguin Story* written by Williams in a manner that can only be described as complacent. 'The free-lance phase of Penguins is over,' wrote the author in a stentorian peroration; 'the adventurous sallies have given way to the solid responsibility of building up a comprehensive Popular Educator.' The capitalization was undoubtedly the author's, and the statement of intention. It must be doubted that it was the publisher's for Allen, deprived of opportunities for 'adventurous sallies', would have been as unhappy as Casanova in the Piombi, and none knew it better than Allen himself.

Four years later, to greet the Silver Jubilee, another volume appeared, with *Penguins Progress 1935–1960* on the title-page and spine and, lest the reader could not calculate, *Twenty Five Years* on the cover. In editorial planning it was less obviously narcissistic than either *The Penguin Story* or Segrave's *Ten Years of Penguins*. This time a number of writers were enlisted to offer, each on behalf of his own kind, congratulations to Penguin on the occasion of their Silver Jubilees. There was Compton Mackenzie for authors, Professor Michael Grant for teachers, Elliott Viney for printers, Richard Hoggart for readers and Reuben Heffer for booksellers, all men who had themselves contributed to Penguin history and all men who were prepared to admit that they and those for whom they spoke had profited greatly from Penguin success. The introduction was written by the Chairman of Cassell's. The cricketing metaphors that he used must have mystified Allen who only once in his adult life took any part in a game of cricket – playing for Penguin against their printers – and on that unique occasion was only once active, when he jumped over the ball as it approached him where he was fielding at very long leg. Though Desmond Flower wrote for himself and not for the body corporate of publishing, his admiring and affectionate tribute was generous compensation for the absence of any contribution written specifically in the name of those who had profited as much as any and more than most from Allen's audacity and who owed him some form of collective apology for their collective antagonism and timidity a quarter of a century earlier.

Within the book world only one important group, the library service, remained ostentatiously silent. Relations between libraries and publishers have always been tinged with suspicion. Librarians are apt to think of publishers as no better than other sordid men of commerce who gloat over their account books but care nothing for the books that make their balance-sheets such pleasant reading. Publishers castigate librarians as book-misers who would rather see thousands of volumes on their own shelves than dozens on the shelves of readers. On both sides these suspicions had been for the most part ill-founded. But during a period which coincided almost exactly with the history of Penguin they had been given point if not substance by the vociferous, active and virtually unanimous opposition of the library profession to every attempt to secure for authors and publishers some method whereby they could be recompensed for the lending-out of their books by libraries. Allen had taken little part in these wrangles, though twice he added his signature to letters to the press which were well-disposed towards his fellow-publishers and unequivocally sympathetic to the authors' cause. As he had the most to lose he was the most vocal and the most active objector to the custom, practised in so many public libraries, of casing paperbacks in durable covers which he like any just man (and like any indignant author) looked upon as an exaggeration of the inequity which allowed librarians to exploit and the public to enjoy freely the fruits of the co-operative labours of author and publisher. He went to law on the issue and won an action that did not endear him to the library profession. There were, however, more subtle reasons for the lack of enthusiasm for Allen and for Penguin that was common if not universal among public librarians. By opening the way to new and vast opportunities for book-ownership the paperback revolution seemed to threaten book-borrowing. The accessibility and 'friendliness' of Penguins and other paperback series was perceived by many librarians as doom to their cherished status as the principal and most intimate benefactors of the reading public.

The fears were at very least premature and probably worthless. Paperbacks helped to destroy the old subscription libraries and the 'twopenny libraries' but in that process their part was insignificant when compared to the part played by the public libraries themselves. Though any attempt to establish cause and effect must be complicated and is probably futile, it is possible to argue from the statistics that the explosion in the book buying habit after 1935 and the simultaneous growth in book borrowing is more than a coincidence.

Intended as they were primarily as exercises in public relations, it is not surprising that the anniversary publications in 1956 and 1960 were, like *Ten Years of Penguins* in the previous decade, short on self-criticism; if, in retrospect, the noise of so much drumbeating is close to being offensive, much is redeemed by the care and impeccable taste that went into the presentation of the giveaway histories. *Penguins Progress 1935–1960* stands high among Penguin productions; despite the need to accommodate illustrations in colour and black-and-white by several artists, decorations, photographs, substantial and sometimes severe text matter, are all manoeuvred into a unity and so managed as to sustain that lightness and cheerfulness that had come to be typically Harmondsworth. The one concession forced by the complexities of *Penguins Progress 1935–1960* was that it was not produced in the conventional Penguin size; yet it is immediately and infallibly recognizable as a Penguin.

Allen's concern for the production and his frequent interventions in the course of its preparation prove that in 1960 as in 1935 his interest in book design was among the most prominent of his characteristics as a publisher. Tschichold and after him Schmoller had changed the face of the Penguin, not its smile or its unpretentious elegance; but without Allen's constant encouragement neither Tschichold nor Schmoller could have kept Penguin from succumbing to the pressure for economy and thus from the shoddiness that was general, if not quite universal, among paperback houses.

The self-indulgent custom of presenting to themselves handsomely wrapped birthday-gifts is not peculiar to Penguin. To those who simultaneously give and receive it is all the more gratifying because the cost can be set to the publicity account and thus be borne by the Inland Revenue. Nor was it in the Penguin story peculiar to the fifties; all that can be said is that in the fifties custom came close to being mania and the cause is not difficult to find. Allen was almost as old as the century and awareness of the years was upon him; reminiscence had become more comfortable than prognosis, looking back made all the more delectable by the knowledge of difficulties overcome and status achieved, and given added piquancy by the awareness that among those who read the record of his glories there would be many who at the outset had forecast doom, who had done their utmost to fulfil their prophecies and who had cursed his triumph. But his ebullience had always been tempered by doubts; the years and increasing success brought not, as might have been expected, erosion of uncertainty but an access of fear that, at the last, his achievement might prove illusory, that when he died Penguin would collapse and, with its founder, be forgotten. From time to time he articulated the reasons for this unease, offering to his acquaintances the egocentric but impeccable argument that, as Penguin was so dependent on his personality and leadership, its character must change drastically with his disappearance, so drastically, perhaps, as to be no longer identifiable as his creation. Then he would mock out of existence his terror. Penguin, he would say – and the argument was no less egocentric and equally impeccable – was Allen Lane but so also was Allen Lane Penguin; when he no longer existed it could no longer matter what happened to Penguin.

Yet beyond doubt he was determined to leave behind him some memorial; if not Penguin as he had made it, then at least some visible and enduring record that would prove that the Penguin he had created had existed, had been powerful and energetic. This obsession with the opinion of posterity as much as his concern for the approbation of contemporaries or the mischievous pleasure that he took from recalling the folly and malevolence of his ill-wishers persuaded him to raise in his lifetime so many memorials to his genius.

Of these the most extraordinary was the huge group portrait, 'After the Conference: The Penguin Editors' commissioned from Rodrigo Moynihan in 1955. It purports to show gathered together all the series editors, with Allen, Dick, Williams,

Eunice Frost and Glover. It was extraordinary, not so much because it offered to the viewer a deliberate, solemn and formal interpretation of Penguin as an institution entirely out of keeping with the casual and swashbuckling reality, as because it was intrinsically dishonest. In all the twenty years of Penguin history there had never been a 'conference' of editors (the 'weekly meetings' included only full-time staff), most of the editors were strangers to each other, some were out of the country or otherwise engaged on the one occasion, 'After the Conference' became historical evidence, when the painter took films in preparation for his painting. Some, who were not present when the picture was given a private viewing at the Leicester Galleries, have not to this day met most of the men and women in whose company they will hang, presumably for all time, in the main lobby at Harmondsworth. Some, having discovered that like Allen they are not after all immortal, are now not likely to come together unless a Penguin editorial conference is arranged by an authority higher than either Allen Lane or Rodrigo Moynihan. The scene, a room made elegant by arches and pillars is the Senior Common Room of the Royal College of Art, a setting that has no association with Penguin history except as the backdrop for Moynihan's 'After the Conference'.

The aesthetic quality of the painting must be judged by others; some of the critics were far from kind. When it went on public view at the Royal Academy one of those honoured by inclusion made himself unpopular both with Allen and with the artist by remarking in the stage-whisper for which he was infamous: 'Better a team photograph, all of us in rows with A.L. in the centre clasping a Penguin marked 1955 and the small fry of the team cross-legged on the ground at his feet.' The picture is a fabrication, but it does show all those responsible for Penguin's editorial policies in a period which many have come to see as the golden age. There is Williams, massive in the foreground, and for some reason more prominent even than Allen himself. Rieu is larger than life (just tribute to a man who translated not only Homer but also the Four Gospels), Pevsner somewhat diminished in scale. Eunice Frost and Glover stand out from the rest but in the crowd there is Gordon Jacob, Mallowan, Carrington, Ayer, Eleanor Graham of Puffins and Fishenden the Technical Editor of King Penguins. Lehmann peeps out from behind a pillar and Morpurgo hangs like a gargoyle from the opposite wall.

Even more important: though 'After the Conference' is in the eyes of any purist a lie, it uncovers a profound truth about Allen. He wanted and could afford his monument. He could have followed the example of many another tycoon and many another petty businessman, sitting for his portrait and hanging it at Harmondsworth as perpetual reminder of the Founder, but though he knew that Moynihan needed no prompting to avoid the solecism of losing Allen in the murkier recesses of the picture, he was genuinely concerned to leave a reminder of Penguin as a venture in which many men and women had played their considerable part. Like Captain Franz Banning Cocq before him, if he was certain that the light would shine most brilliantly upon him and make inescapable the realization that he was the catalyst and the commander, he was also determined to have around him his Company memorialized for all time. (In this unlike his self-immortalized predecessor, Allen did not charge members of his 'Night Watch' 'more for the one person and less for the other, depending upon the place which they had in it', but Moynihan's grouping seems to indicate that, either under advice or by instinct, he had made some assessment of the comparative worth to Penguin of each individual in the group.)

Allen had, indeed, much to celebrate as he considered Penguin in the fifties and early sixties, but he could not hide his face entirely in the comforting sands of commemoration. Growth had brought with it many of the problems that come with size – complacency, lack of delegation, difficulties in communication – problems made more intractable by his own seemingly autocratic, changeable and frequently secretive manner and by the arrogance that some who had served him longest and were closest to him had adopted either because it was natural to them or because they believed it the best way of representing Allen to junior colleagues.

There is in the Penguin archives a memorandum, undated and unsigned but written to Allen almost certainly in 1954 or 1955, possibly by Dick but more probably by Glover, which sets out, sagaciously and with uninhibited frankness, some of the grievances of the younger members of the staff. These included many that were in publishing not peculiar to Penguin: long hours, short holidays and poor pay; but these commonplace grouses are of infinitesmal significance when compared to the theme which runs throughout the 2000-word document and which is hammered out most vigorously by the use of such phrases as 'supercilious manner' and a 'we and them custom' to describe the attitude of Allen and his senior staff to their inferiors.

> The senior people and those who have been longest with the firm have a different kind of background ... to these young University intellegentsia [who] have, naturally and rightly, ambitions and interests which are not shared by and mean little to the others. They appreciate ... that seniority and experience count for a very great deal in the running of this, or of any, business. But they cannot forget – and, after all, why should they? – that talents of a different kind are needed for looking after the physical side of the business – accounts, warehouse, sales and so on – and for the 'spiritual' side – the production of our books ... including the editorial work, the personal relationships and negotiations, the contacts with the outside world. And they feel ... that not as much use is being made of them as could be made. I have heard it said, for example, that if the BBC can discover that Miss W ... is worth picking out of 200 candidates to do a responsible job for them, why couldn't more use have been made, and more expectation shown, of her here?

The writer gave a shattering answer to his own question:

> We have three people in the front offices (and I'm perfectly ready to grant that I myself may be a fourth) who all in their respective ways have unusually strong personalities; who all have an 'urge for power'; who none of them happen to be very tactful or psychologically penetrating in their methods of dealing with other people, particularly their subordinates; and who are all, I think, consciously or unconsciously, jealous of the people who work with them knowing too much or taking too much responsibility.

And, ducking under Allen's guard, he took his chance, delivering an undisguised left jab and, immediately, a powerful right hook:

> You've got such an overwhelmingly definite personality yourself that they have set you up as a model, as it were without being at all like you.

It does not appear that Allen ever replied to this critique. He had no great love for the formalities of inter-office communication, preferring to seek out in his own office any who addressed him in this way. There, perching himself on the corner of the other man's desk, if the matter raised was to him embarrassing or prematurely posed, he would begin with a frank smile and an open admission that this was something which deserved serious discussion and then slip somehow past controversy into confidence, leaving his protagonist at the last happy in the thought that he alone was privy to Allen's plans and dreams, for minutes – sometimes for hours or days – after Allen had disappeared unaware that his provocative questions had not been answered. But on the issue of restlessness among the younger staff Allen did not need to answer; nothing in the memorandum was news to him. It was disconcerting but not dramatically so and he was not inclined to allow it to increase the number of his sleepless nights. Indeed, he regarded friction among his subordinates as not only inevitable but even desirable: friction struck-off sparks; Penguin must be kept alight; if there was no spontaneous friction then he was ready to arrange it. Further, rivalries, jealousies, wrangles and disputes were all part of the ordeal by fire of candidates for power. Those who could not survive were no use to him and did not deserve a place in Penguin; senior or junior, there were always others clamouring to take their place. If he had ever been determined to run a happy ship that was no longer a persuasive consideration; now uppermost in his mind was the need to hold a crew loyal to the Penguin flag and to him as their captain. If he was in the least perturbed by rumblings from the gun-room, it was only because he was alert to the risks of gambling with relationships; resentment might explode into concerted mutiny.

As yet he had no real cause for worry. The stance of most of the staff was exactly as he would have wished and would have devised had he himself been responsible for all the choreography: aggressive competition one with another but still abundant enthusiasm for the unique mission of the firm and unequivocal loyalty to him. When there were outbursts of discontent or anger, they were directed against his immediate subordinates; for him, even when his behaviour was outrageous, there was only amused resignation, a chuckling, affectionate acceptance that amounted at times to pride in the knowledge that, in his attitudes to those who worked for him as in his publishing activities, A.L. was not bound by the conventions of lesser men. Those who could not live according to this pattern went elsewhere and there was indeed, as he expected, never any shortage of able volunteers eager to fill their shoes.

That he did behave outrageously is undeniable but, because he was still obsessed with Penguin and still almost without any interests except publishing that could hold his entire attention for long – not even interest in his family – the demands that he made upon his employees never touched his conscience; it never occurred to him that they were in any way inordinate.

Everyone who ever worked for Allen in his prime has some story to tell about his callousness. Bob Davies, for example, who had been taken on as an office-boy during the last month in the Crypt, remembers vividly the Allen of those days 'dark, slight, clipped and very, very abrupt, as if he hadn't got a second to live'. Davies had come back from the war to find himself promoted to the dubious honour of serving as Penguin's only sales-representative on the Continent. Allen himself planned Davies's itinerary. No one else in the firm knew the international railway time-tables as did he – except possibly Glover, who knew everything but never went abroad for Penguin and played no part in anything connected with sales. Allen also chose the hotels at which Davies must stay. 'All of them grotty,' says Davies; even for himself when on holiday and even when he was rich Allen had a perverse liking for third-rate hotels. (Hence the remark made by Paroissien's son, Paul, when as a young boy he and his parents went to France with the Lanes: 'Uncle Allen, couldn't we spend a little less on drinks and a little more on rooms?') Davies, thus regimented, would be sent off: Victoria to Newhaven, Newhaven to Dieppe, on to Paris, to Brussels, Amsterdam, Copenhagen, Oslo and then back to Harmondsworth for an hour with Allen and at the end of it only an urgent command to set off out again. 'He didn't understand that you'd been away for five weeks, that you had dirty laundry, that your wife wanted to see you. He was married to the firm and he expected all of us to follow his example, to give up all thought of domestic life. . . .'

After two years on the continental circuit Davies pronounced himself and his wife 'fed up with the existence'. He wanted a change but, if there was no other job available, he insisted that he must stay in hotels better than Allen's favoured Paris doss-house, the Bourgogne. Allen promised to give the matter some thought. He thought but did nothing for another two years.

Then Paroissien, who had himself been so often summoned home from Baltimore, asked for an assistant. The job was offered to Davies and he accepted. Immediately Allen began to haver; there was no one to take Davies's place in Europe; someone would have to be trained; Paroissien did not need an assistant; Paroissien needed an assistant, but not yet. So it went on for another eighteen months, Davies prompting and Allen postponing a decision until at the last Davies told him that as his wife was upset by the uncertainty, as he could not settle his daughter's education nor even buy curtains for his house, he had made the decision for Allen. He would not go to Baltimore.

Allen scowled and said nothing but, as so often when crossed, soon despatched his herald, in this case Eunice Frost, to deliver his ultimatum. A.L., she said, was dismayed by Davies's uncooperative attitude, particularly as Paroissien's need for an assistant was now imperative and the firm ready to arrange for Davies to go. Davies stayed adamant even when he was bearded by Allen.

For three years Davies received no increase in pay. He tells this story, as so many others tell similar stories about Allen, without any trace of bitterness, almost as if he were apologizing to Allen's ghost for remembering a discreditable incident as he brings back to mind Allen's spontaneous generosity whenever any member of his staff or their families were seriously ill – so much at variance with his miserliness over incidentals and his implacability in professional dealings; as he reminisces delightedly about Allen's shrewdness, his instinct for finding the right price for a book, his readiness to subsidize out of the profits from best-selling Penguins prestigious series, such as King Penguins, in which he believed even if he knew that they could never do much for his balance-sheet. It is episodes which illustrate Allen's vigour and not those which emphasize his harshness upon which Davies dwells most often: the furore and the publicity when the Melbourne Customs held up *The Golden Ass* because (not without justice) they classed it as pornographic; his brilliance as a salesman; and, always, the excitement he generated. 'Whenever he was about,' says Davies, 'there was excitement. It was as if he was himself some kind of generator giving off electricity. And we all felt it; not just the front office but all of us, clerks, accounts staff, packers, van drivers, lookers-out, even the ladies serving in the canteen, we all knew when there was something special going on, were all thrilled. It was *our* firm.' And he adds, somewhat wistfully, 'That *was* publishing.'

This extended example of the contradictory but overwhelmingly admiring view of Allen that is held to this day by a man who would not object to being described as one of Penguin's long-serving and stalwart warrant-officers is undoubtedly archetypal. It could stand, little amended, as representative of the *ex post facto* opinion even of many who served, more publicly, as holders of short-term commissions. Allen's recurring nightmare almost from the end of the war did not include any devil-dancing from such as these, men he knew he could manage, could either use or cast out. His besetting worry – it became in the sixties for a while an obsession – was that he had no successor. Paroissien, Eunice Frost, even Williams (for all his involvement elsewhere:) these were all capable aides but, if each for a different reason, it was not possible to see any one as his Heir Apparent. He complicated the situation by his ambivalence about the future. When he arranged commemorations of Penguin achievements, he was never able to make up his mind as to whether he intended them to stand as reminders of archaic marvels that had vanished with him or as ineradicable reminders that would prompt the public to seek his memorial, not in the commemoration itself, but in the continuing glory that was Penguin. As he teased at the enigma of the succession, he was pulled one way or another – and sometimes, it seemed, torn in half – by two contradictory but equally powerful forces. Common sense, the conventional wisdom of commerce and the unanimous opinion of the many advisers he consulted persuaded him that he must settle the future of Penguin before the moment arrived when he could no longer himself manipulate that future, but the egoist in him argued that he could not, and need not, be interested in a future in which he could play no part. After him let the flood come; in this mood he saw no reason to select his own Noah.

In 1965, writing to Williams, Allen rationalized his lack of concern for the future. Penguin, he insisted, 'we have made very much in our own image', and, he continued:

> What happens after our time is beyond our control. As good gardeners or farmers we can only do our best to see that the soil is kept in good heart, free of weeds, and that the crops are not forced but allowed a natural growth

in the knowledge that if these principles are followed our successors will continue to have the satisfaction from it that we have had ourselves.

This bland dismissal of any genuine responsibility for the future fought against his countervailing determination to legislate in advance at very least the character of that future by choosing his successor. The conflict might have been more easily resolved had he countenanced even the thought that he must allow his crown prince some measure of authority that would prepare him, the Penguin staff and the world at large for the coronation, and had not Allen known that his own machinations had made certain that, even if he brought his successor to the walls of Carnarvon Castle and gave him not just stated but also real power, his principal lieutenants, every one of whom had advised some action of this kind, would nevertheless pay only lip-homage to his Prince of Wales and, more than likely, would conspire to make the election nugatory.

Instead of decisiveness there was indecision or rather a plethora of confusing, obviously mutable and generally impulsive decisions. Uncertainty about future direction was one, and not the least, among several causes for the sapping of confidence which became obvious in Penguin during the sixties. The list of putative successors is long and the qualifications of those pricked out remarkably diverse. Some never knew that they were being considered. Some, like Arthur Crook, the Editor of *The Times Literary Supplement*, knew but rejected the honour. Some, Christopher Dolley and Ron Blass among them, were insiders, men already serving Allen in senior posts. Some had no knowledge of publishing but great expertise in other commercial activities, whereas several, Woodhouse and Boyle prominent in their number, had no previous experience of publishing but much experience of public life. On two occasions, separated by almost three years, Allen turned to Morpurgo. It was in a sense, yet another sentimental gesture, this salute to one of the few members of that generation of young men of Penguin's golden generation who had not become entirely divorced from Penguin nor removed from Allen's intimacy; it constituted also in Allen's mind a nice resolution of his dilemma because it committed him to no resolution. By offering the custodianship of the future to a representative of the past he thought to ensure that when the king died the cry would not be 'The King is dead; long live the King' but rather, 'The old order changeth, yielding place to the old.' (Whether he was right in his assumption none can tell, certainly not Allen's biographer who must nevertheless take to himself the dubious distinction of being the only man who twice mounted the steps and twice was tripped before he reached the throne.)

Allen's flirtations with possible successors were never wholehearted; on almost every occasion he left himself an escape route which was seldom obvious to the other man until the preliminaries were over: a vagueness about share-holding or pension rights, a reluctance to commit himself to any precise status for the chosen person in the time between proclamation and accession, and hesitant and conflicting answers to all enquiries about the duration of that misty period. Generally he let the heir assume that he was the only runner in the race but he judged well his man; if he felt that competition would encourage ambition and persuade the candidate to accept some disadvantage in the proposed deal, Allen would not only admit that he was one of several – though always first among equals – but would actually name the opposition. To one, an employee of long standing, he showed all the kingdoms of the earth and suggested that they could be his to inherit – if only his wife were more suited to be the Queen Consort of Penguin. The implication was obvious, and indignantly rejected. Indeed, with but two exceptions, the decision to break off negotiations came from the other party. Allen was left with the comfortable feeling that he had done his best to do his duty, and all that he could for a worthy acquaintance.

Almost at the last, when serious illness forced upon him cleareyed awareness that, despite all his manoeuvrings and all these decisions no sooner made than unmade, nothing had been settled for a future that was now imminent, his attitude to the succession changed. By then he was no longer so much concerned to determine whether or not there should be a successor and if so who should be the confirmed candidate, as he was fearful that others were planning to make the decision for him. The suspicion which had so often soured his opinion of one who had but recently been his favourite was intensified by his consciousness of his own increasing helplessness to direct events and by the accident that there was in office at that time an individual as mercurial and as ambitious as Allen had ever been. He had given Tony Godwin his position in Penguin. Though there is no evidence that he had ever intended Godwin to be his heir nor even that he had ever promised to him anything of the kind, he woke to the realization that Godwin had accumulated much more power than Allen had ever conferred upon him: he had made himself, not only in the eyes of the uninformed, the obvious successor. Allen feared that he had encouraged not an heir but a usurper; if he were not checked, that even without his blessing Godwin would take the place that Allen had not yet abdicated.

> Dost thou so hunger for mine empty chair,
> That thou wilt needs invest thee with mine honours,
> Before thy hour is ripe?

Alarm roused Allen to the last and certainly the most bitter quarrels of his life; quarrels made all the more fierce by the two antagonists being a match for each other in acerbity. Unfortunately Godwin possessed neither that disarming capacity for self-deprecating laughter that made Allen's more heinous activities seem so often no more than boyish mischief nor (or so it seemed) that over-riding affection and admiration for Allen which, despite all provocation, had blunted the swords of many of his opponents.

With this late exception Allen found stimulation and some pleasure in the quest for an understudy. He was no longer himself often intimately involved in dealings with publishers or authors over individual titles but negotiations, haggling and wrangling with men who were, many of them, his peers as bazaar merchants was like manna in a world that, but for this, would have seemed a desert. The process was stimulating and he could dignify it, even to himself, as the ultimate and most sensational application of his abiding principle that the worth of aspirants for authority should not be measured by reputation, appearance or the recommendation of others but must be treated in action, first, in a skirmish of wits and thereafter, as no more than a temporary commander of some Penguin forces in the field. From his point of view even better: those with whom he was now engaged were not, like their predecessors, novices who looked to him to start them on a career, for these were all men of some eminence with substantial and sometimes sensational careers already behind them. It was for him to discover, for them to prove that what was good enough for politics, commerce, the philanthropic foundations, academic institutions or conventional publishing was good enough for Penguin.

Throughout his adult life Allen had on occasion looked for supports to decision beyond the evidence of his own eyes and the promptings of his own instinct. In 1929 he had consulted an American astrologer about his future. His life, she had assured him, 'would be successful but uneventful for the next twenty-one years' and she advised him to take 'the line of intelligent non-resistance'. He 'craved travel'; that she could discern in his horoscope; 'but there is a strong indication that your best prospects seem to come through remaining in the land of your birth'. 'There is,' wrote Miss Evangeline Adams, 'little to indicate that you should go into business for yourself.'

Allen, notoriously careless with personal correspondence, nevertheless kept Miss Adams's letter in his files for the rest of his life. It would be more flattering to his memory and more consistent with his reputation for shrewdness and for mischievousness if it could be assumed that the document was preserved as a self-mocking reminder of youthful folly or as a sensational example of bad marksmanship but there are, hoarded among the disappointingly few private records of forty years, a disproportionate number of astrological predictions – which become increasingly percipient as his growing fame made simpler the task of the soothsayers. When he came to the great search for a successor, he proved his obstinate and naïve faith in astrology by having cast the horoscopes of all the more promising candidates.

In the war years he had discovered a more substantial aid to decision-making, and ever after sought the opinion of a graphologist on any person with whom he was engaged in any sense that he regarded as potentially significant. This he did even when the relationship was essentially intimate. For each member of his family, not once but many times, he had both horoscope and handwriting analysed. Without revealing that it was his own he sent examples of his calligraphy to several experts and one, writing in 1956, produced a palpable hit: '[this] mode of appearing and tackling things, although it is forceful, has become . . . almost stereotyped . . . others expect him to present himself according to an anticipated pattern. He feels the need to be a magnetic centre.' When he was about to enter into the one enduring liaison of his mature years he first took the precaution of submitting an example of Suzanne's handwriting to his current graphologist, accompanying it with a frank statement on what he had in mind (but not the lady's name). The reply he received encouraged him and, even if it may be difficult to guess what course he would have followed if the graphologist had advised him to avoid the entanglement, the acumen which he recognized in that part of the assessment which related to the lady's artistic qualities was, at least in part, responsible for the unprotesting manner in which subsequently he accepted her leadership in his forays into collecting and for his complacency, which he accorded to few others, when she offered her opinion upon editorial policy or upon the personalities of Penguin.

As he had looked to astrologers so also did he look to graphologists to give him more information than he could glean for himself about all his prospective heirs-apparent. Not all the resulting dossiers have survived; of those that remain none can be identified beyond question. Because the covering-letters have all been destroyed (either by Allen or by some other person intent on preserving confidentiality) it is not even possible to use chronology as an aid to intelligent guess-work. There is no name anywhere in the collection and among the reports bearing upon the succession only one is dated: January 1968. The graphologist writes of a handwriting-sample: 'It may easily be the most important one you have shown me for years. . . . I can imagine vividly what makes him attractive to you but also what you may not overlook. . . . He is cautious, genuinely timid and needs to proceed without drawing attention to himself. He is not agressive but will make a good *representative* rather than a leader.' Because this is the last item in a file that makes uncomfortable reading it is not difficult to narrow the possibilities; from an identity parade of four candidates, only two come close to suiting the time and to matching this description. But it is conceivable that graphology is not an exact science and that the expert was not as proficient as she or Allen imagined. The list must be left with four candidates. He who the cap fits must be allowed to wear it – in private.

Not all of the many plans devised for the eventual control of the firm involved the selection of an individual. Several times Allen moved towards an arrangement with his fellow publishers. Some of the schemes were no more than reactions, somewhat late in the day, to the growing competition from other paperback houses and to the fact that more and more publishers were establishing their own paperback imprints. All that Allen offered, in deals that approximated to the 'special relationship' agreements of international diplomacy, was particular attention to the lists of his treaty partners. All that he asked in return was an assurance that Penguin would be given first refusal on any titles. There was not on either side any will to add long-term implications to a scheme designed to meet immediate needs; no staff reorganization was envisaged, no surrender of editorial initiative and no exchange of shares. Even so, though several pacts of this kind were sealed and all of them with much banging of drums by the Publicity Department, in every case even the short term proved remarkably brief and the schemes died without a whimper from Harmondsworth or Bloomsbury.

There was, however, in Allen's mind the rough sketch of a plan for a more formal and enduring alliance with other publishers. Memories of the futility of the trade's calm attempt to cooperate against him by raising a rival paperback series did not encourage him to look in this direction for the perpetuation of Penguin ideas and ideals, but as counter to the sorry history of Guild Books, jaded even in infancy and dead before maturity, he had the vigorous example of Pan Books, Penguin's outstanding competitor and controlled by a board which included representatives of leading publishing houses. He toyed with the notion of following in the steps of Pan. When he toyed he talked; when he talked he bargained; when he bargained he made promises; and more than once he convinced himself and those on the other side of the table that when he promised his fingers were not crossed behind his back.

He did in fact commit himself to arrangements of this kind with other publishers on a limited scale, with Longman for collaboration in exports and, one after another, with several

Americans for the exploitation of the United States market.

How many was his transatlantic 'several' it is impossible to say; even W. E. Williams, who still at the time when his editorial and personal influence was waning was nevertheless the one man who was invariably present as both *claque* and licensed critic at all significant negotiations, can come no closer to a statistic than 'at least five major American publishers'. Computation must depend on a complicated equation which includes a factor for the intensity of cooperation proposed and another for Allen's interest and sincerity. Because these two factors are susceptible only to subjective measurement the consequent resolution of the equation would be even less precise than that offered by Williams, but the sum of the recollections of all those close to Allen in the fifteen years from 1950 to 1965 adds to one persisting memory; of distinguished-looking, grey-suited, clean-shaven men emerging from Immigration and Customs at Heathrow with, a pace or so behind them, their lawyers clutching expensive brief-cases.

Williams suggests that the Americans usually took these negotiations more seriously than did Allen who 'always liked to have a simmering pot on the fire', but the regularity of his attention to some kind of American alliance does demonstrate his unsatisfied hankering for sensational success in the United States and his shrewd awareness that, with the expertise of American publishers on his side, he could achieve much more than Paroissien had been able to secure for him; just as his breaking-off of negotiations, often just when they were close to maturity, proves that he was not ready to abdicate in favour of some American tycoon.

Earlier there had been the hesitant agreement with D. C. Heath. Then, just before Paroissien was brought back to England, there was concluded what seemed to be to that moment the most promising American alliance, this time with a new house, Atheneum.

The history of this concordat is typical. It contains so many of the elements of impulsive attachment to individuals, no less impulsive rejection of favourites, pertinacity, acumen and inconsistency that were common to all Allen's negotiations. It had its prologue in Allen's association with Morris L. Ernst, the combative New York attorney who wrote in his autobiography 'gracious good fortune has given me many opportunities to pitch for freedom . . . once in England years ago I thought of giving a party to some of the British authors whose works I have defended – Havelock Ellis, Marie Stopes, Radclyffe Hall, James Joyce – to name but a few'. Ernst had been Allen's friend since the days when the Lane brothers bought the British rights of *Ulysses* and for much of that time had been one of his American legal advisers.

When Ernst first heard of Paroissien's recall he commended to Allen his son-in-law, Michael Bessie an editor at Harper Bros. (who were also Ernst's publishers); it was with Bessie, acting as the representative of Harper, that the haggling began.

The opening dialogue was spoken at the Frankfurt Book Fair, that great annual celebration of book trade internationalism. There, in September 1958, Allen, Paroissien and Bessie sat down to hammer out an agreement between Penguin and Harper. Refinements were added at a subsequent meeting in New York but the negotiations collapsed because the Harper representatives would not give up their demand for a substantial block of Penguin shares.

A few months later Ernst intervened again. His son-in-law was leaving Harper to join two fugitives from other houses (one of them the son of Alfred Knopf and his formidable wife, Blanche) in their own business. Michael Bessie was ready to take on Penguin representation in the United States 'on any suitable terms'. Allen looked upon this offer with favour, in part because he wanted Paroissien at Harmondsworth and had no one to replace him in Baltimore, in part because he saw advantages in cooperation with a new firm that must be less determined than any old-established house to go its own way even with the Penguin list. This new firm was managed by men who, for all that they were young, energetic and ambitious, were nonetheless already old hands in publishing – and well-capitalized. Not the least of his considerations was personal; he favoured arrangements which allowed him to work with men he liked. If liking did not always survive the experience of collaboration, the thought that sentiment and sense were coincident added to the pleasures of anticipation. He liked Bessie.

The various parties to the deal with Atheneum shuttled around the world in a manner that was, even for Allen, well-nigh hysterical; in less than three months there were meetings between the principals in New York, Vienna, London and Baltimore; and almost before Atheneum had its own note-paper printed the new firm's new salesmen were on the road with a list of 200 Penguins and not one Atheneum title in their bags.

Bessie stipulated that Atheneum be allowed to offer to American wholesalers and to retail booksellers more generous discounts than had hitherto been the custom of Penguin Books Inc. This Allen conceded, despite reservations expressed by Paroissien. He also agreed to finance advertising on a scale much greater than anything that had previously been allowed to Baltimore and that was out of keeping with practice at Harmondsworth, where buying space in the press was still regarded as an exceptional breach of Penguin principles. Further, he accepted for the United States what had been tried and rejected in Britain: that direct selling should be positively encouraged.

All these concessions to his new partners proved wise, effective and almost certainly the only way to place the American Penguin in a situation where it could hope to compete with the entrenched opposition, all of whom employed similar methods and all much more extravagantly than Penguin–Atheneum. At the end of the first year of joint operations the book value of Penguin sales in America had risen to $875,000, an increase of more than twenty per cent on Paroissien's projection. Profits had marched in step with the sales because Allen realized that, for all that he was attempting to compete with popular series, the quality and style of the Penguins that sold best in the United States made them in the eyes of the buying public more nearly analogous to the more expensive and specialist paperbacks appearing for the first time in large numbers on the American scene. He had authorized a general increase in Penguin prices to offset the increased costs inherent in the Penguin–Atheneum arrangement. In 1960, even when enhanced discounts were taken into account, the trade price per book went up by 10 per cent, the largest increase for nine years.

Allen had not become overnight a soft negotiator. Not unnaturally Bessie wanted a long-term agreement; Allen would offer no more than three years. Even within that term he kept the right to abrogate the arrangement with no more than four weeks' notice. The liaison with Atheneum was 'a trial marriage with a view to a permanent relationship'; the phrase was Ernst's but the sentiment was very much Allen's also. He knew that other American houses were eager to take on Penguin representation. Though he was delighted with the figures that Atheneum presented to him, he was soon aware that Atheneum was exerting very little influence on that part of the American business, almost 50 per cent of the whole, which was built from educational sales. Furthermore, by the beginning of 1961, he was already concerned lest Atheneum work to reduce the status of Baltimore to little more than a Southern warehouse. His suspicion became terror when Paroissien predicted in March 1961 that, if Bessie and his colleagues were allowed to continue unhindered, within a year Penguin Books Inc. would be wholly dependent on Atheneum.

Allen's disquiet had been aroused even earlier by reports of some of the methods used by Atheneum to boost sales. Rebel and innovator though he was, he had always respected and generally accepted the discipline of the British book trade and he had insisted that Baltimore should conduct its sales policy in the severe manner of Harmondsworth without resorting to 'special deals' and other concessions to booksellers willing to offer volume sales. In America arrangements of this kind were not only customary but both obligatory and entirely honourable. Allen nevertheless disliked having them made in his name. This distaste had been one of the causes of his breach with Weybright and Enoch; it now began to disrupt his relations with Atheneum.

His capacity for suspicion was enlarged by remarks made by Bessie, probably in all innocence, about possible editorial collaboration; as ever, instead of bringing his doubts into the open, Allen decided to test the realities of the situation by encouraging the Atheneum board to enter the confessional. He would offer them something, see how much they hoped to grab and then either exploit their ambitions to his own advantage or else place them so situated that they had to withdraw from all connection with Penguin, leaving him publicly innocent and decently aggrieved, the deserted partner in the failed trial-marriage.

Paroissien, who had been privy to all the earlier negotiations with Atheneum, was not admitted to the second round of talks. It was as if Allen mistrusted his own ability to put on a convincing charade in front of one who had seen it all before; most of the information that came to Paroissien came not from Allen but from Bessie. When Bessie asked, as had every other American publisher who sought collaboration with Penguin, that Atheneum be given a stock-holding in Penguin Books Inc. Allen agreed nonchalantly, muttering something about 49 per cent. This vague assurance was reported to Paroissien as a firm promise, and even that most loyal of Allen's subordinates could not resist offering to Bessie a warning against taking Allen's negotiating word as his contractual bond.

The discussions spluttered on until the term of the original agreement came to an end. Then no more was heard of negotiation or agreement.

With Houghton Mifflin the negotiations were just as involved but the outcome seemingly more conclusive for they did acquire Penguin stock. But the conclusiveness was false. Immediately, as Williams wrote later: '. . . . he began to regret it and did not rest until he bought back his independence' from Houghton Mifflin. . . . 'They had observed the terms of the treaty meticulously, but Allen's basic allergy to all alliances was bound to prevail. Once a pact was agreed he began to develop suspicions of a subtle plot to erode his power.'

At the last he settled once more for a Penguin Books Inc. untouched by American associates, managed by Harmondsworth-trained deputies and run substantially on the same lines as the parent company.

Active though he was in all these manoeuvres in the United States, there was in Allen's attitude to them an amalgam of curiosity and dispassion. This, he knew, was not the ground on which the future of Penguin would be won or lost; he manipulated with cunning and he observed with care, but his involvement was no greater and no less than that of an experienced coach who sets his reserves to test in play tactics which by their success or failure will serve as lessons that can influence the manner in which he prepares his first team. The metaphor is useful and can be extended. His first team was Penguin Books Ltd. His experiments with the succession were not unlike the hesitancies of a coach who seeks a captain who can be depended upon to lead well and to carry out his intentions once the coach is silent and helpless on the touch-line.

No such frivolous metaphor is appropriate to one proposal that was advanced. The idea that Penguin should be taken over by a trust controlled by a group of academic institutions aroused his whole-hearted interest; in this way he could ensure that after his death Penguin would preserve its unique characteristics and continue to develop in the direction that had been evident since the publication of the first Pelican. It was not a new idea; from about 1950 Allen himself had been suggesting that he would like Penguin to be taken into protective custody. Since that time, Williams alone and Williams and Allen together had sporadically discussed the possibility with officers of various foundations. Woodhouse and Morpurgo, who both had close connections with the largest of British foundations, having been successively Assistant Director of Nuffield, separately wrote papers for the Trustees of the Foundation, but the inspiration for the most promising and definitive round of discussions, which took place in 1967 after Penguin had become a public company, came undoubtedly from Richard Hoggart.

The source made the notion even more attractive than it might otherwise have been. Hoggart's *The Uses of Literacy* was one of the few modern sociological books that Allen had read (even before it was published as a Pelican in 1957). If, mistakenly but conveniently, he equated Hoggart's working-class background in provincial Leeds with his own bourgeois heritage in provincial Bristol, nevertheless he did appreciate that *The Uses of Literacy* was, as it were, the Penguin gospel according to Hoggart and a fair representation of that gospel as Allen would have had it propounded.

There are in Hoggart's book very few references to Penguins; some of them are sardonic, as when he describes the prevalent tendency to seek 'entry into the cultured life' by 'a reading of cultured publications which is from one aspect improper, which is inspired by too vague an expectation'.

> For some people [Hoggart writes] the late *John O'London's Weekly* obviously met a strongly felt need, one stronger, I think, than it could have legitimately claimed to meet. Others are proud of reading J. B. Priestley and writers such as him, because they are 'serious writers with a message'. Others have learned that Mr Priestley is a 'middlebrow' and only mention him in tones of depreciation. They tend to read bitterly ironic or anguished literature – Waugh, Huxley, Kafka, and Greene. They own the Penguin selection

from Eliot, as well as some other Penguins and Pelicans; they used to take *Penguin New Writing* and now subscribe to *Encounter*. They know a little, but often only from reviews and short articles, about Frazer and Marx; they probably own a copy of the Pelican edition of Freud's *Psychopathology of Everyday Life*. They sometimes listen to talks on the Third Programme with titles like 'The Cult of Evil in Contemporary Literature'.

But generally Allen was right: elsewhere in the book Hoggart did justify his conviction that *The Uses of Literacy* absolved Penguin of the accusation of debasing British culture levelled against most of the media. Later (but too late for Allen because it was spoken at his memorial service) Hoggart made explicit his faith in the Penguin ideal, and in terms that Allen would have liked to use as his own had he been capable of equivalent articulacy:

> Penguins' basic attitude towards the life of the mind underpins their attitude towards their readers. They made assumptions about possible relationships which to some people are beginning to seem old-fashioned, touching maybe but probably mistaken. They assumed that you can make contact with others by trying to speak straight to them, and that it matters to try to connect is not just a deluded speaking into the void. Again, this tradition in Britain is long and has a special flavour. Remember that extraordinarily characteristic range of discursive voices which we hear all the way up through the nineteenth century, and in this century hear again, strikingly, in Forster and Lawrence and Orwell. Their tones differ a great deal but at their best have common roots. They are in touch with the palpable detail of that day-to-day life they share with their readers; they are out of step with the big battalions; and they care very much about making contact with individuals. But – and this is the acid test – they care more about what they are trying to communicate than about the act of communication in itself. They know in their bones that when care for communicating takes precedence over care about content, then the activity becomes mindless – 'togetherness' with intellectual pretensions. One has to care first about what one is saying, care also about sharing it with others, recognize how difficult that sharing is, but be willing at times to break the connections rather than lose hold of the truth ... and then you may indeed 'communicate' well.
>
> Something of this particular concern Penguins have managed to show. A sense of caring about the mind and its disciplines; a sense, too, of caring that people should know which implies a respect for people in themselves, whatever their background; a respect for what they might aim to become if they were shown other perspectives. In all this, Penguins have stood for the idea that our potentialities are greater than the pressures of our time and place and circumstances might have led us to assume.

Back in 1967 Hoggart's benediction was of itself almost enough to convince Allen that his plan for Penguin was appropriate and worthy of active consideration, and there was more encouragement to come. First Lord Goodman, in his generation the most energetic and skilful of all intermediaries in ventures of this kind, set himself to developing the scheme in detail; then the Vice-Chancellors, the Masters and Principals hurried in, all applauding, all ready to collaborate. Lord Butler of Trinity College, Cambridge, Sir Alan Bullock of Oxford, Sir Roger Stevens of Leeds, Professor Asa Briggs of Sussex, Lord James of York, each and everyone committed himself and the institution over which he presided to the Hoggart proposals as elaborated by Goodman.

The unanimity of approval from the academic world, next only to the unbridled affection of the reading public, was probably the greatest compliment ever accorded to Allen and his work. It proved beyond a doubt that in thirty years Penguin had become something far greater than a publishing house, that it was itself an institution which some of the wisest men in Britain were not prepared to see reduced in status or integrity.

Allen responded warmly. He would sell to the university consortium his 700,000 Penguin shares, still the controlling interest, at two-thirds of their market value, a proposition that removed any possibility that the University Grants Committee would oppose the deal; not even that fastidious body could raise its collective eyebrows against an arrangement so patently advantageous to the various university chests. All that he demanded in return (in addition to the not inconsiderable sum involved in the purchase of his shares) was that he should continue as Chairman for as long as he pleased and that the new holding company should have no control over the day-to-day management or the editorial policy of the firm. Even on this point he conceded, as safeguard for their interest and to ensure that there be no violent change in management techniques or publishing philosophy, that two or three representatives of the consortium should be added to the Penguin Board.

There was, however, one obstacle which the promising horse could not be made to jump. It was agreed that no participating institution could be allowed to make a quick profit by selling the shares that they were buying at cut price, but universities, in public manner solid and unchanging, are in truth chameleons. Vice-Chancellors are not what they appear to be to the uninformed, among whose number Allen was one, unimpeachable and unquestionable commanders; they are susceptible to the whims of councils, senates, committees and sub-committees. All the Vice-Chancellors in the consortium were nevertheless convinced that they could carry their underling-masters but none dared commit his successor or a succeeding generation of committeemen. Three or, at the best, four years was all that they could promise, and this eventual uncertainty was exactly what Allen was trying to avoid.

Like all the other schemes this, the most hopeful of all, collapsed, and Allen was dead before he could venture on another.

In all probability there would have been no schemes at all, no search for a Prince of Wales, no alliances with publishers, no University Trust, had Allen had a son.

The history of publishing is embellished with many successful dynasties. True, in recent years and for reasons that are far from obvious to one who is more sophisticated in the book business than he is in the mysteries of the City of London, there has been a large-scale invasion of the trade by major financial holding companies seeking to add publishing houses to the vast financial empires created originally from the sale of London's last independent transport system, from the American electronic industry, or from land speculation in Mexico. It is true too that in much the same period, roughly the last quarter of a century, the multiplicity and complexity of take-overs within the book world has made the task of tracing the genealogy of some firms as difficult as unravelling the relationships between members of European royal families when most monarchs, most princes and almost every petty princeling were in some way related to Queen Victoria. Even so the *Almanach de Gotha* of publishing is to this day plush with names that ring with eighteenth- and nineteenth-century sonorities. The John Murray who is thought to have roused Thomas Campbell to make what has since become the most-quoted and the unkindest remark about his kind, 'Barabbas was a publisher,' was already the second in his publishing line; there is still a John Murray in the principal's office in 50 Albemarle Street, the offices to which Campbell's publisher (who was also Byron's and Washington Irving's) moved from Fleet Street. The Black who presides over A. and C. Black Ltd is the great-grandson of the man who founded the firm in 1807. There are members of the Collins family on the board of the house that has carried their name since 1819; there are Macmillans in Macmillans as there have been since 1843; a Blackwood at Blackwood's as there has been since 1804; and it is only ten years since for the last time there was a Longman at the head of that 250-year-old firm. The family nature of publishing is no less obvious in some houses which have achieved their prominence in this century. There is an Unwin at the head of Allen and Unwin; a Blackwell runs Blackwell's; Victor Gollancz passed his business to his daughter Livia; there is a Faber at Faber's, and a Hodder-Williams on the board of Hodder and Stoughton.

Allen himself was the second generation at John Lane The Bodley Head. The simple stratagem which thrust him into the Lane dynasty to which he did not truly belong was not a deceit practised uniquely by Uncle John; among Allen's distinguished contemporaries there were at least two who changed their names to match the imprints that they were to control.

From time to time Allen indulged himself with dreams that he might be the progenitor of a line of Lanes at Harmondsworth. Such imaginings were rare for, having fathered his first child when he was already forty, he could hardly hope that Clare or Christine would be ready to succeed him when the time came for his withdrawal from the Penguin scene. A man who was generally most comfortable when in the company of women, he was also, like many of his kind, definite and uncomplimentary in his opinion of woman's ability. He knew what he expected of his daughters and it was not that they be like him, energetic, ruthless and innovative mistresses of a great business. The fact that they were likely one day to be no longer Lanes did not deter him; that could be arranged as he and Uncle John had arranged it. When Clare and Christine married he did look wistfully, if only momentarily, at both their husbands and talked, tactlessly but again only for a moment, of settling their future by the convenient process of conferring the dignity of his borrowed name on one or other son-in-law. His most enduring notion of a perfect daughter was that she be decorative, perhaps a little flighty and, when he chose and had the time, ready to gossip with him and to join him in a cheerful conspiracy against the world at large.

The age of the girls, his peculiar idealization of daughterhood and his lack of confidence in the business abilities of womankind compounded his indecisiveness about the succession; although it is just possible to catch moments when he was implying that all this would have been different had there been a son, there is no strong evidence to support this view and at least some justification for extrapolating from his relations with his daughters and for speculating that, with a son as with his daughters, his behaviour would have followed an erratic pattern similar to that of his dealings with those he adopted for a time as his professional sons.

The first demonstration that Allen was prepared to overlook the unfortunate disadvantages of their sex and to consider one of his daughters as his publishing heir was tentative and risible. It was also premature: Clare was only eight years old when he announced to her that she would never be qualified for a significant career unless she made a habit of reading *The Times*. Daily he brought to her his newspaper but his attempt to prepare her for a life as a businesswoman ended when he discovered that her attention waned once she had finished with Births, Marriages and Deaths. Two years later he sought her opinion on Tolkien's *Lord of the Rings* and was much put out by her distaste for a book on which Puffin had an option. Later, when she was eighteen, Allen took Clare with him on a world tour. Clare's two-finger exercises on the typewriter soon disabused him of any notion that she could serve as his itinerant secretary; his flicker of hope that on tour she might prove herself to be after all heir to the Penguin throne was effectively snuffed out when she persisted in refusing invitation after invitation from willing hosts eager to give a good time to the girl whom the Australian press was forever describing as Princess Penguin. In a manner that was by no means typical of him he wailed at her, 'You owe it to the firm' but, perversely, when Clare proved her interest, her adulthood and her independence by criticizing to his face his ruthless treatment of his senior Australian staff, he left her in no doubt that it was none of her business.

Nevertheless it was on that world tour that he established for the first time a comfortable and enduring relationship with one of his daughters. He had always been patient and affectionate towards Anna, his tragically handicapped child, but his attempts to act the part of a good father to his two healthy, noisy and energetic daughters had been erratic and often markedly inept. With other people's young – and particularly with their small daughters – he was invariably charming and kindly but other people's children made no great demands upon his attention and did not threaten his concentration upon his favourite offspring, Penguin Books. From time to time, as when he took them holidaying in North Devon, cycling in France or playing Murder with a house-party at Priory Farm, he roused himself to be a marvellously relaxed companion for Clare and Christine, and in his treatment of them he was never pompous. But when they were small he paid them little attention except when showing them off to strangers or alternatively posturing before strangers as an uncaring, even as a brutal, father; as they grew to adolescence and came to make demands upon his time his valiant efforts to give them what he knew they needed – and what he himself truly wished to give – were too often inhibited by his inability to close his mind to publishing or farming. Battered by a twelve-year-old's insistent and insignificant conversation, he would pretend interest for a while, then his eyes would glaze over so that even the child knew his mind was elsewhere. In this, as in almost nothing else, he was pathetic, hoping and hoping desperately that he would receive much more than he could give, wanting to be a good father but shackled by his unwillingness, and perhaps by his inability to amend the habits and traits that spilled over from his public life into his home, too self-conscious to match the requirements of his paternal ambitions.

Consideration of the formal education of their daughters he left almost entirely to Lettice. It is a symptom of that uncertainty which contradicted his assured manner that he, the greatest 'popular educator' of his generation, was so overawed by his wife's educational background that he seldom questioned her decisions about the girls' schooling. He, who had among his professional advisers some of the greatest authorities on education in Britain and who was forever seeking advice on other matters – even if he seldom took the advice given – never looked beyond Lettice for guidance about the girls' education.

For Clare Lettice chose well enough. When it came to

Christine's turn to go away to school Allen and Lettice were separated; neither had the will to make for her a choice different to that made for Clare. Christine was unhappy where Clare had been content, but it was years before either parent realized that she merited a more academic school. By that time Allen and Lettice were back living together comfortably enough but in what all the world knew to be a somewhat ambiguous arrangement. Then, at last, Allen stirred himself and, with Lettice's consent, turned to professionals for their opinion, took it, and himself made the arrangements which moved Christine to the North London Collegiate School.

There was, however, one aspect of the girls' upbringing which benefited from Allen's paradoxical nature. His faults were many, but conceit was not one of them; though they shared their lives, rather inequitably, with Penguin he never attempted to persuade them that he was in any way eminent or extraordinary. Clare insists that she had no idea that her father was a public personality until he was knighted (she was then ten years old); that even then it was not his pride but her own pleasure in being able to show off to her schoolmates which awakened her to his fame. (Her first letter home after the accolade was addressed boldly to 'Sir and Mrs Lane'.)

Like many another liberal Allen would argue, with what was from him surprising vehemence, against the principle of inherited wealth, but his antipathy was peculiar in that it was almost entirely impersonal and unrelated to his own circumstances. He did not allow his daughters to act or to think of themselves as heiresses – and this was probably his most beneficient and significant contribution to their upbringing – but his severe sumptuary regulations were not imposed as a practical manifestation of pedagogic theorizing and parental wisdom nor as evidence to his parsimony, real and persuasive though that could be. He did not give to his children the possibility of indulging themselves with the pleasures and privileges of the rich because he was not convinced that he was rich enough to support such frivolities or assured enough in his fortune to be certain that he would leave behind him heiresses. His remarkable unsophistication about his financial status persisted until he was almost sixty. Clare was almost adult and Christine well into adolescence, before their father came to comprehend fully the monetary value of his Penguin holdings. Before that time all that he had known to be his without challenge was the power that he had as the head of the firm and the immediate and tangible perquisites that went with that power. Some person or some institution must inherit that power and those perquisites.

His uncertainty about the future of Penguin complicated, and was complicated by, his consideration of the future of his children. Generally convinced that no woman, and perhaps least of all one of his daughters, whose foibles he had endured or enjoyed for upwards of twenty years, could ever serve with success as dictator at Harmondsworth, even that blessed certainty was occasionally punctured by flashes of hope which illuminated a sentimental picture of Clare or Christine seen, not as they were, not as they were likely to become but as they might be if only they were prepared to submit themselves to a long regime of indoctrination by himself, the only publishing Gamaliel he could trust. And these moments of whimsy tended to confuse even more his already distracted consideration of plans for the eventual disposition of his empire. Lest decision become irrevocable he put off making arrangements both for Penguin and for his family; postponement became inactivity and in the end both his family and his firm suffered.

Nevertheless, in those years when he discovered that his daughters were no longer children, he discovered also, and also for the first time, the advantages of fatherhood. There was much that was inconsistent in his attitude; he was alternately delighted by their independence and infuriated because neither was willing to design her life according to a pattern of his devising but that he could not make coherent either to them or to himself. He was, however, flattered by the attention paid to them when they were seen in public in his company; his pride was heightened and his heretical sense of humour was titillated when it was reported to him that some who recognized him but did not know his daughters took them to be his Lolitas and that others, acquaintances of the girls who had never before seen their father, congratulated the girls on the conquest of a prosperous and elegant elderly 'protector'.

There was, in his pleasure in the company of his daughters, an element of narcissism; he imagined that he was seeing himself when young, that he was re-living through them the glorious uninhibited days in Talbot Square, a period of his life which had become with reiterated reminiscence more golden and more liberated than it had ever been in fact. He was amused by their indiscretions; so amused that he could not resist recounting them to any who would listen, often with embellishments and, when indiscretion threatened to become disaster, he was patient, understanding, generous and even ready to abandon momentarily his hitherto habitual obsession with publishing to rush to the aid of his girls.

Gossip, and often gossip of an acrid kind, had always been his favourite diversion, but John's death, the departure of Dick and the loosening of his ties with Williams had deprived him of that part of his audience which was best qualified to appreciate his sharply-flavoured conversation. Sometimes he turned to Robert Lusty, a fellow publisher, a friend but no rival, and a man who could always be trusted to offer some tit-bit of trade news in exchange for Allen's more indiscreet information and more outrageous opinions. Sometimes, and particularly when they were together on long journeys overseas, he used Blass as his confidant, but Blass was in the firm and already Allen saw him as a runner in the race for the succession. Allen was not often prepared to offer the advantage of intimacy to any who were in that frame, even if they were outsiders in his betting. Now he found to his satisfaction that the girls were amiably prepared to listen as he regaled them with unflattering and often slanderous comments about his competitors and his closest associates. Godwin, Dolley, Boyle, even Clare's godfather, Bill Williams, and their uncle Dick: all those who enjoyed for a time his public support he stripped in private for the delectation of his daughters. Across the dinner table in one of his favoured restaurants he blackened the characters of his allies, questioned their ability and denied their integrity. To Clare on one occasion he announced that he had come to resent in the man who was then his choice for the succession his unprofessional and discourteous habit of making appointments which he did not intend to keep; Clare was happily unaware of her father's notorious reputation in this very respect and he not notably gifted with self-knowledge. It was all for him highly amusing and because, by his reckoning, it was unlikely if not unthinkable that his daughters would become involved in the organizational struggles or the partnerships in which his targets either had been or were likely to be at some time enmeshed, the choice of Clare or Christine as crony was also convenient, even more appropriate than his earlier selections for that role: John, Dick and Bill Williams. The girls listened, nodded wisely, smiled indulgently – and settled to the next course.

Allen had added his two very attractive daughters to his collection of elegant possessions. Even he was prepared to respect them in their own right as individuals but that right was still by his measure limited. In Christine he thought he saw something of his own shrewdness; enough to convince him that she was capable of serving as a trustee when he set up a charitable foundation but not enough to persuade him to make her his publishing heir. Clare for too long he idealized. She was beautiful, and in no beautiful woman could there be a hidden business tycoon.

Clare was also gentle, much too generous to be allowed authority, and he persisted in thinking her flighty long after her essential integrity had erased her frivolousness but not her energy or her ebullience – qualities which she inherited from him. He revelled in her beauty, took personal but not professional comfort from her gentleness and was not displeased by her imagined flightiness. But it was many years before he was prepared to admit that she too could be hard-headed and was therefore qualified to serve with Christine as a trustee of the Allen Lane Foundation.

At the very last, when death was certain, he looked once more at his two daughters and almost convinced himself that they were competent to make the definitive arrangements for Penguin that he had consistently avoided. By then it was too late for him, for Clare and Christine, and for Penguin, and who is to say that, had he been given a few more days of life, he would not have changed his mind again?

CHAPTER NINE

WHEN Penguin Books came of age in 1956 Allen was close to his fifty-fourth birthday and still he looked – and acted – as if he were ten years younger. A tendency to put on weight he combated by bouts of abstinence, which for him meant substituting a generous intake of wine for what had hitherto been an overliberal indulgence in spirits, and by increasingly frequent submission to the expensive regime of a health farm. When neither champagne nor carrot-juice could hold back the advancing avoirdupois of advancing years he disguised the evidence from most observers by impeccable grooming and the immaculate art of his tailors, Kilgour, French and Stanbury. His energy seemed unbounded; still he bustled round the world, leaving behind him wherever he went an impression of vigour unabated, the hope of new, exciting ventures still to come from the man who had revolutionized readership and book ownership and leaving behind him also an ever-increasing multitude of admirers – and an ever-enlarging if informal association of former Penguin employees. The recognition made explicit by his knighthood and by his many academic honours had eroded the lingering doubts about the validity of his achievement; if he was still far from sure that the achievement could be enhanced or perpetuated by any but himself, public applause and public demand bolstered his will to make the attempt. At Harmondsworth, Baltimore and Melbourne his suzerainty was unchallenged, his leadership still compulsive even upon his more remote or more junior colleagues, and the ebullience and originality of Allen Lane still a major factor in recruiting into the Penguin service bright, energetic and able young men. His mastery of the detail of Penguin practice, as of the broad scope of Penguin policy, seemed as sure as always. After twenty years his eye was as sharp as in the days in the Crypt. A soiled copy discarded when it should have been re-vamped for sale or a stock-sheet not completed would bring down upon the culprit an explosion of wrath; if the offender was sensibly absent, then Allen held to his principle that Penguin must not be rigidly departmentalized, that all his employees were mutually responsible for error as for triumph, and so he would turn his anger on whosoever was convenient. As before in the story of Penguin, detail was his relaxation but planning his life's work and the schemes that he was now dreaming up – for example a vast natural history series – were even more elaborate and even more extravagant than anything proposed before; so elaborate and so extravagant that the most experienced editors, who had long since discovered that Allen's wildest schemes were apt to prove wily publishing projects, were convinced that what he now had in mind was beyond even his capacity for making lunacy profitable.

It was from his profession that he had always drawn the greater part of his happiness, and the zest that he had invariably applied to publishing was in no way reduced either by prosperity or by the ever-increasing complexity of his business. But now, in late middle age, he seemed to have discovered outside Penguin some measure of the contentment that had hitherto eluded him, a combination of ease and excitement that he needed if his private life was to satisfy his inclinations as did his public career. The arrangement with Lettice was little more than a truce convenient to both parties but he respected her taste and he enjoyed her company, provided that he did not have too much of it and that she did not make too many demands upon him. He had found a school for Anna and, though the tragedy of her condition still bore heavily upon him, he had the comfort of knowing that he had made her financial future secure. With Clare and Christine his relationship was equable and generally delightful. The companionship and sexual pleasure for which he had always hankered he had found at last with Suzanne, his German lady; he revelled in the discovery with the abandon of a man half his age and with as little discretion as a boy who cannot resist showing off his attractive conquest to his envious contemporaries and who stumbles upon the truth that bragging about his prized acquisition is by no means the least of the gratifications of his first affair.

This period in Allen's life when he was generally contented and contentedly busy he saw as the inevitable reward for years of struggle, tragedy, unmerited ingratitude and incomprehensible obstreperousness on the part of those in his professional family who owed him most. Even his puzzlement about the succession was part of the prize. As Jesus, Son of Sirach has it (in the Book of Ecclesiasticus according to E. V. Rieu), 'There are some who are unremembered . . . and it is as though they had never been born or left children to succeed them', Allen could now be confident that he would not be one of these, the anonymous of history. Somehow he would be numbered among those whose achievement would be 'handed on to their descendants and their inheritance to future generations'.

Just because his life had reached a plateau of contentment Allen dared not look ahead or tempt the Fates by consulting their intimates; in the four years between *The Penguin Story* and the twenty-fifth anniversary *Penguins Progress*, although he bombarded his graphologist for advice about others, either he never once asked his astrologer to draw back the curtain on his own future or else he was so dejected by what she revealed that he broke with his otherwise unvaried custom and destroyed the foreboding horoscope.

The period of euphoria was short. The uneasy armistice with Lettice could not survive either the continuing and increasingly virulent clash of personalities or Allen's ostentatious disloyalty. Even more devastating: Clare and Christine married and both chose their husbands without consulting Allen and without due consideration to the interests of Penguin.

Clare's marriage to Michael Morpurgo particularly disturbed Allen; it revived his old and fevered suspicion that some cunning conspirator might take away his freedom to make his own dynastic arrangements. He struck out in a manner that can be variously interpreted as either vindictive, mean or shrewd, but that none can categorize as in any way truly relevant to the circumstances. Allen sent his emissaries to demand of Clare's new father-in-law that he, a salaried book-trade administrator and modestly successful author, match the allowance that Allen, by that time self-recognized as a millionaire, proposed to offer the young people. The ultimatum, conveyed by Paroissien and Williams, was rejected, as it deserved to be; the message they were asked to take back to Allen was blunt and, considered in tranquillity, unnecessarily rude. No more was heard of the inequitable settlement but the two men, who had been close friends for almost twenty years and who were soon to become grandfathers of the same grandson, never met and never wrote to each other so much as one formal note – a severity which at least one of them holds forever on his conscience.

Before long Allen came to accept Clare's marriage, as later Christine's, and in time learnt respect and even liking for his sons-in-law and pride in his grandchildren, but he could never bring himself to concede that his proprietorial hold upon his daughters was no longer entire. The intimate dinners with Clare and with Christine continued, less regularly than before but still not infrequently. The girl's husbands regarded their exclusion from these occasions with amused tolerance; now that they had lives that were truly their own, the girls enjoyed the meetings more even than in the past when their dependence upon their father had made attention to his gossipy and uninhibitedly malicious reporting of trade affairs as much a matter of duty as of pleasure. Now adult and at one remove from his influence, they could admire him as did others not too deeply enmeshed in his activities. In their new freedom they discovered, for the first time in their lives, that he was both vulnerable and lovable. Sadly, he was almost incapable of demonstrating affection. Always, even with his daughters and grandchildren, he had to hide – as much from himself as from them – his capacity for sentiment lest it be mistaken for sentimentality.

Unable to sustain the close relationship with his daughters that he had enjoyed for such a very few years he found himself at the same time distanced as never before from most of his Penguin colleagues. Dick was in Australia; Eunice Frost was ill; no one in the office except Allen knew what was wrong with her or how serious was her ailment and he kept the knowledge to himself but cossetted her with great generosity. Tanya Schmoller was off rearing her own family. Glover had retired. There was Paroissien, back from Baltimore and installed as Deputy Managing Director in a handsome office across the corridor from Allen's; but contiguity, his enhanced seniority and the fact that at Harmondsworth his determination to guard his private life from constant invasion by Allen and by Penguin business was much more obvious and much more irritating to Allen than when he was in America had an effect contrary to that which Allen had promised or intended. Paroissien was no longer the intimate adviser, indeed Allen treated him often as if neither he nor anyone else connected with the firm needed to treat with him at all. There was also Hans Schmoller, who, like Eunice Frost, Williams and Paroissien, had at last been made a director, but Allen's attitude to Schmoller had always been ambivalent. He admired his typographical skills but he was convinced that he had lifted Schmoller from obscurity, looked upon him as a noble Roman would look upon a freed slave, expected from him gratitude and, as tangible evidence of gratitude, a readiness to accept willingly all the unenviable duties that Allen would not undertake for himself – and Allen could not find comfortable intimacy where he offered only patronage. Many others who might have been his intimates had been removed from Harmondsworth, either by their own volition or by Allen's actions.

The new men, young but high in the Penguin hierarchy – such as Charles Clark and Dieter Pevsner – were no less able than their predecessors, their enthusiasm for Penguin and for Penguin standards was no less intense, but they were not his contemporaries, nor even, as had been the first post-war generation, his near-contemporaries. Though their respect for him was obvious, he was disturbed by the suspicion that its basis was historical rather than immediate, that they looked upon him more in awe for what he had done in the past than in admiration for what he was doing, or in excited anticipation for what he might still do for Penguin and for them. For his part, he could neither bring himself to confide in them nor find the appropriate manner for instructing and directing them. Hitherto, unashamedly and with deliberate intent, he had refused to accept any employee as a permanent fixture in the Penguin scene; now he thought he glimpsed in every one of these newcomers an eagerness to climb on his shoulders, up and, if need be, out of Penguin, and he resented what he saw. At some time or another over the years he had quarrelled with almost every senior member of his staff but, now that he felt himself to be removed from his colleagues, all that stormy history was conveniently erased from his mind.

The seniors of previous Penguin generations were elevated to the rank of intimates; these had been his fellow-pioneers, his fellow-architects in the building of Penguin.

Only for one of the new generation could he feel as, his recollections coloured by nostalgia, he now believed that he had always felt for those who had come – and gone – before. Kaye Webb had followed Eleanor Graham as editor of Puffins, and for her Allen's publisher's respect was coupled with personal affection. The admiration was reciprocated and he found much more gratification in her dedication to Puffins. Kaye gave him what, at that time, he needed. She was an informed but patient audience.

Eleanor Graham had done marvellous things for Puffins and for children's books generally but she was cast in the conventional mould of children's book editors. Kaye Webb was quite different and for Allen, as man and as publisher, much more compatible. Young, energetic, attractive, the ex-wife of the cartoonist Ronald Searle, she was herself a successful journalist and moved regularly and easily in that society composed of publishers, prosperous writers and editors in which Allen was the most eminent member.

That Penguin must at some time invade the juvenile market had been, almost from the outset, inevitable. Once the decision was made to launch Puffins, Allen had no cause to be positively dissatisfied with Eleanor Graham's achievement but he was aware that he knew nothing about children's books. For this reason and because there could be no spirited communication between him and his editor, his attitude to Puffins had been in Miss Graham's time more complacent than enthusiastic. He suspected that the list was conventional, even 'fuddy-duddy', because he believed that Eleanor Graham was conventional and did not doubt that she was 'fuddy-duddy'; that, he thought, was all that he could expect, and the ordinariness of Puffins – in every respect but their price – was, after all, in much the same kind as the ordinariness of Penguin reprints in the first two or three years of the firm, and therefore to be tolerated. Kaye Webb brought with her a novel venturesomeness. Books were published which were brighter, some of them, according to the customary rules of publishing for children, almost risqué, and few of them open to the criticism, so often levelled against books for children, that they patronized their readership. Kaye Webb sought liveliness, she wanted to sell and she was eager to employ brisk and thrusting sales-techniques. Under her leadership the Puffin concept changed so that the whole sub-group became in editorial terms, in presentation and in marketing more and ever more obviously an integral part of Penguin, its total philosophy consistent with Penguin doctrine.

So Allen began to take notice. For many years in debates with more cautious members of the Penguin hierarchy he had advanced the 'swings and roundabouts' theory of marketing, arguing that many titles must be included in the Penguin list just because they were worthy of their place and the list would not be complete without them. If they lost money *tant pis*, the losses could be made up from the profits on other books. Whole series – among them King Penguins and the Pocket Scores – he had justified on this premise and many a children's book had been accepted for Puffin with a nod from Allen and a murmur of 'swings and roundabouts'. With the advent of Kaye Webb Allen found a new theme, in analysis not so very different but in expression much more explicit and much more forward-looking. Puffins, he would say, were the persuaders, the educators, the means to establish the firm's corps of future Penguin readers; it was he who defended the series most vociferously against the attacks of his seemingly more hard-headed colleagues when they complained about Puffin losses, and it was he who accepted with good grace Kaye Webb's plea that the price of Puffins be kept low when all other Penguin prices were rising rapidly. Nevertheless his new enthusiasm was made even brighter when he saw in the sales sheets resplendent figures for Puffins. Then he would write brief notes to Kaye Webb: 'Well done' or 'Excellent sales on last month's Puffins' and, once, he went overboard for Kaye Webb. She was, he wrote in one of his notes, not only a GREAT EDITOR but a GREAT PUBLISHER. 'I felt,' says Kaye Webb, 'as if I wanted to have this note framed and hung above my desk' and she adds in a phrase that many who worked for him would find themselves forced to echo, 'It was his habit of doing things like sending these notes that made one work oneself to death on his behalf.'

The arrival of Kaye Webb gave him some respite from loneliness, but she was not always on hand at Harmondsworth and could not and would not be his companion on his many tours overseas. He needed a professional intimate and he needed a travelling companion, and none of the younger men could fill that role. He turned finally to Ron Blass.

The understanding that developed between the two men was founded on many factors but not least upon two seemingly contradictory elements in their relationship. Allen alone had been responsible for elevating Blass in the hierarchy, and yet Blass had no pretension to rise any higher or to take elsewhere the skills that he had acquired at Penguin. This alone might have made Allen despise him as he despised others whom he had made but, like Allen himself and like no other senior member of the staff, Blass was virtually married to the firm, always ready to subordinate such private life as he had to the interests of Penguin, always prepared to follow Allen's whims and to set off at a moment's notice on long trips in Allen's company. He had joined the firm before the war in a humble capacity and Allen imagined that he saw in his rise to authority a repetition of the story that he had come to accept as his own early history; if not exactly rags to riches then certainly insignificance to power. With Allen's help Blass had made himself unquestionably one of the book trade's experts on distribution, but he was not and never pretended to be an editor. This too made him a comfortable companion for Allen, always uneasy with editors who might be supercilious and patronizing about his inferior education and about what he thought to be his comparative inability to deal in literary small change. Almost all who had come close to the succession were editors; therefore Allen assumed that all editors had their eyes on his throne. A sales manager was safe.

Allen chose Blass as crony but not as Crown Prince. At the end of the day, because all others had proved themselves either unworthy of his confidence or impatient with his vacillating, Blass was left, virtually unchallenged, higher in Penguin than he had ever dreamed or than Allen had planned when first he settled him in the Penguin aristocracy. Blass is to this day the one powerful survivor from the days when Allen was himself the undisputed monarch.

Already in the early sixties, and despite Kaye Webb and Blass, Allen was lonely where he most needed to be companionable: at work. His interest in Penguin slackened. He was often ill but none, not even he, could foresee that an ailment diagnosed as jaundice was a precursor of cancer. He was more often just bored. His elaborate schemes were designed almost despairingly, as much to bring novelty into his own life as to offer something new to readers, but now no longer with that certain appreciation of publishing possibilities that he had shown in the past. Tired, and tired above all by success, even publishing itself was beginning to pall. Had it not been so he, and perhaps no other man in Penguin, might have seen what at the time (and for many years to come) none at Harmondsworth comprehended entirely: that the balance of power between the media was shifting once more, and to the disadvantage of the book and particularly of the kind of book represented by Pelicans and Specials, the dynamic centre of the Penguin list. Allen's efforts over twenty-five years had kept books competitive with other modes of communication. His Pelicans and Specials had marched easily as companions with radio and with television in its infant days but by the end of the fifties television was adult, all-pervasive and omnipotent. Information, enlightenment, political campaigning: all that capacity for exciting the minds of the public which Allen had indulged to make his projects uniquely potent was now everywhere evident, immediately accessible in every sitting-room and available to every man, woman and child who could turn a switch. Books were not finished; still they possessed qualities of permanence and adaptability that could not be matched even by television; because of Allen they must still be regarded as one of the mass media; but the universality of television and the readiness of the public to accept pictures on a small screen as tablets handed down on Mount Sinai had reduced the status of the printed word yet again.

Aware that advance was not as easy as it had been for twenty-five years, yet no longer either capable of seeking the cause nor competent to find a new way forward, Allen retreated into halls hung with the trophies of his past triumphs. He was by this time the unchallengeable, if not always the unchallenged, king of the London book world but he needed to be reassured; the man who in the past had defied the leading publishers in the land was now on occasion guilty of seeking the approbation of their successors. Twenty, even ten years earlier he would have denied to himself and would have castigated in others social pretentiousness; now he aspired to be the focus of attention at the Garrick Club, that Zion for publishers as it is for successful actors and the more gregarious members of the Bar. At the Garrick he listened as he had never listened before to the advice of his rivals, but his concentration upon publishing topics was no longer entire nor was his pleasure in book world gossip all-satisfying. Not even the Garrick could suffice, and he turned more and more often for companionship to the febrile expatriate society of the south of Spain.

Allen Lane and Penguin had been from the first indivisible. Now the organization had become too large and too complex for one man to control – too large and too complex even for Allen – and though he was not ready to abdicate he was forced to admit to himself that delegation was inevitable, even if his admission was so half-hearted that he would invariably rush back to take command whenever a crisis occurred and even if, now as often in the past, he so arranged his return that his was the glory of surmounting disaster but not any obloquy that might go with defeat.

The trial of *Lady Chatterley's Lover* was one of those episodes which re-awakened Allen. The fevered attention of press and radio made *Regina* v. *Penguin Books Ltd* as exciting as a Cup Final even to tens of thousands who had never before heard of Lawrence and who thought little and cared not at all about public morality or the cause of literary freedom.

Once the case was fairly launched, this excitement was not only communicated to Allen but also by him re-charged and passed back to the public. Yet, originally, when the decision was taken to publish *Lady Chatterley's Lover*, Allen was not looking for publicity and had no thought that he might be risking martyrdom. Penguin had already published most of Lawrence's novels; the Million was designed as no more than a consolidation of existing strength, timed, as so often with Penguin projects, as an anniversary celebration – in this case the thirtieth anniversary of the author's death. What could be more sensible or more obvious than that among the ten titles selected should be the two novels which had as yet appeared neither as Penguin nor elsewhere as paperback: *Women in Love* and *Lady Chatterley's Lover*?

Allen and his colleagues were not naïve. There would be some stir caused by the appearance in a cheap edition of a title that had gathered a certain notoriety; so they planned to abandon arithmetical niceties by printing not 100,000 copies but twice as many. However, a prosecution was unthinkable. Since the war the climate of opinion on 'obscene publication' had become much more generous and the process of liberalization had been completed (or so it seemed at the time) by Mr Justice Stable's generous and wise direction handed down in *The Philanderer* case and by the Obscene Publication Act of 1959.

The gentleness of time had settled Lawrence among the indisputably great writers of modern fiction. Death had made him respectable, so respectable that even the staid and cautious guardians of the school examination syllabus had for some years thought a few of his novels suitable for study by adolescents. There was not one word in *Lady Chatterley's Lover*, not even a four-letter word, that had not appeared in books produced by publishers whose reputation was beyond reproach. It needed no great courage, no reforming zeal and certainly no ulterior and commercially sordid inspiration to persuade Allen to include *Lady Chatterley* in the Lawrence Million for he foresaw no danger, no great advantage and no extraordinary excitement. He and his editors were so unconcerned that they did not even take the precaution, not uncommon in the publishing process, of seeking the opinion of legal advisers. *Lady Chatterley's Lover* was little more than another reprint to add to the several thousand already in the Penguin list.

They had not reckoned with two factors: the authorities wished to test the months-old Obscene Publications Act and there still lingered in the minds of some in high places a paternalistic conviction that what can be proper for the rich may be harmful to the masses. Allen Lane, Penguin and *Lady Chatterley* were brought to trial as much because A. P. Herbert, Gerald Barry, Norman Birkett and Roy Jenkins had forced the Government to take on board an Act which it did not much like as for any sin that they might have committed. Their most heinous offence was that they had priced the book not at thirty guineas but at 3s. 6d. When the case came finally to the Old Bailey the leader for the Crown made the implication explicit by a suggestion that was precise if also notably inept even in a prosecution that was conducted with remarkable ineffectiveness. *Lady Chatterley's Lover*, he proposed, was not a book that any upright citizen would wish his maidservant to read. Almost certainly there was not one member of the jury whose morning tea was brought by 'a maidservant' and probably not one person in court, except perhaps Mr Griffith-Jones QC himself and Mr Justice Byrne, would have used such a word at any time unless he was writing eighteenth- or nineteenth-century social history.

The first hint of trouble reached Harmondsworth not from the police or the Director of Public Prosecutions but from the printer who had been contracted to manufacture the book. Only a few days before stock was due in the warehouse he appeared in Schmoller's office and announced, in some embarrassment, that his board had refused to allow him to go ahead with the work. Only one senior Penguin executive was much troubled by this defection but his timidity and what Allen took to be the unjustified faint-heartedness of the printer aroused Allen's indignation. What had hitherto been no more than a routine exercise became a battle over principles. Another printer must be found – and immediately! There would be no withdrawal!

With no difficulty at all Schmoller arranged for a printer, but the delay made it impossible for Penguin to publish on the date previously announced and so they were forced to advertise the postponement in the trade press.

It is likely that this announcement alerted the Director of Public Prosecutions; it was in the days which followed its publication that Penguin heard that the Director was sniffing at their doors.

Even under the 1959 Act not only the author and the publisher but also the printer and booksellers could be found guilty of publishing an obscenity. Lawrence was conveniently dead but, rather than risk proceedings against a bookseller, Allen accepted that Penguin must take the whole burden by tempting the Director to do his worst. Twelve copies of the book were handed to the police, technically an act of publication. The privilege of performing this uncomfortable duty was conferred on Schmoller, the most junior director; as so often when there was a possibility of embarrassment Allen was conveniently absent in Spain when 'Scotland Yard came to Harmondsworth'. But even at that moment not he, nor any member of his staff nor any informed member of the trade could believe (as Roy Jenkins put it in a letter to the *Spectator*) that 'our prosecuting authorities' had learnt nothing 'from the illiterate mistakes of their predecessors' and, he might have added, from the recent failure before both lower and higher courts of an American case against the very same book. They had, in fact, learnt nothing.

Allen was now utterly involved, indefatigable and, therefore, as happy as he had been for years. Men of letters, among them some of the greatest living exponents of their craft, teachers, churchmen, sociologists, a Privy Councillor and even his old rival Sir Stanley Unwin (who probably to his chagrin was not cross-examined by the Prosecution when the case came to court): all stepped forward to give witness in support of Lawrence, Lady Chatterley, her gamekeeper and Allen Lane.

On 20 October 1960 the case opened at the Old Bailey. For six days those who could get into court (and, by way of the newspapers and the BBC, the whole nation) were titillated by the unequal struggle between the Prosecution, unaided by one witness, confused both in purpose and direction but supported, it seemed, by the Judge, and a brilliant Defence led by Gerald Gardiner QC (soon himself Lord Chancellor) and assisted by a procession of articulate, clear-headed and unawed witnesses. A few minutes before three o'clock on 2 November the foreman of the jury proclaimed Penguin Books Ltd not guilty of publishing an obscene article. 'His voice was drowned by an outburst of clapping and one or two noises that sounded scandalously like cheers from among the elated *literati* at the back of the Court.'

Mr Justice Byrne had his own reasons for not following precedent by awarding costs to a successful defendant in a test case; he did not offer them to Gerald Gardiner or to posterity.

In some senses the importance of the trial of *Lady Chatterley's Lover* has been exaggerated, by folk-lore, by serious commentators and, not least, by the shrewd activities of those responsible for Penguin. The authorities still learnt very little from the verdict and even thereafter contrived time and time again to subvert the intentions of the 1959 Act. The debate about the proper stance of Government to literary licence and artistic liberty is as heated today as it was in 1960; neither side much helped by what went on at the Old Bailey. The most significant moment in the case was when Roy Jenkins managed to slip in, before he was interrupted by the Judge, a half-sentence which indicated that, in the opinion of the principal architect of the Act, the prosecution was 'against the intentions of Parliament'. For Penguin the advantages gained from the case were more oblique than direct and were not fully apparent until the next year when the firm became a public company. As for Allen himself: once the case was actually in court and the period of stimulating preparation over he was reduced for most of the time to the status of an intrigued observer. He, 'the accused', was cross-examined only cursorily by the Prosecution and almost exclusively about a remark, which he was alleged to have made to a *Manchester Guardian* reporter, to the effect that he did not consider *Lady Chatterley's Lover* 'a great novel'. He could not remember that he had said any such thing, though, had he done so, his opinion would have coincided with that of most of his expert witnesses; despite the intellectual cavortings of Judge and Prosecution, it should have made no difference to the outcome of the case. If failure to achieve greatness is a crime, then most of the entries in the dictionaries of literary biography should be transferred to the *Newgate Calendar*.

One phrase from the interview as reported in the *Manchester Guardian* Allen did accept as accurate. He had undoubtedly said that for his part as publisher of *Lady Chatterley's Lover* 'either I'll go to prison or I won't'. He repeated it in court, gratuitously but boldly and to great effect, yet it was certainly over-dramatic and, just as certainly, he knew it. In the post-war period, even before the 1959 Act, several distinguished publishers had been prosecuted for publishing obscene books; some had been found guilty but not one had suffered a penalty harsher than a fine.

The *Lady Chatterley* case merits its place in legal history for one reason above all others, and that a reason that has little to do with the life and character, personal or professional, of Allen Lane: it stands as a proud justification of the jury system. Those who were in court during the first five days of the trial grew with each day more confident that good sense would prevail, that the verdict would follow the spirit of the new Act and would go with Penguin. Then towards the end of the fifth day the Judge began his summing-up and immediately optimism faded. All those with a smattering of legal wisdom recognized that there were parts of Mr Justice Byrne's direction to the Jury which could serve the Penguin cause well should the case come to appeal. If need be it could be argued that the Judge was misdirecting when he insisted that 'our criminal law ... is based upon the view that a jury takes of the facts and not upon the view that experts may have' for the new Act categorically admitted 'artistic or scientific merit' as a justification for publication and specifically allowed for the calling of 'experts' to vouch for that merit. But the Penguin claque at the Old Bailey was not looking for an appeal; all hopes were centred on immediate acquittal. The judge's partisanship had been only too obvious from the beginning of the case; Penguin's supporters had watched helplessly but in a fury when he allowed to the Prosecution liberties that were unpardonable; when, for example, he made no move to call a halt as Griffith-Jones played the arcane trick, no longer according to Hoyle or the Obscene Publications Act, of reading to the jurors out-of-context but undeniably rough passages from the novel. Yet for all his unrestrained and undisguised prejudices Mr Justice Byrne was a senior, distinguished and much-respected member of the Bench. Not even the most suspicious Penguin sympathizer expected him to push himself forward as stand-in Leader of the Prosecution. This he did, and in that role he was much more effective than the man he supplanted. By theatrical use of pauses, with pejoratives, with nicely timed and carefully accented rhetorical questions he undermined the whole tenor of the case for the Defence. The authority of each of the witnesses in turn was reduced by implication or by some explicitly derisive description. Veronica Wedgwood, one of the world's leading historians, he described as 'the author of some dozen books', Norman St John Stevas as 'perhaps a little presumptuous' and the educator James Hemming as 'an adviser to publishers' and therefore, presumably suspect; he was also a 'doctor of philosophy' (the Judge seemed to be saying, as if he thought it significant, *not* a doctor of medicine). Indeed, all expert opinion was derided by the Judge at the very beginning of his direction, and with an out-worn gibe: 'As we all know, in these days the world seems to be full of experts. There is not a subject you can think of where there is not to be found an expert who will be able, or says he will be able, to deal with the situation.' Even, if with a suitably deferential bow, he questioned the expertise of a most distinguished brother-judge, Mr Justice Devlin, who when trying another novel, *The Image and the Search* (under the old Criminal Libel legislation) had directed that the defendant 'must be found guilty if it can be proved that he seeks by his writing to corrupt the fundamental sense of morality essential to the healthy life of the community'. This was good law, said Mr Justice Byrne, so far as it went, but it did not go far enough. For him it should read 'anyone who by his writing *tends* to corrupt...'.

For Penguin Books, too, for all that he admitted that they had behaved with dignity appropriate to their good reputation, the Judge had his sneering half-truths, implying that they waited to publish *Lady Chatterley's Lover* until they could be sure of the shield of the new Act and so upon the spears of complacent experts. He followed Griffith-Jones (and his maidservant) by insinuating that he was trying Penguin not for publishing an obscene libel but for producing a naughty book at a price that would make naughtiness accessible to the masses. *Lady Chatterley's Lover*, he complained, would find 'its way into the bookshops and on to the bookstalls, at 3s 6d a time, into public libraries... for all and sundry to read'.

Before the Judge finished his summing up on the sixth day it was clear that it was not just Penguin that had been on trial but also all the witnesses for pretending to be expert, D. H. Lawrence for running off with another man's wife, and Lady Chatterley for committing adultery – with a gamekeeper! And, if the Judge's direction was accepted by the Jury, all the defendants must be found guilty. Hence the despondency of most on-lookers.

But 'twelve good men and true' (three of them women) read the book, considered all that they had heard in court and accepted from the Judge only one direction:

> You are the sole judges of the facts. They are nothing to do with me.... If during the course of the observations which I shall have to make to you I express an opinion, or I appear to express an opinion, you will pay not the slightest attention to it, unless it happens to coincide with your own opinion.

There was, however, throughout the case, even as it was

conducted by the Prosecution and the Judge, an undercurrent of respect for Penguin, an acceptance of the fact that, whatever crimes the firm had committed, the benefits that over the years it had conferred on society made it somewhat different from other publishing houses. This distinction was ostentatiously symbolized by the empty dock. Throughout the trial Schmoller and Allen, the 'prisoners at the Bar', sat with their solicitors in the well of the court. No such courtesy had been granted to earlier defendants in obscenity cases; recently, at his trial for publishing *The Philanderer*, even Frederic Warburg, that most fastidious and gentlemanly member of the profession, had not been excused the additional ordeal of standing where murderers, rapists and pimps had stood.

The concession to Penguin was in a sense an accolade. If it was conferred by an authority for which he had no great affection and in a situation that he had not designed or coveted, it added something, a quality that was close to smugness, to the renaissance that Allen experienced in the preparation for the case and in the trial itself. Others might have thought him finished, his zeal and initiative sapped by success; at times he had been close to thinking it himself; but here he was, still indubitably a leader and recognized as such even by his persecutors. Challenged, he could still respond with all the fire of his youth.

It was, in truth, as much recollection of antique battles as the immediate excitation of the case which aroused him; in private conversation and in the many interviews which he gave at the time of the trial, as in his frequent references to it in the years still to come, he rarely failed to remind his audience that it was he who, almost thirty years earlier, had risked prosecution by publishing Joyce's *Ulysses*, on occasion he would slip in a gratuitous reference to Uncle John and *The Yellow Book*; once he contrived an analogy with the trial of Oscar Wilde, inaccurate in substance and as analogy entirely inapposite.

Yet in one further respect the *Lady Chatterley* episode proved that Allen was not content to see current drama exclusively through binoculars focussed on his own glorious past. It showed that Penguin under his direction was neither moribund nor reduced in its capacity to exploit even the most difficult circumstances. No other publisher but Allen (except, of course, Uncle John) would have had the wit – some would say the impertinence

– to publish for general circulation a transcript of his own trial. The case ended on 2 November 1960; *The Trial of Lady Chatterley* edited by C. H. Rolph, appeared three months later – even by the standards of pre-war Specials no slouching effort – and still that was not enough to satiate Allen's glee at this triumph. For years he had sent each Christmas to his more intimate friends and closer colleagues a handsomely produced, lavish, privately printed book, some 'little trifle' as he described it, such as a leather-bound *Ancient Mariner* specially illustrated by Duncan Grant. At Christmas 1960 many of the hitherto-privileged recipients watched the post anxiously and by New Year were tracking back over 1960 to discover what they had done to offend Allen. Then, early in the spring of 1961, their doubts were dissipated by the arrival of a copy of the limited edition of Rolph's book (with an appendix covering the debate in the House of Lords subsequent to the case) and an explanatory note from Allen:

> Some of my friends were concerned because they did not receive a card from me last Christmas. . . . I have taken one of the few vows of abstention in my life, and have resolved that I will no longer burden the December mails with expressions of wit and sentiment.
> Instead of a card [his word for prime examples of the book-maker's craft], I propose, as the spirit moves me and the occasion warrants, to send a book or keepsake, the current offering being a limited edition, printed for private circulation only, of *The Trial of Lady Chatterley*.

Reverberations from the case continued for many years, and not only in Allen's reminiscences. It inspired a popular ballad by Sydney Carter:

> Was it in the barn-yard dear or was it in the ricks
> Or was it up in Bloomsbury from four o'clock to six
> . . . What did the gamekeeper do today to lucky Lady C?

(At Clare's twenty-first birthday-party the same brilliant balladeer dedicated to Allen another of his songs:

> There's no fun at all for a mixed-up old man
> And the older I get the more mixed-up I am. . . .)

Seven years after Allen's death, his *cause célèbre* was once more the subject of heated correspondence.

The occasion was an event which in itself had little connection with Allen or Penguin: the belated recognition given to that brilliant Cambridge teacher if controversial critic, F. R. Leavis.

Wherever Leavis went, whatever he said, did or wrote, it was inevitable that acrimony would erupt and even his appearance in the Honours List, as a Companion of Honour, was no exception. In the course of a letter to *The Times*, Michael Rubinstein, a member of Penguin's solicitors who had taken part in the *Lady Chatterley* case, complained that the critic had been unique in refusing to stand as a witness in support of Allen at the Old Bailey and that he had 'not disclosed' his reasons. Rubinstein may not have known that, already in 1962, when Allen proved by publishing Leavis's *The Common Pursuit* that his concern for the quality of his Peregrine series was more compelling than any inclination to impose sanctions on a man who had failed to stand by him, Leavis had offered no reciprocal charity. Instead, on the grounds that Allen had performed a disservice to literature by fighting and winning the *Lady Chatterley* case, he rejected the invitation which every other living Penguin author had accepted with delight and refused to sign a copy of his book for Allen's private collection. (His cause would have been more dignified had he demonstrated his principles by refusing to be published by this miscreant publisher!) On the other hand, if Rubinstein did know about this silly episode, he must have assumed, as would most sane men, that even Leavis would have recognized that Allen had atoned for his Lady Chatterley sin, and proved his dedication to literature, by reprinting *The Common Pursuit* three times.

Mrs Leavis would have none of it. As ever quick to champion her husband, and with her habitual loyalty strengthened because Leavis was too ill to defend himself, she rushed to combat Rubinstein's slander. It was, she insisted, just one of the many 'outbursts of jealousy and spite directed against him in the press'. Leavis, she continued, had his reasons for staying away from the Old Bailey when Penguin was in jeopardy: he had 'refused to countenance the case that *Lady Chatterley* is great literature and a good novel . . . and deplored, above all, that the trial . . . could only harm Lawrence since the novelist would become identified with this most unrepresentative work'. Leavis had explained himself in private to Rubinstein and in print in a review of *The Trial of Lady Chatterley* published originally in the *Spectator* and reprinted as 'The New Orthodoxy' in a collection of his essays.

Thus far her advocacy was respectable if not entirely consequential; not one witness had claimed greatness for *Lady Chatterley's Lover* and few had called it a good book; their case rested on other considerations. It was not surprising to any who knew the history of relations between the two men, that she then turned her wrath upon the ghost of T. S. Eliot. The austere poet-publisher had agreed to serve as a witness but the Defence had held him in reserve, to be used only if it was necessary for him to recant in public his thirty-year-old denigration of Lawrence, published in *After Strange Gods: A Primer of Modern Heresy*. The Prosecution either did not know that in 1933 Eliot had written on Lawrence in terms that might have been in 1960 useful to its case or else had judged correctly that if challenged Eliot would say in court what he had in fact said to Allen's solicitors: 'I am not necessarily to be assumed to agree with all my earlier opinions, some of which I now regard as being immature, ill-considered and ... too violent.' Eliot was left, undisturbed if uncomfortable, in the corridors of the Old Bailey. But not undisturbed by Mrs Leavis almost twenty years after the trial and thirteen after his death:

> ... he may well have thought it necessary to do penance for writing defamatorily of Lawrence when it was safe to do so ... [he] lacked moral courage, and it is not very wise of his followers to attempt to use him as a means of attacking a man and a critic and a thinker so notably Eliot's superior in this respect.

Having dealt with Eliot, her indignation over-stimulated by this ready flow of venom, she turned upon another spectral victim, Allen Lane. Leavis, she wrote, had been suspicious of Allen's motives in inviting the prosecution. He had refrained from disclosing his doubts in print but he had made it plain to Allen's solicitors when he had been asked to join his fellow-critics as a witness for the Defence. 'I can see no reason for Sir Allen's knight errantry,' he had told Rubinstein, 'unless he has a Golden Fleece in view'; in her letter to *The Times*, Mrs Leavis went on to prove to her own satisfaction – and probably to the satisfaction of many readers – that Leavis's suspicions had been amply justified by subsequent events. 'This smart commercial venture... brought such immense sales to the Penguin reprint of *Lady Chatterley* as to make its publisher a millionaire.'

Allen was once again on trial for publishing *Lady Chatterley's*

Lover. This time the Leader for the Defence was not Gerald Gardiner QC but Hans Schmoller.

His letter, published in *The Times* on 4 January 1978, was one of the best of the many good things that Schmoller did for Penguin. It began with an irresistible dig: like Leavis, Allen had also been created a Companion of Honour and just as Mrs Leavis was determined to guard the reputation of her husband so also were Allen's associates keen to protect his good name. The body of the letter dealt categorically and effectively with the accusation that publishing *Lady Chatterley's Lover* had been a 'smart commercial venture'. Had it not been for the publicity engendered by the trial Penguin profits from the book would have been no more than £5000. Though the promotional efforts of the Director of Public Prosecution, Treasury Counsel and Mr Justice Byrne had boosted the sales from the projected 200,000 to a phenomenal 3 million and had increased the profits to £112,000, even from that prodigious sum – in itself greater than any that ever came to the firm from any other title, nor even from the best seller of all, Rieu's *Odyssey* – from the account must be deducted the £13,000 costs which the Judge had refused to pass to the Crown. Of what was left more than half went to shareholders other than Sir Allen Lane CH. Allen may have laughed all the way from the Old Bailey to Martin's Bank, but he could hardly be said to have been carrying the Golden Fleece across his shoulders.

Schmoller's riposte was deft. Yet, if in a sense that she neither intended nor understood, Mrs Leavis had stumbled on a truth: *Lady Chatterley's Lover* had helped to make Allen a millionaire, not by its sales, phenomenal though they were, but because the excitement created by the trial was still alive in the imagination of the public when, a few months later, the decision was taken to turn Penguin into a public company.

It would enhance his reputation for shrewdness – and would also strengthen the Leavis' contention – if it could be shown that Allen had foreseen the benefits that must come from staging a much-publicized trial as curtain-raiser to the drama of a flotation of shares and that he had somehow manipulated this useful conjunction. Allen was nimble, even cunning and adept at making others dance to his fiddling but he was not a magician; only a highly proficient necromancer could have been certain that the Director of Public Prosecutions would recognize the tune that he was playing, would know the appropriate steps and would perform them as he intended. Not even Merlin could have been confident that, once the dancing began, an Old Bailey jury would join in and follow obediently the choreography. Both the documentary evidence and the recollections of those who were closest to him at the time run counter to any such conclusion and tend to deny even the more limited accusation, levelled at him on several occasions after 1961 by his unflagging detractors, that the sale of shares was a direct consequence of the trial, yet another example of Allen's opportunism, or, as the more timid of his critics put it, still more support for the view which they had expressed frequently over the years, that Allen Lane was no genius but an ordinary mortal watched over by some unfastidious ally who prompted him to act always at precisely the right moment.

Not only the immediate evidence, which reveals that the notion of turning Penguin into a public company had been discussed for, at very least, four years before the *Lady Chatterley* trial, but also the total thrust of Allen's financial operations before 1961 deny all possibility that his dealings then were either Machiavellian or opportunist. He was a brilliant publisher and a leader of rare quality but there his business capability stopped; although he saw to it that his social and private life was made comfortable by his public success he was, for a man who had achieved so much in business, uninformed and almost remarkably naïve in the ways of the City. In the early days of the firm he had seldom dealt directly even with Penguin's own bankers; that had been left to Dick. Allen's only part in the financial affairs at Penguin had been to decry and over-ride the acute if conventional advice of his brother and other, even more cautious counsellors. He never studied the business journals and read the City columns only on those occasions, before 1961 infrequent, when there was in them some mention of Penguin. He had never played the stock market and previously had owned shares only in his own firm.

At the last the decision to go public was virtually forced upon him. The cash-flow problem which had dogged Penguin in its early days had been solved (if temporarily). The firm was rich in saleable book stock and in copyrights, and richer still in land and buildings. It is a reflection of Allen's hitherto unshakeable self-identification with the yeoman class that, for his company as for himself, he favoured tangible assets to what he described (with no great originality) as 'Monopoly money'. In 1961 Penguin owned: at Harmondsworth, 51,000 square feet of offices and warehouses built on a 3½-acre site and 8 acres of agricultural land; within a three-mile radius of Harmondsworth, 25 acres, 9000 square feet of warehouses, five flats and two houses (one of them Silverbeck); and at Melbourne 9000 square feet of office and warehouses built on a half-acre site and near by, ripe for development, a further four acres.

Except for those houses which had been settled for more than a century on fabulously valuable sites in the City of London, no other publisher owned as much in buildings and in land (and of those City-dwellers very few were still possessed of their privileges: most, including the Oxford University Press, had been driven from the City by the Luftwaffe).

But property is capital only in the abstruse calculations of accountants; it is not a form of wealth which can be used to finance development. Allen could not stand still; even he had plans to buy more land and to build more buildings; there was no way forward without a powerful infusion of new money. Martins Bank would help; Martins Bank had always helped and had good reason to be pleased with the fruits of generosity; but the nagging of his advisers persuaded Allen that the public would help more effectively.

There was also in his mind a vaguely held belief that, by making this change in the status of Penguin, he would stem his irresolution about the long-term future of the firm and might somehow make easier the task of those who carried responsibility for the business after he had retired. In a letter to one of his favoured candidates Allen did his best to explain himself; at the time (the letter was received before news of the flotation) the recipient was mystified as much by Allen's syntax as by his logic, but years later events have made more obvious the drift of his thinking: 'Penguin is a private company but its really me. I don't mean that as a boast but you know and I know that it would be easier for you or anyone else to be answerable to shareholders than to the Owner.'

Once he had accepted the idea of an offer of shares Allen

entered into the preparations with all the vigour and enthusiasm that he had given to publishing projects, to the briefing of counsel and witnesses prior to the *Lady Chatterley* case, or to his beloved building schemes. He called frequently at the offices of his solicitors, or of the solicitor for the share offer, of the two merchant bankers (Helbert, Wagg; and Shroder) who were to handle the offer. A quick study, he bandied with City editors and financial journalists the jargon of their craft as if he had been familiar with it all his life. In a series of lengthy trans-Continental telephone conversations with Dick, whose association with the institution that he had helped to establish was already tenuous and would be ended in the moment when Penguin became a public company, he cajoled, persuaded and was eventually adamant that his brother had no alternative but to dispose of his shares in the firm in which he was, with a $16\frac{2}{3}$ per cent holding, next to Allen, the most substantial proprietor.

In March 1961 the authorized share-capital of the private company was increased from £262,500 to £500,000. In the same month Dick transferred his holdings to Allen at a price of £220,000. On 20 April 1961 Penguin became a public company.

Prospective purchasers were offered 690,000 4-shilling shares at 12 shillings a share. A further 60,000 shares were reserved for Penguin employees.

Just as when Allen was launching some new and bold publishing venture, the excitement of preparation obliterated all recollection of any doubts that he may have had about the wisdom of his actions; even his austere financial advisers betrayed uncharacteristic optimism, but neither he nor they had any right to expect the deluge of applications that followed upon the advertising of shares. The prestige of Penguin was undeniable; even, there was in public feeling for Allen's unique creation something warmer than recognition of prestige, something compounded of affection and gratitude; but by the unemotional measure of the balance-sheet Penguin's record was far from sensational. Despite increased retail prices, in only five of the previous ten years had the profits for Penguin and its overseas subsidiaries exceeded £100,000 before taxation and the remarkable profits for 1960 (£365,000 before taxation) owed much to an accounting adjustment and even more to Griffith-Jones and the *Lady Chatterley* case. In but half of those same ten years had Penguin declared a dividend and only in the last two had the dividend exceeded 5 per cent. Yet tens of thousands, most of them small investors, were eager to prove that the City's use of the word 'sentiment' is more accurate than the City knows. Undoubtedly some were shrewd enough to foresee that the tides of publicity, from *Lady Chatterley* and from the run-up to the offer, would make initial trading brisk and thus open the way to a quick profit, and some others were buoyed in their expectations by the 10 per cent dividend paid in 1960, but a majority of those who applied for shares did so, almost certainly, not from altruism (the past and the prospects of the company were good enough to offer security if not affluence) but from some instinctive feeling that they wanted to enjoy actual ownership in an institution which they regarded as already peculiarly their own in all senses but financial.

The flotation was hugely successful. In all its previous history Harmondsworth had seen nothing to equal it for excitement, except perhaps the morning of Bernard Shaw's birthday. The issue was dramatically over-subscribed and within a day dealings on the market had the 4-shilling share up from the 12 shilling issue-price to more than 18 shillings.

Almost everyone was delighted.

Allen had signed a seven-year contract to serve the new company as Chairman and Managing Director. His position as majority shareholder was unassailable: he could trump the 750,000 shares owned by several thousand institutions and individuals with 1,250,000 shares registered in his own name and a further 475,000 held by trustees (all but one directors of Penguin and the exception Allen's cousin) for the benefit of his daughters. The staff were happy. Most had taken up their shares, and for them that sense of dedication to Penguin which had always existed was enhanced by the realization that they were now working for themselves. Merchant bankers, brokers, solicitors: all had made their percentage without too much effort. Only Dick had some right to feel aggrieved. When the details of the share issue reached him in Australia he discovered that his shares in the private company had been worth £250,000 at the issue price – a notional loss of £30,000 – and £375,000 at the end of the first day's dealing – a notional loss of £155,000! £220,000 is no bad return on a £100 investment paid originally because of a burglar, but Dick had given much of his life to Penguin. He was out and Allen was still in and Allen was now a millionaire.

Allen was slow to grasp the implications of his new fortune. Not for many years had he been forced to deny himself any necessity or even any luxury that he coveted; Silverbeck and his flat at West Drayton belonged to the firm, the firm owned his cars, paid the rent at Whitehall Court, settled most of the accounts for his entertaining and his travels. Now he could spend more on experiments at Priory Farm, look without considering the cost for another farm and for land in Devon, invade the auction market and the sales-rooms for more paintings and more antique snuff-boxes to add to his already considerable collections. He took some comfort from the knowledge that the future of the girls – and particularly Anna – was now secure, but he was not yet alert to the probability that riches on the scale which was now his have a remarkable capacity for self-propagation. It needs only application and shrewd manipulation to make them reproduce at a rate that would have been inconceivable to him even a few weeks earlier when he had been, like many another successful businessman, obviously prosperous and comfortable but not personally blessed with capital free for speculation. His outbursts of generosity, though discordant with his customary meanness and seemingly unpremeditated, were almost always directed towards his colleagues and his kin, even at times towards comparatively distant blood relations. Though, once big money came his way, he talked of establishing some form of charitable trust, he neither saw himself as an imitator of Nuffield or Gulbenkian nor yet understood that he had the wealth to start a new career as a philanthropist. Even when at last the size of his fortune became apparent to him such aspirations to indulge in charity as he discussed with his friends and with his solicitor were limited by the consciousness of his own most intimate tragedy. He planned to establish a trust to make easier the lot of handicapped children.

However, the success of the share-issue had an immediate and enlivening effect upon his Penguin activities. The transfusion of new capital removed the financial inhibitions to yet another elaborate construction-programme and made it possible for him to pass many months contentedly immersed in what was his favourite pastime of collaborating in an architectural project.

The need for more warehouse space had been apparent before the rights-issue, even before the *Lady Chatterley* trial, but the cost and the diversions created by these two events had made it necessary to postpone all thoughts of new building. With the case won and funds available the light in Allen's eye brightened, but there were other diversions. It was not until late in 1962 that he began to cover used envelopes with calculations and drawings.

Blass was chosen to be his collaborator within the firm. (Not the least of the causes for Blass's rise in the hierarchy was that he shared with Allen an enthusiasm for building, for trees and for gardens, that, even more than Allen, he was capable of translating plans into practice, that he was prepared to give long hours and close attention to supervising builders or landscape-gardeners.) However, when in the summer of 1963 Allen left for a long tour of North America, still nothing had been finalized; no architect had been commissioned and no builder contracted. Those who were left behind, thinking to implement Allen's wishes as quickly and inexpensively as possible placed the specifications in the hands of a construction company which offered to its clients a comprehensive arrangement, everything from design to completed building. Allen returned home, looked suspiciously at the plans and grudgingly accepted that they might serve.

Then, in 1964, the Labour Party took over government. When it introduced a land levy it was apparent to all who, like Penguin, had building projects in hand that the only way to avoid the imposition was to prove that construction had already begun before the effective date of the new legislation. This consideration added weight to the argument that the contractor's design be accepted forthwith and building be started without delay.

Only Allen hesitated. The proposals he castigated as plans for something little better than a glorified shed. When his colleagues remonstrated that a glorified shed would serve well enough as a bulk-warehouse, he replied that a shed was not good enough for Penguin. Then, as happened to him so often, he met a man at a party, in this case Ove Arup, and he put to Arup his problem. Encouraged by the architect's interest he refused to sign the contract with the construction firm and turned instead to Arup and his partner, Philip Dowson. Again his colleagues protested: one of the most eminent architects in the world to design a mere warehouse! And their protests became strident, and it seemed unanswerable, as they pointed out that the delay caused by abandoning the contractor and beginning all over again the planning-process must make inevitable the payment of the crippling land-levy.

Allen was adamant: he would have Arup and Dowson. As for the levy, that too he would arrange. Less than a week before the effective date, workmen dug preparatory trenches on the site.

Penguin did not pay the levy, and Allen had for enduring memorial one of the very few warehouses which is both efficient and aesthetically satisfying.

It was to be the last of his major building projects. Already before it was finished Allen had discovered another pastime which soon became so absorbing that it reduced his need to turn for relaxation to architecture, set back his interest in farming and came close to usurping the place at the centre of his existence which had been held for forty years without challenge by publishing. He discovered the delights and thrills of making money make money.

A late beginner – he was almost sixty when he opened his portfolio – Allen responded eagerly to the scrupulous tutelage of Anthony Hornby of Cazenove's but the attention which he paid to his investments in the five or six years before his final illness was inspired, not by calculation and certainly not by necessity (his advisers would have handled the calculations with experienced efficiency and he had no need for more money), but by the fever of a collector. He gloated over his investments as he had never gloated over his antiques or paintings; he was frequently on the telephone to his broker and often, perhaps too often for his broker's comfort, he found the impersonality of the telephone dispiriting and so presented himself at the Cazenove office. His talk turned regularly to his investments – a topic which many, and above all those who had none – found as infuriating as conversation about diet (another subject on which he was increasingly fluent). He boasted about his successes in the market as he had never boasted about his achievements in publishing. 'I've only to open my portfolio,' he told one uninterested and disinterested listener, 'to see it double before my eyes.'

There was, behind all this euphoria about money, a strain

which at the time very few could identify and which Allen, determined as he was to preserve his reputation for ebullience, was of all men least capable of confessing even to himself: a sense of sadness for liberty that had vanished under the weight of affluence. As never before in his professional life and as had been noticeable in his private manner only rarely (the prime example his earliest encounter with Lettice), Allen seemed to be vulnerable. For this, no doubt, poor health was in part responsible and physical deterioration made it ever more difficult to sustain his capacity for ubiquity and for sustaining unimpaired that quality of resilience which had always been the greatest, the most attractive and the most compelling of his attributes. Reduced vitality served but to compound and to make more intransigent worries that were greater than any uncertainty about his physical condition. Allen's obsession with his personal fortune was largely a self-prescribed panacea for an ailment which he was powerless to cure. The flotation had made him a millionaire but it had not achieved all that had been hoped and intended: an enduring improvement in the health of Penguin.

Within a year it was obvious that the magic wand which had transformed Penguin from a private into a public company had not magicked into existence a *doppelgänger* who could in time take the part of Allen Lane. The responsibility for choosing his successor was still his and he was still incapable of settling upon one candidate – and staying with his choice. None but Allen had expected any resolution of this particular dilemma but all with even remote responsibility for Penguin finances were disappointed when, only three years after the sensational response to the offer of shares, it became clear that, unless Allen was prepared to authorize severe curbs on Penguin publishing programmes, some new and yet more drastic financial reorganization would be forced upon the firm. It had always been among the first of Allen's business principles that he who attempts to stand still runs the risk of being toppled backwards; the thought of restriction was no more pleasing to him in 1965 than it had been twenty or thirty years earlier.

Allen's last decade, the decade of unprecedented affluence, was the unhappiest of his life.

If it is possible, or just, to isolate from all his activities and from the tangle of consequences which flowed from circumstances over which he had little or no control, one act of his which can be marked as genesis to miseries, that act was his invitation, coincidental with the *Lady Chatterley* trial, to Tony Godwin to serve as an editorial adviser. Superficially the appointment was inspired by considerations that were well founded. Godwin had proved himself a brilliant bookseller; there was indeed none other in Britain who could match him for energy and shrewdness; the flair, the literary and artistic taste that had contributed so much to the success of his two bookshops were virtually synonymous with the qualities that were integral to Penguin. Like Allen he had shown that good taste and commercial viability are not antipathetic and, as Allen in publishing so he in bookselling, had managed to win over the public without ever seeming to patronize or condescend. That he had achieved all this even from a small shop in that most competitive of bookselling market-places, the Charing Cross Road, where he had operated in the shadow of famous and long-established rivals, made possibility into a probability that Godwin could help to contrive something of the same for Penguin.

This was a time when, despite all the glories of the previous years, the enormity of the competition was at last perceived at Harmondsworth. Already ten and more years earlier, Penguin had stood by complacently as the first of its substantial competitors established itself as more than an irritating imitator. The fault then had been editorial and largely Allen's (though his attitude had not been questioned by any of his senior editors); it had been a product of his ambivalent feelings about the war. Convinced that war books were somehow beneath the literary dignity of Penguin and of Penguin's readership and that they were likely to prove ephemeral, he had allowed Pan Books to corner the market in a series of phenomenal bestsellers, including *The Dam Busters*, *The Colditz Story* and *The Wooden Horse*. He had failed to take advantage of the immediate popularity of such titles; he had missed the possibility that they were likely to be just as attractive to book-buyers who were drawn to the conventional Penguin range as to tens of thousands who did not buy Penguins or books of any kind; but he had also failed to appreciate that the cinema and the television would sustain the popularity of these books for years to come. Most significant of all, because of his distaste for books about the war, which came perhaps from his more personal unease about all reminiscences by old soldiers, he allowed Pan Books to build unhindered commercial strength and public reputation.

In the late fifties writers turned once more for subject-matter to the war. The public response proved that a new generation of approving readers – a generation that had itself no knowledge of the war – was, no less than its elders, eager to snap up everything that dealt with the war. For all his perspicacity not even Allen could forecast that this enthusiasm would last and grow, that it would be unabated even thirty years after the end of hostilities; though Penguin's reluctance to enter this lucrative field persists to this day, Allen can be blamed only for the original blunder.

It follows that it was not from any inclination to fill a notable editorial lacuna nor yet out of any wish to compete, in particular and even this late in the day, with his most successful rival, that Allen sought to bolster his editorial power and that he looked therefore to Godwin. What impressed him in 1960 was the overall strength of the opposition. Where once, and not so long ago, he had stalked alone there were now more than 150 paperback publishers, some prepared to offer for reprint-rights sums that made Penguin's customary bids look like the offerings of a peanut-vendor among the jewellers in Hatton Garden.

The burgeoning of paperback series – and the prodigality of some of their proprietors – was not the only threat to Penguin supremacy. Book clubs had existed for many years but even the most successful of them had been discounted as a competitor to Penguin largely, and hitherto sensibly, because it was thought that the vast audience which brought Penguins was for the most part composed of readers who did not wish to have their books selected for them and who rejected the notion of committing themselves to playing a passive part in an automatic process. (For many years Allen chose to dismiss as insubstantial evidence to the potential of the clubs the progress made soon after the war by his own, admittedly tentative, direct-order scheme, which embraced many of the characteristics of a book club, and to tolerate as an eccentricity the popularity of Kaye Webb's Puffin Club.) But by 1960 soaring prices for hard covers had driven into the arms of the clubs many who still held to the belief that a paperback is not truly a book. The growing number of clubs, and their increasing specialization, reduced the sense of passivity, allowing prospective members if not a choice of titles then at least a wide choice of clubs.

When at last it came, Allen's awareness of the situation was sharpened by the knowledge that his principal assistant in editorial matters, Eunice Frost, was a sick woman; Godwin was, it seemed, in every respect admirably qualified to take her place. Even had she been still blessed with the energy that was once hers, it could be argued that, because her modernity was already a generation out of style, Godwin's more advanced tastes and the associations with a new generation of writers and artists that he had developed at Better Books gave him advantages over Miss Frost and made him more appropriate to Penguin's current needs.

These were good and bold reasons for the invitation to Godwin. There was also in the magnetism which he exerted on Allen a quality which, though not to be despised, was undoubtedly more sentimental than thoughtful. Godwin's assertiveness, energy, briskness and that strain in him which is best described as chirpiness reminded Allen of himself when he was Godwin's age; he was tempted to believe, as it turned out mistakenly, that Penguin needed a reincarnation of Allen Lane.

He had misjudged his man and he had misjudged the times. In the next six years whenever there was friction at Harmondsworth (and there was much more friction than ever there had been in the past) there was Godwin as catalyst or *provocateur*. He was ambitious, but that Allen had known before ever he took him on and did not see as an inhibition. In the past he had employed many ambitious men and had successfully harnessed their ambitions to his own purpose, and ambition was just one more characteristic which added to the illusion that Godwin was an *alter ego*; but Allen had not appreciated that Godwin's ambition was not far short of megalomania. Nor did he realize that Godwin's sprightliness was sustained by an exorbitant output of nervous energy, that the taut strings of his personality could be snapped under tensions applied by opposition, that when such highly charged extroversion is crossed it is apt to vanish, almost at a moment's notice, and to leave behind a character disposed either to depression or aggression. In sum Godwin had most of the qualities that would have been useful to Allen and to Penguin except stability.

In his handling of Godwin, as in his appreciation of his professional and personal character, Allen made disastrous mistakes. He had thought to add him to the number of his aides, as he had from time to time added so many others, but as with them, he had not considered it necessary to delineate the limits of Godwin's responsibilities and he had not measured the possible consequences of Godwin's dynamism or his capacity for influencing his colleagues, and particularly his younger colleagues. The one inhibition imposed by Allen upon Godwin's power in Penguin was expressed only in negative terms: neither in 1960 nor at any time in the next six years did he promise or hint that Godwin would be his successor as Managing Director.

Not unnaturally this calculated omission distressed Godwin and intensified his ambitions. It was a tactical error which Allen in his prime would never have committed. By comparison with Allen a young man, Godwin, if he had seen for himself the possibility of a future at the head of the firm by Allen's nomination, might have bided his time. When Allen indicated no such intention and not infrequently denied the possibility by adopting, either from within the firm or from outside, other candidates for the role that he coveted and thought was his by right, Godwin resolved to take what was not offered even if it meant destroying Allen in the process.

In the past Allen had dealt effectively with others no less forceful than Godwin but each in turn, though eager for his own advancement, had seen Penguin always in the likeness of Allen Lane and had thought of himself not as supplanter but as an inheritor. Godwin was the first who planned for Penguin reconstructed in his own image. He arrived on the scene when Allen seemed no longer capable of matching his ruthlessness, when through time or his own actions he had lost many of his more sturdy allies. Godwin's vigorous personality, his adventurous editing, even his mode of dressing according to a style that was in truth younger than his years, made him a standard-bearer for that element in the firm which, though no less dedicated to the Penguin ideal than its seniors, feared that the ideal was fast becoming a convention and a handicap, and which suspected many in the older generation, including even Allen himself, of looking back so often upon the achievement that they had not time to look forward to the potential.

Godwin's status in the Penguin organization was at first vague. His climb to authority was accepted by others, among them Allen, not so much as a matter of corporate and considered decision as from recognition of necessity to accept formally a situation that had been allowed to develop. As such it was not unprecedented in Penguin history; Allen's habit of expecting from his colleagues versatility in all publishing techniques, of taking on comparatively senior employees and then allowing them to prove in what direction their usefulness lay, had brought several men and women to the firm who had eventually established themselves, either temporarily or permanently, at the head of departments in situations for which they had not been intended either by contract or by the implied terms of their original appointment. But none before Godwin had risen so rapidly. At least in the first three years of his Penguin career, none had been allowed by Allen quite as much freedom to act for Penguin unmoved by the opinions of his senior colleagues and only tangentially affected by Allen's supervision.

Employed at first as just one of several editorial advisers, he was then given the substantive rank of Fiction Editor, but within months he was signing letters as Chief Editor – although there was at that time still another Chief Editor at Harmondsworth. When Woodhouse left it was inevitable that Godwin's right to the title must be confirmed. When the Board was enlarged, it was no less inevitable that the Chief Editor (with Blass, by that time Penguin's undisputed expert on all matters connected with sales) would be made a 'director below the line'.

By then Godwin's spiky personality and his fiercely held and tactlessly expressed opinions had brought him into open conflict with many he classified or castigated as 'the old Guard', and notably with Paroissien and with Blass; Allen was either unwilling to take the side of older servants or incapable of rejecting the benefits that came to Penguin as a direct consequence of Godwin's vigorous editorial management.

Allen had not as yet lost his capacity for sitting in the stands and watching with delight as his senior colleagues indulged in gladiatorial combat. Both because he revelled in the sight and because he held still to his precept that fraternal strife is an excellent preparation for battle with external enemies, he was not above intervening to incite mischief where without his prompting none might have existed, but he was slow to appreciate that the bitterness within the upper echelon was essentially different from anything that had occurred previously at Harmondsworth. He was even slower to realize that the weapons being sharpened in the struggle against the Old Guard must eventually be turned against the Napoleon of Penguin, against Allen himself.

It was by no means entirely indolence nor yet solely a decline in his perceptive faculties that reduced Allen to complacency and impotence. Godwin was in fact doing for Penguin much of what Allen had hoped that he would do. He had made the transition from bookselling to publishing without difficulty. All the brilliance that he had shown in the Charing Cross Road was apparent at Harmondsworth and enhanced by the greater opportunities presented to him by publishing, and particularly by the especial advantages that flowed from the Penguin heritage. He was a brilliant editor; though such things are difficult to measure, it is at least arguable that he was the finest editor ever employed by Penguin; but even more important, he was in most respects the right editor for the time. In this like Allen, his capacity for judging the relationship between literary quality and commercial viability was generally sound and though, again like Allen, his judgement was not schooled but instinctive, his instinct was sharper than Allen's and worked, as Allen's did but rarely, without the promptings of professional advice or popular acclaim.

The resentment that he felt for the Penguin establishment may have been ill-founded and his frequent articulation and demonstration of that resentment was certainly offensive, but his refusal to accept as immutable some tenets of Penguin doctrine freed him to move out into the market to compete, even at the exorbitant levels which had become commonplace among the firm's rivals. The boldness of some of his coups, though hideously expensive and shocking to some of his colleagues, brought to the list titles which without him would never have come to Penguin and which renewed the possibility of competition on equal terms with more extravagant if less distinguished paperback houses.

All these virtues in Godwin Allen required, and it was this recognition above all which held him for so long complacent even about Godwin's faults. For some years he thought that he saw advantage also in that very characteristic which made Godwin unpopular among his more settled colleagues, believing that Godwin's hold over the younger members of the staff was an effective substitute for the influence which Allen could no longer exercise fluently; that therefore, by way of Godwin, he could sustain the enthusiasm of a new and restless generation. Allen could not accept, however, that Godwin's bohemianism was similar to the unconventionality which he and his brothers had shown in their days in Talbot Square and that it was transposed only according to the different styles of different times.

Godwin was volatile, charismatic, a buccaneer and in so many other characteristics a latter-day version of the old Allen. The characteristics and activities which made him attractive to his younger colleagues were all of a kind that Allen himself had practised thirty, twenty, even ten years earlier, that he still hankered after exercising but could not. As Allen before him, Godwin was never happier than when he was engineering conflict and competition between his subordinates; just as Allen in the past, so now Godwin made life at Penguin fun even in its most tensely dramatic moments. But not fun for Allen. Him Godwin never understood. Allen was the past, Godwin the future. He could not and would not appreciate Allen's need for company, for purpose and for some generous distraction from the sorrows of his isolation and his illness.

For his part Allen was blind to the fact that Godwin himself was a sick man and, no less than he, impatient to complete, at last after false starts, what he saw as his real life's work. After the honeymoon period, Allen's resentment for Godwin grew and blossomed on its own malevolence, but even in the early days of antipathy Allen expressed his suspicions only in terms that were almost ludicrously superficial. He objected, for example (not to Godwin but to all others who would listen), to his Chief Editor's casual appearance, to his loud shirts, brash ties and long hair. Such demonstrations of modernity Allen categorized as uncouth and they were undoubtedly anathema to Allen's fastidious nature, but if all this was but a talisman working advance for Penguin then this Allen was prepared to tolerate.

There was, too, holding them together in the early days of their relationship, one consuming ambition. Both men dreamed of breaking out of their paperback bonds and of establishing within the Penguin complex a hardcover list.

This ambition had nagged at Allen for many years. He had made it explicit when, in answer to Maynard's enquiry about what he would do when he had conquered the paperback market, he had replied that he would then conquer the world of hard covers. It was explicit in his aphorism that books could be sold successfully only at sixpence and six guineas. When, in the early sixties he began to move out of fantasy into hardheaded preparation, he had motives in addition to the desire to fulfil a long-standing ambition, and reasons that were abetted but not originated by Godwin's eagerness.

He needed novelty, something to revivify his fading zest. This he found occasionally but it seldom lasted for long. There was, for example, the adventure, much publicized and perhaps much exaggerated both by him and by the press, when he and Blass, having set off to drive through the African forest with no other guide than a road map for roads that were non-existent, were stranded miles from civilization. He could still find much pleasure in travel and in meetings with his favourite authors (one of the few letters that he thought worthy of preserving came from P. G. Wodehouse, inviting Allen to join him in New York, but not on Election Day 'when all the bars will be closed'). But he needed new interests to take the place of something that had gone out of his publishing life; he felt deprived of that quality he called 'fun'. It was a word that he used often and was for him the personal equivalent of that other and similar word 'cheerful', which synthesized most of his *desiderata* for the books he published. Not all his new-found pleasure in manipulating his stocks and shares could make up for the loss of 'fun' in publishing. Later – almost at the end of his life – he revealed his sense of deprivation, if in a stilted and somewhat back-handed manner, when he added an inscription to a history of Marks and Spencer which he gave to Blass: '.... who will I know enjoy reading this as an example of the importance of having a basic philosophic approach to business principles if one is to achieve a greater satisfaction than can be obtained solely by concentrating on budgets and balance-sheets.'

There was, too, still worrying at the hems of his pride, that antique uncertainty about an achievement in publishing which was almost entirely limited to the production of paperbacks. Even after thirty triumphant years Allen was still burdened by the prejudices which, against all odds, he had done more than any other man to make ridiculous. Now he knew that he had little time left in which to make certain that his contemporaries and posterity would recognize his life's work as equal to, and perhaps superior to, the achievements of Uncle John.

Godwin had other and better-founded reasons for indulging Allen's hard-cover aspirations. Recognizing the power and collective wealth of the opposition, he sought to create for Penguin its private reservoir of titles which, having already proved themselves in the hard-cover market, could then be added to the paperback list. Thus far he was reverting to a publishing principle which had been commonplace before the advent of Penguin, to the time when it was customary for publishers to produce their own cheap editions only after they had exhausted the possibility of the standard version, but Godwin had something more in mind. Penguin was still unique among paperback houses in that a majority of its non-fiction titles were written to the firm's own commission. A few, a very few, had been marketed by the firm in both paperback and hard-cover editions; some, but still not many, had progressed from Pelican paperback to hard-cover exploitation by other publishers; but most original Penguins never appeared in durable or expensive format unless by the piratical intervention of libraries and library-binders. If Penguin had its own hard-cover subsidiary more Penguin titles (and particularly more Pelicans) could enjoy the totality of market opportunities, and all the financial benefit would come to Penguin and to Penguin authors. Much as writers coveted inclusion in the Penguin list, it remained a fact of literary life that few writers were entirely satisfied until they saw their works decently encased in cloth. By offering to them this respectability and increased royalties (without depriving them of the gratification that came from reaching a vast audience with low-priced paperbacks) it must follow that they and their as yet un-Penguined writing colleagues would be even more eager to work for Penguin than in the past.

Allen saw the force of these arguments, and for a while allowed himself to drift in the tide of Godwin's enthusiasm, but this was not the way to the rejuvenation of spirit that he required. In all essentials Godwin's plan was no more than an extension of current Penguin practice, an enlargement of potential but not a sensational innovation.

Later, when Allen had established his hard-cover imprint, it was widely reported that it had its origins in an impulsive moment. It was said that Allen, walking one day down Vigo Street, happened to notice an estate agent's board outside the premises where he had begun his career and Uncle John had ended his, had resolved immediately that he would acquire the building and that only when it was his had he decided that the ghost of Uncle John could be brought back to life by setting up, at the address that he had made famous, a firm which, like The Bodley Head, would specialize in the lavish production of esoteric books. It was a tale that Allen enjoyed and helped to circulate, not less because it contradicted such rumours as had reached the public about his dwindling decisiveness than because it emphasized to his Penguin colleagues that this new imprint had policies and a style independent of the Penguin tradition. There was even an element of truth in the story. Allen was both superstitious and easily overcome by nostalgia. The nice coincidence made possible by the availability of the Vigo Street offices (there still extant on a window was the signature that Allen had engraved long ago when practising for his meeting with the Prince of Wales) was the hand of Fate writing QED to a theorem that was already close to resolution.

Allen Lane The Penguin Press began its career as a virtually independent publishing house inauspiciously, with on its side only Allen's reawakened energy, that charming coincidence of address and its name, deliberately contrived to sound inescapably reminiscent of John Lane The Bodley Head. Godwin accepted with remarkably good grace the subversion of his own plans for hard-cover publishing but it was his duty to point out to Allen what Allen must have known but could not accept: that it would be two or three years before the new enterprise could be properly launched. He and Boyle reasoned with Allen that the very independence from traditional Penguin philosophy could be created and sustained only by adopting for Allen Lane The Penguin Press editorial, production and sales techniques in which Penguin personnel were not practised or adept; there must be a separate budget and, almost certainly, new staff. But Allen was no longer merely impulsive: he was impatient. He must have his new indulgence, and quickly. Consequently the first books which came from Vigo Street were in editorial terms ill-considered. Some were in direct competition with similar but generally better and always cheaper titles already well established in the Harmondsworth list; none was sufficiently notable or sufficiently idiosyncratic to mark the new imprint with a character that set it apart from other hard-cover houses; there were no patent bestsellers to provide cash-flow and nothing which was obviously destined for long-term survival as part of that reservoir of strength without which no publisher can prosper, a powerful back list. Only in one respect were Allen's intentions amply fulfilled. The output of Allen Lane The Penguin Press was from the first both remarkably elegant and, in the characteristics which contributed to that elegance, immediately identifiable as something which could not have come from any other publisher. But elegance of this kind is expensive and contributed to the indifferent financial performance of Allen Lane The Penguin Press. By forcing up costs and therefore retail prices, it alerted both booksellers and the reading public to the suspicion that all this high-toned production was no more than a mask for unworthy contents.

Allen knew that it is never easy to recover from the consequence of initial failure. Though he continued to assert that all would come right in the end and so never accepted that he must write off Allen Lane The Penguin Press as a failure, he was quick to realize that the stimulation which he had thought to find would not come from Vigo Street.

His disappointment he marked up against Godwin. It was a calumny, but relations between the two men were by this time so soured that it was almost inevitable that Allen should blame Godwin.

The battle of wills between the two moved to another field: the issue this time the physical appearance of Penguins. Godwin was determined to create for Penguin a new and essentially contemporary image. For him the reform that was most obviously needed was in that aspect that was most immediately and obviously apparent to the public. If Penguins were to compete for attention and shelf space with a host of rivals they must be dressed to match and master the eye-catching appearance favoured by their more brazen competitors.

His was, in essence, no more than a latter-day restatement of precepts which had governed Penguin design formulae from the beginning, no more than a reiteration of Allen's firmly held conviction that the manner in which a book is packaged is almost as important as the quality of the material contained within the package. For a while Allen conceded that a new look was necessary, but the advent of pictorial covers was also perversely an heretical, almost blasphemous breach of Penguin articles of faith. The Penguin designers, reinforced by several brilliant young artists, notably Germano Facetti, struggled manfully to resolve the paradox. They were on the whole successful, contriving somehow to combine colour, pattern and pictorial excitement in cover-designs that were, even so, unmistakably Penguin. But Allen was determined to nourish a grievance and soon he was mouthing, against his own Production Department, the 'bosoms and bottoms' *canard* that he had raised so often against rivals.

Once more – but this time with rather more justification – Allen marked Godwin as the originator of his dissatisfaction, but there was over-riding even his displeasure, a spirit of lassitude. Unwilling to face the enlargement of conflict which he suspected must come from confronting Godwin and aware that many of Godwin's plans were long term and must be in time beneficial to Penguin, Allen sparked – but as yet did nothing.

Even the most notorious dispute between the two was fought out largely in sulks, silences, demonstrations of strength and despising asides. Though eventually it stirred Allen to action, it did not arouse him to the most definitive act of all: the dismissal of his Chief Editor.

Many times in its history Penguin had published collections of the works of distinguished cartoonists. Allen did not forget that he had manufactured his independence from the restraining influence of his conservative fellow-directors at The Bodley Head in part on the reputation of a cartoonist – on the edition of Peter Arno that he and his brothers had published in tandem with Joyce's *Ulysses*. Since then there had appeared, under the Penguin imprint, many analogous volumes, among them collections of drawings by James Thurber, Charles Addams, Nicolas Bentley, Ronald Searle, David Low and, again, Peter Arno. Therefore, when Godwin secured for Penguin a selection from the work of Siné he had every right to assume that he was following established and profitable precedents. Siné's *Massacre* he regarded as no exceptional addition to the list, but merely one more to add to the hundreds of titles in preparation. He planned for it no fanfares and gave it no further thought once he had delegated to a comparatively junior editor the task of seeing it through the press. Certainly he never envisaged that it would exacerbate the tension between him and Allen. That Allen shared his opinion of the comparative insignificance of this one title is proven by the fact that he, who knew Siné's work only by repute, never troubled to look at the satirist's vigorous drawings until the completed book was already in the Penguin warehouse. Even then, when his suspicions had been aroused by murmurs of distaste from several quarters in the firm and though he confessed himself to be unhappy about the blatancy of some of the drawings, he allowed himself to be swayed by Malcolm Muggeridge's generally admiring introduction:

> ... he is a Gallic, de-sentimentalized Thurber, whose art will, as I hope, find a wide circle of admirers and addicts in this country for its sharpness, quickness and vividness; for the economy of the drawing, as well as a kind of photographic impressionism Sine uses which is all his own – exact, and at the same time formless; like a mushroom cloud whose impending universal *Massacre* provides the backdrop for his own particular one.

Once Penguin representatives showed the book to booksellers the chorus of disapproval swelled and could not be ignored. When several of Penguin's best customers refused to stock a title which they described variously as 'disgusting', 'shocking', 'an affront to good taste' and 'a scandal', the affair had to go before the Board for resolution. Allen was always inclined to favour his sales staff and their bookseller contacts against the more literary and esoteric editors. His predisposition was in this case strengthened by his animosity towards Godwin. When Miss

Una Dillon, one of London's best booksellers and for many years a stalwart Penguin supporter, joined the protests, added that she considered this publication to be an abdication of Penguin responsibility, and announced that Dillon's University Bookshop in Bloomsbury, so long the one place in London where the public could find the complete range of Penguins, would not subscribe this book, Allen resolved that he himself would act as prosecuting counsel before his fellow-directors.

Godwin defended his choice energetically, logically but with what was for him comparatively little truculence. The book was scatological; that he admitted and even Muggeridge had commented upon this (though he had glorified Siné's obsession with bodily functions and water-closets by comparing him to Swift), but it ill-became a publishing house, he suggested, which had not so long before won many friends and vast sales by defending *Lady Chatterley's Lover* against the forces of illiberality now to act as censor itself. It would be a sensational and shattering blow to Penguin's reputation for independence if the firm surrendered to the captious opinions of a few puritanical individuals, however influential those individuals might be.

Allen took his stand on the commercial imperative of avoiding offence to those who controlled retail outlets. It was a legitimate contention but there were other strains in Allen's argument which, had Godwin known more about Allen's record and precepts and had he wished to make the debate more personal and more acrimonious than it already was, he could have used to destroy any validity that survived in Allen's case. If it was inappropriate for the publisher of *Lady Chatterley's Lover* to censor Siné it was even more out of character for a man who had often insisted that he had no need for religion and only despising for all religious institutions to turn suddenly a philosophical somersault and take against a satirist because he was avowedly and overtly anti-clerical. Where now, Godwin might have asked, the heir to John Lane, the man who, almost alone, had built the British reputation of Anatole France? And, had he known what Allen was saying in private about the Siné contretemps it would have been easy for him to make Allen look both ridiculous and pathetic; to some of his intimates Allen was muttering that, if ever a Penguin edition of Siné's *Massacre* found its way into the hands of the people of North Devon (it must be added, an unlikely eventuality), he would never again be welcomed by the farmers and farm-labourers who hitherto had greeted him so warmly in the pub at Iddesleigh, where, as in no other environment, he found relaxation and acceptance that was touched neither by envy nor by obsequiousness.

Godwin did not need to articulate any savage debating points; unspoken, most were still obvious to all involved in the discussion, even to Allen himself, and without them Godwin won the verdict of the Board. Allen accepted his defeat, if not with good grace then at least with no show of resentment more dramatic than a shrug of the shoulders. But Godwin's triumph was short-lived. Allen fretted over the decision. Now he was no longer concerned with the rights or wrongs of publishing Siné nor even with the malodorous effect the publication was having on the good name of Penguin. What dismayed him was the discovery that he had allowed the Penguin Board to become a democracy, that his voice was now but one among several and his opinion no longer omnipotent at Harmondsworth. Throughout most of his years at the head of the firm he would have dismissed even the unanimous opposition of his fellow directors in the manner of Abraham Lincoln: 'Noes, seven; Ayes, one. The Ayes have it.' Godwin and the others thought that those days had gone forever. He would show them how wrong they were.

For a month after the publication-date of *Massacre* he continued to brood. Then he acted.

He wanted no more debates, and the success of his plan depended on secrecy and surprise. Not even his most-favoured colleagues could be expected to condone the *coup* he had in mind. He told no one except George Nicholls, a long-serving member of the warehouse staff whom he had selected as accomplice. One night, long after all other employees had gone home, the two of them entered the warehouse, loaded the stock of *Massacre* on to a van, drove to Priory Farm and there burnt the books on a huge bonfire.

Allen enjoyed every moment of the escapade, and enjoyed even the fireworks from Godwin that followed the bonfire. As Godwin ranted, Allen sat, smiling his infuriating self-satisfied naughty-boy smile, his lips set thinly. Godwin threatened to resign; Allen merely shrugged his shoulders as he had when the Board voted him down, neither accepting nor rejecting the offer. It was not, he was convinced, a genuine threat. There was nowhere else for Godwin to go where he could exert influence equal to that he enjoyed at Penguin, nowhere else where he could exercise his restless imagination as freely as he did at Harmondsworth. He had taught Godwin a lesson, and had shattered the illusion of Godwin not merely as the Chief Editor but as the Chief Executive of Penguin, answerable to the Board, perhaps, but even to the Board only in general terms, and to Allen not at all except insofar as Allen was one of the directors. With this lesson dramatically completed Allen was content to loosen the rope round Godwin's neck, confident in the knowledge that, if Godwin ever again attempted to dance to tunes of his own composition, he would undoubtedly hang himself. As for the rest: the martyrdom of *Massacre* brought from them not so much as a banged table or a whimpered protest.

The story of Allen's night operation was kept from the press and dutifully the book was reported 'out-of-print'.

Allen's assessment of the effectiveness of his disciplining of Godwin was far from shrewd, for Godwin's skills and his genius for self-advertisement had ensured that his ability was widely recognized. There were on both sides of the Atlantic several publishers ready to bid for his services. If it was true that he preferred the power base at Penguin to all others that might be accessible to him, it was no less true that he had neither the need nor the inclination to set himself up as a Saint Sebastian for Allen's arrows. There was open to him, he decided, only one method whereby he could make himself secure at Penguin: he must shoot first. He would dispose of Allen. It was a dangerous ploy, that he knew, but the price was worth a conspiracy and not all the advantage was with Allen.

Even if Godwin could muster all other shareholders (in itself inconceivable) he could not out-vote Allen, but there was ample precedent for manoeuvring the major shareholder out of active supremacy in the company that ostensibly he controlled. Even so, Godwin had no intention of appealing to the shareholders; instead he would work his revolution within the walls of the palace itself. He had strong support among the younger members of the staff. Though their restlessness could have no executive effect, he calculated that a concerted demonstration of discontent from those who were largely responsible for the day-to-day and month-to-month implementation of Penguin policy might incite to action those others, the members of the Board, whose concern was primarily for more long-term decisions. Of these several, he knew, had been more put out than they dared admit by Allen's autocratic piracy in the Siné affair. There was no thought in his mind that, even with their connivance, he could ever succeed in having Allen removed entirely from the Penguin scene but – and here examples drawn from other public companies encouraged him – there were many ways in which a Chairman and Managing Director could be elevated out of power. Allen might be made President or given some other suitably honourable but insubstantial title.

For a while it seemed as if Allen was playing into Godwin's hands. For two or three years he had been talking of retiring; by 1966 the suggestion had become an insistent theme in his conversation and in his correspondence. To Williams, and in similar vein to several others, he wrote that he had tired of the pace and noise of city life and was 'increasingly drawn to the peace and quiet of the countryside', that he intended to make the most use of his remaining years by 'working only on three days at the office and spending the remaining four at Priory Farm'. For years he had prepared for just such an eventuality, even for a retirement at once more varied and less idyllic. If he wished to work he had offices in three countries; there was the farm for energetic relaxation; and, for whatever else he needed, a choice of flats and houses: Silverbeck for himself and, sometimes, Lettice, Priory Farm for himself and, sometimes, Lettice, Whitehall Court and the house in Ireland for himself, and, often, Suzanne, the Old Mill where, in his own words, 'I can be shot of all women' and El Fenix, for himself and everyone he chose to invite. In fact, despite what he wrote to Williams, by 1960 he was spending more time in Spain than at Priory Farm or anywhere else. His sporadic raids on Harmondsworth, which Godwin took to be designed to harass him, were discommoding even to better-disposed colleagues who found Allen's interventions disruptive and his inconsistency difficult to support. Did not all this prove, Godwin asked his more willing adherents, that the future of the Penguin ideal could no longer be left in the unsure hands of the founder? And, to some of those who were not members of his claque, he hinted that it would be a kindness to offer to Allen glory without authority and the chance to live out his life in the manner which he so palpably desired.

Allen sensed little if anything of all this. Almost certainly he decided after a while that he wanted Godwin to leave, but as so often in the past when dealing with recalcitrant or inconvenient associates, he hoped that he would go of his own volition. He expected him to go and was prepared to help him on his way by making his stay uncomfortable, but more than that he was not prepared to engineer.

It is not possible to establish how near Godwin came to achieving his *putsch*. Even a decade and more after the event no man is quick to admit that he once took part in a frustrated conspiracy, nor yet that he stood by idly waiting to see which way the dice would fall. It is even difficult to be certain that Godwin had constructed a plan of operations or a time-table for a *coup*. What is clear is that he made his reconnaissance too obvious; perhaps because he thought to make his forces invincible before he struck, he revealed his machinations to one man too many.

It seems at first inconceivable that Godwin should have thought of Blass as a potential conspirator. Not only were relations between the two far from comfortable but also Blass, more than any one else in the upper echelon, had made his way largely because Allen was prepared to discard the narrow-visioned spectacles of conventional selection processes and was ready to seek out ability in places where others did not trouble to look. The debt that he owed to Allen was acknowledged by Blass and repaid by loyalty (castigated by his enemies as obsequiousness), which had become ever more patent as other favourites disappeared from the scene and as Blass became as much an intimate as an employee. But Godwin reasoned quite otherwise: he needed an ally on the sales side to supplement and support his predominantly editorial cabal. He assumed that Blass, who had not only survived so many explosions but had come out of most of them with his own strength enhanced by the convenient immolation of others, must appreciate that his one chance of retaining influence after this next upheaval, the most seismic in the history of Penguin, must lie in being one of those who lighted the fuse. Further, Godwin had undoubtedly convinced himself and believed that he could convince Blass, that what he planned was the only way to save Penguin and the kindest method of dealing with a once-great man whose inconsistent and irrational behaviour had become a danger to himself and to the institution he had created.

Godwin put his case to Blass, and was amazed by the vehemence with which it was rejected. He then floundered from tactical error to tactical error. He blustered; when Blass issued a counter-challenge, insisting that he must reveal all to Allen, he attacked. Blass (who did not ordinarily attend Board meetings unless to discuss sales operations) was summoned before the directors to face accusations against his administration insinuated into their minds by Godwin. He answered nothing but instead gave to Allen a full account of his conversation with Godwin.

Allen forgot that he was tired and ill. As he had long hoped, Godwin had hanged himself. He had organized a conspiracy – the melodramatic word caught his sensitized imagination then and held it for the rest of his life. Godwin must go. Allen would neither talk to him about his going nor correspond with him; as ever in such circumstances that task was left to an intermediary. Some others must go too, both because they were known to be Godwin's allies and because a failed conspiracy cannot have only one martyr, but the heads that rolled round the floors of Harmondsworth belonged mostly to insignificant members of the staff. A few, more senior, resigned either from loyalty to Godwin or because resignation pre-empted the executioner's axe, but all that truly mattered to Allen was that he was rid of Godwin and master once more in his own house. As Williams put it a few years later in one of his best phrases, Godwin left 'with a handshake which was indeed golden but otherwise very limp'. He had lost nothing of his market value; he was coralled immediately by Weidenfeld and Nicolson and moved later to a handsome job in American publishing. He died in the United States a comparatively young man, still at the height of his considerable powers, but lonely and unhappy.

Not long before his death Godwin saw Paroissien in a New York restaurant. He crossed the floor, asked Paroissien for a moment of his time, and apologized for the fractiousness that had separated them. It was an amazing gesture from a man not given to self-criticism towards another for whom he had never shown any great liking or respect but it was as nothing when compared to what followed after. 'Allen Lane,' said Godwin in a tone that Paroissien had never before heard him use, at once sad and warm. 'Allen Lane: I truly loved that man.'

But one in a long sequence of seemingly inexplicable panegyrics to Allen from men he had fought, harmed or done his utmost to destroy, it is nevertheless perhaps the most heart-felt and most revealing tribute that was ever paid to Allen Lane.

CHAPTER TEN

ALLEN was more exhausted than he was willing to show and more gravely ill than he was prepared to admit, even to himself. Nevertheless, the routing of his enemies acted upon him like some miracle drug. His confidence soared. Not only had he proved that without him at the centre Penguin must disintegrate but also he had demonstrated that his capacity to hold the centre was undiminished, that he could still decide, control and lead.

Temporarily re-vivified by his triumph, he looked at the survivors of his day of the long knives and was heartened by what he saw. The conspiracy had been cathartic, but he saw, dramatically exaggerated. His response had rid Penguin of the consequences of his mistakes; those who were left (and they were, after all, most of the upper echelon) were loyal to him, loyal to Penguin ideals and without doubt capable of continuing and developing the firm according to his precepts.

He counted them off. In the light cast by recent events each of them looked better than had seemed possible during that period when his eyes had been dazzled by Godwin's brilliance. Together they made up a team which was, by his reckoning, still the strongest in British publishing.

Paroissien was close to retirement but Paroissien had served for twenty years, always involved in policy-making, and Paroissien knew more about Penguin at home and abroad than anyone at Harmondsworth except Allen himself.

Schmoller, Allen had always admired for that rare combination of thoroughness and flair which had held Penguin design far above all rivals, but he had never been quite easy with him –

partly because he felt free to patronize; now the very fact that Godwin had considered Schmoller's loyalty unassailable and had not even thought to approach him as a potential conspirator warmed Allen towards him and allowed him to accept, almost as a tribute to himself, the knowledge that his Production Director had grown. He was no longer merely the perpetuator of the Tschichold tradition but in his own right an acknowledged leader of British book-design, acclaimed as *maître* by his peers.

Behind Schmoller stood his wife, Tatyana, for some years not a full-time member of the staff and yet something more than an occasional auxiliary. Cold winds had blown between Allen and Tatyana earlier in the sixties when Allen had demanded of her more consuming attention to Penguin affairs than she was prepared to give but now all that was forgotten: Tatyana Schmoller's dedication was entire and, whenever it was required, she could be depended upon to contribute great competence in handling detail.

Charles Clark had grown in stature with responsibility and he was now making something viable out of the unpromising, and to Penguin eccentric, Penguin Education list. He had launched some brave pioneering ventures. Although Allen was not then, nor ever would be, competent to judge the pedagogic venturesomeness of such series as *Success with English*, the Nuffield A-level books or the Education Specials, his ear was to the ground. He heard the approving voices of the leaders of the teaching profession and his eye, as ever on the sales sheets, was quick to recognize better than satisfactory turnover. Clark could also be relied upon to give editorial sanity and moderation to the generally extravagant editorial policies of Allen Lane The Penguin Press.

Dieter Pevsner and Oliver Caldecott had served well under Godwin as editors of Penguins and Pelicans. Allen knew them to be restless but they had not sided with their former leader. Allen believed that (with a newcomer, Tony Mott) they were capable and for the moment willing to enlarge the lists and to sustain Penguin standards.

Kaye Webb was resolute. Blass, more than anyone else, had proved his devotion but even that would not have reassured Allen had he not known that as a sales manager Blass had no rival. His opinion of Blass's competence could hardly have been higher, but it must have given him a certain sardonic pleasure had he known how much in this his view was shared by Godwin. In a letter sent to Blass just before his unmasking – a letter scarred with underlinings, emblazoned with capitals and littered with mis-spellings – Godwin had written

> ... You must know how I regard you as *by far* the best bloke in Publishing on the whole distribution side – NO ONE to touch you. Well I've always stood by you loyally if it's ever been needed and championed you too. Now I want your help. I want you PERSONALLY (no delegating) to plan and supervise ALPP distribution . . . I know it's an awful imposition. BOY IS 1967 GOING TO BE BIG. . . .

The letter is so effusive that it can be dismissed as part of a softening-up barrage, but that the tribute was genuine is confirmed by remarks made at the time to others, peripheral to Penguin affairs, who knew almost nothing of what was going on at Harmondsworth.

Allen's belief that the stalwarts of his inner cabinet could free Penguin and Allen Lane The Penguin Press from every consequence that might stem from ridding the firm of the participants in the aborted *putsch* was strengthened by his awareness of the unwavering loyalty of many long-serving but less senior members of the staff. For these his affection had always been strong; because their ambitions were limited he had no need to suspect their motives as he suspected some of their seniors and because they played no part in creating Penguin policies their views never came into conflict with his own. In the sixties, for the first time – for all his proclaimed loyalty to the Labour Party and much to Allen's distaste – Penguin was forced to accept unionization. With it he suffered some of the disunity and dislocation of activity and spirit that seem to be an inevitable concomitant of the tension of loyalties between union and management, but none of this had touched the attitude of those who had long known the old regime. For them A.L. was Penguin and service with Penguin more a vocation than a job. Allen knew it and repaid their loyalty with concern and feeling. A letter written from Spain in 1968 is typical of many expressions of his thoughts about the middle and lower ranks of Penguin employees:

> I see that Beale joined us in 1947, which means that he is qualified for his watch this year. I am delighted at his new appointment. It is really a case of

the hare and the tortoise. While the whiz-kids have been whizzing he has been patiently toiling and gaining ground steadily.

At the other, the most exalted, end of his management scale was Sir Edward Boyle, his Vice-Chairman. Boyle had entered the Penguin scene in 1965, like so many before him as the consequence of a casual meeting and, like many others, he owed his position to Allen's collector's instinct, his eagerness to gather round him a body of eminent and not-so-eminent advisers. It had been Boyle and not Allen who had followed up Allen's unvaried but vague suggestion – 'I hope that some day you will become involved with Penguin' – and had forced from him a definitive invitation. It was, as Boyle confesses, the one occasion in his life when he applied for a job. It was also, probably, the only time in Allen's life when he accepted an applicant without equivocation. A former Cabinet Minister in his collection was a prize never before equalled; Boyle was made a director forthwith and, within a year, Vice-Chairman of the Board.

The arrangement had worked better than any who knew both men might have expected. Boyle found Penguin less venturesome than he had hoped and was dismayed to discover at Harmondsworth many of those same inhibitions to action he had known in Whitehall: bureaucratic methods, inter-departmental rivalries, imperial pretensions on the part of section-heads, and even something of that same attention to the petty privileges that are the outward and visible signs of status (the plush director's dining-room, for example, had he but known it, so very different from the Blue Diamond Café, where, only fifteen years earlier, the senior members of the staff had gathered each day for coffee after lunch in the works canteen). But Boyle offered his criticisms to Allen without hesitation, and most of them reinforced doubts that were already worrying at Allen's mind. By Allen's severe professional measure Boyle was not a publisher; though he learnt the craft quickly it was his experience outside publishing and his wide range of acquaintance beyond the world of letters which Allen found most useful, just as it was his informed gossip about political life which Allen found most stimulating. It did not trouble him that Boyle's adherence to the Conservative Party might seem to make him an inappropriate leading figure at Penguin; just as Allen was by this time an unorthodox Socialist (if indeed his vote for Labour had even been more than a dutiful bow to a tradition he had made for himself), so was Boyle an eccentric Conservative. He was, at all events, more comfortable in Boyle's company than he was with many Conservative politicians for Boyle was an 'unbeliever', like Allen but unlike most of party colleagues, a rebel against conventional Anglicanism.

Despite all the factors that brought them together, Allen was not certain that he wished to enhance Boyle's power at Penguin. To himself and to others, he rationalized his hesitation by insisting that, even were he to ask Boyle to exchange his part-time commitment to Penguin for a full-time job, his invitation must be refused. No distinguished politician would abandon the excitement and satisfactions of a varied and very public life for the all-consuming but often routine business of controlling day-to-day affairs at Penguin.

Nevertheless, who better than a former Financial Secretary to the Treasury, a man but recently Minister of Education, to stand in as Allen's alternate at meetings of the highly individualistic Penguin directors?

There was still one huge gap close to the top of the hierarchy; a gap that had never been adequately or definitively filled; but, now that he could not hide from himself the fact that the selection of a successor was immediately imperative, Allen thought that at last he had the answer. He would bring Christopher Dolley back from Baltimore.

Had time been granted to him it is possible, and, according to the record likely, that Allen would have changed his mind about Dolley as he had changed his mind about all previous favourites; that he would have discarded him with as little compunction as he had shown to them. As it was, Allen, who had seldom before thought it necessary to defend his decisions, was almost feverish in his advocacy. He knew that, right or wrong, this must be his final selection; like Captain Ahab he was so 'jamming himself on' that there could be no turning back.

As others close to Allen were forced to accept that Dolley was the ultimate inheritor and that they could no longer depend upon Allen's whim to remove him from power, so also did they find reasons for strident opposition to his elevation. Even some who had hitherto reserved their advice on Penguin affairs for

Allen's ears alone, now voiced their objections openly. Suzanne, for example, was adamant that Dolley was not the man for the job and on more than one occasion said as much in public; once to a room full of Penguin executives, among them Dolley himself: 'Not Chris! Not Chris to follow my little millionaire!' She, Williams and several others argued that Dolley was self-seeking, some said slick, but most of the criticisms levelled against him had an obverse side. Flaws seen in his personal and professional character could be rewritten as virtues – and were so accounted by Allen.

Christopher Dolley was in truth amply qualified for the role for which, once Allen had named him, he was inevitably destined. He was ambitious, of that there could be no doubt, but if Penguin was to develop it needed someone at the head who was not content to mimic Allen in his prime, someone who would impose his own personality on an organization which had been for so long the creation of one man and the representation of that one man's skill and idiosyncrasies. He was decisive, much more decisive than Allen. He had experience of many sides of Penguin and above all – in this like Allen – he recognized that publishing is at once a commerce and an art. Among intellectuals he could be an intellectual and, having been reared in Unilever, he was among businessmen their peer. The mermaids who sang their sweet songs into the ears of so many of his aesthetic editorial colleagues had not chosen him as a member of their audience but he knew the tunes, heard them in the distance, was attracted but not deluded. Yet he was sufficiently imbued with the Penguin ideal to appreciate that immediate profits do not presage ultimate profitability.

No man makes vital decisions quite so readily as the historian. Writing a decade and more after the event it is easy to be wise for Allen. He was no longer in tune with the spirit of the times, he no longer had the physical or mental energy necessary to hold mastery over the complexities of Penguin, and was no longer vigorous enough to hold his creation against the ever-growing forces of the opposition. He should have promoted himself to some position, honoured but without executive power and then allowed Dolley to take over, unhindered by supervision or the inhibiting presence of the founder. Only thus could he have consolidated the achievement of thirty-two years and extended its line into an unhorizoned future. This was, of course, Godwin's formula but varied in certain significant details: by the substitution of a candidate of Allen's choice for a self-elected successor, by the enhancement of dignity that would have come with removing himself from the centre of activity, and by avoiding the disturbance and dissension caused by a *coup d'état*. But rational or ruthless decisions of this kind can be made without question only by an observer who is happily freed from personal and professional responsibility or by a potential usurper. Allen knew that his grip on life was slipping. Penguin was the core and the reality of that life and he held to it tenaciously. He temporized: in due course he would make Dolley Managing Director (at first, as a concession to the past and as a safeguard against too-hasty amendment of policies, *in tandem* with Paroissien) but when that course was due he, and he alone, would decide.

Meanwhile, almost contented by the promise of the vestigial organization at his disposal, he was lulled into the belief that all was well: he could continue as leader and dictator of Penguin. With the rebels expelled and only the tried and faithful left in positions of responsibility at Harmondsworth, Melbourne and Baltimore, he could lead and control from a distance.

It was as if Napoleon had set up in Elba his headquarters for the Hundred Days. Because neither the Board as a whole nor any single member of that Board had sufficient authority to make substantive decisions without Allen's acquiescence, the arrangement was far from satisfactory. Superficially Allen's interventions in Penguin affairs seemed once again to be more interruptions of essential routine than aids to the judgement of those who were carrying the responsibilities that he would not cede unequivocally. Figures were now his consuming passion; it was as though his new-found obsession with his private portfolio had spilled over into his publisher's conscience. Throughout the previous history of Penguin he had always been aware that good performance is the consequence of fastidious attention to the details of editing, production, promotion and distribution, present success a delusion unless plans are forever in hand for future experiment and greater development. Now he seemed content to gloat over the digits that shone out from the sales reports sent to him in Spain.

But Allen had not lost entirely either his flair or his acumen.

The difficulties that were now facing Penguin were more intractable than any that he had met since 1935. Penguin was over-extended. It had more titles in its list than any other paperback house, and kept them in print far longer than its rivals (a fact that may surprise critics who are forever claiming that essential books published by Penguin and by no one else are forever vanishing from the list just when they are most in demand). It spread its interests, both intellectually and geographically, more widely than any even among its most powerful competitors. Its prestige was high and its prosperity considerable. All this, with the additional complication of insufficient working capital, made it an attractive mark for a take-over by one of the great financial conglomerates, British or American, which since the middle of the fifties had looked towards British book publishing as a vehicle for diversifying their commercial interests. There was a strong streak of xenophobia in Allen. Persuaded though he was that Penguin must in time accept some form of take-over by an organization with a stronger financial base, he was nonetheless determined to surrender only to a British master and, as his last significant contribution to the Penguin story, to a British master of his own choosing.

Later, after his death, there were a few, even among those who had been close to him, who with some justice criticized his survivors on the Penguin Board for accepting so hastily the merger with Pearson Longman, the book publishing subsidiary of Lord Cowdray's huge holding-company, S. Pearson and Co. More than a few exonerated the directors from blame but marked the loss of independence squarely against Allen himself, believing that it had been forced upon the Board because he had failed to grasp the implications that his death must have for the financial status of Penguin. It is true that his will was not drawn with all the cunning that might have been expected from the advisers of a man who could command the best legal advice available in England, true too that his hesitancy and his readiness to put out of mind the consciousness of his own mortality had created difficulties which not even the finest legal minds could have circumvented entirely. But the choice of Pearson Longman had been made by Allen himself; it was he who opened the negotiations with Longman and he who continued them after the absorption of that firm during 1968 in Pearson Longman.

When in 1970 S. Pearson and Co. paid £15 million for Penguin this was but the last step in a march which Allen had ordered.

If it is accepted, as accepted it must be because the firm was dangerously short of capital, that new arrangements of some kind were necessary for the salvation of Penguin, then an arrangement with Longman was logical though possibly not incontrovertible. The oldest of all publishing houses, Longman was nonetheless among the most energetic, particularly in export markets, in which it had for many years worked closely with Penguin. Yet in editorial terms it was directly competitive with Penguin only in the limited but hugely-profitable field of school-book publishing, a field to which Penguin was a new-comer, which was tying-up a disproportionate amount of Penguin's slim capital, in which Penguin performance was still unsure and Allen's enthusiasm far from entire. Once Longman entered the Pearson empire the logic of Penguin's move in that direction was almost complete. Here was an organization with vast and diversified interests that included the *Financial Times*, Lazards, the Westminster Press – and Château Latour – which now owned a major book publisher with whom Penguin already had associations and which possessed an unrivalled organization for selling in the expanding markets of Asia and Africa. Pearson was financially impregnable, British and, most tempting of all to Allen, there was much evidence to support the whisper that, unlike the lords and lordlings of some other comparable conglomerates, the directors of S. Pearson and Co. were content to allow to those responsible for each of its subsidiaries a large measure of freedom to practise their own particular expertise without insistent interference or inhibiting supervision.

Allen settled upon Pearson Longman not so much as a saviour but as a victim. He would see to it that they paid dearly for his life's work and his nagging of his Penguin subordinates, his reiterated demands for better and ever better performance, was part of the process of raising the stakes for Pearson Longman.

To each comforting report of booming sales he replied with letters setting new and higher targets. If these letters reveal a falling-off in Allen's dynamism it is because his instructions were never accompanied by advice on how the targets might be achieved; instead they were over-loaded with gossip about life at Carvajal. A letter to Blass contained one curt paragraph insisting that Penguin must increase its turnover by 10 per cent and three pages of instruction on acquiring and despatching to Spain pheasants for Allen's Christmas party (in itself a somewhat surprising request from a man whose sybaritism had never before included devotion to any foods more exotic than shepherd's pie or digestive biscuits). The pheasants were duly shipped and after them, eventually, a set of trading figures even more satisfying to Allen's palate. Even so, back from Spain to his bustling and breathless colleagues came a new target – but no more bids for game birds.

Allen was summoning all his strength for further and perhaps conclusive negotiations with Pearson Longman when, for perhaps the first time in his adult life, he was faced with a crisis that not even his extraordinary resilience could surmount. In July 1968 he was admitted to the Middlesex Hospital to undergo major surgery for cancer of the bowel.

Often in the past his professional boldness had been blemished by the pusillanimity of his personal relations and his reputation for resource and energetic leadership reduced by changeability that at times amounted to shiftiness. But the courage with which he faced two years of a painful and terminal illness was little short of magnificent. It was as if he had discovered, at the last, some inner source of inspiration more compelling than ambition and more durable than success. It was not religion; still he held doubt as his one unshakeable conviction; but there was about him an air of spiritual complacency. He had done all he could with his years and talents, he looked for no more adventures in this life and could not believe that there was another life to come and more adventures to follow. In such time as was left – and he suspected that it must be meagre but feared that it might be extended – he would work to make his pain as little noticeable, as little painful and as little inconvenient as he could to his friends. Saintliness is not a word that can be applied without embarrassment to Allen Lane, and even this long after his death many who knew him well remember him as demonic, but in those last two years he showed qualities of resignation and solicitude of which the saints could be proud. He feared the ministrations of the radiographer – and hated them when they came – but, for the re-assurance of his friends, he turned aside both dread and distaste by referring always to the radiotherapists as 'Dr Who's gang'. Even he managed to overcome the one terror that hitherto he had found insupportable; through months in hospital rooms, and most of the rest of his time spent at Priory Farm preparing to return to hospital, he managed to face boredom without allowing himself to become too often either depressed or resentful.

He received visitors with delight and made delightful the awkward task of sick-room visiting. He listened eagerly to gossip, his eyes brightened if it was scabrous, and if it was slanderous he passed it on to the next visitor, with mischievous embellishments, but the edge of malice had been blunted. Even when the talk was of his more ferocious and unrepentant opponents his antipathy was now seldom apparent. In its place was a savouring of reminiscence that was almost fond for antique rivalries and battles fought long since.

It was as if he had wrought for himself that quality which he had always coveted for his books: an air of dignified flippancy.

Nothing gave him greater pleasure than visits from members of the current Penguin staff. He listened to their reports with no less eagerness but with rather more patience than in the past. His questioning was as sharp as always, but his attitude was dispassionate, his reactions no longer appropriate to the prime source of Penguin energy but more those of a well-informed but remote observer. 'There's a new crisis on at Harmondsworth,' he wrote to Williams after an operation, 'but I'm far enough away to feel detached from it. I think perhaps the tiredness which comes over one after a go like this acts as a protection against involvement.'

He maintained, as much for the benefit of others as for his own comfort, the pretence that he saw a term to his ordeal; when it was over, he could settle himself to an idle, pastoral and idyllic existence freed from the burden of business. The tale was not new; he had been telling it for the best part of ten years. Hitherto it had convinced no one, and least of all himself, because none believed that Allen could live contentedly without the excitement of Penguin; now he and all others close to him knew full well that his chance of living, with or without Penguin, was slim to the point of being non-existent.

The realization that there was no future for him set him to dwelling upon the past. His friendship for Williams revived, and his letters and conversations with the man who had been his closest collaborator throughout the hectic and satisfying years of Penguin struggle and triumph – and, next to his brothers, his most frequent drinking companion – were warmed by contented and often hilarious recollection. With Lettice, too, his relationship improved. In adversity they settled to an easy devotion he had never been capable of allowing in the days when his restless energy could not be fettered by domesticity.

He who had always enjoyed and profited by anniversaries now found that the celebration of achievements past was more therapeutic than the attentions of 'Dr Who's gang'. He had, in fact, one comparatively recent triumph to commemorate, his victory over Godwin and his fellow-conspirators, and he remembered it each year with glee. 'What a two-year stretch we have behind us,' he wrote to Blass at the end of 1968, '... from the New Year [of 1966–7] we swept the revolutionaries out and brought in sense and order.' (For those 'revolutionaries' he had no charitable feelings. Others had sneered at him, had prophesied the inevitable damnation of his schemes and had even fought against him, but they had done so openly; in his triumph these he could remember with magnanimity. Godwin and his cohorts had plotted against him in dark corners; because against him and secretively, then, by his reckoning, against Penguin and in a manner that blasphemed the Penguin doctrine of cheerful and willing collaboration.)

The spring and summer of 1969, the Golden Jubilee of his entry into publishing, was the heartiest and most satisfying of all his many anniversary celebrations. The pleasure that he found in the tributes that were paid to him – and in organizing some of them for himself – came close to working the magic that the surgeons and their hierophants could not contrive. There were private parties for Penguin colleagues, a dinner at the House of Commons, warm appreciations of his career and achievements in the newspapers, interviews in the press, on radio and on television. As never before, he was quick to respond to invitations to speak; each was seized upon as an opportunity to establish for all time the identification of the personality of Allen Lane with the personality of Penguin; and as never before he was almost unbelievably prolix whenever he spoke. But parties, speeches and press comment could not of themselves make a truly

Penguin celebration; there had to be a book and the choice was not difficult. It must be Joyce's *Ulysses*, which became Penguin number 3000. It was galling to have to haggle with the directors of The Bodley Head over the rights which they would not have owned had not he, Dick and John flouted the wishes of their predecessors thirty-three years earlier but *Ulysses* stood, even more obviously than *Ariel*, as the monument to his declaration of independence. It was good to have his Liberty Bell hanging in the Penguin belfry and better still to flaunt as the emblem of respectability achieved this one title, now universally acclaimed as a classic but not so very long ago almost universally condemned.

In the Birthday Honours for 1969 the Queen made Allen a Companion of Honour. Allen claimed that when he heard from the Patronage Secretary he felt as Henry Irving must have felt when he was knighted or Tennyson when he was raised to the peerage. These were historical analogies of which none thought him capable, and perhaps they were produced for him by his Publicity Department, but it was undoubtedly he who soon after saw the implications of his statement. He was certainly the first publisher to be recognized in this way, but he had no wish to allow other publishers to preen themselves in the light of his glory. He corrected himself: the honour was not his alone but his and Penguin's. The corollary was clear: Penguin was different from all other publishers; it was an institution. The inference, unspoken by him, was expressed openly by two newspapers. One called Penguin 'the BBC of publishing' and another 'the publishing arm of the Beveridge Report'.

Cancer outpaced compliments and honours. There were more operations, more frequent visits to 'Dr Who's department' and, early in the summer of 1970, he was taken into the Mount Vernon Hospital at Northwood in Middlesex. Still he managed a bold front. Visitors – and they were many – found him still alert to publishing gossip. Robert Lusty, next to Williams, Blass and his family his most regular visitor, thought him as knowledgeable as ever about all that was going on in the book world; even to Clare he talked of little but the trade and Penguin, but more about Penguin than about the trade in general. He would go back to Harmondsworth, perhaps for just two days a week. The Pearson Longman arrangement could work but not without him. 'They can't cope without me,' and Clare could not know if 'they' were Boyle, Dolley, Blass and the rest, or the mighty Pearson empire.

Then, not long before he lapsed into a seven-day coma, he began to insinuate that he was dissatisfied with the Pearson Longman deal. It was a *volte-face* more amazing than any previous contortion. For the first time he admitted openly and without euphemism that he was about to die. It must be someone's business to see that Penguin remained independent.

Allen died on 7 July 1970.

Next morning the very same newspapers which published long, uniformly eulogistic and generally accurate obituary-notices carried a statement from the Acting Chairman (Edward Boyle), the Managing Director (Christopher Dolley) and the Directors of Penguin Books Ltd announcing an impending merger with Pearson Longman.

Allen's ashes were taken to Hartland Church in North Devon, where lie also the ashes of Uncle John. It was what he had wanted: this symbolic gesture which proclaimed his consciousness of his professional ancestry and which at last made irrefutable his right to be mustered a Devonian.

The obsequies continued, the mourning genuine, warm but unpompous and just as he would have wished could he have stage-managed it himself, all good publicity for Penguin.

On 18 August, at a service in St Martin-in-the-Fields, Paroissien, Lusty and Hoggart gave memorial addresses and Michael Morpurgo read the lesson. It was a nicely balanced cast: a representative of his colleagues, his fellow-publishers, his authors and readers, and his family. The congregation was drawn from sources so various that, wherever he was by that time, Allen must have looked on with a satisfied smirk.

In his later years he had tended to resent the manner in which some of his staff accepted and elaborated the logic of earlier Penguin promotional activities. Not least among the causes for his objections to Godwin and his cohorts had been their addiction to staging large and extravagant book-launching parties. (One such occasion in particular a jaunt to Berlin organized for journalists in order to encourage them to publicize the Penguin of Len Deighton's *Funeral in Berlin* he had described as an ostentatious gimmick shaming to Penguin prestige and out of tune with Penguin budgets.) But not the Godwinites, not Allen in his less puritanical prime, not the Lane brothers in their extrovert days in Talbot Square, nor yet the most liberal offering of Penguin champagne contrived such a reunion of colleagues and former colleagues, such a gathering of celebrities, such a public demonstration of respect from former competitors and forgiveness from ancient enemies as was represented by the congregation of the church in Trafalgar Square. Yet, as Allen would have had it, all was done with dignity but without aggressive solemnity. An awareness of loss was real but even more evident a sense of gratitude.

If Allen would have been flattered, and perhaps not a little surprised, by the unbroken adulation of the obituary notices and heartened by the tributes of his friends, by the attendance and scrupulously tactful management of his memorial service, his mischievous spirit must have been elated by the knowledge that there was 'yet another crisis at Harmondsworth' and that 'they really could not cope without him'. There had seldom been a time when there was not a crisis of some sort at Harmondsworth but now there were several, all interlocked and all created just because Allen was no longer on hand to resolve them.

From the first, and admittedly in the main for those who worked for Penguin, Allen had been the heart and head of the enterprise. If in the last few years long absences and illness had reduced his status to that of a figurehead, still he, Allen Lane King Penguin, was there in the background, the proclaimed constitutional monarch to whom all owed allegiance, his existence the safeguard that could prevent dissension from becoming disaffection; the ultimate arbiter. Now that Allen was dead Dolley was King, by Allen's decision Managing Director. Though all involved knew the erratic history of claims to the succession and suspected that Dolley owed his inheritance to the accident that Allen had not been given time to change his mind yet again, none doubted his capacity both to manage and to direct. But, just because Penguin had become a national and international institution and so much more than a business, it was arguable that it needed at its head a figure who could be what Allen had become, in all the full panoply of the word, a national and international personage. Not all the members of the Board were confident that Dolley had the stature to sustain this role; some doubted that any man other than Allen himself could do what Allen had done for many years: act as both figurehead and controller, as Chairman and Managing Director. A minority were worried lest, for all his ability and whether in one capacity or the other, or in both, Dolley might not hold the loyalty of the staff or the respect of that wider constituency so essential to the future of Penguin, the book trade at large.

There was much canvassing of opinion and much debate. Boyle as Chairman and Dolley as Managing Director seemed an obvious and promising combination, but Boyle had just accepted an invitation to be Vice-Chancellor of the University of Leeds. Although he was willing to continue as a director, he could not commit himself to the diversion of energy which was bound to go with the chairmanship of a firm that must rediscover itself after the death of Allen, its founder and key figure, which must at the same time complete negotiations with Pearson and thereafter, almost certainly, must struggle to retain its independence and unique characteristics.

By this time Williams had retired from the Board. His first action after Allen's death was to ask for an increase in the meagre pension granted to him by Allen, his second to suggest that Jennie Lee be asked to consider the chairmanship. It was, in many ways, an attractive proposition. Not only was she undoubtedly a public figure much admired even by her political opponents, but as Minister of State with special responsibility for the Arts she had been energetic and enthusiastic in many causes which were analoguous to Penguin. But, it was pointed out, the enthronement as Queen Penguin of Aneurin Bevan's widow, herself a Tribunite and for forty years a prominent and vocal Labour parliamentarian, must give additional ammunition to those who, ever since Ethel Mannin had castigated Allen for acting as if he were a hireling of Soviet Russia, had been sniping at Penguin for its allegedly left-wing bias.

The controversy was heated but confined to the Penguin cabinet. It was also largely academic. Pearson Longman would probably have much to say about the reorganization of the Penguin hierarchy, and already the Pearson negotiators were suggesting that part of the price that they would demand in exchange for their substantial investment was the right to nominate the Chairman of a newly constituted board.

There was, however, a crisis more immediate and more public than any haggling over position. Only eight days after Allen's death McGraw-Hill announced to the press that its management wished to consider carefully the proposed Penguin–Longman merger. A few days later they delivered to Dolley and to all holders of substantial parcels of Penguin shares a memorandum entitled ominously 'McGraw-Hill and Penguin'. These were the conventional preparatory signals for a counter-bid; though the memorandum contained little that was specific it aroused consternation among Penguin's directors. Many of the arguments in favour of the Longman deal could be employed with equal force in favour of a merger with McGraw-Hill. Here was one of the most powerful of all publishing houses, with an incomparable selling organization, active world-wide, with a list that was broadly educational and yet not often in direct competition with any part of Penguin except insofar as Penguin was engaged in producing school-books; though McGraw-Hill had launched several years earlier a successful invasion of Britain (and set up its headquarters only a few miles from Harmondsworth – a fact that made it somehow even more sinister to the Penguin Board), its policies were designed in New York. There could be no thought that the Americans would allow to Harmondsworth (and so to Baltimore) the degree of freedom which could be confidently expected from Pearson Longman. In recent years the nightmare consequences of an American take-over had become waking reality to many in British publishing; some even among the most senior and most respected members of the trade had been subjected to the indignity of peremptory dismissal by their new overlords; and stories such as those which came out of Cassell made the executive directors of Penguin fearful for their own security and for the jobs of their senior colleagues. There was also, heavy upon the consciences of some, a feeling that was eventually articulated most vehemently by Dieter Pevsner. Penguin had done much for readers; that was undeniable. It could not be demonstrated that the interests of the Penguin readership would be in any greater danger from McGraw-Hill than from Pearson Longman, but, he argued, no less significant among the benefits which had flowed from

Penguin were the advantages which had been opened to authors, of every kind, and these, he was prepared to assert, must be in jeopardy if Penguin became part of the vast McGraw-Hill empire.

The Americans had prepared the ground well; already they had acquired more than 600,000 Penguin shares, far from a winning stake and only one-third of the controlling shares residuary in Allen's estate and in the various trusts established in his lifetime and under his will. Nevertheless, next to these combined holdings, it was the largest in the hands of any one individual or institution. The threat was made more immediate by the certainty that, to meet estate duties, some of Allen's shares must be sold on the open market – and therefore be accessible to McGraw-Hill. With competitive take-over bids before the public, the value of Penguin shares must rise, the improved price would tempt some shareholders to sell, and some of these sales must go to McGraw-Hill.

Determined upon completing the reverse take-over with Pearson Longman, the Penguin Board hurried through a recommendation to shareholders. On 5 August they issued a proposal to their shareholders, setting out in due form the details of the prospective merger with Longman. In consideration of the acquisition from Pearson Longman of all the Ordinary capital of Longman, Penguin would issue 6,250,000 Ordinary shares thereby making Penguin a subsidiary of Pearson Longman, with the existing Penguin shareholders holding only $37\frac{1}{2}$ per cent of the increased Ordinary share capital and Pearson Longman the rest. Five representatives of Longman and Pearson would join the Penguin Board where, as befitted their majority holdings, they could outvote the four nominated Penguin directors (Boyle, Dolley, Blass and Clark). Dolley was confirmed as Managing Director of Penguin (and would also represent Penguin on the Pearson Longman Board), and it was specifically stated that 'the character and imprints of Penguin and of Longman will be preserved'.

The memorandum to shareholders included an immediate and not inconsiderable inducement to accept the merger:

> As a token of their confidence in the future, your Directors have decided (with the agreement of the Directors of Pearson Longman and subject to no unforeseen circumstances arising . . .) to increase the interim dividend

payable in November from 5 per cent to 15 per cent, and to recommend in respect of the current year an increase in the final dividend from 10 per cent to 20 per cent.

The peroration was in the form that is customary on such occasions but it was for all that virtually irresistible:

> The Directors of Penguin, supported by their financial advisers J. Henry Schroder Wagg & Co. Limited, are convinced that the merger with Longman offers outstanding prospects for the future growth of Penguin as a publishing house and for the well-being of those associated with it, and that this will be to your benefit as a Penguin shareholder. Accordingly, they unanimously recommend you to vote in favour....

No substantial opposition was expected other than from McGraw-Hill. In the week before the Extraordinary General Meeting of Penguin shareholders called for 21 August to complete the preliminaries essential to the merger, the Penguin directors were much taken aback by the news that formidable objections to the merger were being raised from a source in itself potentially powerful and, because of the sympathy that it might arouse in other shareholders, a very real threat to their plans. Clare and Christine were asking questions about the propriety of hurrying through the merger so soon after Allen's death, about the wisdom of this particular merger and even about the necessity for a merger of any kind.

More than one-third of all Penguin shares were held in trusts that Allen had established several years earlier, principally for the benefit of his family, but their role as beneficiaries from these arrangements conferred upon Clare and Christine no power to influence events. However, as themselves trustees of the smaller but still magnificent Allen Lane Foundation, which derived its funds exclusively from Penguin, they had some voice in the control of a substantial parcel of shares. Both in this capacity and as Allen's daughters their opposition to the proposed deal might prove to be a persuasive rallying-cry for all who either resented or suspected the arrangements that were in train.

Later the motives of Clare and Christine were branded as sentimental. So in a sense they were: it was not so easy for them to accept that their father's life's work, vigorous and always independent, should be submerged in a huge and, to them, amorphous consortium nor to concede with easy conscience that his individuality and esoteric creation must be subordinated to the authority of those responsible for a conventional publishing operation. But sentiment has some place in business; Allen himself had been sentimental about Penguin. The unique status of the firm owed as much to public sentimentality as to the dispassionate evidence provided by annual reports and balance-sheets. Even so, all that Clare and Christine were asking was that the shareholders, among them the Trustees of the Allen Lane Foundation, be given time to consider alternatives before deciding whether or not the Pearson Longman arrangement was right for Penguin.

Christine's activities were somewhat inhibited by the fact that her husband David Teale, was employed at Harmondsworth. His future, therefore, to some extent depended upon those who were recommending the merger. It followed that the task of raising the standard was left largely to Clare.

Even those who knew Clare best, who did not accept in its entirety the portrait of her that Allen had loved to present as a pretty if rather flighty girl who had developed into a beautiful and responsible mother of three children, were surprised by the energy and skill she displayed during the few weeks allowed to her for preparing the case for delay and second thoughts. She had learnt more than either she or Allen had realized from watching her father at work; from him she had gathered a wide range of useful contacts and from him she had acquired the art of using them. In one way or another several private banks were already committed to support the merger; Clare went herself to the most famous of the uncommitted, to Rothschild, and though there she found no immediate encouragement, neither did she receive advice sufficiently strong to deter her from prosecuting her efforts.

Her early attempts to bring the trustees of the family trusts to accept her point of view were fruitless. She had hoped for much from Paroissien but he, with entire reasonableness, insisted that he could see no advantage to Penguin or any of the trusts in hesitation and argued with some force that it was unlikely that from any source but Pearson could Penguin shareholders discover a deal so satisfactory, retaining $37\frac{1}{2}$ per cent of the equity whilst contributing only one-quarter of the net assets in the merged corporation. Eunice Frost, like Paroissien no longer a director of Penguin but, also like him still a trustee of the family trust, was more hesitant. No less than his daughters she had been shocked by Allen's death; for her, even more than for them, the thought of Penguin shackled was traumatic, but she could not conceive of Penguin existing at all without Allen. Such tentative alternatives as Clare could propose at this stage were to her just as unpalatable as those proposed by the Board. She was too numb to fight.

Unable to discover within the Penguin family any encouragement, Clare looked outside for a sophisticated adviser. She discovered an expert and energetic champion in Peter Rosenwald, an American living in London whose considerable experience of the machinations of the City included particularly appropriate knowledge of the financial background to the publishing industry. Rosenwald's interference in the affairs of Penguin exposed him to much criticism and some vilification from the supporters of the deal with Pearson Longman. His abrasive personality, his brisk transatlantic manner and his undisguised disdain for his opponents, whom he regarded as representatives of an Establishment which he thought responsible for much that was effete and ineffective in British commerce, raised even higher hackles already head-high because of Clare's impatient intervention. But his zest for her cause was genuine and charitable. At a time when he could have been engaged upon highly remunerative activities he devoted himself entirely to advising Clare and Christine, without thought of immediate or eventual financial reward. His sense of justice was aroused and his business acumen persuaded him that some as yet indefinable but perhaps sinister compulsion was hustling the Penguin Board into making too-hasty decisions that must be irrevocable but that were not necessarily either inevitable or in the best interests of Penguin, British publishing or Allen's various trusts. Above all his dedication was personal to Clare. In so many ways so utterly unlike her father, she had nevertheless something of that same capacity which had helped to make Allen supreme among his contemporaries: the ability to win the loyalty of shrewd and unsentimental advisers.

Rosenwald scoured the City and the book trade for alternatives to Pearson Longman. As he saw it, he had neither the responsibility nor the time to produce a scheme demonstrably preferable to the merger. It was not even part of his brief to deny that

Pearson Longman might prove to be at the last the safest haven; all that he needed to do in the few days before the Extraordinary General Meeting was to establish that other viable possibilities existed, and so win a stay of execution.

His tentative investigations did not give him cause for pessimism or euphoria. Though he could discover no institution that was ecstatic at the thought of involving itself with Penguin, several were eager to hear more, among them yet another American company, the proprietors of the *Encyclopaedia Britannica*. He was able to report to Clare, and by way of Clare to some Penguin directors, that it was by no means inconceivable that a sensible arrangement could be negotiated which would either ease the immediate financial problems of Penguin, offer greater independence than could be won from Pearson Longman or McGraw-Hill or, at very least, by increasing competition with the two bidders already in the field, raise the value of Penguin shares.

The Penguin Board was unmoved by an opinion that was inevitably circumstantial and hedged with provisos. As Clare and Rosenwald assessed the possibilities there was left to them only one course: to exercise her rights and duties by putting her case for delay to her fellow-trustees of the Foundation and the trustees of the other trusts that were Penguin's main shareholders.

Already she had been rebuffed by some of them, but it was not unthinkable that others would be susceptible to persuasion nor inconceivable that with this group she might carry a majority. Almost without exception, the trustees were men and women who had worked with Allen for many years; just as Clare and Christine were driven to act from a sense of dedication to Allen and out of respect for his determination to always stay a free agent, master of his own creation and of his own fate, so also might similar sensibilities influence the judgement of these, his old colleagues. Though at the time she did not know it, all that she was asking was that they bring back to mind the precedents which Allen had set time and time again – and follow his example. So often in the past Allen had brought negotiations to the point of determination and then withdrawn, so often he had played one aspirant for power against another, so often he had promised much and conceded little. For Allen no negotiation was complete and no agreement binding until it was signed, sealed and delivered – and sometimes not even then. Vacillation was with him a habit but also a useful ploy; more often than not his brinkmanship had wrought benefit for him and advantage for Penguin.

But the odds against Clare were heavy. Not only had she come late onto the Penguin scene – too late even for those of the trustees who were no longer immediately concerned with Penguin affairs – but also Boyle was in the ambiguous and potentially embarrassing position of being both Acting Chairman of Penguin and Chairman of the Allen Lane Foundation.

Nevertheless Clare went to a meeting of the trustees, called only ten days before the Extraordinary General Meeting of Penguin shareholders, armed with a persuasive brief prepared by Rosenwald and supported by Rosenwald and her husband. If she had expected not an easy victory, if in her most confident moments she had hoped for nothing better than postponement of the Extraordinary General Meeting, she had not thought to be met with hositility and outfaced by technicalities. Rosenwald's status in the whole affair was questioned, and it was ruled that he had no authority to speak in her behalf. It was conceded, however, that the Trustees would listen to the paper which he had prepared. The task of reading it was given to Michael Morpurgo.

The document that Rosenwald had produced was nicely balanced to force discussion without provoking indignation. He suppressed all tendency to aggressiveness and expressed his doubts in tones that, at once gentle but firm, were entirely appropriate to his client. The case was Clare's but the expertness of the advocacy was his and his alone; without him neither Clare nor her husband could have mustered their arguments with such cogency. An experienced duellist, he offered to his adversaries all the proper courtesies, conceded a pass here and there and then darted in, his rapier pointed at some undefended or indefensible target. There were, he argued, several courses open to Penguin. The first was that selected by the Board – the merger with Longman – and then the lunge, the rider already rejected in the memorandum to shareholders: 'to invite other bidders for control of the company with the intention of getting the highest possible price'. Secondly, 'to seek a minority bidder whose stake in the company would be purely financial' and, again a thrust, 'who would help to preserve the independence my father fought so long and hard to maintain'. Thirdly, to raise additional capital 'by means of a rights-issue or some other form of financing'.

This third possibility, Clare and Rosenwald conceded, might be rejected out of hand. To invite a deluge of bidding must have the most disastrous effects upon the firm and upon the Foundation's assets. As for the other two, Clare admitted freely that she did not know which was best for the body of shareholders and for the Foundation but, she said: 'What I do know is that with additional time, each alternative could be more fully explored and only then can I feel I have completed and fulfilled my trusteeship.' The brief went on to demonstrate that, even in the short time that had been available to him, Rosenwald had already explored extensively if not fully, that he had questions which merited an answer, and suggestions which deserved consideration. Could it be asserted beyond doubt that in the past the overseas sales of Penguin books by Longman had been adequate? If not, why should shareholders accept the contention that they would become beneficial just because the two firms were merged? Was there in truth compatibility between the basic educational level of the materials distributed by Longman in the less developed countries and the sophisticated books, educational only by the broadest definition of the word, which were central to Penguin efforts in Britain, Australasia and the United States? What were the 'significant benefits' promised as a direct consequence of rationalization? Was rationalization itself anything more than a vague term for a fashionable but uncertain concept?

Speaking for Clare in Michael's voice, Rosenwald then went on to ask some incisive questions about the merger itself. Was the stock valuation based upon real or, as is common practice in publishing, upon written-down value? Was it proper to class copyrights as intangible assets and therefore to be ignored in assessing the worth of Penguin? When had the figure for freehold and leasehold properties been set at £1,395,000 (the implication being that this valuation was long out of date).

Even at a figure approaching £1½ million Penguin's property holdings represented both the justification of Allen's faith in land and buildings and, so it seemed to Rosenwald, a hint of a way out of immediate cash-flow problems. Had the directors considered a lease-back or some similar arrangement based on the real estate?

The paper ended with a polite but unhesitating reiteration of Clare's doubts, followed by one last deft thrust:

> My reason for suggesting the possibility of a delay is that I continue to have reservations about the merger, and I believe many of you would also welcome additional time to think. Personally I have the utmost faith that the management has acted wisely and that the management would understand that a delay was not a vote of no confidence but simply the result of the haste with which we have been asked to commit proxies to a merger which we must fully understand.
> There is [however] one further issue which *I* do not understand ... Will the trustees be represented on the Board of the merged company... ? And if not, can I in good conscience say that my Trust should have all its assets in a company over which the trustees have no say and which could, conceivably make decisions adverse to the beneficiaries... ?

It was all very reasonable, all perspicacious, all irritatingly inconvenient to those who were genuinely convinced that the merger with Longman was in the best interest of Penguin, who had themselves taken over the negotiations which Allen had begun, and who had thought that all that stood between them and finality were the formalities of an Extraordinary General Meeting.

There was some elusive discussion and some acrimony. These were rough times, it was said, in which there could be no place for sentiment. And what authority had Clare, who had no knowledge of her father's profession, to hint that she and her sister could interpret his wishes more accurately than his closest colleagues? There were no direct answers to Rosenwald's direct questions. No trustee supported Clare and the last vestige of Lane influence in Penguin affairs was shrugged off without a vote.

Ten days later, on 21 August 1970, after almost exactly thirty-five years of magnificently independent existence, Penguin Books Ltd, became formally part of Pearson Longman.

This could be – and in some senses should be – the last line in the biography of Allen Lane, more definitive than the announcement of his death and more conclusive than the effusive obituary notices. Here, it would seem, is enshrined the ultimate statement of failure, the irreversible negation of his freedom to fashion a unique creation, without supervision or the inhibiting controls of more orthodox business. This, it must appear, was the end of self-determination and consequently of all that Allen had uniquely contributed to publishing and to society at large. Indeed, within a pathetically short time the profile of Penguin management changed radically. Clark went off to succeed Lusty as Managing Director of Hutchinson; some of the senior editors left; in 1973 Dolley resigned as Managing Director; when Schmoller retired in 1976, of the top echelon at Harmondsworth, apart from Kaye Webb in her virtually autonomous Puffin domain, none but Blass survived of those who had been reared in the Allen Lane tradition. Lower in the hierarchy old hands muttered dispiritedly that the excitement had vanished and with it the intense dedication to Penguin. The American headquarters was moved from Baltimore to New York – in itself a concession to the conventions of the trade and heretical to Allen's philosophy. Only in Australia could it be said that all went on much as before, and there only because the changes at the head were as frequent as they had been in Allen's time.

Yet such awareness of disintegration as there was remained for some years largely domestic and passed unnoticed by the public. In the three years after Allen's death Penguin output burgeoned on a scale unprecedented since the war years: 540 new paperbacks in 1970, 620 in 1972, and, within that increase, the number of Pelicans almost doubled. In the past Penguin had achieved fantastic sales figures for some titles but usually by virtue of steady selling over many years. Only in sensational and notorious circumstances, such as those which fostered the sales of *Lady Chatterley's Lover*, had any Penguin burst suddenly into the paperback bestseller lists to compete there with titles like *The Caine Mutiny* or *The Dam Busters*. Now suddenly Penguin topped the list with *The Great Gatsby* and *Watership Down*. There were 5000 Penguins in print; if the list continued to grow at the current rate, by the end of the decade the figure would be 7000.

It was not the merger which confounded Penguin's planners, not the lack of an authoritarian personality to fill the place left vacant by Allen's death, nor yet the disappearance from the scene of most of his protegés which brought Penguin to the edge of disaster. At the beginning of the seventies all British industry was battered by sudden and sharply rising inflation. Penguin, which had built its financial success upon a combination of slim item-profits and large turnover, suffered more dramatically than most. Trading profits slithered. Production and distribution costs soared. In 1973 alone production costs rose by 15 per cent, and in the next year the increase in total operating costs, forecast at 10 per cent, was up to 20 per cent and still rising. Already £4.5 million was tied up in books in the warehouse and the working capital committed to stocks was increasing by £1 million a year, more than three times Penguin's net profit. Borrowing stood at £2.6 million a year. Jim Rose, the Chairman appointed by Pearson, and Dolley's successor, Peter Calvocoressi, looked gloomily to a future, not more than three years off, when they must somehow find an extra £2 million.

Not infrequently Allen had speculated on growth, had bought his way out of financial troubles by publishing more titles and thereby increasing turnover, cash flow and profits. His successors tried the same panacea, and were frustrated by inflation.

Salvation would not come from the parent company. In four years Pearson Longman took only £240,000 from Penguin – less than the shareholders had received in the last four years of Allen's life – and they, like Penguin, were suffering from the effects of inflation and from a shortage of accessible cash.

Publishing has much in common with gambling; like good punters, publishers are careful students of form, but in publishing as in racing, roulette or poker there are no infallible systems and no certainties. The player either takes a risk or quits the game, and the one impulse which separates publishers from their more raffish fellow-gamblers is that publishers believe that they place their bets for the good of society. In the circumstances of 1974, however, Penguin could buy no more chips; only a drunken poker-player would have looked to the bank for a loan. Rose was sober but he was not ready to stop playing. Instead, early in the year, he instituted a policy of retrenchment. The programme for the year envisaged the publication of 780 new books; this he slashed to 520. Even more drastic: he announced the total extinction of Penguin Education.

Still more dramatic economies were not, however, sufficient to halt financial deterioration at a time when nothing boomed except inflation and the size of wage claims from the unions. Consequently, beginning in the last months of 1974, the management hacked at the body corporate of Penguin in a series of blows unprecedented in their severity. The new book programme was reduced further, to 450 a year and, it was decided, must be held at that figure at least until 1977. Sixty contracts were cancelled. Print-runs would be shortened. Old titles would be allowed to die if there was even the slightest doubt that reprints would move steadily. To make some saving in capital invested in stocks, even some titles constantly in demand would be allowed to go out-of-print for short periods. Conversely, to an even greater extent than hitherto, Penguin must rely on its back list. Most bitter of all the economies proposed: the staff must be reduced by 10 per cent; this in addition to the jobs already axed at the close of Penguin Education.

Every one of these Geddes-like measures aroused anxiety among Penguin addicts and indignation from special interest lobbies. Both anxiety and indignation were inflamed by the protests of the unions and above all by the inevitable reaction of Penguin editors, of all groups within Penguin the most affected by the cuts and of all groups the one uniquely gifted to articulate its resentment. Threats of strikes, appeals to the government conciliation service, forthright refusal to accept as accurate the financial profile presented by the management, letters to the press, to authors and to agents: every conceivable method of opposing and obstructing the Chairman's plans was employed. A tribute to Allen's memory as powerful as any that had been written in his obituary notices, somewhere in every letter of protest, in every whisper of complaint and in every reasoned case presented by the opponents to the cuts there was a reference to the intentions of the Founder (written now with an upper-case F and even spoken as if capitalization was irresistible) and to the unique nature of Penguin.

The anguish and anger of the objectors is entirely comprehensible. Though flattering to Allen, their appeals to his spirit were on almost every issue founded upon unsound precedent or indifferent understanding of his record and personality. It was said, for example, that the closure of Penguin Education was vicious infanticide; never before in its history had Penguin retreated from an area of publishing which it was close to conquering. Yet twice in its early life Allen had considered murdering this child. Over the years he had executed the Illustrated Classics, the Modern Painters, King Penguins, the Scores and all his periodicals. It was argued, most vocally by schoolteachers and academics, that the reprinting restrictions imposed by Rose undermined the especial educational virtue of the Penguin and Pelican list. Undeniably there is truth in this complaint, but Penguin records show that it was raised as early as 1939. The one great difference between 1939 and 1975 was that in thirty-six years Penguins and Pelicans had advanced from being occasional if useful additions to students' reading lists to the point where, notably in some university departments, they made up virtually the entire foundation of books on which the curriculum was based. Allen himself had devised the notion of reliance on a substantial back list; this as much as anything else made Penguin unique among paperback houses and Rose was only planning to extend minimally the principle which Allen had established. It could be urged with some authority that Allen had never looked for bestsellers, that he had always insisted that Penguin success depended upon steady sales of seemingly unsensational titles and that he had regarded obvious winners with some suspicion, as capital burdens and as distractions from the true Penguin task. Yet when bestsellers came, when, for example, he had *Aircraft Recognition* in his list, he was the first to exploit the happy accident. He would have enjoyed and enlarged the benefits that flowed from the coincidence of Penguin's rights in *The Great Gatsby* and the appearance of a highly successful and much-publicized film version. Against the cry that, by cutting in half his editorial staff the Chairman was reducing Penguin to 'sausage-machine editing' (the phrase was actually used in a serious article in a quality newspaper), the defence could point to the fact that twenty years earlier Allen had published more than 200 titles in one year, almost half the figure now projected, with editorial support less than one-eighth as strong as it would be in the new regime. Above all, no honest man could maintain with sound historical evidence what several indubitably honest men attempted to assert: that, because of his loyalty to his staff Allen could not have loosed a purge on the scale of that unleashed by Rose. Allen was loyal, but sentiment had never prevented him from ridding himself of unwanted employees; his reasons for not wanting them had been, not infrequently, far less worthy than Rose's.

Even the lamentations of authors were by no means original. Several years earlier Priestley had spoken up for all his fellow-craftsmen who felt aggrieved because they were denied publication by Penguin. Nevertheless the volume and stridency of their wailing was of itself by 1975 a far more powerful acclamation of the prestige of Allen's achievement than had been similar grievances expressed ten, twenty or thirty years earlier. Then for many kinds of author there had been only one paperback home, Penguin. By the time Rose announced his 450-book annual target, there were around London dozens, even hundreds, of other paperback publishers. Many of them had their cheque-books open, waiting for authors and ready to write in sums Allen would never have offered in the heyday of Penguin or that Harmondsworth would consider even now. Yet still many writers – and probably a majority – looked first to Penguin.

All Rose's critics called upon the ghost of Allen Lane. Rose, too, had he felt the need, might have turned to Allen for support. Years before, when Allen decided that he could no longer hold the price of Penguins at one shilling, a few of his most valued colleagues had used one of the weekly meetings to mount a sustained attack on this proclamation of heresy from the Pope himself. It was, they said, an overt denial of all that he had intended when he founded the firm, a contradiction of the spirit of Penguin, a betrayal of Penguin's faithful readers that must leave the firm no longer unique.

Allen listened, his eyes staring out of the window, the look on his face, so well known to all who worked with him, part mocking and part almost insultingly patient, until one of his senior editors, more pretentious than the rest, produced what he thought to be the summary of all their arguments: 'We owe it to society to keep our price at one shilling.'

Allen's eyes turned back from studying the sky. He looked at the spokesman, then at each of the protesters in turn. His lips pursed and then, quietly, he closed the discussion: 'I do no good to society by going bankrupt.'

Rose saved Penguin from 'going bankrupt'. There were crises still to face. There always had been crises at Harmondsworth and probably there always will be; but somehow Penguin, though now selling its books at prices that might make even Allen blanch (and which, incidentally, represent a percentage increase from 1935 far greater than the inflation rate or the increase in the average price of hard-cover books) still adheres to many of the principles which Allen had established, and still holds as does no other publisher the respect and affection of readers and authors.

There has not been a new King Penguin, no genuine replacement for Allen Lane, no dictator-leader acceptable alike to the staff, to the authors and to the book trade, no outstanding personality known, if not by name then certainly by his works, to readers all over the world. Probably there never will be: the conclusion is inescapable that it was Allen Lane who was *sui generis* and Penguin only because Allen Lane *was* Penguin. A successor can hope only to sustain, with just such amendments as may be demanded by the times, those virtues of quality, accessibility, variety, style and cheerfulness which Allen had cherished and which made Penguin, alone among publishers, the emotional property of readers.

Penguin survives. Critics whine that it is no longer what it was. Perhaps this is so and must be so, but even those whose eyes are dimmed by nostalgia or by envy can still see enough to perceive that it is still, unlike any other publishing house, an institution and recognizably Allen's creation (even from time to time, as Ethel Mannin did, they imagine that they see the snow from Soviet boots in the corridors of Harmondsworth!).

In less than half a century, from beginnings that were almost accidental, this one firm has changed the face of the book trade, has helped to make and break governments, has had a profound and beneficial effect on teaching methods in schools, colleges and universities, has given to authors vast new opportunities for passing on their art, their ideas and their knowledge, has opened a wide range of subjects to an audience which before shied away from topics which seemed the exclusive property of an esoteric, sophisticated and intellectual minority. Above all, Penguins, Pelicans and Puffins – the whole priceless but low-priced and unpompous Harmondsworth aviary – have led the way to making book ownership a possibility and a reality for all manner of men, women and children everywhere.

Much of this stems from the influence of one man: Allen

Lane. Perverse and capricious he undoubtedly was, enigmatic, unreliable and often careless of the consequences of his actions but there was in him that quality which is difficult to define but impossible to miss, the quality that can only be called genius.

If you seek Allen's memorial it is there in the Penguin list. It is just as evident in the lists of Penguin's emulators – and they prosper in almost every country in the world. Look around you, and you see it in the enhanced gaiety of bookshops and on the book-shelves of readers everywhere.

This is no mean monument, and such as stands to the enduring and universal honour of no other man of his profession, of few of his generation – and to not so very many of any trade or of any time.

A PERSONAL AFTERWORD

PUBLISHING HOUSES, no less than other industrial and commercial institutions, are eager to celebrate in print their achievements. The histories of book businesses are apt to suffer, more even than the histories of less obviously literate firms, from an awkwardness which exists always in the relationship between the commissioning agent and the author he hires to tell the story of his work and the work of his predecessors. In this unlike his equivalent in other industries, the publisher is not only the patron but is also the guardian of his hireling's future and himself an experienced editor. In almost every publishing history that I know it is clear that both parties - the publisher and his chosen historian - began with an honest determination to be objective. It is just as clear that thereafter the author was dogged by awareness that pipers must play the tunes that are put into their heads by their paymasters or else risk finding all concert-halls barred against them forever. The publisher - even with the best will in Bloomsbury - has not been able to resist the temptation to enlarge the editorial process so that it takes on the appearance of censorship. In consequence, and with very few exceptions, publishing histories are bland, uncritical paeans to the shrewdness and benevolence of a race of men unhampered by the frailties and avarice commonplace among lesser beings.

In histories written on a larger scale the publishers themselves - the men who own or manage publishing houses - appear but seldom. Generally no more than shadowy figures in the histories of the literatures they have helped to foster, even their names are rarely mentioned in the histories of the societies they have helped to create, to support or to change. Many write their autobiographies but, when it is turned inwards, the critical faculty fails and the perspicacity they applied so freely and generously to the works of their authors is blunted. More often than not publisher–autobiographers seem to be following the example of one of their kind – and he among the most distinguished as also among the most eminent and most implacable of Allen Lane's adversaries – who, on hearing the comment that his book about himself must have been much improved had he confessed to occasional fallibility, replied without hesitation or intentional humour: 'But I am not writing fiction.' Biographies of publishers are much more rare than autobiographies; there is as yet no life of Barabbas; of those that have been written most are debilitated by that same unease which is apparent in books about publishing houses. Even if the hero is conveniently dead, it is not easy for an author to shake off the effects of the ambivalence which prevails in dealings between his profession and the profession of his subject. As seen by an author, a publisher is at once champion and antagonist, philanthropist and Shylock, candle-holder and bottle-washer, banker and exploiter, a friend but even so an inconvenient interloper in the process of communication. Publishers on their side are convinced that most authors are ignorant of the techniques of the publishing craft and suspect, often with justification, that many sustain this ignorance by a lofty conviction that comprehending the technical and commercial practicalities of publishing is somehow beneath their dignity and an unnecessary distraction from their prime duty, to set words, ideas or narrative to paper. Understanding the means whereby their handsomely embellished paper is to be reproduced, promoted, distributed and made profitable – to both publisher and author – is a process to which they need give only such thought as is, in their opinion, unavoidable.

Allen Lane was above all else a publisher and, as I have attempted to demonstrate, the most original of this century. As I have also tried to show, the influence he exerted by way of his publishing ventures has been felt far beyond those areas of activity which, in the past and in his own times, have habitually been influenced by his habitually influential profession. Within a very few years the house he founded had been elevated by the public to the status of an institution. It has been held in affection by millions and its name has entered the popular vocabulary as –

for the first time in all publishing history – a truly household word. Yet Allen himself remained – and remains – if not exactly anonymous then certainly not well known beyond the limits of the book trade and the world of letters. He left behind him no autobiography. His achievements and his character are given surprisingly little notice in the autobiographies of his contemporaries except in that by his American associate, Victor Weybright. The several histories of Penguin published in his life-time were all unashamedly publicity ventures, and none dealt in any depth with the life or career of the founder. There have been, so far as I am aware, only two more generalized studies which have considered his influence on society and the book trade: Hoggart's *The Uses of Literacy* and my own pamphlet *Paperbacks Across Frontiers*. Both were written when his career was far from complete. (I am grateful to Richard Hoggart and to Chatto and Windus for permission to quote from the first, and to the Bowater Corporation for permission to quote from the second.) W. E. Williams's *Allen Lane: A Memoir* is by the author's admission more a brief account of a friendship than an attempt to write the life of Allen Lane.

For all these reasons, and no less because his energetic and enigmatic personality exercised a rare fascination on all who met him, since his death in 1970 it has been obvious to some that he could not be left to the shadows and to eventual oblivion; he merited a biography and a wider audience might welcome the chance to glimpse something of the character which so affected his friends, his colleagues and his rivals. Many talked, but Sir Robert Lusty acted. It was he, Allen's friend and mine for many years, who first declared that the role of serving as Allen's biographer must be mine. It has been Bob Lusty's enthusiasm and encouragement and the thoughtfulness and editorial wisdom of Charles Clark, his successor as Managing Director of Hutchinson and also a friend since the days when we worked together for Penguin, which has largely sustained me during the years when the obstacles that stood between me and the completion of this book were many and not all of them raised by the intrinsic nature of the task.

Looking back, with the work done, I see that I had no alternative but to accept Bob's invitation. Over the years I have heard many men and women say that, of all with whom they have come in contact, none has intrigued them more than Allen Lane. I can but add my voice. Fortunate though I have been in the number and variety of my acquaintances, I can think of no individual who has fascinated me more, perplexed me more, exasperated me more than Allen, and of very few whose influence upon my life has equalled his. Nevertheless, natural indolence held me from falling easy victim to the flattering insinuation that the coincidence of my experience in publishing, my familiarity with Allen and with most of those close to him, with my painfully acquired knowledge of the peculiar problems endemic to writing the life of a contemporary made my selection as Allen's biographer almost inevitable. But even when I tried to exercise what was, for me, unnatural modesty, I could not bring myself to deny that for this particular work I had some qualifications and some advantages that must be denied to almost any other putative biographer I could bring to mind. Some of the strategems that I attempted in order to reduce my eagerness were immediately thwarted by the generosity of those who I might have expected to conspire with me to make my excuses valid.

I am a member of that generation which, on August Bank Holiday 1935, was suddenly given access to a new world, at sixpence a time entrance-fee, and which, only a few years later, discovered in Penguins and Pelicans a sound shield against boredom, loneliness, fear and the horrors of separation from all the customary supports of a civilized society. My admiration and affection for Penguin had not been dimmed by twenty years of close association with the continuing work of the firm, but neither gratitude nor respect could persuade me that I should write yet another of those unflaggingly eulogistic business histories of which I am habitually suspicious. This long involvement with Penguin, though it had given me an insider's knowledge, had also sharpened my awareness that Penguin itself has not always been the surest defender of Penguin principles.

Such doubts as existed in my mind about my freedom to write as I thought fit, without censorship either explicit or implicit, were considerably reduced by the knowledge that my book was to be commissioned, in the first place, not by Penguin but by a publisher who had no interest in slavering over the glories of Penguin. Even so, I could not work without the acquiescence of those who have taken over the leadership of Penguin from Allen Lane and I was by no means certain that they would accept without reservation the return to Harmondsworth as a potentially critical chronicler an investigator from another Penguin era who was known to be not always sympathetic to the latter-day variations on the Penguin theme. I misjudged my men. Jim Rose, Edward Boyle (with whom my relationship might have been made even more embarrassing by the coincidence that he is not only Deputy Chairman of Penguin but also Vice-Chancellor of the University in which I have a Chair), Ron Blass, and all their colleagues greeted me as a member of the family who has an undisputed right to study and use the family papers. Everything was opened to me (including the Directors' drinks-cupboard) and it was made clear to me that, though this latter-day generation is eager to learn more about its own heritage than has been handed down by word of mouth and is anxious to know more about the founder of its tradition than survives in folk-memory, it had no wish to perpetuate fable and no intention of influencing my opinions by *fiat*, by overt persuasion or by innuendo.

Thus relieved of one fear, I held still to an even more substantial case for hesitancy. It was not my wish to write a business history, however objective; though I knew that it was neither necessary nor possible to separate the life of Allen Lane from the history of Penguin, I could but face with trepidation the thought that writing a life of Allen Lane must bring me to an attempt to unravel many of his relationships, some with individuals I held in great affection, and must even force me to rehearse the history of my own association with Allen.

Beyond all else I could not accept Bob Lusty's invitation unless with the approval of Allen's daughter, my daughter-in-law. I knew that Clare's feelings for Allen were more than dutiful. I could not be certain that she would relish her father-in-law meddling with the reputation of her father, more especially as she knew that my attitude to Allen was not and can never be entirely adulatory. Clare's response to my hesitant enquiries was unhesitatingly enthusiastic. She might not agree with all my assessments but she agreed without reserve that I must write his life; that my assessments must be made without reserve or consideration for her susceptibilities and without any form of supervision by her or by any agent other than my historian's conscience. As the book has progressed she and her husband, my son Michael, have helped me in all manner of ways, practical and emotional. My gratitude to them is immense.

Already, in the text, I have referred to the technical difficulty imposed upon me by my own appearance as a character in my book, but technical problems can be overcome by technical means. Much more intransigent were difficulties raised by the complex nature of my relations with Allen. From my previous experience in writing the biography of a contemporary I had discovered that this *genre* carries only the most superficial resemblances to writing biographies of men who have been conveniently dead for a hundred or a thousand years. The contemporary biographer is not supported by the comforting editorial hand of time. Documentary evidence is unhealthily abundant but it has not yet been gathered into libraries and archives, not yet sorted, calendared and catalogued nor its value assessed. There are few secondary sources against which the biographer can measure the validity of his assumptions or check his facts. He is forced to rely on notoriously unreliable oral evidence; he is dogged by what might be called 'the witness to the accident' syndrome and must somehow plot his course through waters made treacherous by the instinct, common even to the most honest men, to blow themselves up to the stature of stars when they were in truth at best supporting characters. But, when I wrote the life of Barnes Wallis, although my subject was still happily very much alive and although he had been a friend for forty years, I myself had made in all that time but one minor intervention in his public life – and even that peripheral to his professional career. Before I began my research I had no knowledge of his private affairs and had at no time been intimately involved with his family. With Allen Lane, in one way or another, I had close connections for a quarter of a century. He it was who gave me all my early training in publishing, and he who first persuaded me that the profession of publisher and the profession of author are not antipathetic (and thus, I hope, released me from the weight of the accusation which I raise, perhaps glibly, against most authors: that they know little and care less about the publisher's craft). I was first his employee, then his associate and for many years his intimate and confidant, but not long before his death, and just at the time when my contact with him produced for me its most enduring and happiest benefit (though not for that reason alone) I quarrelled with him, bitterly and irrevocably. My admiration for his achievements remained and remains, but I could not be certain that I could keep personal prejudice from colouring my biography, whether that prejudice be inspired by enthusiasm or distaste.

Many who had the right to be concerned about my interpretation of events and personalities reassured me by their willingness to cooperate in my research, by their generosity with documents and by the openness with which they answered even my most impertinent questions. Above all it was Lettice Lane who, having more authority for suspicion than all others, persuaded me by her quiet but unhesitating collaboration to accept as dogmatic a precept which, had I not been intimately involved, I would have recognized without tuition: that a biographer is not called upon to be remote. It is his duty to tell the story as he sees it, as fairly and as completely as he can but with passion where passion is felt.

Similarly my resolve was strengthened and my difficulties reduced by the unqualified cooperation of Dick Lane. On several occasions he and his wife Betty gave me the freedom of their beautiful home near Melbourne. Dick's hospitality has always been prodigious; on these occasions he added to hospitality by suffering without protest hours of inquisition and by handing over to me a draft of his reminiscences.

Thus, finding in almost every presumed advantage the seed of an inhibition I moved on to discover that almost every inhibition was an illusion.

As example: I had no doubt that my long association with the firm gave me both knowledge of Penguin affairs and an insight into Penguin methods such as a more distant investigator could have acquired only with the greatest difficulty – if at all. But I was timorous lest this very privilege reduce my capacity to judge fairly, lest my preconceptions overpower my inquisitiveness. In more practical terms, I was concerned that there might be raised against me a not-unnatural resentment for a one-time colleague turned inquisitor.

Of that first reservation, I can only say that as I worked I discovered much that I had never known and discovered also that I must discard or amend opinions that previously I had thought inviolate. Of the second, I am now convinced that my fears were groundless. From the days in the Crypt there has existed between Penguin employees, past and present, a sense of comradeship (even in rivalry) such as I have noticed elsewhere only in the products of a good school or regiment. This warmth, as much as their determination that Allen's story should be told, eventually made my task a little easier than I had expected, and much more pleasant. Indeed, it has been the renewal of old friendship and antique collaboration, and the chance offered to make new associations within Penguin which has been among the greatest delights that have come my way in the process of writing this book. Not only Dick Lane and Ron Blass but also from among the many who worked with me for Penguin, Len Beales, Noel Carrington, Bob Davies, Bob Maynard, Jill Norman, Jack Summers and Kaye Webb have helped me with their reminiscences, with frank answers to my brutal questions, and with their unvarying insistence that I tell the story as I see it.

In this context all have been cooperative but none more so than Eunice Frost, Harry Paroissien, Hans and Tanya Schmoller.

Eunice Frost holds to an affection for Allen and for Penguin as it once was more devoutly than any of us. I am fully conscious of the fact that reliving a happier past was for her a painful process, but she was unhesitating in her determination to assist my search. I am deeply grateful for her honesty and for her kindness to me.

Harry Paroissien – 'The Aged P' of those cheerful days soon after the War when he, then in his forties, was the old man of the front office – has been for longer than anyone else close to the centre of Penguin power. He gave me much time, much information, many papers and a scrupulous guided tour through the confused scene of Penguin Books Inc.

To Hans and Tanya Schmoller my obligation is immense. Like all others I approached they provided me with the unbridled recollections of many years of close contact with Allen (recollections in their case made somehow more immediate because they were offered as we sat surrounded by their collection of Penguins, probably the largest in private hands*).

* Now given to the library of the London School of Economics

That same spirit of fellowship which I found among my former Penguin colleagues and their successors at Harmondsworth was extended to me without reserve when I visited the Penguin offices at Ringwood near Melbourne, though not one of the staff there was known to me before I made the first of my two visits. Reluctant though I am to single out individuals from the many who offered me hospitality and assistance, I feel that I must offer thanks in particular to Rozanne Turner, not only for her spirited and efficient organization of my itinerary but also for the gift of friendship.

Apart altogether from publishing considerations, a series of coincidences have brought to Australia several who were closely associated with Allen: Lettice his widow, Dick his brother, Bob Maynard, one of his earliest Penguin employees, and his sister Nora, who entertained me nobly in her home across the harbour from Sydney and gave me much valuable information about Allen's childhood and youth. My progress in Australia was made comfortable by the generosity of the Humanities Research Centre and Burgmann College, both within the Australian National University, and Professor A. D. Hope, who must be the only poet in the world with an office in a building named for him (also in the Australian National University), added to my repertoire a revealing anecdote about Allen's dealings with authors.

I have known in my time almost every personality who appears in this book as in any way connected with Allen after 1935, and not only those who worked for Penguin. I cannot pretend that it was for this reason that Philip Unwin, Peter du Sautoy, Ronald Boswell and Frank Morley allowed me to use freely tapes of their recollections of Allen but to them my thanks and to Peggy Rafferty, Tom and Monica Girtin and Eric Norris. Livia Gollancz scoured the records of her firm for evidence about her father's tempestuous relations with Allen, and David Machin searched through the archives of Jonathan Cape Ltd for materials that might assist me to an understanding of the more cheerful relationship with the late Jonathan Cape. Peter Rosenwald provided me with much documentation for my account of the controversy over the Pearson Longman takeover.

Beverley Ricketts of the Australian National University painstakingly transcribed tape-recordings of many interviews, my secretary Christine Conlin typed the manuscript, and a former student, Elizabeth George, assisted me in my searches through Harmondsworth files.

For an author to thank his wife is so conventional that it has become almost a cliché. In this case, however, my sense of obligation must be rare, for my wife's contributions to the preparation of this book have been in a peculiar way intimate in that she has been not only a support but also a witness. Allen was, for many years, a frequent visitor to our home. He called upon her for advice about the upbringing of his daughters, in moments when it was we who were suffering stress he treated her with great generosity and at the last she suffered the pain that came with the break in a long-standing friendship. Yet she remembers him always with affection.

And so also do I.

INDEX

academic honours, A.L.'s, 226, 305
academic world, tribute to A.L. by, 296
Adprint, 144, 148
adult education movement, 96, 120, 123
advertising, 100, 114, 166, 203, 205, 222, 249, 291
Air Ministry, 165
Albany, A.L.'s residence in, 57, 64
Albatross Modern Continental Library, 181, 182
Aldington, Richard, 127
Allen, Ashton, 104
Allen and Unwin, 298
Allen Lane Foundation, 304, 372, 373, 375–7
Allen Lane Incorporated, 248
Allen Lane The Penguin Press, 343, 344, 355, 356
Allingham, Margery, 90, 155
ambition, A.L.'s, 61, 111, 124, 190
Anderson, Sherwood, 35
anonymity, A.L.'s comparative, outside book world, 389
architecture, A.L.'s interest in, 152
Arlen, Michael, 58, 128
Arno, Peter, 75, 346
Arup and Dowson, 331, 332
astrology, and A.L., 286, 287, 307
Atheneum, 289–93
Auden, W. H., 170, 265
Australasian, Penguin companies, 202, 229, 230, 235, 245–7, 251–63, 305, 360, 377, 379, 395
  autonomy granted, 263
  growth of activities in, 263
  sacking of manager, 262–3
Australian National University, 395
author, A.L.'s ambition to be, 141
authors,
  pride in Penguin publication, 267, 371, 383, 384
  seeking, 58, 214
Avon paperbacks, 201, 243
awe of intellectual superiors, A.L.'s, 152, 193, 225–6, 269
Ayer, A. J., 268, 276

Ballantine, Ian, 180, 183, 187, 201, 231
bank loans, 103, 108, 111, 113, 128, 135, 235, 380
Bantam Books, 201
Barry, Gerald, 315

Barton, Sir Sydney, 140
Bates, Ralph, *Lean Men*, 133, 134
bathrooms, A.L.'s fascination with, 50, 64, 68, 69, 73, 80, 88, 138, 141
Beach, Sylvia, 75
Beales, H. L., 119, 120, 124, 175, 394
Beardsley, Aubrey, 22, 26, 28–31, 34, 35, 39, 44
Beerbohm, Max, 28, 34, 42, 50, 265
Bennett, Arnold, 131, 265
Berne Convention of 1908, 82–3
Bertram, Anthony, 171
Bessie, Michael, 290–3
Birkett, Norman, 315
Black, A. and C., Ltd., 298
Blackwell's, 298
Blackwood's, 30, 129, 298
Blass, Ron, 204, 263, 283, 303, 312, 313, 331, 338, 341, 351, 352, 355, 356, 362, 365–7, 371, 379, 391, 394
Bles, Geoffrey, 60
Bloomsbury set, 170
Bodley Head, The, 12, 16–107, 142, 184, 266, 298, 343, 345, 366
  aestheticism of, 21–3, 25–7, 29–31, 34, 35, 37, 39, 44, 47, 97
  A.L. and, 45–106 *passim*
  A.L.'s desire to revive, 52, 73
  American market, 35, 40, 42, 44, 51
  American office, 31–2, 35, 36, 45, 51
  artists, 22
  authors of fame, publishing, 22
  bid by A.L. to recover controlling interest, 107, 108
  break of Lanes with, 106, 107
  change of premises, 24
  conflicts within, 52–4, 72–4, 77, 86, 96, 104, 106, 107
  crises in, 19, 25–7, 29, 31–4, 40, 43, 44, 51, 78, 106
  empire-building by A.L. within, 72–5
  financial problems, 44, 51, 52, 59, 62, 64, 73, 74, 94, 105, 107
  foundation of, 20, 30, 31, 36
  innovations by A.L., 35
  Keynotes, 34, 35, 82
  Lane brothers as Directors, 65; strength in, 67, 68, 72
  left-wing books, 61

Bodley Head, The—*cont.*
  legal proceedings against Hesketh
    Pearson, 54, 55
  libel actions, possible, 53
  Managing Director A.L., 55
  paperback publication, 85
  poetry, publishing of, 37
  private company, conversion to, 51
  promotion of A.L. to Board, 51
  publishing technique, 21, 33, 35, 37–9, 43,
    44
  reorganization of, 77
  sales department, A.L.'s work in, 50
  shareholding, A.L.'s inheritance of
    majority, 55
  success of, 21–5, 33, 37, 39, 40
  translations, 26, 31, 38–41, 44
  voluntary liquidation, 107
  writ, serving of, 41
  Yellow Book, The, 27–32, 34, 41, 44, 67, 78,
    130, 170, 321; contributions to, 27
Bogue, David, 22
Boni, Charles, 84
bonuses, annual, 135
Book Clubs, 335, 336
Book Collector's Quarterly, 64
Book Export Scheme, 210
book ownership, increasing, 83, 384
books,
  inexpensive, 81–4
  mass media, 12, 235–8, 313
Bookseller, 109, 126, 188, 195, 205
boredom and A.L., 99, 128, 223, 224, 246, 259,
    313, 364
Boswell, Ronald, 51–4, 61, 65, 107, 395
Boyle, Sir Edward, 270, 283, 303, 343, 357, 358,
    367, 369, 371, 391
  Acting Chairman of Penguin, 376
  Chairman of Allen Lane Foundation,
    376
  Vice-Chairman of Penguin, 357, 358
Brett Young, Francis, 128
Briggs, Professor Asa, 296
Bristol and A.L.
  early years in, 12–16, 50
  Grammar School, 12, 14, 15, 17, 55
  University, honorary degree, 226
Britain in Pictures, 144
Brooke, Rupert, 34, 37
Broomcroft, A.L.'s life at, 13, 14
building, A.L.'s enthusiasm for, 128, 152,
    223, 330–2
Buildings of England, The, 213, 264, 267
Bullock, Sir Alan, 296
bully, A.L.'s tendency to, 152, 199
bureaucracy, A.L. and, 160, 167, 178, 357
burial of A.L. in Devon, 367
Butler, Lord, 296

Byrne, Mr Justice, 316, 317, 319–21, 325

Caldecott, Oliver, 355
Caldwell, Erskine, 227, 228
callousness of A.L., 24, 124–6, 152, 160, 173,
    181, 193, 200, 211, 213, 226, 246, 260–3, 280,
    281
Calvocoressi, Peter, 380
Canada, 161, 162, 241, 242, 244–6, 253
  A.L.'s determination to open in, 242–5
Canterbury Tales, The, 249
Cape, Jonathan, Ltd, 47, 87, 89, 107, 109,
    127, 395
capital, nominal, of Penguin Books, 128
Carr-Gomm, 51, 52
Carrington, Noel, 171, 172, 276, 394
Cassells, 272, 370
caution of A.L., 239
Cazenove, 332
Cerf, Bennet, 76, 77
Chalmers-Mitchell, Sir Peter, 119, 120, 122
Chamberlain, Houston Stewart, 44
Chambers, 129
Chapman, Frederick, 38
Chapman and Hall, 57
charm of A.L., 126, 136, 160, 212, 259
Chatto and Windus, 84, 89, 104, 108, 389
Cherry-Garrard, Apsley, *The Worst Journey
    in the World*, 116
Chesterton, G. K., 34, 42, 127, 195
children's books, launching of Penguin,
    171–3
Christie, Agatha, 58–60, 80, 90, 267
  Penguin editions, 60, 89, 94
Christmas gifts by A.L., 322
cinema and book-buyers, 322
Clark, Charles, 309, 355, 371, 379, 389
Clark, R. &. R., 219
Coghill, N., 249
Cole, G. D. H., 117, 118, 122
Coles, Joan, 126
collaborators, A.L.'s choice of, 181, 215
collector, A.L. as, 19, 49, 152, 153, 233, 287,
    330, 332
Collins, 60, 82, 83, 93, 98, 144, 298
Communist countries, 237–9
Communist Party, 131–4, 369, 384
Companion of Honour, A.L. as, 325, 366
complacency and Penguin, 277
confidence and A.L., 61, 99, 111, 143, 145, 168,
    173, 245, 354
Constable, 81, 116
contentment of A.L., 186, 199, 307
contrition, A.L.'s lack of, 190
Copyright Act of 1842, 82
Copyright Act of 1911, 83
Cornhill, 129
cost philosophy of A.L., 102, 144, 264

costing, 62, 80, 82, 85, 94, 96, 109, 145, 203, 250, 252, 253, 255, 266, 287, 291, 311, 315, 341, 384
costs, printing, 111
courage of A.L., 236, 363, 364–7
Crime Club, Collins's, 83
Crook, Arthur, 283

Daily Herald, 192
Daily Mail, 53
Davidson, John, 27, 37
Davies, Bob, 280–2, 394
death of A.L., 367
decision-making, A.L.'s uncertainty in, 245, 246, 250, 281–6, 282–304 *passim*, 300, 307, 331, 333, 343, 359
Deighton, Len, 368
delegation by A.L., 169, 198, 271, 277, 314
Dell paperbacks, 201, 243
Dent, J. M., 83
design
 importance of, 15, 21, 35, 85, 88, 92, 97, 143, 146, 152, 153, 172, 204, 217, 218, 225, 226, 230, 232, 243, 271, 274, 291, 344, 345, 354, 355
 pictorial covers, 345
detail, A.L.'s lack of attention to, 24, 124, 137, 223
developing countries, as a missed market, 236–40, 377
Dillon, Una, 347
Director of Public Prosecutions, 316, 325, 326
Dodd, Mead & Co., 73, 219
Dolley, Christopher, 283, 303, 358–60, 367, 370, 371, 379, 380
 successor to A.L., 358–60, 368, 369
Douglas, Lord Alfred, 26–8
Dowson, Ernest, 37, 39
Doyle, Conan, 50, 129
Dreiser, Theodore, 34, 35
dress of A.L., 173, 234, 305
Drummond, Lindsay, 59, 65
du Sautoy, Peter, 395

ebullience of A.L., 48, 52, 78, 111, 123, 126, 169, 181, 186, 214, 219, 230, 275, 304, 305, 333, 362, 363, 389
eccentricity and A.L., 231, 232
education and A.L., 12, 14, 15, 17, 213, 226, 312
 improvement in levels of readers', 83, 213, 244, 249, 252, 253
Egerton, George (*alias* Mrs Egerton Clairmonte), 34
egotism and A.L., 282
Egyptian Mail, 208
Eliot, T. S., 37, 77, 265, 295, 324
Ellis, Havelock, 290
Encounter, 295
Encyclopaedia Britannica, 375

enemies of A.L., 125
Enoch, Kurt, 181–3, 187, 201, 202, 227, 229, 230–3, 248, 292
Ernest Benn Ltd, 61, 84, 91
Ernst, Morris L., 76, 289, 290
erratic behaviour of A.L., 19, 61, 194, 199, 210, 218, 219, 259, 277, 363
Everyman Library, 82, 102, 143
Exchange Control, 217
executive power, proposed removal of A.L. from, 349–51, 359, 360
experimentation by A.L., 125

Faber and Faber, 37, 77, 88, 98, 298
Facetti, Germano, 345
Fairbank, Alfred, 153
Fairley, Tom, 188, 205–7, 209
family
 life of A.L., married, 185–8, 208, 224, 280, 298, 300–4, 306, 308
 relationships, 12–14, 17, 18, 55, 60–2, 64, 137, 168, 173, 174, 176, 177, 186, 218, 254–6, 260, 308, 365; deterioration in, 177, 178, 189
Faulkner, William, 127, 128
Film Review, 129
financial modesty of A.L., 301, 302
First Edition Club, 64
First World War, 15, 16, 44, 45, 47, 50
Fishenden, R. B., 149, 276
flair, A.L.'s, 137, 218
Flower, Desmond, 64, 272–3
Forces Book Club, 162–5, 168
Forster, E. M., 265, 295
France, 67, 238
France, Anatole, 38–40, 43, 44, 78, 347; death of, 40
Frankfurt Book Fair, 290
Franklin Books, 237
French classics, collaboration with Kurt Enoch, 182, 183
friends, A.L.'s close, 60, 99, 137, 173, 190
Frost, Eunice, 126, 127, 147, 151, 159, 167, 171, 187, 191, 200, 202, 209, 212, 214, 227, 276, 281, 282, 308, 309, 336, 373–4, 394

Galsworthy, John, 50
Gardiner, Gerald, QC, 317, 325
Garrick Club, 314
Germany, 67, 238
Gibbings, Robert, 143
girl friends of A.L., *see* woman friends of A.L.
Girtin, Monica, 395
Girtin, Tom, 395
Glasgow, Mary, 189
glass engraving by A.L. and the Prince of Wales, 49

Glover, Alan, 192–4, 202, 209, 214, 215, 219, 221, 224, 276, 277, 280, 308
Godwin, Tony, 285, 303, 334–56, 365, 367, 368
　conspiracy to dispose of A.L., 349–52, 354, 355
　death of, 352
　dismissal, 352, 356, 365
　resentment by A.L., 340, 341, 344–51
　resignation threat of, 348, 349
　similarities with A.L., 336–40
　Siné dispute, 346–50
　tribute to A.L., 353
Golden Ass, The, 281
Goldsack, Sydney, 93
Gollancz, Livia, 395
Gollancz, Victor, 62, 84, 90, 91, 98, 122, 133, 206, 298; antagonism to Penguin, 91
Goodman, Lord, 296
gossip, A.L.'s love of, 48, 184, 303, 304, 308, 364, 366
Graham, Eleanor, 276, 310
grandchildren, A.L.'s, 308
Grant, Professor Michael, 272
graphology and A.L., 286, 287, 307
Graves, Robert, 228, 265
Great Gatsby, The, 379, 382
Greene, Graham, 90, 228, 294
Griffith-Jones, Mr, QC, 316, 319, 320, 328
Guild Books, 157, 163, 197, 298
Gulbenkian Foundation, 330

Hall, Radclyffe, 290
hardbacks,
　high cost of, 336
　movement into by Penguin, 264, 341–4
Hardy, Thomas, 266
Harland, Henry, 27, 34
Harper Bros., 290
Harrap, 164, 165
Harrison, G. B., 113, 149
Hart-Davis, Rupert, 24
Hay, Ian, 127, 155
Hazell, Raymond, 48, 70
Hazell, Watson and Viney, 48, 91, 103
health farms and A.L., 106, 305
Heath, D. C., and Company, 249, 289
Heaton, Peter, 249
Heffer, Reuben, 272
Heinemann, 45, 50, 129, 239, 267
Hemingway, Ernest, 89, 265
Hemming, James, 319
Herbert, A. P., 315
Hill, Ralph, 224
Hodder and Stoughton, 83, 84, 109, 298
Hogarth Press, 170
Hoggart, Richard, 272, 294–6, 367, 389
holidays, A.L.'s family, 300

Holy Trinity Church crypt, 104–6, 110, 126, 134, 139, 168, 199, 255, 280, 306, 394
Home Guard, 166, 167
Hope, Professor A. D., 258, 395
Hornby, Anthony, 332
Hornung, E. W., 128
horse-riding and A.L., 48, 49
Houghton Mifflin, 293
Huebsch, Ben, 95
Hutchinson, 379, 389
Huxley, Aldous, 90, 127, 228
Huxley, Sir Julian, 117, 239, 294

Iddesleigh, 180, 348
idealism of A.L., 61, 194
Iliad, The, 249
illness and A.L., 257, 284, 285, 313, 332, 333, 340, 352, 354, 363–7
Illustrated Classics, 142–4, 152, 382
Image and the Search, The, 320
impatience of A.L., 52, 79, 169
impetuosity of A.L., 61, 246
impulsiveness of A.L., 79, 173, 181, 289, 343, 344
innovator, A.L., as, 35, 96, 111, 168, 169, 173, 181, 230
Insel Verlag, 143
instinct of A.L., 199, 212, 216, 218, 225, 251, 339
integrity of A.L.
　commercial, 160
　questioning of, 74
interpreter, A.L. as, 38
intimacy of A.L. with others in book world, 47, 48, 78, 169
intriguing nature of A.L. 389–90
investments of A.L., 332, 341, 360
Ireland, A.L.'s property in, 350
Irish Parlour Library, 82

Jackdaw Books, 109
Jacob, Gordon, 224, 225, 276
Jacobs, W. W., 101, 128
James, Lord, 296
Jeans, Sir James, 117
Jenkins, Herbert, 42, 45
Jenkins, Roy, 315, 317, 318
John Murray Ltd, 30, 81, 98, 129, 297
Jonathan Cape Ltd, 47, 87, 89, 107, 109, 127, 395
Joyce, James, 75–7, 265, 290, 321, 346, 366
judgement, A.L.'s, 19, 98, 125, 135, 181, 260, 336, 337, 339

Kelmscott Press, 21
Kent, Tatyana, *see* Schmoller, Tatyana
kindness of A.L., 199, 224, 256, 257, 261, 280, 300, 306, 308, 330, 396
King Penguins, 142–9, 151–4, 169, 171, 172, 191, 267, 276, 281, 311, 382
　booksellers' resistance to, 146

pride of A.L. in, 153, 154
Redouté's *Roses*, 148
Kite, Peter, 104, 204
Knight, the gentleman's gentleman, 70, 71, 141
knighthood for A.L., 11, 235, 301, 305
Knopf, Alfred, 290
Krishna Menon, V. K., 119, 122, 124–6, 130, 133, 141, 268, 270

Labour Government (1945), 195, 196, 270
Labour Government (1964), 331
Lady Chatterley's Lover, 41, 77, 266, 314–25, 328, 329, 331, 334, 347, 379
  bestseller, 325
  printer of, 316
Lamb, Charles, 81, 82
Lancaster Gate Terrace, No. 8, 16, 36, 44, 49, 50, 52, 56, 57, 69, 71, 184
Lane, Anna, 224, 300, 306, 330
Lane, Annie, 36–8, 40, 41, 43, 44, 50–2, 55, 56, 61; author, 41, 42
Lane, Christine (Mrs Teale), 188, 298–304, 306–8, 330, 372–5
Lane, Clare (Mrs Morpurgo), 185–7, 298–304, 306–8, 322, 330, 366, 367, 372, 373, 391, 392; merger, resistance to, 372–7
Lane, John (brother of A.L.), 13, 18, 56, 64–7, 69–71, 74, 80, 81, 85, 91, 95, 99, 103, 104, 106, 111, 114, 122, 124, 128, 135–42, 145, 147, 151, 158, 159, 167, 168, 173, 174, 176–9
  'brain' in Penguin Books, 137, 138
  death of, 185, 186, 189, 190, 254, 303
  Director of Penguin Books Ltd, 107
  will of, 186
  working for The Bodley Head, 65–107 *passim*
Lane, John ('Uncle'), 12, 15–52, 58, 61, 67, 68, 74, 77, 85, 97–9, 128, 143, 184, 231, 250, 265, 298, 321, 342, 343, 347, 367
  Bath, move to, 16, 44
  death of, 51
  early career of, 20, 30, 31
  illness, 40, 51
  Lancaster Gate Terrace, 16, 36, 44, 49, 50
  marriage, 30
  religious views, 38, 39
  shortcomings of, 23, 24, 27, 35, 36, 44, 45, 51, 52
  similarity of Allen Lane with, 18, 19, 24, 41, 58, 85, 128, 152
  success of, 21–5, 30, 31, 33
  and Wilde, Oscar, 23, 24, 26–9, 31–4, 38
Lane, Lettice (*née* Orr), 174–7, 190, 208, 224, 257, 300, 301, 306, 307, 333, 350, 365, 393, 395
Lane, Nora, 13, 17, 18, 56, 95, 111, 136, 140, 141, 158, 159, 173–5, 247, 395

Lane, Richard (Dick), 13, 14, 16, 18, 50, 55, 56, 60–2, 64, 66, 69–71, 74, 80, 81, 85, 89, 91, 95, 99, 103, 104, 106, 111, 113, 114, 122, 124, 128, 129, 135–42, 145, 147, 151, 158, 159, 161, 167, 168, 173, 174, 176–9, 184–6, 189, 190, 198, 204, 215, 217–19, 227, 229, 252, 254–6, 259, 260, 262, 263, 275, 277, 303, 304, 326, 366, 393–5
  abdication from Penguin Books Ltd, 261, 303
  to Australia, 245, 247, 254–6
  challenge to Allen Lane, 254–6
  costing disputes, 62, 255
  Director of Penguin Books Ltd, 107, 255
  insurance claim, 128, 235, 329–30
  marriage, 256, 259
  relationship with A.L., 14, 55, 60–2, 64, 168, 173, 177, 186, 218, 254–6, 260, 308
  transfer of holdings, 328, 329
  working for the Bodley Head, 65–107 *passim*
Laski, H., 122, 133
Lawrence, D. H., 220, 265, 267, 295, 314–21, 323, 324
Le Gallienne, Richard, 20–2, 27, 34
Leacock, Stephen, 35, 42, 43, 155
Lear, Edward, 28
Leavis, F. R., 266, 267, 322–4
  Common Pursuit, The, 323
Leavis, Q. D., 323–5
Lee, Jennie, 369
Left Book Club, 122, 206
Lehmann, John, 30, 130, 133, 169–71, 207, 276–7
Leighton, Sir Frederick, 27, 29
Lewis, Sinclair, 101, 102, 127
libraries, public, 83, 97, 265, 273, 274, 342
Linklater, Eric, 89, 91, 265
Little Review, 75
Littlewoods, 160–1
Locke, W. J., 40, 43, 44, 50
London, A.L.'s early days in, 17
loneliness of A.L., 136, 138, 140, 158, 173, 174, 251, 312, 313
Longmans, 30, 239, 288, 298, 362
Lord of the Rings, The, 299
Lusty, Sir Robert, 188, 303, 366, 367, 379, 389

MacGraw-Hill, bid to merge with Penguins, 370–2, 375
Machen, Arthur, 34
Machin, David, 395
Mackenzie, Compton, 89, 94, 95, 265, 272
McLean, Ruari, 204, 211
Macleod, Fiona, 34
Macmillan, 98, 239, 266, 298
Mallowan, Max, 80, 215, 276
Manchester Guardian, 237, 318

Mannin, Ethel (Mrs Porteous), 56, 57, 99, 110, 132–4, 369, 384
Manvell, Roger, 188
Mardersteig, Hans, 182
marriage of A.L., 18, 174, 176, 177, 180, 190, 306, 365
   failure of, 190, 233, 301, 307
   separation, temporary, 301
Martins Bank, *see* bank loans
Massacre, 346–9
Mathews, Elkin, 20, 24, 25, 35, 36, 43, 45
Maurois, André, *Ariel*, 38, 40, 89, 192, 366
Maxton, James, 132, 133, 270
Maxwell, William, 219
May, J. Lewis, 36, 39, 60
Maynard, R. W., 104, 160, 161, 201, 202, 204, 229, 245–7, 251–4, 256–61, 264, 341, 394, 395
   attacks on, 260, 261
   to Australia, 202
   daughter of, 257, 259, 261
   family tragedy, 256, 257
   severance with, 261, 262
Memorial Service, 295, 367, 368
memories of A.L., 381–5
memory, excellence of A.L.'s, 46, 48
Messer, Peter, 204, 211
Michael Joseph Ltd, 188
millionaire, A.L. a, 329, 330
Mitford, Nancy, 44, 265
Monkhouse, C. A. W., 116
Morley, Frank, 395
Morpurgo, Clare, *see* Lane, Clare
Morpurgo, Jack, 204, 206–11, 216, 220, 222, 224, 277, 283, 284, 294, 307, 308
   severance with Allen Lane, 308
Morpurgo, Michael, 307, 308, 367, 376–8, 392
Morris, William, 21
Mott, Tony, 355
Mount Vernon Hospital, 366
Mowrer, Edgar, *Germany Puts the Clock Back*, 129, 135
Moynihan, Rodrigo, 275–7
Muggeridge, Malcolm, 346, 347
Muirhead, L. Russell, 142
Murray, John, Ltd, 30, 81, 98, 129, 297
music and A.L., 14, 58, 59, 226

name, change of family, 12, 17, 45
narcissism and A.L., 302–3
National Book League, 220
National Library (Cassell), 82
Natural History Series, 306
Nelson's Classics, 82, 84
New American Library, 230, 231, 243
New Century Library, *see* Nelson's Classics
New English Weekly, 101
New Statesman, 100
Newnes Group, 172

Nicholls, George, 348
Nichols, Beverley, 56, 89
Norman, Jill, 394
Norris, Eric, 104, 395
Nuffield Foundation, 294, 330

Obscene Publications Act 1959, 315–21
Observer, 100
obstinacy of A.L., 96, 116
Odyssey Press, 75
Odyssey, The, 215, 216, 244, 249, 325
Old Bailey, 315–20
Olney, S. H., 104, 161, 167, 187, 191, 202
opposition, A.L.'s thriving on, 190, 191
optimism of A.L., 111
Orr, Lettice, *see* Lane, Lettice
Orwell, George, 100–3, 108, 170, 207, 265, 295
Oxford University Press, 97, 239

Pan Books, 197, 264, 288, 334, 335
paper,
   black marketeering, 160–1
   supply of, 162, 164, 168, 180, 203
   use of, 156, 157, 160, 161
paperbacks,
   adverse reception by booksellers and publishers, 86, 87
   book-borrowing, threat to, 273, 274
   competitors, number of, 335
   conception of, 35, 80, 81
   founding of, 84, 98
   impact of, 85
   Penguin's monopoly of, 191, 264
   publishers launching own series, 109
Paperbacks Across Frontiers, 236–7, 389
Paroissien, Harry, 204, 210–12, 231, 235, 243, 244, 246–52, 263, 280–2, 289–93, 308, 309, 338, 352–4, 360, 367, 373, 394
   to America, 231
   deputy to A.L., 251, 308, 309
Pearson, Hesketh, *The Whispering Gallery*, 52–5
Pearson, S. and Co., 361, 362
Pearson Longman, 361–3, 366–80, 395
Pelican Archaeologies, 214–15
Pelican Books, 118, 121–3, 131, 134, 143, 144, 147, 148, 165, 168, 169, 172, 175, 182, 189, 193, 197, 206, 214, 231, 232, 239, 243, 244, 253, 267, 294, 295, 342, 355, 379, 382, 384, 390
   adult education, role in, 123
   editorship of, 119–24, 126, 127, 135
   famous writers for, 267–8
   launching of, 114–17
   success of, 139
Pelican History of Art, The, 213, 264, 265, 267
Pelican History of England, The, 253
Pelican Shakespeare, 249
Pembangunan, Indonesian publisher, 237

Penguin
- ancestry of, 18
- authors' interest in, 108, 109, 127, 149, 150
- beginnings of, 11, 18, 77–81, 84–91, 94–8
- Board, Siné dispute, 346, 348
- Book Club, suggestion of, 206
- cartoonists, 345, 346
- catholicity of, 127, 267
- choice of name, 88, 89, 118
- cloth bound, 264
- colour printing, 144, 147, 149, 154, 172, 217, 229, 230, 243, 274
- coming of age, 272, 274, 305
- competition element, 190, 197, 203, 218, 223, 230, 250, 252, 264, 267, 271, 288, 334, 335, 345, 383
- dependence on A.L., 275
- direct selling, 206, 209, 291, 335
- displaying of, 91, 146, 197, 218, 243
- distribution, 80, 84, 103, 135, 158, 201, 312, 360, 380
- dummy, 91–3
- editorial policy, 96, 110, 113, 114, 127, 129, 131–3, 142–4, 149, 153, 166, 169, 172, 187, 190, 192, 193, 203, 209, 214, 219, 227–30, 235, 243, 244, 252, 253, 265, 267–9, 271, 275, 276, 287, 288, 292, 296, 306, 311, 315, 334–9, 344, 346, 355, 360, 362, 382
- educational/cultural image of, 96, 120, 122, 123, 149–51, 166, 193, 213, 215, 216, 232, 235, 236, 239, 243, 244, 249, 252, 253, 265–7, 272
- exports, 210, 211, 218, 235, 242, 248, 250, 288, 362
- financial aspects, 103, 107, 108, 111, 128, 135, 154, 164, 180–3, 199, 230, 235, 249, 250, 263, 281, 291, 326–7, 330, 333, 362, 363, 368, 380, 381, 383
- first ten titles, 89–91, 96
- in French, 169
- friction within, 336, 338–40, 349, 350, 352
- future of, *see* successor to A.L. at Penguin
- future planning, 98, 99, 106, 111, 130, 139, 142, 187, 191, 198, 217, 262, 282–3, 306, 338, 360
- generic term for paperbacks, 222–3, 230
- golden epoch, 213
- Great Portland Street, 107, 111, 126, 139, 168
- hardbacks, aid to sale of, 127
- Harmondsworth site, 111–13, 128, 134, 135, 139, 142, 147, 152, 167, 179, 183, 194, 199, 202, 204, 209, 213, 214, 218, 229, 243, 276; requisition of buildings, 165, 166
- illustrated, 264, 274
- inflation, hit by, 380–5
- international writers, 265, 267
- job demarcation, lack of, 104, 105
- later difficulties of, 379–85
- library cloth covers, 265, 273, 342
- literature, all periods covered, 265
- long run of titles, 361
- marketing, 91–3, 96, 98, 108, 144, 147, 187, 217, 218, 311
- 'millions', 219–23, 267, 314
- 1939 list, 155
- offices in central London, 214
- over-extension of, 361
- profits lowered, 380
- property, value of, 327
- Public Relations Manager, 203, 205, 206, 208–10, 222
- publication of, 94, 95, 97, 98
- publicity, 203, 205, 206, 222, 259, 275, 281, 288, 314–25, 328, 329, 367, 368
- publishers' approaches, 109
- purpose of, 102, 109
- quality maintenance, importance of, 98, 109, 110, 113
- reorganization, post-war, 198–200, 202–4
- retrenchment, 380
- royalties, 89, 91, 111, 164, 265, 342
- salary levels, 111, 211, 217, 221, 261, 262, 278, 281
- scepticism about, 86, 96, 102, 103, 108, 127, 145, 146, 153, 195, 196, 215, 216, 273, 275, 326, 365
- scholars on editorial staff, 149, 192, 193
- second list, 102
- Selfridges, display at, 91
- Shaw ten, 221
- silver jubilee, 272–4, 307
- size, problems of, 277
- staff competition, 279, 284
- staff grievances, 277–9
- staff loyalty, 194, 271, 279, 293, 351, 354–6, 369
- staffing, post-war, 199–204, 211, 212, 215
- storage, 103–6, 110, 111
- strike threats, 381
- success of, 96–9, 109, 111, 135, 139, 144, 151, 191, 230, 235, 252, 271, 275, 328, 361
- suggestions from readers, 117, 118, 205, 206, 209
- tenth birthday, 195–7, 272, 274
- third list, 101
- translations, 215, 216, 244, 249, 265, 267
- two-volume publications, 116
- unsensational titles, concentration on, 382
- war stories, 334, 335
- war-time impact on readership, 164–5, 187; uses, 157, 161–5, 168, 171, 172
- weekly meetings, 214, 224, 276
- world-wide sales, 157, 160, 231

Penguin Book of Australian Verse, The, 258
Penguin Books Canada Ltd, 245

Penguin Books Inc., 128, 129, 139, 180, 181, 183, 186, 201, 217, 227:9, 232, 235, 243–6, 248–51, 291–3
   Baltimore, move to, 243, 248
   differences with, 231–3, 244
   extension of home firm, regarded as, 227–31
   New York, move to, 379
   pornographic books, 227–8
Penguin Books Ltd
   bid for, 361–3, 366–78
   counter-bid for, 370–2
   formation of, 107
   public company, 318, 325–9, 333
   share flotation success, 329, 335
Penguin Blue Guides, 142
Penguin Classics, 215, 216, 244, 249, 267
Penguin Education, 355, 362, 380, 381
Penguin Education Specials, 355
Penguin Guide to English Literature, The, 267
Penguin Handbooks, 267
Penguin Histories, 209
Penguin Modern Painters, 188, 382
Penguin Music Magazine, 129, 224
Penguin Music Scores, 224–6, 267, 311
Penguin New Biology, 129, 213
Penguin New Writing, 30, 129, 130, 169–71, 207, 295
Penguin Nuffield A-level books, 355
Penguin Parade, 129, 209
Penguin Poets, 169, 267
Penguin Science News, 129, 213
Penguin Specials, 130–2, 134, 135, 139, 143, 144, 147, 148, 155, 157, 165, 168, 169, 171, 197, 198, 268, 313, 322
   political bias, 131, 132, 196, 268, 269
Penguin Story, The, 232, 272, 307
Penguin Success with English, 355
Penguin's Progress, 203, 205, 209, 219, 222, 272
Penguins Progress 1935–1960, 272, 274, 307
perception of A.L., 339
Peregrine series, 266, 267, 323
periodicals, 129, 130, 132, 134, 382
persuasiveness of A.L., 160
perverseness of A.L., 231, 234, 385
Pevsner, Dieter, 309, 355, 370
Pevsner, Sir Nikolaus, 149, 151–4, 193, 264, 276
Philanderer, The, case, 315, 321
Phoenix Library, 84
Pierions, Irene, 210
Pocket Books, 139, 180, 201, 222, 223, 243
Pocket Classics (Collins), 82
politics and A.L., 61, 119–22, 124, 125, 130–4, 175, 196, 268–71
pomposity, A.L.'s lack of, 124
portrait, group, 'After the Conference', 275–7

posterity, A.L.'s concern with, 275–7
Pound, Ezra, 75
pragmatism of A.L., 122
Prescott, Mrs, 92, 93
press, 71, 100, 114, 166, 203, 220, 222, 223, 257, 273, 314, 317, 341, 349, 365–7, 381, 382
pride of A.L., 245, 271, 275
Priestley, J. B., 294
   affronted, 265–7, 383
printers,
   problems of, 144
   schedule of, 130, 131, 268
printing, A.L.'s acquaintance with, 47, 226
Priory Farm, 178–80, 190, 234, 256, 300, 330, 348, 350, 364
procrastination and A.L., 24
profits tax, introduction of, 167, 168
promises, A.L.'s breaking of, 24, 124–5, 200, 210, 240, 246, 258
property owned by A.L., 234
Public Prosecutions, Director of, 316, 325, 326
public speaking by A.L., 166, 167, 365
Publishers Association, 162–4, 206, 209
publishing, A.L.'s waning interest in, 313, 314
publishing dynasties, 297–8
Puffin Books, 206, 276, 299, 310, 311, 335, 379, 384
Puffin Picture Books, 169, 171–3
Puffin Story Books, 169, 173
puritanism and A.L., 230
Purnells, printers of Penguin Books, 107

rabbit-breeding episode, 16
radio, 12, 166, 167, 222, 295, 313, 314, 317, 365
Railway Library (Routledge), 82
Random House, 76
Rapley, Bill, 104, 105
Raverat, Gwen, 143
Raymond, Harold, 108
Raynes Park, A.L. living at, 17, 50
Reader's Digest, 112, 192
reading habits of A.L., 89, 90, 103
Reclam, 84
Redesdale, Lord, 44
Redouté, P.-J., *Roses*, 148
Regina v. Penguin Books Ltd, 41, 314–25, 328, 329, 331, 334, 347
religion, A.L.'s attitude to, 347, 363
resilience of A.L., 333
responsibility, A.L.'s increased war-time, 167, 168
restlenessness of A.L., 246, 250
retirement of A.L., proposed, 350
Rickett's, Beverley, 395
Rieu, E. V., 151, 215, 216, 244, 249, 276, 307, 325

Roberts, D. K., 129
Rodd, Sir Rennell, 53, 54
Rolph, C. H., 322
Rose, Jim, 380–3, 391
Rosenwald, Peter, 374–8, 395
Roth, Samuel, 76
Rothschilds, 373
Rouse, W. H. D., 249
Routledge & Kegan Paul, 82, 84
Royal Academy, 276
Royal Naval Reserve, 138, 158, 159, 173, 177
Rubinstein, Michael, 323, 324
Russian Review, 129

St James Gazette, 21
St John Stevas, Norman, 319
Saki, 42, 43
Sayers, Dorothy, 89–91
Schindler, 187
Schmoller, Hans, 204, 211, 274, 308, 309, 316, 321, 325, 354, 355, 379, 394
Schmoller, Tatyana (*née* Kent), 204, 211, 355, 394
Seaman, Owen, 25
Secker, Martin, 89
Secker and Warburg, 40
Second World War, 142, 143, 149, 155–92
secrecy of A.L., 277
Segrave, Edmond, 109, 126, 188, 195–8, 205, 272
Sender, Ramon, 133, 134
Senior, Elizabeth, 144, 147, 149, 151
sentimentality and A.L., 271, 308, 373
servants of A.L., 56, 70, 71, 141, 159
Shakespeare plays, 113, 114, 126, 149, 249
shareholding, sale of A.L.'s to university consortium, 296
Shaw, Bernard, 22, 33, 50, 59, 108, 114–19, 122, 127, 221, 228, 249, 267
  Million, 219–23
  ninetieth birthday, 219–21, 329
Shilling Library (Bohn's), 82
shrewdness of A.L., 46, 64, 119, 152, 158, 165, 234, 236, 240, 257, 270, 304, 325, 349
shyness of A.L., 61
Signet-Mentor Books, 230, 243, 249
Silverbeck, 138, 139, 141, 142, 147, 159, 166, 176–9, 184, 185, 190, 208, 209, 214, 234, 247, 257, 264, 330, 350
Simon, Oliver, 216, 217
Simpkin Marshall, 210
Siné, *Massacre*, 346–9
Sitwells, the, 228, 265
Skipsie, Joan, 126
Smithers, Leonard, 28, 30, 32
sociability of A.L., 46, 48, 50, 55–8, 61, 66, 68, 70, 71, 98–9, 114, 136, 142, 159, 173, 183, 188, 194, 214, 258, 259, 330, 363, 365
Socialism and A.L., 61, 121, 269, 270, 356, 358

sophistication of A.L., 47–8, 158
South Africa, 240, 241
South America, 209, 213
Southern Languages Book Trust, 237
Southwark Street, move to, 64
Spain, A.L.'s property in, 234, 314, 317, 350, 356, 360, 362, 363
Spectator, 100, 317, 323
sport, A.L.'s dislike of competitive, 14, 48, 272
Stapledon, Olaf, 117
Star, 22
Stevens, Sir Roger, 296
Stopes, Marie, 290
Strand Magazine, 13–14
successor to A.L. at Penguin
  arrangements with other publishers, 288–94
  concern about, 191, 282–99, 302–4, 307, 312, 327, 333, 337, 358, 368
  and his daughters, 298, 299, 302
  trust controlled by academic institutions, 294–6
Sudermann, Herman, *Song of Songs*, 40, 41, 77
Summers, Jack, 104, 204, 394
Sunday Times, 100
Symonds, J. A., 22, 24

take-overs, 297, 361–3, 366, 367, 370–8
  fear of American, 370, 371
Talbot Square, No. 16, 64, 65, 68, 79, 88, 99, 106, 114, 135–7, 142, 168, 176, 178, 255, 303, 340, 368
  alterations to, 68, 69, 152
Tauchnitz series, 181, 182
Teale, Christine, *see* Lane, Christine
Teale, David, 373
Telesford House School, 14, 55
television, 313, 334–5, 365
Ten Years of Penguin, 195–7, 272, 274
Territorial Army, 48, 49
theatre-going and A.L., 58–60
Thirkell, Angela, 128
Times, The, 12, 26, 29, 54, 128, 135, 235, 299, 323–5
Times Literary Supplement, The, 100, 283
torpedo episode, 178
trade unionism, 121, 356, 381
Transatlantic, 129, 188, 205, 207
travel overseas, A.L.'s, 62, 67, 70, 72, 76, 77, 139–41, 144, 146, 147, 159, 180, 181, 209, 213, 223, 240, 244, 246–8, 250–2, 257–9, 261–3, 299, 303, 312, 330, 331, 341
Travers, Ben, 48, 59
Trial of Lady Chatterley, The, 322, 323
trust, university, 296, 297
trust for handicapped children, 330
Tschichold, Jan, 216–18, 225, 274, 355
Turner, Rozanne, 294

Ulysses, 75–8, 228, 290, 321, 346, 366
UNESCO, 239
unhappiness of A.L., 333, 341
Universal Bibliothek, 83
Universal Library (Routledge), 82
University Grants Committee, 296
unmannerliness of A.L., 258, 259
Unwin, Philip, 395
Unwin, Sir Stanley, 94, 108, 317
USA, 31–2, 35, 36, 40, 42, 44, 45, 51, 62, 67, 70, 73, 75, 76, 78, 84, 95, 128, 129, 139, 143, 158, 180, 181, 183, 188, 191, 201, 207, 208, 213, 217, 222, 227–9, 231–3, 235, 237–53, 289, 305, 331, 360, 370, 371, 377
    alliances with American publishers, 289–93
    Ford Foundation, 237, 238
    sales policy, 292
Uses of Literacy, The, 294, 295, 389
USSR, 237–9, 270

vacillation of A.L., 208–10, 375, 376
Verlag, Insel, 143
Vigo, Street, Penguin property, 343, 344
Vigour, 260, 281
Viney, Elliott, 272
vulnerability of A.L., 191, 308, 333

Walkley, A. B., 22
War Office, 162–5, 207–9
Warburg, Frederic, 315, 321
warehousing, 166, 331, 332
Watership Down, 379
Watson, William, 22, 27, 29, 30, 32, 37
Waugh, Evelyn, 127, 267, 294
Weaver, Harriet, 75
Webb, Kaye, 151, 310–13, 335, 355, 379, 394
Wedgwood, Veronica, 319
Wells, H. G., 34, 117, 122, 127, 267
West Drayton, 166, 223, 330
West Indies, 240
Westminster Gazette, 29
Weybright, Victor, 125, 188, 201, 202, 227–33, 244, 248, 292, 389

Whispering Gallery, The, 52–5, 74
Whitehall Court, 233, 234, 330, 350
Wilde, Oscar, 16, 20, 22–4, 26–8, 31–5, 38, 39, 42, 44, 67, 265, 321
    criticisms of publishers, 22–4, 28, 29, 31
    Importance of Being Ernest, The, 31
    imprisonment of, 31–3, 35
    Mr W.H., 32
    Salome, 23, 24, 26, 27, 31, 32, 34, 38
    Sphinx, The, 23
    Yellow Book, The, and, 28, 29
will of A.L., 361
Willans, General, 162, 163
Willett, 51, 52, 54, 55
Williams (*alias* Lane), 12, 145
Williams, Sir William Emrys, 119–25, 127, 135, 147, 151, 162–5, 170, 171, 175, 188–90, 192, 196, 203, 209, 216, 218, 220, 232, 233, 247, 263, 266, 268, 269, 272, 275, 276, 282, 289, 293, 294, 303, 304, 308, 309, 350, 352, 359, 364–6, 369, 389
    Allen Lane: A Memoir, 389
    Army education, 157, 162–4, 189
    Arts Council, 189, 190, 269
    journalism, 189
Wilson, J. G. (Bumpus), 91
Wodehouse, P. G., 101, 341
woman friends of A.L., 48, 56, 57, 59, 60, 136, 235, 287, 306, 350
Woodhouse, C. M., 270, 283, 294, 338
Woolley, Leonard, 117, 153
Woolworths, 80, 92, 93
Workers' Educational Association, 83, 123, 124, 196
World's Classics, 82, 102, 143
Wyld, Peter, 204, 211
Wylie, I. A. R., *To the Vanquished*, 134

yachting and A.L., 137
Yeats, W. B., 134
Yellow Book, The, see Bodley Head, The
Young, Edward, 88, 89, 97, 104, 138–9, 160, 202, 293
    One of Our Submarines, 271, 272